STRATEGIES FOR
CLASSROOM DISCIPLINE

STRATEGIES FOR CLASSROOM DISCIPLINE

Meryl E. Englander

New York
Westport, Connecticut
London

Library of Congress Cataloging-in-Publication Data

Englander, Meryl E.
   Strategies for classroom discipline.

   Bibliography: p.
   Includes index.
   1.   Classroom management.   2.   Students—Discipline.
3.   Rewards and punishments in education.   I.   Title.
LB3013.E54   1986   371.1'024   85-28287
ISBN 0-275-92093-3 (alk. paper)

Library of Congress Catalog Card Number: 85-28287
ISBN: 0-275-92093-3

First published in 1986

Praeger Publishers, 521 Fifth Avenue, New York, NY 10175
A division of Greenwood Press, Inc.

Printed in the United States of America

∞

The paper used in this book complies with the Permanent Paper Standard issued by the National Information Standards Organization (Z39.48-1984).

10   9   8   7   6   5   4   3   2   1

This book is dedicated to professional teachers
in their pursuit of excellence in the trenches of
the toughest game in town

PREFACE

Time on-task is one of the most critical teacher-controllable variables for academic achievement. For instance, Marliave (1979) reported that evidence from classroom observations shows that over 10 percent of the variance in achievement can be directly accounted for by academic learning time. Off-task behavior, particularly if it is combined with intrusion on other learners, distracts not only students but also teachers from their academic endeavors. Allegedly, in some schools teachers devote as much as 80 percent of their time and energy to the management of classroom behavioral problems. Gallop (1982) has conducted an annual national poll for 14 years to identify the desires and concerns of the public with regard to education. The polls repeatedly show that the most prominent desire of the public is that students develop morally. The schools also show that the perceived most critical problem is lack of discipline. Discipline is listed as the number one problem by 27 percent of the respondents as compared to 6 percent for busing and 11 percent for poor curriculum. If concerns for drug abuse are added to the concerns for discipline, the percentage goes up to 47 percent. The public's meaning of morality and discipline is not clarified by the poll, but it is safe to assume that they want youngsters to learn how to behave, to be self-sufficient, and to be socially responsible.

Fear has become a prominent and pervasive feeling in many of our schools. About one third of our large high schools have armed police officers patrolling the halls during the entire school day. In addition, about 30 percent of our large high schools admittedly have undercover agents who report to either the local police or to the FBI. Testimony of violence in our schools is filled with tales of homicide, rape, assault, vandalism, and robbery. More money is spent on the prevention and repair of vandalism than on textbooks (Bayh 1975; DeCecco and Richards 1975).

Graham (1978) reported that a student is less safe from assault and robbery in urban schools than he or she would be on the streets. To be more explicit Graham noted:

> For the typical secondary school student, then, we can estimate the risks as follows: he or she has about 1 chance in 9 of having something stolen in a month; 1 chance in 80 of being attacked; and 1 chance in 200 of being robbed . . . a typical teacher in the Nation's secondary schools: has around 1 chance in 8 of having something stolen at school in a given month; 1 chance in 167 of being robbed and 1 chance in 200 of being attacked. (p. 4)

In contrast to national studies of violence in the schools, most teachers report that though such violence does occur it is isolated. A few schools have extensive trouble, but in a typical school there are only a handful of pupils who are serious offenders. This is not to suggest that the norm is to be on-task, obedient, or passive. Many children in many classes are misbehaving. However, most often it is misdirected behavior. The typical teacher reports such classroom off-task behaviors as tardiness, excessive talking, rudeness, out-of-seat activity, flaunting authority, age-typical mischief, and acting-out-of-feelings. The most frequent inference offered by teachers for such behaviors is lack of motivation or need for attention.

Duea (1982) noted that a national survey of administrators listed the following problems in the order of severity: student apathy and lack of motivation, smoking, insubordination, use of marijuana, use of alcohol, tardiness, truancy, class cutting, vandalism, and theft of student property. Even if such behavior is more mischievous than dangerous, it is still a nuisance and counterproductive in classrooms. Fortunately, most discipline problems are within the realm of change if managed by a skilled teacher.

Regardless of the nature of the offense, the most common reaction to misbehavior in the schools is punishment. The punishment may be as mild as a scowl or as harsh as paddling and suspensions. The severity is mostly a function of who administers the punishment and who receives it rather than the nature of the offense itself. Nevertheless, in about 80 percent of the cases the teacher reacts punitively. Although punishment is a frequent, highly sanctioned way of reacting to misbehavior, it turns out usually to be ineffective. Punishment has not been found successful as a deterrent in either laboratory studies or in field-based research. On the contrary, systematic studies of punishment in the classroom suggest that it probably has a boomerang effect: The frequency and seriousness of misbehavior increases and academic achievement decreases in punitive situations.

We are not without effective countermeasures. Recent research regarding interpersonal relations, learning theory, personal dynamics, and the management of behavior offers us the knowledge to effectively change undesired behavior and simultaneously facilitate personal growth. Our purpose is to identify, describe, integrate, and operationalize these means. Five qualifications guided the development and organization of this material.

1. *Multifaceted Approach.* Teachers need a variety of techniques in the same way that a medical doctor needs a variety of drugs, an auto mechanic needs a variety of wrenches, or a quarterback a variety of plays. Each teacher, each student, and each situation is unique. There is enough commonality so that overall principles can be used, but we also must advo-

cate multiple and flexible treatments. The effective teacher cannot rely on any given strategy for managing classroom behavior. Nine alternatives to punishment were selected and are presented herein because each meets to some degree the other four qualifications.

2. *Goal Directed.* With respect to behavior, the teacher has two goals. First, it is necessary to maximize the time that each student spends on task. The more time that an individual spends reading, writing, calculating, comparing, contrasting, connecting, analyzing, and memorizing, the greater the academic achievement. Second, since the function of education is to enable students to become respectful, productive citizens it follows that teachers ought to strive to help each individual become a responsible, self-respecting, self-directed person who is able to behave within the mores of the society. Our task is to enable the reader to more effectively move toward these goals.

3. *Unified Framework.* If we are to use a variety of techniques to keep students on task and to encourage them to learn self control, we must have a coherent plan. Just as rigidity is limiting, uncorrelated variety and inconsistency is disastrous. In order to logically analyze situations, select alternative treatments, and learn from the effects, we must have an organized framework within which the concepts and cause-effect relationships make sense. The parts of such a framework ought to be discrete but connected so the user maintains a sense of coordinated action. Such a framework should be logical and consistent within itself. To sum up, the framework needs to be complex enough to meet the challenge of functioning classrooms but simple enough so that we can readily grasp the respective techniques, their relationships, and the conditions for their application. The relationships of self concept behavior, interpersonal relationships, and environmental feedback offer such a framework.

4. *Research Base.* When confronted with a problem, teachers like everyone else, tend to recall or use personal experience to reach a solution. The experience might be repeated acts which were used in the past or which occurred in classrooms when the teacher was a student; or it may be that which other teachers offer as advice. Reliance on personal experience is natural and common. Such processes may be useful and often work. However, ineffective and even counterproductive conditions oftentimes are created, and frequently the teacher is unaware of the effects or the cause of the effects. If we rely primarily on personal experience, errors may occur for several reasons:

a. A number of variables or factors that are unrecognized by an individual may powerfully influence the consequences.

b. An individual typically has only a few such experiences, and effects which occur accidentally one time may not reoccur in the future.
c. Other more effective, efficient means for achieving desired ends may be overlooked.
d. Conclusions may be based on expectations or on personal prejudice rather than on what really occurred.
e. Other more critical consequences may occur unnoticed.

To counteract these natural tendencies, educators subject their hunches, models, and theories to the rigors of research.

Admittedly, social research is not on a par with natural and physical science research. Social science research has lagged because the variables are considerably less precise, more numerous, and more complex. Furthermore, social science research has only been minimally funded. Nevertheless, we will refer to whatever research evidence is available because knowledge based on research is more dependable, even in the complexities of classroom interaction. Conclusions based on research are superior to personal experience to the degree that

a. the former is carefully designed to take into account the known multiple variables which might influence the results.
b. the data are collected objectively and biases are controlled.
c. care is taken to make the evidence valid and reliable.
d. procedures are explicit so others may replicate the conditions and obtain the same result.
e. procedures are replicated in various settings to test the applicability of the processes to other circumstances.
f. care is taken in advocating the process so that the procedures will generalize and be equally effective elsewhere.

5. *Theory Into Practice.* What a teacher knows is not as important as how the teacher acts in managing classroom behavior. It is teacher action, not teacher knowledge, which influences the way the referent students feel, learn, and behave. Therefore, though what is espoused by teachers in managing student behavior ought to be based on coherent theory, it must also be translated into behaviors. To whatever degree possible, the teacher as learner ought to practice the skills in near real situations. Our goal is that teachers will learn "that" "how" and "when". To these ends, each of the strategies is presented with practice in terms of a variety of examples, simulated situations, exercises, suggestions for reader role playing, exemplars, and encouragement to employ the respective techniques in operational classrooms.

A CAUTIONARY NOTE

We teachers tend to be idealistic in that we are overly demanding of ourselves, our teaching methods, and curricula. Our expectations are too high. We too quickly discard processes if they do not work a high percentage of the time. Three points are worthy of note:

1. Teaching, as it transpires in a typical classroom, is one of the most complex, difficult processes in which anyone could become involved. Our students are each unique so that we must simultaneously interact with myriad abilities, expectations, goals, habits, attitudes, and fears.
2. Expect success but tolerate failures. Few adventures succeed every time. Some movies, dinners, and dates don't measure up to our expectations. Professional athletes, such as basketball players, after years of practice only score on about 60 percent of their shots. Your success average on the strategies proposed herein may be .200 on the first ten attempts. Stay with them, and the average will improve, though it will never be 100 percent.
3. Adapt as well as adopt. Each of the strategies encompasses some critical elements which must be included, but other aspects will be of more use if bent to your style and circumstances.
4. Each of the given strategies will work sometimes for some people. There are no panaceas. Each teacher must develop expertise in several ways of interacting with students and behaviors to have a repertoire of discipline tools. In given situations, some will be more effective than will others.

ACKNOWLEDGEMENTS

A comprehensive book, such as the one presented here, is the product of the efforts of many people. Foremost are the teachers and researchers who created, tried, and made known the many processes and results discussed herein. Each of the strategies and each of the references represents the ingenuity and efforts of numerous people. I am grateful for their contributions. The teachers and administrators noted in the exemplars of ongoing school practices merit particular credit because they have exhibited the courage and insight to put ideas to work. Finally, several people were very helpful to me through their encouragement, suggestions, and criticisms.

ORGANIZATION

The material has been written for use by teachers, administrators, and educational consultants. It is presented in three parts:

Part I.   A Confrontation With Punishment. The reasons we punish and what is known about punishment are analyzed. Stringent guidelines are offered for administering punishment.

Part II.   The Conflict Cycle/Intervention Strategies. A multiple set of hypotheses for misbehavior is offered in terms which school practitioners can relate. Four general strategies are discussed and illustrated. Several school related behavioral problem situations are presented for the respective strategies.

Part III.   Potpourri. Whereas the Conflict Cycle/Intervention Strategies offers an integration of four major discrete strategies, Part III will identify, describe, illustrate, and present situations for several other independent, proven strategies.

CONTENTS

LIST OF TABLES

LIST OF FIGURES

PART I

A CONFRONTATION WITH PUNISHMENT

Rules exist throughout nature and in every human social context. When we observe an apparent violation of one of nature's alleged rules we seek an explanation. Much of our scientific knowledge was discovered in this manner. However, when human rules are violated, instead of seeking an explanation we tend to respond punitively toward the offender.

Part I is composed of Chapter 1, Punishment: A Complex Affair, and Chapter 2, Effects of Punishment: Classroom Research Findings. Part I addresses the nature of punishment and the reasons for its prevalence, conditions necessary for success, as well as the pitfalls and the apparent consequences in educational settings. Punishment has advocates as well as opponents. Although I oppose the use of punishment, particularly when I am the recipient, the search for evidence was open-minded and thorough. Except to indicate an attitude, little attention has been paid to off-hand conclusions such as "punishment hurts the child's psyche" or "without punishment the world would become chaotic," unless evidence is offered to support the conclusion.

1

PUNISHMENT: A COMPLEX AFFAIR

TEACHER RESPONSE TO RULE VIOLATIONS

Every organization, including schools, must have rules. As it happens in these same organizations the rules are sometimes violated for a variety of reasons. From the point of view of the teacher or parent or whoever is nominally responsible the question is: How can one best respond to the issue of rule violations? Some responses are fruitful, some ineffectual, some possible but impractical and others counterproductive. The answer to the question is not simple.

For purposes of orientation we will consider two classroom incidents:

Mr. Jung was teaching a sixth grade class. He was expecting a visitor and had planned a special activity. After the visitor arrived Jung asked the students to start their assigned seatwork. After everyone had seemingly settled down and the room assumed an on-task atmosphere, Jung invited Group A to begin their special computer project. With a final glance around the room Jung joined them and soon became engrossed with the subgroup.

Meanwhile, Willie, sitting in the last row, had subtly moved his desk to the rear windows, tilted his chair back against the wall and began to swing the drapery cords. Because the sun was shining through the windows the cords cast a moving shadow on the opposite wall. In addition, the cord hitting the window caused a flapping noise, audible throughout the room. Jung and almost everyone else looked up. Two points are important here: Whatever the teacher does at this moment is more critical than is anyone else's reaction. Furthermore, the teacher has a number of options. In this incident Jung might have:

1. Chosen to ignore the situation and just quietly returned to work.
2. Signaled other children to ignore Willie and return to work.
3. Sent Willie a nonverbal hostile stare.
4. Sternly told Willie to move his seat back where it belonged and go to work.
5. Informed Willie that he would receive an F for the assignment if he did not immediately return to work.
6. Sympathetically inquired, "Willie, are you bored?"
7. Quickly moved to the back of the room and roughly moved Willie and his seat back to its normal position.
8. Sarcastically called his behavior to everyone's attention: e.g., "Oh, look class, our little clown is doing his rope trick."
9. Quietly moved to the back of the room and asked Willie if he had noticed the shadow patterns by the cord. Then directed Willie to the encyclopedia to look up the phenomena, vibrating strings, with the assignment to present his findings to the class that afternoon.
10. Punished Willie with detentions, a whack or two with a paddle, or a visit to the principal's office.

Whatever option Jung selects depends on three factors: (a) the nature of the offense, (b) the desired consequences, and (c) inferences that Jung makes about Willie's motives. We react differently when one student maliciously strikes another as compared to when students speak out without first raising their hands. Likewise, we respond differently when the objective is safety in handling tools as compared to when the goal is a quiet workplace. The effect of making inferences about individual students is less apparent. To clarify the issue let us consider another incident and see how you might respond.

Each of your students is working on special projects, some of which involve animals and other attractive elements. The students are given 15 minutes at the beginning of the period to attend to their projects, but most of the class time is devoted to other activities. Today all students are supposed to be in their seats focusing on the textbook. However, you glance over at the special project area and note that a student is there doing something. The student and your inference about each are:

1. Jody is a new student from Utah. Apparently he doesn't know that when working on the text he is not supposed to be in the project area.
2. Ann knows the rule but is so forgetful that she just forgot something that she intended to do earlier.
3. Fritz knows the rule but he does such things just to get attention.
4. Scott is a way-out kid. He just got bored and restless with the assignment.

5. Fran is an independent thinker. Fran thinks that all rules are stupid so she just does whatever she pleases.

6. Deb knows the rule and is deliberately violating it. She gets a kick out of being defiant.

7. Jon is taking a calculated risk. He is sneaky and assumes that he can get away with it because no one will notice.

8. Kris is bright, interested, and obedient. She probably just finished the text material and is eager to get on with her project.

On a separate sheet of paper note how you would respond to each of the students given the suggested inferences. The work sheet in Table 1.1 is offered as a model format showing a variety of ways that a teacher might respond to each student. On your paper place a check mark under each student's name to indicate which of the teacher options you would select.

Treatment Tends to be Inconsistent

If you and the others in your group responded to this out-of-seat violation as did every group to whom this exercise has been previously administered, the following occurred.

First, as an individual you responded somewhat differently to each student. That is, you reacted to the given inferences about the students and their motives and thereby treated each differently, although ostensibly all had broken the same rule. Second, if you compared your responses to the others in your group we would find that any given student would be treated differently, depending on which of you was responsible for the particular class in question.

Only occasionally do two teachers agree on the respective treatments for all students. Thus, if several teachers are confronted with the same rule violation, the responses to the misbehaving student differ even if all the teachers make the same assumption about the student's motives. The variation from teacher to teacher apparently occurs because teachers differ in their goals and beliefs about how to best achieve their goals. The following episode illustrates the point.

Teacher reaction to problem behavior

A group of teachers was told about a boy who had a history of being in trouble. The boy was from a minority ethnic group and lived in the ghetto of a large city. The teachers were told about several incidents in which the student was involved and then were asked what they would do if this boy were

Table 1.1. Selected responses to rule violations (Worksheet)

Teacher options include	Students who violate the rule							
	Jody	Ann	Fritz	Scott	Fran	Deb	Jon	Kris
Ignore the behavior								
Repeat the rule (e.g., "In this class we—").								
Send nonverbal, hostile, message (e.g., scowl, snap fingers).								
Quietly ask student to return to his seat.								
Reprimand with intensity (e.g., "GET BACK TO YOUR SEAT!").								
Warn the student (e.g., "The next time that you—").								
Use humor (e.g., "Looking for a good grade back there?").								
Take away a privilege (e.g., "You know the rule, no recess today.").								
Take student firmly by the arm and firmly escort her back to her seat.								
Compliment others (e.g., "I like the way most of you are working on your assignment.").								

in their class. The teacher's responses are paraphrased and categorized below:

Teacher 1—He doesn't respect anybody, law or order. We must teach him to respect authority; therefore tighten up, punish him.

Teacher 2—He has lived with violence all of his life. He has had to learn to deal with it. He is hard on the outside but internally, he is sensitive and soft; if we love him and accept him he will turn out all right.

Teacher 3—He is hopeless. School has no meaning for him. What we need is an activity program. Give him errands to run, something to do to make him feel that he belongs.

Teacher 4—He is just going through a period, a stage of life. All children do this from time to time. I was like that and I turned out all right. Be tolerant, accept his behavior, and he will outgrow it.

Teacher 5—He is a bad apple. We must protect others so they will not become contaminated by him. Isolate him, exclude him from contact with other people.

Teacher 6—If you only knew the parents you would understand his problem. Our best chance is to work with the parents.

Teacher 7—This kid gets to me. I'm fed up with him. I would set him up and then crack him but good.

Teacher 8—He is bored. School activity has no meaning for him. We must get him interested in something meaningful. Put him in shop courses and in places where he can use his hands.

Teacher 9—He never learned appropriate behavior. He needs reinforcement for good behavior. Give him a gumdrop every time he approaches acceptable behavior.

Teacher 10—Ignore him. We are required to keep him in school but that does not mean we have to waste time with him. Let him daydream or whatever he wants to do, just so he does not disrupt others who want to get something out of school.

When a student violates a rule, teachers react. However, the reaction differs between students depending on the inference each given teacher makes about the student. Teachers respond differently, depending on their respective goals and beliefs regarding how to best achieve these goals. Furthermore, we respond differently depending on the severity of the deviant behavior. This variability in rule violation treatment has several consequences.

Inconsistency is Detrimental

Even though a rule is carefully stipulated, the students need to discover what the consequences will be if the rule is violated. How will this particular teacher react? How will I be treated as compared to others? Apparently, the only way to learn the answers to such questions is to violate the rule several times. The need to know is not necessarily for the sake of being able to outfox the teacher. People need to have a sense of organization, consistency, and predictability.

Furthermore, the individual student can only guess as to why she is treated differentially. These guesses often include: "She has it in for me." "John did it yesterday and nothing happened, the teacher has favorites," or "It doesn't matter what I do, I get into trouble." All such conclusions typically lead to further misbehavior.

To compound the problem each teacher has a different set of rules and different interpretations of the allegedly existing school rules. Hargreaves et al. (1975) observed and interviewed teachers in two secondary schools over an extended period of time. They found that there are few written and stipulated school rules comparable to the traffic laws that govern the operation of automobiles. There are some unwritten but commonly accepted rules, such as students cannot shout in class. However, the vast majority of rules are at the discretion of individual teachers. Rules are numerous, complex, and unique to the teacher, who may allow certain behaviors under some circumstances, but not others. For example, talking quietly to other students is permissible during roll call, but not when the teacher is talking. Because school rules are so complex they must be learned in the context of particular situations.

If apprehended, students can expect that the teacher will respond punitively. Englander (1982) conducted two studies to identify teacher responses to misbehavior. In the first, 40 elementary student teachers were asked during the sixth week of practice teaching to note three rule-violating behaviors and consequent teacher reactions. The observers reported that for 120 rule violations the teachers responded punitively 108 times. In the other 12 instances the teachers appeared to ignore the misbehavior.

In the second study all of the teachers in a school district were asked to respond anonymously to an inquiry sponsored by the parent-teacher association. One hundred and seventy-six teachers representing all school levels responded. The instrument was composed of a list of 20 misbehaviors, ranging from tardiness to physically attacking a teacher. The teachers were asked to select from 15 alternatives how they would respond to each of the misbehaviors. In this study 78 percent of these responses were punitive.

Thus, in both studies, the vast majority of the teacher responses to misbehavior were punitive.

Consistency Is Not Always Just

An alternative to inconsistency is to establish rules and legislate precise consequences. Thereby, everyone will know the rules and what to expect when rules are violated. This principle has advantages but it also has drawbacks. An episode that recently occurred in a high school will illustrate the point.

> It was 3:15 and I was walking down the hall of a well-established high school in a "good" neighborhood. A bell started to ring and before it stopped a flood of boys and girls came gushing into the hall from every direction. Since it was almost impossible for me to move I stepped to one side and decided to wait a moment until the passage cleared. Across the hall a girl was bending down, apparently digging something out of the bottom of her locker. A boy came along, stopped and patted her a couple of times on the buttocks and said something to her. She stood up, and in a single motion, turned around and slapped his face very hard. He retaliated by immediately slapping her. About that time a second boy was walking by and when he saw the first boy slap the girl he rushed over, swung the boy around and hit him. In a moment the two boys were fighting furiously. A male teacher appeared. He separated the boys and taking each by the arm escorted them to the principal's office. The teacher reported the fight, filled out a form and left. Over the "But . . . buts" of the boys, they were charged with violating the no fighting rule and suspended for three days. The suspension of course, is part of their respective permanent record. The school made no note of the girl or her role in the episode.

Did justice prevail? Would it have been more just had the girl, who struck the first blow, been apprehended and automatically suspended for her role in the episode? What did each of the three students learn from the incident?

Individual programs enhance, differential punishments confuse

It is not only natural but professionally appropriate for teachers to make inferences about students and act on these inferences. The concept of individual differences is a cornerstone of teaching and curriculum development. The difficulty does not lie in our differentiating the students but in the nature of our responses. In normal teaching and curriculum situations the responses to individual differences are an attempt to match the needs of an individual with growth-facilitating conditions. However, in situations involving deviant behavior we tend to respond individually, but punitively. Differential punitive treatment for rule violations is likely to arouse confusion and resentment. From the fighting incident in the hallway we sense that a set punishment for given acts may also be inconsistent. Furthermore, the rationale for our entire legal system is that each case is unique. The issue of how we can best respond to off-task and rule-violating behavior deserves careful consideration.

PUNISHMENT AS THE SOCIETAL NORM

The Heritage of Punishment

To punish or not to punish is *not* the typical question. Punishment is a common phenomenon throughout our society; it exists. The use of punishment as a primary response to misbehavior is supported by history, the courts, public opinion, and common child-rearing practices.

We have had a long history of responding punitively to transgressions. Harsh punishment was endemic in the ancient world and continued to be so throughout the medieval period. Ancient Egyptians used the concept of the rod as a synonym for instruction. The Middle Ages and in early America the Christian ethic was reinforced with harsh retribution.

General Support of Corporal Punishment

Attitudes continue to be very supportive of the use of corporal punishment in the schools. The United States Supreme Court in 1975 and again in 1977 reaffirmed that right of educators to use their own discretion in the use of corporal punishment. In only four states is it expressly prohibited. Chase (1975) reports that a series of Gallup polls showed that roughly two-thirds of the parents and teachers alike favor the use of corporal punishment in the schools. Even students see merit in corporal punishment. Elardo (1978) interviewed elementary schoolchildren and found that many prefer paddling to other forms of punishment in order to "get it over with." However, one articulate child said, "Sometimes you get falsely accused of doing something. If you get paddled and later prove you did not do it, you can't get unpaddled" (p. 18). Many of these children also reported the opinion that paddling does not change behavior.

The degree of prevailing attitudes toward corporal punishment is reflected in a study reported by Reardon and Reynold (1979). A number of assertions were presented to a broad sample of parents, principals, teachers, and school board presidents. They were asked if they agreed or disagreed with each of the assertions.

Look carefully at the individual assertions and the "I agree" responses of the respective groups as shown in Table 1.2. The agreement across groups is remarkable. Only in the statement, "Most of the people in the community served by my school support the use of corporal punishment" were the subgroups significantly different. It is apparent from this data that corporal punishment in the schools is strongly supported. Paradoxically, the Soviet Union, which most Americans perceive to be authoritarian and brutal in its treatment of people, outlawed corporal punishment in the schools over a century ago.

In spite of the general support given for the use of punishment as a viable means for promoting desired rule-abiding behavior, the issue is clouded. Popular notions of how, when, and who to punish are muddled. Furthermore, neither tradition nor common practice is sufficient reason to continue the practice unless objective evidence demonstrates it to be an effective and efficient treatment for altering behavior.

We need to look more closely at what research has to offer regarding the processes and outcomes of punishment.

MULTIPLE FACTORS DETERMINE THE EFFECTIVENESS OF PUNISHMENT

Respected researchers (Azrin and Holz 1966; MacMillan, Forness, and Trumbull 1973; Walters, Park and Crane 1965) contend that behavior can be changed through judiciously applied punishment. However, we will discover as we review the bases for their conclusions that research does not give carte blanche support for administering punishment. The evidence strongly demonstrates that punishment is an effective means for controlling behavior if and only if certain specific conditions prevail.

In order to obtain a sense of the multitude of potential variables and their relevance let us consider a simple case in Jane Doe's class.

Ms. Jane Doe's mixed first and second grade class is supposed to be doing seatwork in arithmetic. As it happens crayons and drawing paper are

Table 1.2. Endorsements of statements regarding corporal punishment in the schools of Pennsylvania

Items	Parents (*n* = 558)	Teachers (*n* = 972)	Principals (*n* = 1,278)	Supt. (*n* = 461)	School board presidents (*n* = 216)
Corporal punishment will cause changes in behavior	74.9	75.8	75.6	76.0	75.0
Corporal punishment builds a student's character	35.5	29.5	30.9	32.3	45.1
Students learn self-discipline from corporal punishment	54.9	49.7	52.3	49.1	61.9
Discipline cannot be maintained without corporal punishment	43.8	38.9	36.7	37.8	58.4
Corporal punishment is less harmful than other forms of humiliation	57.0	58.4	61.3	61.6	67.3
Teachers use corporal punishment when they have no other way to respond to difficult situations	63.8	64.9	62.1	62.9	57.8
Corporal punishment is the only thing that will work with some students	76.0	76.8	70.3	66.4	81.9
Student attitudes are generally made worse by corporal punishment	28.8	19.8	24.1	31.7	15.8
Most of the people in the community served by my school support the use of corporal punishment	36.9	42.0	65.6	62.0	73.2
Complete elimination of corporal punishment would have serious consequences	73.1	76.2	71.8	67.2	79.2
Corporal punishment is not effective unless administered at the time of incident	83.5	81.5	74.1	69.6	83.3
Some students receive corporal punishment while others do not for the same offense	72.1	68.5	63.7	73.7	66.7

Data is presented as percentage in agreement with the respective statement.
Source: Reardon, F.J. and Reynold, R.N., pp. 308–09, 1979.

on many desks because the next activity is art, which most of the class enjoys. Ms. Doe wants and expects the whole class to be working on arithmetic problems.

The question is, what will be the impact of punishment if a student sets aside the arithmetic book and picks up the crayons? There is no blanket answer to the question. It depends on a combination of the following variables: (a) the relationship between Ms. Doe and the students who are being punished; (b) the setting in terms of time of day and previous activities; (c) the history of the acts of putting aside arithmetic to begin coloring with crayons: has it been punished before or rewarded? Have the rewards and punishments been consistent or spasmodic? (d) cognitive messages that accompany the punishment; (e) the intensity of the punishment; (f) the timing of the punishment with respect to the behavior it is to suppress; (g) the suddenness or shock of the punishment; (h) the relative attractiveness of arithmetic, of obeying the teacher, of coloring with crayons, and of expressing oneself through art or disobedience; (i) the perceived probability of being caught; (j) the consequences for peers when a given student is off-task, and (k) the criteria for agreeing that punishment works, that is, do we mean stopping the misbehavior or staying on task tomorrow when the student is again tempted? Research has not addressed all of these variables, but we can report enough good evidence for some to give us a basis for drawing conclusions.

Recent Research is Scarce

Despite wide use and controversy, little research has been generated on the effects of punishment. For example, experiments have never been published that identify the effects of corporal punishment on normal individuals in a typical classroom. Most of the studies have been done with animals, young children, or in special education classes. The reader will note that much of the research reported here was done in the 1960s. Nevertheless, this research was systematic and we have no reason to believe that is any less valid now then it was at that time. It represents our best knowledge on the subject.

EXPERIMENTAL RESEARCH FINDINGS

The nature of research, or at least researchers, is not only to find out whether a gross strategy like punishment works but to identify the critical factors that determine how it works. We will look at the findings of five selected factors to illustrate the conclusions. The respective factors are timing, complexity of task, intensity, escalation, and frequency.

Timing. Bill, sitting in the back of the room, is in a real jam. He has to do well on this examination. He has been sailing along pretty well but the sixth question has him stopped cold. In desperation he leans over to take a peek at Mary's paper. Bingo! He gets a clue to the answer, quickly finishes the question, and goes on to number seven feeling pretty good. Unfortunately for him, his quick peek did not go unnoticed. Mr. Albert, the teacher, was closely monitoring the situation from across the room. He unhurriedly walks over to Bill's desk and just as Bill starts number seven, Mr. Albert reaches down and puts a red zero on the test. The scowl on Mr. Albert's face completes the message. A reasonable punishment for cheating, but too late if it is Mr. Albert's intention to change Bill's cheating ways.

Aronfreed (1968) conducted a number of studies to ascertain the differential effects of timing on punishment. In this particular study Aronfreed worked one at a time with fourth and fifth grade boys. The boys were given ten pieces of candy for participating in the study. In each of ten trials they were presented with a pair of toys. The boys were told, "Certain toys are reserved for older boys."

In each case one of the toys was quite attractive, a detailed replica of the real object. The other was a plastic inexpensive toy with very little detail. The task for the boys was to select one of the toys and describe its function. If the attractive toy was selected the experimenter loudly said: "NO!", one piece of candy was taken away and both toys were immediately removed. If the unattractive toy was selected the experimenter did nothing other than listen attentively to what the boy was saying.

The critical point of this experiment was the timing of the punitive action. A total of 80 boys, 20 for each of four groups, participated in the study. For group 1 the punishment was administered as the boy's hand approached the attractive toy. For group 2, punishment was administered immediately after the toy was picked up. In group 3, the punishment came six seconds after the toy was touched, and for group 4, the delay between picking up the toy and the punishment was 12 seconds. Does the timing of the punishment make a difference? None of the 80 boys touched the attractive toy with the researcher present after the third trial. They got the message but the real question remains, will the boys refrain from playing with the attractive toy when authority is not watching?

One-Half Yield to Temptation

After an eleventh pair of toys was placed on the table, the researcher suddenly left the room saying he had to run an errand that would take 10 minutes. In each case the boy was told that the door would be closed so he wouldn't be disturbed and the researcher would knock when he returned. Did the timing of the punishment differentially affect the boys' behavior while they were unsupervised?

In group 1, in which the boys were punished for approaching the attractive toy, half of the boys did not touch the attractive toy at all. The majority of the boys in group 2 picked it up within five minutes. Almost all of the boys in group 3 picked it up within two minutes and all of the group 4 boys picked it up immediately upon being left alone.

The effectiveness of punishment depends on how soon it is administered. Apparently, a delay of 12 seconds or until the recipient has all but completed the behavioral sequence renders the punishment relatively ineffective. Note also, it has minimal effect on half the boys even with optimum timing.

Punishment Effects are Nullified

Walters et al. (1965) elaborated on the Aronfreed (1968) studies by consequently showing a film in which a model was treated differentially. A group of 80 boys was first subjected to punishment under the various timing conditions. One-half of the boys were punished immediately as their hand approached the more attractive toy. Punishment for the other boys was delayed until they had finished telling about the toy.

The total group was then subdivided into four subgroups, each with 20 boys. In each subgroup ten of the boys had been punished early while the rest received the delayed punishment. Three of the four subgroups were shown a film. The fourth subgroup was temporarily otherwise occupied. The film showed an adult female, presumably a mother or a teacher, indicating to a boy that he was to sit at a table and read a book and that he was not to touch the toys, which were on the table. The woman then left the room. After she departed, the boy in the film set the book aside and proceeded to play with the prohibited toys. The toys were similar to the attractive toys of the punishment training segment of the study except that three were unassembled. While unsupervised the boy in the film assembled, part by part, these three toys; a sword, a truck, and a rifle. He then played with the toys despite the woman's warning. The film had three different endings. In ending number one the woman reentered the room. She sat down beside the boy, handed him some of the toys from the table and then affectionately played with him. In the second ending the woman returned, angrily pulled the boy up from his chair, snatched a toy from his hand, and spanked him before angrily sitting him down again in the chair. She once again gave him the book to read. In the third film the woman did not return and the film ended with the boy playing happily with one of the toys.

Thus, there were four film conditions: condition 1, no film; condition 2, deviancy rewarded; condition 3, deviancy punished; and condition 4, deviancy undetected. The early and delayed punishment boys had been distributed equally among the four film conditions in such a way that there were eight equal groups of the ten boys. The groups could be labeled early punishment–deviancy rewarded film, early punishment–deviancy punished film, delayed punishment–deviancy rewarded film, and so on, such that all eight combinations were included (see Table 1.3).

Table 1.3. Interaction of witnessing consequences of others' deviant behavior and timing of punishment

| | Previous punishment experience of observers | |
Observed consequences of deviant behavior in film	Punished prior to touching toy	Punished after describing toy
No deviancy observed	50% obedient	Nearly all deviant
Deviant behavior rewarded	Nearly all deviant	Nearly all deviant
Deviant behavior severely punished	50% obedient	Nearly all deviant
Deviant behavior is undetected	Nearly all deviant	Nearly all deviant

Source: Constructed by author from data from Walters et al. (1965).

As in the Aronfreed (1968) study, the boys were then returned one at a time to a room in which an attractive toy and an unattractive toy were available. As in the earlier study each boy was left alone for ten minutes. One-half of the boys from the early punished–deviancy punished film and the early punished–no film subgroups did not touch the attractive toy. The punishment had suppressed the natural tendency to pick up such a toy, thus confirming Aronfreed's conclusions. However, seeing the deviant child in the film (either suffering no consequences or being affectionately treated by the woman after violating a rule) modified the effect of the other early punishment subgroups. Most all of them picked up and examined the attractive toy. It should be noted that even under these conditions the early punishment group hesitated longer than did the late punishment group before picking up the attractive toy. On the other hand, apparently if a child who has effectively been trained not to violate a rule sees offenders go unpunished, then he too will violate the rule.

The results of this study strongly suggest that if we are to use punishment as a strategy for rule enforcement then it must not only be done very early in sequence of behavior but everyone else violating such a rule must also be punished. Any witnessed omissions could wipe out the effect of the punishment. These are two critical but difficult conditions for a teacher to achieve.

Punishment Inhibits Learning

This study also subsequently introduced another facet of punishment that we have not discussed—after-effects.

At the completion of that portion of the study just discussed the 80 boys were given the opportunity to play with the toys used in the study. In particular, the researchers were interested in the way the children worked with the unassembled rifle, sword, and truck. Those 40 children who had witnessed the boy in the film going unpunished for assembling and playing with the forbidden toys were significantly more successful at assembling the toys than were those children who had not seen the film. Apparently observing a model in a film performing a task is an effective means for learning a novel psychomotor lesson. However, those who had seen the film version in which the model was punished did significantly less well in assembling the toys than did those who had seen the model go unpunished. In fact, the boys who saw the model-punished film did no better in constructing the toys than did those who hadn't seen the film at all. Apparently, observing the punishment late in the film inhibited constructive learning, which presumably had already taken place. Recall this when you read in Chapter 2 about the Kounin and Gump studies regarding the effects of punishment in normal classrooms.

Three conclusions are warranted from the studies on timing of punishment. The effects are greatest if punishment is administered *before* the act is carried out. Delay for as little as six seconds severely limits the effects. Second, seeing others go unpunished tends to nullify the effects. Finally, and perhaps most important, to observe someone else being severely punished is debilitating with regard to the application of concurrently learned skills.

A closer look at the issue of intensity of punishment is instructive.

Intensity

If you were in the hall of West High School, one of the things you would note is the difference in noise level from one room to the next. More specifically, you may hear Mr. Soft say rather quietly but firmly, "OK, you guys, knock off the noise, sit down, and get to work." This is a mild punitive comment, compared to Mr. Ruff, who booms out: "JOE, SIT DOWN!" The directive to Joe is supplemented by a not-so-gentle shove. "EVERYBODY GET TO WORK!"

Setting aside all factors other than intensity, will Mr. Soft's or Mr. Ruff's admonishments have the greater effect on the future behavior of their respective students? Mr. Ruff's higher intensity would, if the form of punishment were electric shock. Sudden, high-intensity electric shock completely shuts off future use of behavior that has just preceded it, while lower levels have a lesser effect. The intensity of sound, however, has a more complex effect. Azrin and Holz (1966) report that a blast of noise of 105 decibels has relatively little suppressing effect on behavior, but if the intensity were 135 decibels behavior repetition is cut about 50 percent. A decibel is a unit of energy, not necessarily a direct measure of loudness, although they are related. The typical speaking voice is between 45 and 75 decibels. A level of 135 decibels would be very intense, much greater than that exhibited in any classroom. Mr. Ruff's booming voice will not likely exceed the 105 decibels that allegedly had minimal effect. He probably does not reach the 135 decibels needed to affect the behavior of even half of the class.

The Complexity Factor

Aronfreed (1968) found an interaction of intensity of punishment and complexity of task that may be closer to life in the classroom. He reasoned that discrimination of situations is often the critical factor in effective behavior. That is, it is important to discriminate between situations in which given behaviors are appropriate or inappropriate. Classroom rules are seldom as simple as the traffic controls where speed limits are posted and red means stop and green means go. For example, student conversation is generally prohibited when the teacher is addressing the class or during individual seat work. However, during group work or lunch periods we approve of quiet talk. During recitation we want loud, clear talk. Student talk is sometimes prohibited, sometimes tolerated, and sometimes mandated. Students are required to learn the subtle differences within situations that signal the respective behaviors.

Aronfreed (1968) conducted two related studies. In Study I, each of 72 boys was presented with two toys, one of which was painted red, the other yellow. The task for the boys was to select one of the toys and describe it and tell about its various uses. Each boy was given 10 pieces of candy for participating and randomly assigned to one of two groups. Whenever the boys in subgroup A reached for the red toy he was scolded: "NO!" and one piece of candy was removed. When a boy from subgroup B reached for the red toy he was told: "NO!" and a piece of candy was withdrawn and an additional blast of loud noise was sounded. The boys in both groups quickly learned their lesson and after the third trial the red toy was ignored. Just as in the other studies that we have discussed after the tenth trial the experimenter left saying he had to run and errand and would return in ten minutes.

From the Azrin and Holz (1966) studies we would anticipate that the more severely punished boys of subgroup B would be more inhibited than would the less severely punished boys of subgroup A. The Azrin and Holz findings were confirmed. In subgroup A, 27 of the 37 boys transgressed and picked up the red toy when left alone after the tenth trial. That is, only 27 percent of the mildly punished boys resisted temptation—not a very impressive effect. Among the more severely punished boys of subgroup B only 15 of the 36 boys picked up the forbidden toy. Nearly 60 percent suppressed the temptation. Although the intense punishment was not totally effective, it worked better in these circumstances than did the mild punishment.

In a second study, the conditions were the same, except that a total of 86 boys were assigned to either subgroup A or B and the toys were differentiated by complexity rather than color. The no-touch toy had internal mechanisms and appeared to be slightly more realistic than did the touchable toy. However, one had to look closely to differentiate the toys.

Interestingly, a striking reversal occurred when the differences between the toys were more subtle, as in Study II. Under the conditions of harsh punishment only 12 of the 43 boys resisted playing with the forbidden toy, while 25 of the 43 mildly punished boys resisted the temptation.

The data contrasting the two studies is shown in Table 1.4. When the discriminating task is simple, severe punishment has the greater effect. However, when the discrimination between right and wrong is more difficult, the mild punishment is more potent. This calls into question the expected effects of harsh versus mild punishment in school. First, the behavioral cues in school are not as simple as the difference between red and yellow. Second, perhaps the difference is not so much a matter of the task but of the individual student being able to make the discrimination. A given situation for a bright child with much experience may be easily differentiated, but for the younger, physically handicapped, less able, or culturally different child, a particular discrimination may be more complex. Yet, we know that these disadvantaged students are the ones who receive the harshest punishment.

In summary, intensity of punishment seems to be a complex factor. If the discrimination of right from wrong is simple then high intensity is more effective. However, if discrimination is more difficult by reason of the task or the student's ability, then the effects are reversed, and low intensity is more effective.

Table 1.4. Interaction of intensity of punishment and complexity of task for inhibiting punished behavior

Complexity of task	Subgroup A (mild punishment)	Subgroup B (severe punishment)
Simple discrimination	27%	58%
Complex discrimination	58%	28%

The percentages shown here refer to the proportion of boys who did not play with the forbidden toys when left alone.

Source: Constructed by author from data from Aronfreed (1968).

Escalation

The intensity of punishment has another dimension, escalation. Have you heard about the teacher who advocated his own brand of progressive education? "First I ask them, then I tell them, and then I bop them!" This sequence is fairly typical as illustrated by the following example:

Teacher: Mary, honey, is your work completed?

[*a minute passes*]

Teacher: Mary, will you please stop talking!

[*another minute passes*]

Teacher: Mary, stop that and get to work!

[*another minute passes*]

Teacher: MARY!!!!!

Teacher (finally): OK MARY, NO RECESS FOR YOU TODAY!

And if Mary, as is often the case, persists, possibly the punitive action will escalate to a trip to the principal, the paddle, or worse. When a mild reprimand is administered without success it almost inevitably is followed by harsher punishments.

Bad news! If the intensity of the punishment is increased gradually over successive trials, it is unlikely to suppress the response. Maximum effect of punishment only occurs if it is sudden and substantial. Animals hit with an 80-volt shock are likely to completely and irreversibly suppress previously rewarded behavior. However, if the initial shock is less than 60 volts and it is gradually increased in successive trials, the behavior will be maintained, even if the voltage goes up to 130 volts. The most effective punishment comes harshly and suddenly. In other words, to be effective Mary should have been paddled on the first incident without warning.

As it happens, that is illegal. The Supreme Court ruled in 1975 that although teachers may corporally punish students, they must use less abrasive measures first and then warn the student that if the specific behavior continues he will be paddled. According to the Azrin and Holz (1966) research findings this procedure renders the punishment ineffective. Perhaps this explains why we constantly warn and punish the same students. Some never seem to learn.

We will consider one more factor that may influence the effects of punishment: frequency.

Frequency

"John, how often do I have to reprimand you for playing around with that microscope?" the science teacher grumbled irritably. "I've given you an F in deportment every day this week and here it is Friday and you still haven't learned." Is John slow, the teacher's grumbling immaterial, or is this the way that repetitive punishment works?

As we have noted, the effect of punishment depends on a number of factors such as timing, intensity, and escalation. So too, the effect depends on the rate of repetitiveness of punishment. This phenomenon apparently has not been very systematically studied with human beings, so our conclusions are very tentative.

The evidence from animal studies are quite clear: *every* instance of the behavior to be suppressed ought to be punished if the behavior is to be controlled. If the punishment occurs only periodically then the behavior will continue at the unpunished level until it is time for the punishment to recur. When the animal senses that the punishment is due, the rate of misbehavior drops off noticeably.

In the classroom we know that disruptive students continue to play around until they sense that the teacher is about to really come down hard with punishment. Then their misbehavior temporarily drops off. To be really effective the teacher would need to be right there, poised to punish the particular behavior every time it occurred, preferably at the beginning of the misbehavior sequence.

The more frequently a given behavior is punished the less often it will occur. Therefore, during a series of repeated punishments the frequency will decrease. However, established behavior is never completely suppressed. Laboratory studies with animals show that each occurrence of a behavior must be immediately punished. This is particularly important if in the absence of the punishment the behavior is somehow rewarded. If punishment is to succeed it must be administered repeatedly, at every occurrence of the misbehavior.

Summary of Laboratory Research

The point of delving into the research is not to summarize everything that has been published. We have looked at the research most frequently referenced by those who advocate the use of punishment for changing behavior. We hoped to be fair while establishing the point that while punishment does suppress behavior it is complicated and its effectiveness depends on a number of factors. No single factor ensures that punishment will shut off the undesired behavior. Each condition specifies that the punishment will be more effective if a given prescription is followed. The effects of the various conditions are additive. Therefore, to really work punishment needs to be administered expertly with attention to a variety of conditions.

Finally, we noted that in the experimental settings with carefully controlled conditions nearly half of the students yield to temptation even under the most ideal conditions.

Necessary Conditions for Effective Punishment

Azrin and Holz (1966) listed a number of principles deduced from research for effective punishment. In order to eliminate a given behavior by punishment one would have to adhere to such principles as:

1. The person administering the punishment should arrange the conditions in such a way that no unauthorized escape is possible. No flinching, or closing one's mind is allowed the student.

2. The punishment should be as harsh and intense as possible.

3. The same form of punishment should be used every time the undesired behavior occurs.

4. The punishment must be delivered immediately, preferably during preparatory stages of misbehavior.

5. The punishment should never be introduced gradually but be administered at maximum intensity on the initial occasion.

6. Extended periods of punishment should be avoided; lengthy, mild punishment such as missing recess for a week have a boomerang effect.

7. Great care must be taken to make certain that the delivery of punishment is not associated in any way with pleasure or reinforcement for then the punishment stimulus might acquire conditioned reinforcement properties. Thus, the punishment might actually be sought.

8. Strict control must be exercised to make certain that the behavior is not reinforced. That is, if we punish a student in order to stop him from talking to a friend in class then we should never let talking to that friend be a source of satisfaction.

9. Motivation for the undesired behavior should be reduced.

10. Alternative behaviors that could obtain the same reinforcement (goals) as the undesired behavior should be allowed.

None of the research reported thus far was conducted in the typical settings of normal classrooms. Human recipients of the punishments were at their best in small groups, but most often they were alone in a one-to-one situation with the experimenter. Kindergarten children were used occasionally in small groups, or in some instances older children in special education classes were used. The punishments used in controlled studies are atypical in that teachers do not use electric shocks or buzzers of given decibels. Therefore, it behooves us to now look at effects of punishment within classrooms.

RECOMMENDED READINGS

Dobson, J. *Dare to discipline.* Wheaton, IL: Tyndale House, 1970.

Lefkowitz, M.M., Eron, L.D., Walder, L.O., and Huesmann, L.R. *Growing up to be violent.* New York: Pergamon, 1977.

Rutter, M., Maughan, B., Mortimore, P., and Ousten, J. *Fifteen thousand hours.* Cambridge, MA: Harvard University, 1979.

2

EFFECTS OF PUNISHMENT: CLASSROOM RESEARCH FINDINGS

VERBAL DESIST MESSAGES

Jacob Kounin has conducted the most diverse, intense, and realistic research regarding the management of school behavior. His research includes age groups from kindergarten through graduate school. His techniques include highly controlled experiments, casual observations, intense interviews, questionnaires, and extensive unobtrusive observations in the natural settings of classrooms.

Kounin (1970) and his associates focused one of their major studies on two facets of verbal punitive techniques which they labeled *desist techniques*. The first was to ascertain the relative effect of variations in clarity, firmness, intensity, focus, and orientation of desist messages. Each of these variables will be described in some detail. The second concern was the impact of the desist modes on other students who happen to witness the teacher's admonishments. That is, if two students were sitting side by side and one of them was reprimanded for a given behavior, Kounin investigated not only the effect of the reprimand with respect to prescribed conditions on the recipient student but on her neighbor as well.

The properties of the respective desist techniques are as follows:

Clarity. A statement was coded as maximally clear if it stated (a) who was deviant, (b) what to stop doing, (c) what to do, and (d) why the behavior was inappropriate.

Firmness. A statement was coded firm if it conveyed an "I mean it! Now!" message. Firmness also included behaviors such as the teacher moving toward the student, looking firmly during and after the message, using a physical assist such as holding the chair or leading the student by the arm as opposed to half-heartedly asking students to stop or angrily giving commands and then turning away as if defeated before the student has carried out the directive.

Intensity. An intense message is one that by volume and strength intrudes into the awareness of the students in sharp contrast to ongoing noise. The message is ladened with affect: a threat or sarcasm.

Focus. Desist messages differ in content. For example, they could focus primarily on the deviant behavior, "Stop talking!" or on the alternative desired behavior, "Do your arithmetic." Focus is not unrelated to clarity but Kounin wanted to see if a positive or negative focus had differential effects in and of itself.

Orientation. This factor concerned the pro-child versus the anti-child issue. A pro-child message could be, "Oh, don't do that, the scissors could hurt you," while the anti-child message would be "Hey, dummy, if you do that one more time I'll . . . ." Messages were also coded for being neutral.

Kounin and his associates conducted a number of studies in their investigation of the impact of these variables on behavior. The one of most interest to us is that conducted in naturally functioning classrooms. Two cameras, each housed in a box so as to make them relatively inconspicuous, were placed in each of 30 classrooms. One camera had a wide-angle lens that picked up most of the ongoing behavior regardless of where it occurred in the classroom. The second was such that it could pan the classroom by remote control and pick up selected details. The cameras were left in the rooms for an extended period of time and only periodically turned on to record teacher and student behavior. Camera control was maintained in a van parked outside of the school. It would have been difficult for either the teacher or the students to have known when the cameras were alive and recording.

Literally thousands of hours were spent analyzing the tapes. The effectiveness of the teachers' techniques was measured in terms of the students' immediate and ten-second-delay behaviors following the specific desist messages.

Findings

Kounin (1970) concluded from these in-class observations that there was no relationship between variations in the qualities of desist message as described here and the ensuing student behavior. The degree of teacher clarity, firmness, intensity, focus and orientation appeared to have no consistent effect on student work involvement, or rate or extent of deviancy. Variations in control techniques were not only insignificant as determinants of target student behaviors but were equally immaterial for affecting the behavior of witnessing children.

Kounin (1970) reports as a summary of all of these studies that the only quality of a desist technique that consistently showed an effect was that of anger and punitiveness. Rough, angry, and punitive teacher response to misbehavior in kindergarten resulted in an increase in disruptive behavior, apprehension, and restlessness, along with a decrease in ongoing task involvement. High school students reported emotional discomfort, personal distress, and distraction from witnessing angry reactions to misbehavior. These student reports were substantiated by observations. Students with highly punitive teachers were more aggressive, more confused about the difference between right and wrong, and were less oriented toward learning and achievement than were those students of less punitive teachers.

PUNITIVE VERSUS NONPUNITIVE TEACHERS

Kounin and Gump (1961) conducted an earlier study to determine the effect of punitiveness on students. They identified the most punitive and least punitive first grade teachers in each of three schools. The teachers were all judged to be competent, with good organization for well-behaved classes. In each case the teachers had well-defined learning objectives. There were significant differences, however, in their reaction to misconduct. Whereas the nonpunitive teachers responded to student misbehavior with explanations and other reorientation procedures, the punitive teachers seemed ever ready to administer punishment. Their threats of hurtful consequences to misbehavior were extreme but within the norm of teacher response.

Inasmuch as the students came from the same neighborhoods and were randomly assigned to the teachers within their respective schools it is fair to assume that the classes were not significantly different at the beginning of the school year.

The data was gathered by asking the children (a) what are the bad things that could happen in school? (b) why are some behaviors bad and (c) what could happen if someone behaves badly? One hundred and seventy-four girls and boys were independently interviewed.

Student Perceptions

The data shows that the children of punitive teachers compared to those of nonpunitive teachers (a) manifested more aggression, (b) were more unsettled and conflicted about school misconduct, (c) showed less concern for learning and other school-unique values and (d) showed some, but not consistent reduction in rationality about misconduct. The punitive teacher students were more concerned about physical assault while the nonpunitive students focused on school rules. For example, in one school the question was asked, "Why shouldn't you play in the storage bin?" Nonpunitive teacher's student: "Because somebody might get hurt." Punitive teacher's student: "Because you might push a kid off and there could be a sharp rock down there and he could hit his head against it and crush his skull and he would bleed and his brains would fall out and he'd die."

The punitive teacher students tended to project blame more often. They disowned involvement and referred to accidents more frequently, although the description of misdeeds showed more malice and forethought than did the misbehavior described by the nonpunitive teacher students. By a margin of 2 to 1 the nonpunitive teacher students gave work-oriented reasons for not misbehaving (e.g., "It's bad to make noise because somebody could make a mistake in his work."). Finally, it was noted that the reasoning of the nonpunitive teacher students was more abstract—at a slightly higher value level as measured by Kohlberg's moral development system (see Chapter 6, "Moral Development").

STUDENT RESPONSES TO TEACHER DIRECTIVES

Several studies have looked more precisely at the effect of intensity of punitive teacher reactions. For instance, O'Leary and Becker (1968) asked two trained observers to sit in a first grade class to identify the effects of different teacher directives on out-of-seat behavior. The observations took place during 12 rest periods on successive days. The findings are summarized in Table 2.1. The teachers, under experimental conditions, varied behavior as noted in column 1.

The conclusions from this research are twofold: Intense reprimands, loud and public, as opposed to quiet and personal, *increase* the frequency of undesired behavior from 39 to 53 percent. Second, praising desired behavior while ignoring inappropriate behavior is as effective in eliminating inappropriate behavior as are reprimands.

Table 2.1. Effect of teacher behavior on student misbehavior

	Teacher behavior	*Student behavior*
Normal baseline operation	Teacher gave sit-down directives and comments, about one per minute.	54 percent of activity was out of seat, making faces and yelling.
Experimental condition 1: reinforcement	Teacher praised appropriate student behavior (one per minute), with an average of two reprimands per period.	32 percent of activity was out of seat, etc.
Experimental condition 2: quiet reprimand	Teacher quietly reprimanded inappropriate pupil behavior (about one per minute). Only referent child could hear it.	39 percent of activity was out of seat, etc.
Experimental condition 3: loud reprimand	Teacher loudly reprimanded inappropriate pupil behavior (about one per minute). Everyone in the room could hear it.	53 percent of activity was out of seat, etc.
Experimental condition 1: reinforcement	Teacher praised appropriate student behavior (about one per minute).	35 percent of activity was out of seat, etc.

Source: Constructed by author from data from O'Leary and Becker (1968).

In another study, Becker, Englemann, and Thomas (1975) monitored a well-behaved, normal elementary class. During arbitrarily selected periods, the pupils misbehaved about nine percent of the time. Misbehavior included (a) noise such as crumbling paper and shuffling feet; (b) gross motor activity such as rocking, flailing arms, and getting out of seat; and (c) orienting behavior such as turning around, looking at others, chatting with other students.

The teacher was then instructed to increase her control of the class with the following disapproving transactions: (a) physical contact such as putting children in their seat; (b) verbal directives with sarcasm and raised voice threats such as "If you don't settle down, then you can stay inside during recess"; and (c) facial signals such as frowning, head shaking, and giving the "evil eye."

The effect of the change in teacher behavior was that the misbehavior *increased* from 9 to 31 percent. The increased control more than tripled the misbehavior.

In another classroom, a first grade with two teachers and 48 students, the directives were more specific. Two observers sat in the back of the room and tallied the number of children out of their seats during ten-second segments of time. This was continued for 20 minutes for each of six days. Thus, a total of 720 segments of time were sampled. The average out-of-seat behavior was three children per ten-second period. It was also noted that one of the teachers asked the students to return to their seats or sit down about seven times per 20-minute period. Apparently the teachers overlooked much of the out-of-seat behavior. The teachers were directed to change this and increase the frequency of asking the children to sit down. The teachers complied, and for the next 12 days averaged 27.5 "sit down" directives per 20-minute period. The children's out-of-seat occasions were recorded. The frequency of being out of seat increased to 4.5 times per ten seconds. In other words, in response to the teachers quadrupling the frequency of telling them to sit down, the students stood up 50 percent more frequently. In order to see if something else was operating in the classroom, the whole procedure was repeated without saying anything to the children or changing any other factors, with the same results.

Something else very important was noted. The children were not being obstinate or disobedient. When the teacher asked pupils to return to their seats, they complied. As a consequence of this obedience the teachers "felt" that the sit-down directives were working. Second, it would seem that sit-down directives may have served not only as a message to sit down, but as a reinforcement for standing up. That is, it may be that since "sit-down" followed standing-up behavior, it tended to increase the probability of stand-up behavior. It sounds odd, but neurologically it could very well have that effect. The sit-down message serves as a reinforcing agent. Thus, although the students follow the directive, the tendency to stand up and move about has been strengthened by teacher attention. Regardless of grade level, when teachers admonish misbehavior a sequence of three events tends to occur over and over again:

Scene A			Scene B		
Student misbehaves	Teacher sends desist message	Student obeys	Student misbehaves	Teacher sends desist message	Student obeys

The scenes are repeated because it is rewarding to everyone. The student gets attention whenever he misbehaves. Likewise the teacher is reinforced because each time an order to STOP or START is given, the student, although grudgingly, does so. Since both parties are reinforced the scene ends, but within minutes it is replayed, and so it goes all day long.

Although punishment is logical and common, the evidence suggests that it is not a very efficient means for changing undesired behavior. Laboratory studies have shown that punishment procedures are very complex and their effectiveness depends on a number of components like personal relationships, timing, intensity, frequency, and suddenness. Studies within classrooms strongly suggest that punishment has a boomerang effect, actually increasing the behaviors we wish to extinguish. Redl (1980), a noted student of the causes and corrections of deviant behavior, offers an explanation.

STUDENT RESOLVE: PROMISES AND PITFALLS

Necessary Conditions for Successful Punishment

Punishment is administered externally, but what counts most in punishment is not what we do to the child, but what the child does with the experience to which we have exposed her. If a given child is to constructively utilize the experience, Redl (1971) reasons that the following sequence of events (without omission) is necessary:

1. The child experiences a displeasure as a consequence of the punishment. It may be a irritating sound, the haranguing voice of a teacher or parent, the sting of a slap, or the withdrawal of affection or privileges. Redl believes that the critical first step to the effectiveness of punishment is that the recipient is hurt, feels displeasure.

2. The displeasure arouses an upsurge of anger in the child. A person becomes angry as a normal reaction to frustration and pain. The anger may or may not be expressed, it may even be unconscious. However, for the punishment to be effective, the recipient must be angered.

3. The recipient clearly perceives the difference between the source and the real cause of the displeasure. The source of the pain is obviously the authority who administered the punishment. The cause of the displeasure, the person's own behavior for which the authority imposed the punishment, must be equally obvious.

4. The punished individual then directs the anger that has welled up within her, not against the source of her displeasure but at its cause: she gets mad at herself.

5. She transforms the energy of the anger directed toward her into self-analysis. She comes to realize that she could have avoided the hurt had she only controlled her own impulses and behavior.

The fury or hatred directed toward the self must be neutralized and made available for productive use. The neutralized energy is used for two purposes: (a) the person regrets what she did and (b) she vows not to behave that way again. In essence she says, "I'll not be dumb enough to let that happen again."

6. In future situations the image left from the punished incident will be available and will mobilize self-control before the individual repeats a similar act. The previous punishment experience enables the person to gain insight into her own behavior and also leaves her with the energies to resist future temptation.

The reader ought to test the reasonableness of this sequence against his own thinking. If punishment is to work, could any of the above steps be omitted?

The logic of Redl's position is consistent with Aronfreed's (1968) studies and interpretations of timing. If punishment occurs early in the sequence then the inhibiting anxiety is associated with such factors as intentions and muscular preparations for the deviant behavior. This is the point at which the person must control his behavior if he is to escape the consequence of misbehavior.

The Pitfalls

If such a sequence of events is necessary for punishment to be effective, then the question remains, what is the probability that the sequence of events will occur as suggested? Redl lists several pitfalls and raises questions about each.

Punishment may not be displeasurable

Will the child experience displeasure from the punishment? It obviously depends on the individual, the circumstance, and the nature of the punishment. More particularly, MacMillan et al. (1973), who allegedly support the use of punishment, suggest that:

One point regarding punishment concerns the perception of the child, the recipient of the punishment. Whether a particular stimulus is aversive is determined by its effect on the behavior it follows. No matter how noxious or aversive a particular consequence may seem to the punisher, it is the recipient's perception which determines the effect of the consequences of behavior. (p. 86)

We can suspect that exclusion from a lesson may not be a bad experience if a student is asked to sit in the hall and thus miss what *he perceives* to be a very dull, laborious lesson that threatens him with the danger of failure. Furthermore, an outraged verbal attack by the teacher is not all bad if one was just trying to provoke the teacher to start with. A moral masochist *loves* to feel sorry for himself. Punishment is really a source of joy if it nourishes a grudge against authority or other targets in the world that the student feels have done him wrong.

It is difficult to know what is aversive for each individual. One person's poison may be another's nectar.

Directed anger

It is likely that the source of the punishment will be differentiated from the cause in terms of the target for the anger? We have all seen children kick a table or some object in revenge for "what it did to me." Young children often fail to differentiate the source of pain, such as the impact between his body and an object, and the cause, his own clumsiness when no one else is involved. In the face of pain, older persons sometimes regress to that earlier stage. The differentiation is particularly difficult if the offender does not sense what he did as being wrong or at least not natural under the circumstances. Talking to a good friend in class, walking around when one is tense or bored, or running in the hall so as not to be late are easily perceived as natural events rather than a cause for punishment. If one senses that he has been punished unjustly, the anger is directed toward the source, not to the underlying cause.

Self-recrimination

If the differentiation of source and cause is made, is it likely that the typical student will turn his aggression and ill feelings toward himself rather than toward the punishing adult, the other kid with whom he has been fighting, or the system? Is he more apt to be angry with himself or sorry for himself? If it is the latter, the punishment won't work.

Cognition

Is the punished student typically able to sift out and transform her anger to productive energy for insight and self-control? Even when an individual is angry with herself she may pour her fury out at people and events around her as an ego defense mechanism. People frequently can't stand the guilt or self-debasement and thereby act out the anger with other deviations. The hyperactive student may explode in an orgy of diffuse and frantic aggressions just to discharge the very feelings that punishment creates. On the other hand some students internalize the anger to such an extent that they are overly repentant, discouraged, and debased, with the result that they withdraw or develop rather negative self-images. For punishment to work effectively the individual needs to vent some anger by mumbling under her breath, slamming a door, briefly fantasizing a revenge, or walking it off, but some anger and energy must be used to analyze what went wrong and what can be done in the future to avert the consequence.

To Sum Up Redl's Position

Punishment is a complex technique with a number of natural pitfalls and perhaps dire results. What the teacher does in cutting off recess, cuffing a student, giving a low grade, or shouting abuse may be simple, direct, and clear-cut. What the student does with this experience on the other hand is anything but simple or clear-cut. It involves the most sensitive aspects of the intellect, including emotional control, social awareness, and the person's value system. Punishment does not teach anything unless the recipient is able to learn.

It is interesting to note that the recipients of most punishment are those persons who might encounter the greatest difficulty incorporating Redl's contingencies for effective punishment. Most punishment is meted out to those who are younger or already suffering from mental and emotional handicaps. It takes insight, sorting out, connecting, projecting into the future, remembering, and generalizing to constructively use punishment. We are most apt to punish those who are least apt to take these necessary steps.

CORPORAL PUNISHMENT IN THE SCHOOLS

Most In-School Punishment is Noncontroversial

The research that we have reviewed suggests that the frowns, multiple desist directives, placement in isolation, and referrals to the principal's office have little effect in suppressing misbehavior. Such responses are too mild, inconsistent, late, and escalating. However, such teacher behavior is commonplace and everyone seems to accept it as part of the system.

Corporal Punishment As An Issue

Paradoxically, although corporal punishment is an issue and is quite common in public schools, few assertions can be either supported or refuted with hard evidence. Maurer (1974) reports that no experimental study regarding the use of corporal punishment in normal classrooms has ever been published. Researchers are restrained by ethical and humane considerations from inflicting physical pain. Research would require that on a random basis some students would be treated with pain induction while others would be protected. Researchers have refused to do this. So, we really do not know of the effects, although thousands of our students are subjected to physical punishment while others are spared.

We do have well-established data regarding attitudes toward corporal punishment. Given our mores, the general orientation of the courts, and human reasoning, it is not surprising that the majority of people are in favor of punishment, and corporal punishment in particular, for controlling off-task school behavior. We ought to note however, that with the exception of parents, schools are the only institution in which corporal punishment is legal. Mental institutions, state and federal prisons, local jailkeepers, juvenile halls for incorrigible youth, and the military services are all prohibited from using corporal punishment. Striking one's spouse is against the law. The society morally and legally sanctions the beating of children but only by parents and school officials.

Currently four states specifically prohibit the use of corporal punishment in schools, but only in New Jersey and Massachusetts is the prohibition absolute. In 12 states no statute mentions the physical punishment of children. Interestingly, the child abuse laws in many states are merely amendments to animal abuse laws. In those states that directly sanction the physical punishment of students the language is imprecise: "Punishment must be reasonable" is typical for describing limits and "maintenance of control" is usually mentioned as justification. State laws are typically based on the concept of *in loco parentis,* wherein a teacher is considered the parent substitute. Paradoxically, in 1975 the Supreme Court ruled that at the discretion of the school principal, a teacher could strike a child with or without parental approval.

In 1977 the Supreme Court ruled that students are not protected by either the Eighth or Fourteenth Amendments against undue, unjust, or overly harsh punishment. The Eighth Amendment is to protect convicted criminals from cruel and unusual punishment. If a student has not been criminally charged and convicted he is thereby not protected by the Eighth Amendment. In ruling on the Fourteenth Amendment, which normally protects citizens by requiring due process, the Court noted that teachers are primarily nurturant and would not willingly hurt a student. Furthermore, it was argued that parents are in daily contact with their children and keep a watchful eye on school policies. After all, school administration is within local control and politics. Finally, the court pointed out that local civil and criminal courts offer the means for bringing legal retribution to any teacher who is overtly abusive.

Incidentally, the Supreme Court decision was based on a five-to-four majority. The available evidence raises some doubt as to the rationale offered for not guaranteeing students due process via the Fourteenth Amendment.

The Supreme Court assumed that over-abuse by teachers would be monitored by parents, who then could sue the teacher in civil court. Records of all court activity in a state are difficult to obtain. However, it is reported that a parent has never won a case against a teacher in either Vermont or Florida. There was a case recently in Indiana in which parents won and were awarded $1.00.

These are not vendettas against teachers. The point is, when teachers begin to administer punishment, serious consequences can occur, not for the teachers but for the students. No one has or is able to give stringent guidelines for the administration of punishment. In most cases the teacher is free to administer punishment at will, guided only by professional skill and knowledge. Effective punishment requires a great deal of skill and attention, more than most of us possess.

Corporal Punishment is Easily Abused

There are few legal guidelines to guide teachers in the use of corporal punishment. Typically, it is at the discretion of the teacher who most often has to play all roles. He makes up the law (rule), accuses alleged offenders, judges them innocent or guilty, and prescribes or administers the punishment. Students may be and sometimes are paddled for being tardy, forgetting a pencil, or not saying "Sir" when addressing a teacher. The following incident recently occurred in a middle school. Students were coming down a stairwell and into a large corridor through double doors. A large male teacher was standing outside of the doors with a girl, who may have been either a young teacher or a mature student. The male teacher held a whip-like switch about three feet long. When his companion nodded toward specific female students as they filed through the doors the teacher snapped the switch against the bare calves of the "fingered" girls. The girls noticeably winced, grabbed their legs and looked up angrily. When they saw who the teacher was, they just rubbed their legs and hurried on. About 12 young girls were whipped in this manner. The incident was described to the principal, an articulate, outstanding administrator. He responded angrily, "That is an outrage, far beyond the intent of paddling." However, he didn't request the identity of the teacher and presumably nothing came of the outrageous act. In fact, there was little that he could do, for he was on record as approving corporal punishment in principle. Once the principle has been established, the details of the who, why, how, where, and when of the punishment are often left to the discretion of the individual teacher.

Procedures are Stipulated

In 1975 the Supreme Court recognized the dangers of the situation and stipulated four procedures for corporal punishment:

1. The use of corporal punishment must be approved, not in each individual instance but in principle, by the principal before it may be used in a particular school.
2. Except for those acts of misconduct that are so antisocial or disruptive in nature as to shock the conscience, corporal punishment may never be used unless the student was informed beforehand that specific misbehavior could occasion its use, and subject to this exception, it should never be employed as a first line of punioshment for misbehavior.
3. A teacher or principal must punish corporally in the presence of a second school official, who must be informed beforehand and in the student's presence of the reason for the punishment.
4. An official who has administered such punishment must provide the student's parents, upon request, a written explanation of his reasons and the name of the second official who was present.

Legal Restrictions are Often Abused

In 1977 when ruling that students were not protected by either the Eighth or the Fourteenth Amendments, the Court did acknowledge that in searching for evidence regarding the case in question they found many violations of these conditions. The Court made it very clear that it has to be the community of local parents and the teaching profession that establishes guidelines and monitors the appropriateness of corporal punishment. Such issues do not lie within the legal system.

Corporal Punishment is not Uncommon in Schools

Wise (1977) summarized a statewide study of punishment in California schools. One thousand school districts participated. Reportedly,

> Over fifty percent of the schools use the paddle, approximately thirty-five percent use the hand and the remaining districts use belts, light straps, yardsticks or other implements not described. In 1972–73 there were slightly more than 46,000 cases of corporal punishment in California. As in other studies, boys were found to receive corporal punishment more often than girls. Thirty-one percent of the corporal punishment was received by minority children. Most districts reported they would not use corporal punishment if parents objected. (p. 9)

Rose (1984) surveyed 324 principals selected at random from 18 states to ascertain the popularity of corporal punishment. Seventy four percent of the principals indicated that corporal punishment is used in their school. Students at all grade levels were punished for such behaviors as disrespect for teachers, general misconduct, horseplay, refusal to work, tardiness, vulgar language, fighting, and throwing objects.

The Last (?) Resort (Committee to End Violence Against the Next Generation, 1983) indicated that in 1981 over a million cases of corporal punishment in schools were reported nationally.

School officials often contend that suspension from school is a more serious punitive action than is corporal punishment. The academic year of 1972–73 was a bad year for suspensions as well. The Children's Defense Fund (1975) reported that over 1 million American students were suspended that year, for a net loss of 4 million school days. That is equivalent to losing 22,000 student–school years in one year. We have to find a better way.

Why were the students suspended? Since suspension is considered more serious than corporal punishment, one would expect that the reasons would be pretty serious. Approximately one-third of the suspensions were for fighting. Since these undoubtedly were not first offenses it is reasonable to suspect that they were serious. However, nearly two-thirds (63 percent) were for rule infraction (victimless crimes): truancy and tardiness (25 percent), smoking (6 percent), and such other violations as dress codes, no books, and rudeness. Three percent were for property destruction, drugs, alcohol, and criminal activity.

Corporal Punishment is not Universal

Some states, districts, and schools prohibit corporal punishment. Advocates contend that order, freedom to learn, and adult control would be lost if corporal punishment were prohibited in schools. Statistics from California, Texas, and Florida suggest that there is a dire need and widespread use of corporal punishment. However, in Washington, D.C., New Jersey, Massachusetts, as well as in many schools in Florida, Texas, and California, the use of corporal punishment is prohibited. These schools are allegedly no more chaotic or less productive than are comparable schools where corporal punishment is accepted. What is the difference? The difference is what is allowed. If corporal punishment is approved in a school, the teachers are less pressed to discover alternative means for encouraging appropriate behavior. Once paddling starts, it escalates because the precedent and pattern is set. Everyone is aware of it and expects its use. The power is in the hands of the individual teacher. Either by direct threat, subtle cues, or the fantasy of the students, unless the teacher is unusual, the paddle hangs over the classroom. When used, the physical aggression of the teacher becomes a model for more acting out on the part of the students. Recall the Kounin studies regarding the difference in student views as a function of teacher punitiveness. Several such studies have demonstrated that teacher punitiveness not only influences the general atmosphere of the classroom but the degree and quality of student participation in the academic program.

Corporal Punishment Backfires

Evidence suggests that the use of corporal punishment has an effect quite the opposite of its intention. For evidence let's take a trip to England. The divisional education officers of West Riding County selected 15 "good" schools and 15 "poor" schools on the basis of in-school overt behavior and out-of-school delinquency. In addition to behavior, data was identified regarding the socioeconomic status of the community in terms of the per capita tax rate and the use of corporal punishment in the schools. The results reported by Nash (1963) are surprising:

> It is notable that the schools were corporal punishment was absent had the best records of behavior and delinquency, despite being in areas with the lowest average ratable value. It is also notable that behavior deteriorates and delinquency increases as corporal punishment increases. (p. 401)

Corporal punishment is often defended in schools with such statements as, "That is what they get at home; it is the only thing they understand!" As it happens, corporal punishment at home may have severe consequences. From his own research as well as from several studies reported in the literature, Welsh (1979) concluded that a very strong relationship exists between the severity of parental punishment and delinquency. He further concluded that the excessive aggression of lower socioeconomic youngsters is best explained by the excessive use of corporal punishment by their parents. Schools only exacerbate the consequences if we, too, corporally punish.

CONCLUSION: TO PUNISH IS NATURAL AND COMMON BUT IMPRACTICAL

Punishment is a term, like several others in our vocabulary and personal lives, that arouses opinion, emotions, and commitment. Almost everyone lines up on one side or another. Part of this is because it is a critical part of our heritage and our individual selves since we have all experienced it, lived with it, and attribute some of our being to it.

Punishment is a very common procedure for controlling the behavior of others. Parents use it, our legal system is built on it, to some extent our sense of justice rests on the principle: The guilty should be punished. Threat of failure for nonproductivity and penalties for misbehavior are common in our school systems. Finally, we readily and naturally respond to those who offend us or are the cause of frustration for us in a punitive manner.

Behavior that is followed by positive reinforcement tends to recur. This principle has been clearly demonstrated by scientific research. It is equally logical that behavior followed by punishment will tend to be weakened and surpressed. We have reviewed some of the scientific research but the results are mixed at best. Two of the most revered research psychologists, Robert Thorndike and B.F. Skinner, who have been most adamant about the importance of reinforcement for obtaining and maintaining desired behavior, have challenged the countereffect of punishment. Both deny that punishment has a lasting effect for eliminating undesired behavior.

What is to be the conclusion? Mine is, if punishment works it does so only under very precise and complicated conditions, much too complicated for us to consistently use in classrooms. The controls that one must utilize to optimize the effectiveness of punishment are not possible in day-to-day operations either within families or schools. I (and, I suspect, you) will continue to respond in punitive ways to frustrating situations. However, I don't expect that the consequence of this punitive action will have the desired effect of helping others function more productively. I therefore will be searching for alternatives. Fortunately, as we will note in future chapters, there are other, less complicated, more promising alternatives.

RECOMMENDED READINGS

Brodinsky, B. *Critical issues report: Student disruptive problems and solutions.* American Association of School Administrators, 1980.

Hyman, I.A. and Wise, J.H. *Corporal punishment in American education.* Philadelphia: Temple University Press, 1979.

Johnson, N.B. West Haven: *Classroom culture and society in a rural elementary school.* Chapel Hill: University of North Carolina, 1985.

Rossman, P. *After punishment, what?.* Cleveland, OH: William Collins, 1980.

PART II

THE CONFLICT CYCLE/ INTERVENTION STRATEGIES

ALTERNATIVES

Wise (1977) points out that advocates of the use of corporal punishment make three assertions that are pivotal in our consideration of school discipline: (1) Corporal punishment should in most cases be a last resort used only after all other means of appropriate punishment have been tried and failed. (2) The offending student should be given a choice: "This is the bottom line—would you rather be paddled or do you wish to be suspended from school?". (3) Faced with the choice of corporal punishment or suspension, students almost always select corporal punishment. This choice is evidence that suspension is more serious and damaging because students really want an education and prefer to be in school where people care what happens to them.

In view of the evidence presented in Chapters 1 and 2, the assertion that corporal punishment should be used as an escalated treatment after all other alternative punishments have failed is untenable. The escalation in and of itself severely limits the probability of success. Furthermore, the aura of physical attack on any person by another is degrading. We need to recall that corporal punishment is outlawed in every phase of American life except the home and school. There is no empirical evidence available of positive effects of corporal punishment. Finally, the use of corporal punishment as an early resort is so common that the national organization, End Violence Against the Next Generation, named its journal *The Last ? Resort.*

The use of corporal punishment as a last resort in a list of punishments

41

overlooks the obvious: the use of nonpunitive alternatives. The positive alternatives that we will study are less complicated, embody less risk, lead to more desirable ends, and have better side effects than does punishment. Happily, the nonpunitive alternatives also leave teachers more relaxed, energetic, and endeared.

That the student will choose the paddle when given a choice overlooks the obvious point: There is no real choice between the paddle and a three-day suspension for which the added condition is that a parent must accompany the student back to school for reinstatement. Either alternative is degrading. The paddle is quicker, a bit less public, and the repercussions are internal. In the name of education and justice we must offer more legitimate choices.

If, in fact, students do want an education in order to live more satisfying, social, productive lives then that should be the core factor in our planning and execution of a discipline program.

A number of strategies have been developed, tested, and utilized in a variety of school settings. If used appropriately these processes will enable educators to facilitate productive student behavior.

Each of the strategies presented here has a particular function and none are successful for all students in all circumstances. Collectively, they offer the teacher an assortment of means for dealing with most behavioral problems. The material of Part II offers a theoretical rationale for selected strategies, describes the respective elements of each strategy, illustrates by example how each can be put into operation within the school setting, and presents exercises by which the reader can develop the necessary skills for using the strategy in his own teaching.

Chapter 3, "Self-Concept: The Inside View of Behavior," outlines a paradigm of behavioral problems, the conditions that cause them, and an explanation based on self-concept theory. Four explicit professional interventions are identified. The point of the respective interventions is twofold: (a) to replace degenerative misbehavior with productive on-task behavior and (b) to enable the student to resolve her conflicts and thereby continue growth toward maturity. Each of the other chapters in Part II focuses on a set of intervention strategies.

Chapter 4, "Deal With Feelings: Intervention Strategy A," discusses the means for responding to an individual who is confronted with a debilitating problem.

Behavior must be governed by rules. If the rules are not imposed and enforced by authoritarian means then the individual must assume the responsibility for controlling his own behavior. Two chapters address confrontation for self-control. Chapter 5, "Promote Student Responsibility: Intervention Strategy B$_1$," presents the means by which teachers enable students to assume responsibility for governing their own behavior. Chapter 6, "Facilitating Value-Moral Development: Intervention Strategy B$_2$," describes several ways in which educators can help students to develop appropriate behavior-guiding value systems.

The teacher can to a degree control the environment and thereby directly influence student behavior. Psychologists have thoroughly studied the interaction of environment and behavior. Chapter 7, "Environmental Control of Behavior," offers an overview of the behaviorist point of view regarding the change and maintenance of behavior. Chapter 8, "Reinforcing Desired Student Behavior: Intervention Strategy C$_1$," describes five methods by which behavior can be controlled through consequences. In essence, we get the behavior we pay for. Chapter 9, "Behavior Control through Antecedent Control: Intervention Strategy C$_2$," includes the means whereby teachers can alter the environment in such a way to induce more appropriate behavior.

Students with poor self-concepts achieve less and misbehave more than those students with positive integrated self-concepts. Therefore, self-concept is an important focus for improving student on-task behavior. Chapter 10, "Building Congruent Self-Concepts: Intervention Strategy D," gives a brief overview of specific attributes of self-concept. In addition, several programs for building congruent self-concepts are described and illustrated.

Caution! The positive alternatives are not as simple to execute as lashing out at a student. They require sensitivity, skill, and self-control. Just as with punitive action there are certain conditions that increase their effectiveness. Just as with punitive alternatives positive intervention alternatives are not always successful. The teacher must not anticipate that any given strategy, no matter how expertly employed, will always achieve its objective. Particularly in the beginning, the positive alternatives will probably succeed less than half the time. So be it: few human efforts whether they be shooting baskets, writing, movels, selecting good movies, or teaching reading, have a better average.

The first axiom of teaching ought to be, "I will succeed but not easily nor every time." Human beings are much too complex, the tasks of education much too complicated, and the conditions under which we labor too crude for any teacher to expect continual success. We sometimes fail and then either blame ourselves, the students, or the techniques and materials. We too quickly reject strategies that don't immediately succeed. We must tolerate failure but always seek to analyze and correct it. The strategies developed here will enable us to do so. Success is possible.

RECOMMENDED READINGS

Brodinsky, B. *Critical issues report: Student disruptive problems and solutions.* American Association of School Administrators, 1980.

Rossman, P. *After punishment, what?* Cleveland, OH: William Collins, 1980.

Rutter, M., Maughan, B., Mortimore, P., and Ousten, J. *Fifteen thousand hours.* Cambridge, MA: Harvard University, 1979.

3

SELF-CONCEPT: THE INSIDE
VIEW OF BEHAVIOR

THE CONSTRUCT OF SELF

Each person lives in a multidimensional existence. Space and time enable each individual to know where and when she exists. A third dimension, the individual's perception of her, enables her to know who and what she is. Just as each person is always at some spatial place in some temporal time, she is also in an awareness of herself. This third dimension is the most important and also the most complex and elusive.

Philosophers, teachers, administrators, and researchers hold some aspects of perception of self to be important. Socrates in 400 B.C., started as his guiding rule, "Know thyself." His teachings were based on the premise that a wide person would never deliberately choose a course of action that was bad for himself. Shevelson and Stuart (1980) point out that self-concept was described and prescribed for virtually every funded program for the disadvantaged. Thus, we may assume that the improvement of self-concept in its own right is widely considered to be a valued goal of education. Hansford and Hattie (1982) note that within the last decade over 700 studies have been published relating the self with academic achievement. Not only do a great many researchers but teachers tend to believe that positive self-regard is a critical factor in academic success. In textbooks of personality, self-psychology is not only presented as a coherent total theory, but almost all other models of people in some way pay tribute to the individual's perception of self.

It follows from these conclusions about the concept of self that it would be a meaningful and comprehensive basis for us to organize our thinking about school discipline.

All human beings, with the possible exception of infants, have a sense of *I am, I do, mine,* and *me.* The infant begins to discriminate the *me* from not-*me* very early in life. The sense of self that evolves from that beginning includes all that which is relevant to I, me, and mine. That is, if a person has a hat for which he has a strong affinity and that hat has been stomped, it is likely that the person will feel that he, himself, has been mistreated and react accordingly. If an observer were aware that the person hardly discriminated between himself and that hat and understood the effects when one's self is threatened, then the person's behavior would be comprehensible.

Formal studies of self-psychology suggest four underlying propositions. These four propositions will help us to better understand behavior and create those conditions that foster more appropriate behavior. Explicit references for the propositions will not be given. However, they were derived from the writings of Lewin (1951), Snygg and Combs (1959), Coopersmith (1981), and Rogers (1978), respectively. The four propositions are: (a) An individual's self-concept is the center of his universe, around which all other perceptions evolve. (b) The fundamental goals for which each individual strives are the maintenance, enhancement, and protection of the self. (c) The individual knows and continually judges himself in terms of his perceived competence, power, acceptance, and virtue. (d) Feelings of adequacy and comfort are a function of three dimensions of self-concept: felt self, the ideal self, and the other-oriented self.

Self-Concept: The Locus of Perception

People do not react to situations as they exist but to situations as they are perceived to be. Perception of events then becomes a major factor in determining individual behavior. Furthermore, the individual's self-concept is the center of her universe, around which all other perceptions evolve. Behavior depends on how the person perceives herself and how she perceives whatever situation she is in.

The person's perception of himself

Much of a person's behavior is determined by who he believes himself to be.

For example, if an individual believes he is Napoleon, then he will act in terms of his perception of Napoleon. Likewise, a person who perceives himself to be a benevolent father, a strong-willed administrator, a virtuous watchdog of special phenomena, or a tough kid who can take care of himself, will govern his behavior accordingly in a variety of situations. At least in our culture, people use themselves as a reference for judging others—whether they are old, fat, right, or wrong. Persons with low self-esteem tend to view others as weak and the world as threatening. As Oscar Wilde put it: "All criticism is a form of autobiography." Likewise, those persons with high self-esteem perceive the world and others positively. It is as if when looking at the rest of humanity and the world through our respective windows, we are to a great extent looking at a mirror.

To put the point more succinctly, the individual is part of everything that he perceives, as such he is the center of his universe, and his perception of himself in that universe determines a personal interpretation of it.

The person's perception of a situation

At any given moment, a situation as perceived by the individual is her universe. It is unique to her, knowable only to her in all of its detail. If she perceives her universe as supporting and enhancing, then she responds positively. If on the other hand she feels threatened, she responds accordingly. The perennial student reference to the relevancy of subject matter is really a statement about her perception of self. History, French, and mathematics are relevant only if they are perceived to have an immediate effect on "me." That is, relevance is not in the subject matter but in the mind of the beholder.

From a different perspective weapons and strategies of war held by the alleged enemy are cruel and inhuman because they threaten us and our extended selves: friends, family, possessions, and country. Similar weapons and plans held by our country are perceived to be wise, humanitarian, and protectors of peace because they are perceived to be used in our defense. Who the enemy and we are depends, of course, on who is speaking.

Our reaction to events is a function of how close the event is to us. If we hear of an airplane crash in which several people perish, we respond differently depending on whether the crash occurred in a foreign land, in our country, or our state. If we fly frequently, particularly with that airline, we would be more interested in details. If we have a relative (extended self) away from home and flying, we are going to listen to the reports very closely. People's attention, interpretation, and response to events are extensively shaped by the closeness of the event to the self. The importance of an event, task, or item depends on the degree that it threatens or enhances the perceiver.

If the self-concept, as alleged here, is a critical factor in the interpretation of external events then it is important for understanding, predicting, and changing student behavior.

Self: The Flagship of Motivation

The point we wish to develop here is that the fundamental goal for which each individual strives is the maintenance, enhancement, and protection of the self. To some degree these goals appear to be incongruent because maintenance and protection are conservative actions while enhancement is a thrust toward change. However, the underlying motive is a desire to be someone of significance and each of the three forces functions to achieve this end.

Self-maintenance

The maintenance of oneself as a significant being is an ever-present critical motive. In the physical sense, we call it self-preservation—the avoidance of death and pain. Psychologically, one of the reasons most of us fear death is because with death the self becomes nonexistent and this realization is distressing. To a lesser extent anything that diminishes the sense of self is debilitating and is to be avoided.

The self-concept is an anchor to reality in an otherwise fluctuating universe of events. It is a stable frame of reference. Almost all of us would agree that although we have changed we are the same persons as we were yesterday, last year, or three-quarters of a life ago. In contrast to myself as a child, every cell in my body is a different one, my shape and size are different, my knowledge of the universe is markedly different, but I am still me. Some of my traits may have changed radically, I now assume different roles, and people treat me differently than they did, but I am still me. I still own what I was and if confronted with an example of behavior I may respond, "That could not have been me, I wouldn't do that," or "That's me, alright."

Surprisingly, we act so as to perpetuate ourselves as we perceive ourselves to be, including those aspects of ourselves that we disdain. Hamachek (1978: 69) sums it up thus:

> Although it [personality] is a complex network of interrelated ideas, attitudes, beliefs, experiences, and feelings seeking expression in a single source, it is more apt to function as a unified whole than as fragmented

parts. The person we are today is probably pretty much like the person we were yesterday and rather similar to the person we will, in all probability, be tomorrow. You may or may not like your personality, but it is nevertheless you as you have come to know yourself as a person. Although we may wear other hats, assume different roles and behavior for short periods of time, each of us ultimately expresses that self which he or she truly is. *A person cannot help but be himself or herself.*

If an individual is scapegoated, ignored, and abused by others he feels hurt and depressed. Very often, however, an objective observer would quickly note the individual's behavior toward others is such that he invites rejection. If told that he is causing his own miseries he may agree but then continue to offend others. If others can be induced to alter their behavior toward the scapegoated individual, to be supportive and friendly, the former scapegoat's first reaction is joy. But that doesn't last. He tests the new treatment by others. He tends to become even more obnoxious as if to force others to once again reject him. They usually do and he is once more unhappy with their ill treatment but at the same time he feels somewhat comfortable because he can again be himself.

The self-concept that most people are maintaining is primarily positive and its maintenance is desirable. However, as we shall see this striving to be oneself is not a rigid perpetuation of a fixed self.

Self-enhancement

The maintenance of a sense of personal organization as an entity is more than mere survival. The individual is striving to possess a sense of adequacy, a belief in his capability to deal effectively with the exigencies of his life, both in the present and in the future.

The world is in constant flux. To stay modern each of us must be flexible. Societal mores, opportunities, demands, and styles change almost on a day-to-day basis. Over and beyond the societal changes with their concomitant requirements, each developing person is challenged by new sets of tasks to be achieved. Each time an individual masters a skill a new demand is thrust on him. For example, a child is first asked to recognize numbers, then count, then add, then subtract, then multiply. No matter what he knows, there is always more to know. This is true of all phases of social, emotional, and intellectual life. Thus, changes in the organization of the self are necessary if the individual is to maintain himself. Because human beings are aware of the future, each anticipates the new set of demands even as he is mastering the current ones. Each recognizes the need to not only maintain his sense of self in the present but also in the future. This anticipation is a force toward enhancement, to be able to meet the challenges of the future. Thus, there is an internal thrust for personal growth in the sense of one's potential.

To feel adequate the individual strives to be consistent, to maintain his status, whatever it might be, through continuity from the past, through the present into the future. The thrust for enhancement is a motive to be capable of dealing effectively with new challenges. The healthy self seeks new challenges, new opportunities to build status, to achieve more control over the environment.

The individual strives to grow personally, to become more like his ideals, to be more like what he senses he is able to be. In both cognitive and personal development there is a reaching out. We need to recognize, however, that this reaching out requires giving up familiar behaviors, ideas, and perceptions. Thereby it is risky and is resisted. Such changes generally require a facilitating environment.

Self-protection

Perceived threats are a major factor for the self. If the threat is very great, attention is sharply focused on the threatening event, often to the exclusion of everything else. A variety of behaviors can be best understood as reactions to feelings of an endangered self. Retreat to a safe place when confronted with a ferocious dog is an apparent way of protecting oneself from a physical threat. Less obvious but more common are the multiple ways people act to protect the self from psychological threats. When psychologically threatened, individuals tend to defend their actions, views, property, beliefs, and anything else with which they feel affiliated. Thus, in an argument, particularly when losing, we seem not to hear what others are saying. We just more forcibly put forth our own position. Students, particularly adolescents who are struggling with the question of their identity, dig in their heels at any suggestion they are in error and must change. People in duress do not tend to understand or accept admonishments or suggestions of errors in their behavior or logic. The more people are exposed or threatened the more tenaciously they hold on to their perceptions and ideas. We attribute such behavior to stubbornness and uncooperativeness, but most often such individuals are just trying to protect the self.

Protection of self is akin to self-maintenance and self-enhancement in that all three strive toward self-significance and integrity. If the individual perceives that any event such as a remark by another person is demeaning or lessens his significance then we can expect him to act in defense of himself.

Self: Monitored and Evaluated

Humans seem to have a propensity to judge the quality of everything. The tendency to evaluate oneself is so pervasive that much of the literature about self does not discriminate between self-concept and self-esteem. Self-concept refers to knowledge about oneself. It refers to self-description or how one knows oneself. Self-esteem refers to acceptance and conclusions as to one's worth and merit. Allegedly most of us frequently slip into evaluative modes when we think of ourselves, so it is easy to think of self-concept and self-esteem as synonymous. The two terms are different, however. Self-concept is a cognitive phenomenon. It is not unlike other kinds of knowledge. Self-acceptance, liking and valuing oneself, is the crux of happiness, positive attitudes, and mental health. The evaluation of self is partially cognitive but it is closely aligned with affective meaning. Wells and Marwell (1976) conclude from an extensive review of a variety of studies that measures of self-esteem clearly differentiate those persons whose behavior reflects "good adjustment" from those who demonstrate its counterpart in lack of confidence, a dependency on others, shyness, defensiveness, unimaginativeness, inflexibility, inability to act under stress and failure, criminality, and underachievement.

A critical question with regard to self-esteem is the identification of factors or dimensions by which people judge themselves. The conclusions are arbitrary, but from the aggregate of research and writing the following proposition is advanced: Each individual knows and continually judges herself in terms of her perceived competence, power, acceptance, and virtue.

Researchers have identified several specific dimensions within the global measure of self by which individuals seem to evaluate themselves. Wells and Marwell (1976) report the following factors: competence; mastery of the environment; control over reward contingencies; sense of social adequacy; interpersonal competence; desirability in terms of personal features, appearance, and style; and a sense of moral worth.

Any given list of attributes is bound to be both arbitrary and subject to idiosyncratic definition. Over time and among a variety of perspectives the self has frequently been described and studied. Most of the processes and instruments have been selected and utilized for the convenience and specificity of the particular writer. The result is a hodgepodge of names and attributes. Therefore the reader must recognize the tentativeness of the identified attributes when a list is offered. Given these limitations, it is still useful to us as practitioners to have specific attributes in mind as we talk with and observe our students. Coopersmith (1981) has identified four sub-categories of attributes that seem reasonable in terms of the various studies as referents for self-evaluation. They are: (1) competence, feelings of efficacy, a sense of being able to cope with the demands of various situations summed up by "I can do." (2) Power, a feeling of control or influence. A sense of self-determination as opposed to being at the mercy of fate, whim, or the power of others. (3) Acceptance, feelings of belonging, and being liked. A sense of status and role among others. (4) Virtuousness, feelings of standing for something. A sense of adherence to a valued code of moral standards or ethics that transcends the person himself. Any future reference to self-esteem in this book will be based on these four criteria.

Self: Congruency as the Mark of Success

Feelings of adequacy and comfort are a function of the congruency of the felt self, the ideal self, and the other-oriented self.

Psychotherapists have found that each of us uses given criteria differently in describing and evaluating ourselves. The evidence is not all in yet by any means, but it is likely that each of us would feel most adequate if we believed ourselves to have strength in all four categories of attributes. For example, no matter how powerful or competent an individual feels, he would be less than whole if at the same time he felt isolated, without ties to other people. Thus, all categories are important to all of us. Within the respective category, however, we each have unique references by which we judge ourselves. That which is important to one person will not be to others. This point is neatly summarized by Rosenberg (1979: 28, 29) who has been one of the most prominent researchers in self-psychology. He notes:

> If people are reasonably free to choose their own values we are led to an interesting paradox of social life: almost anyone can consider himself superior to almost everyone else, as long as he can choose his own basis for judgment. Take four boys. One is a good scholar, the second a good athlete, the third very handsome, and the fourth a good musician. As long as each focuses upon the quality at which he excels, each is superior to the rest. At the same time, each person may blithely acknowledge the superiority of the others with regard to qualities to which he himself is relatively indifferent.

The quotation suggests another facet. In addition to the selected attribute, the importance of one's own values as the criteria of judgment is emphasized. The implication here is that the judgment and the criteria are within the individual. Self psychologists continually refer to events as perceived by the individual. What really exists is not nearly as important as the perception of that reality by the individual. Each individual responds to his interpretation of reality, not the reality itself.

Let's briefly sum up what we have established. People tend to evaluate themselves. The evaluation is in terms of competence, power, acceptance, and virtue. The behaviors and criteria used to judge oneself are unique to the individual. As noted in the foregoing paragraph, the judgment of one's adequacy is made internally by the individual. The question is, what does he use for criteria? Perhaps this student's comment will help us. "I thought that I had done okay but it really made me feel good about myself when the teacher said that my paper was one of the best in the class." There are four important parts of this statement, (1) a self-referent phrase ("I had done okay"), (2) a reference to an outside source ("the teacher said"); (3) an implication of a valued status ("one of the best in class"); and (4) a sense of adequacy ("made me feel good about myself"). Embedded in such statements are three notions of the self: What I am (my real self); what I value and would like to be (my ideal self); and what I perceive others think of me (my other-person self). Good mental health seems to be related to the congruence of these three selves.

Erikson (1969), a highly respected psychoanalyst whose writings on the development of identity are classic, points out that during adolescence an individual needs to feel a sense of unity about his self-conceptions as well as continuity (consistency) over time. This unity is the agreement between the way one perceives oneself to be and the way one senses that significant others perceive him to be. If this unity or continuity is missing, a feeling of diffusion rather than identity prevails.

The contention here is that while each individual thinks of himself in terms of separate attributes, he does so from three different points of view. First, he considers himself as an entity ("I am"). Second, he considers himself in terms of how he perceives others rate him as an entity ("They think I am"). Finally, he uses his ideals of himself as an entity ("I ought to be"). Satisfaction, completeness, and feelings of security depend not only on how positive the respective perceptions of self are, but also on the congruency of the three selves. It is possible that positive feedback in an area in which he feels weak or indifferent may be disruptive to his sense of well-being rather than enhancing. It depends on how the perceived message fits the other dimensions of the self-concept.

At the risk of being redundant, let's look at this issue from a different perspective. On an objective scale an individual may have scores in a number of different attributes, as shown in Figure 3.1.

Figure 3.1. John Doe's scores on four attributes

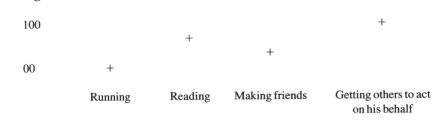

To understand John's reaction the actual scores are not much help. First we need to find out what John perceives the scores to be. Second, we need to identify what John desires to be with respect to each of the variables, and finally we need to know how John thinks people who are important to him view his scores. In other words, to completely understand John's reaction we need not only to have the objective scores but his perception of the scores from three additional vantage points. If this sounds complicated, it is because humans are complex.

Summary

Let's sum up our brief discussion of the self. Every individual with whom we can communicate has an awareness of himself as an entity. This conception of self is unique and more important as a determinant of behavior than is the perception of any other object or event. The concepts of self are said to center on four categories of attributes: competence, power, acceptance, and virtue. One's sense of well-being rests with the stability and congruence of the self-concept.

Can we utilize those propositions to better understand and help our students to more appropriate behavior?

THE CONFLICT CYCLE

Each of the students in our respective classes is an individual whose self-concept acts as an anchor or guideline for behavior. If an individual has a relatively stable and internally congruent self-concept then she will function in a fairly consistent pattern with a sense of satisfaction. This does not necessarily mean that the individual's behavior is productive or otherwise good from the point of view of others. We, as teachers, may desire a mode of behavior that is different from that exhibited, but that is our problem, not the individual student's. The student's objective is to be true to her perceived self. To do so she interacts with the rest of the universe, as she perceives it to be, so as to maintain, enhance, and protect that self.

The balance or congruence among the three components of the self is precarious. Most people in the modern world, particularly school-age youth, do not live in a tranquil world. Signals from within, boredom, or a demanding ideal self urges the individual to try more and be more than she is. Furthermore, the evaluative thrust of human nature is insatiable in needing confirmatory evidence of competence, belonging, control, and virtuousness. It is as if people frequently inquire, "Hey me, how am I doing?" and "Are you qualified for the next demand?" The data for answering these questions is the product of one's behavior and feedback information from others. All data is subject to the interpretation and criteria of the person himself. The interpretation is biased by (a) the ideals and expectation of the individual, (b) the significance or importance of the product or persons offering feedback. When all is congruent, the interpreted data is such that his status of I am, they think I am, and I want to be, are matched, then good feelings prevail. If the individual senses otherwise, he moves into a conflict cycle.

The conflict cycle is a model to depict the causal relationships of a distressed self-concept. The model identifies four sequential events: an emotional response, acting-out defensive behavior, a punitive environmental response, and a perpetuating tendency. Each of these events will be briefly described.

Emotion: A Signal to be Heeded

When an event is perceived to be contrary to expectations or hopes for oneself or is just demeaning, the individual feels distressed. As Staub (1980: 109) points out, behind almost every emotion there is a hidden cognition. For example,

When we are angry, it is apt to be because we have made a judgement that someone has treated us unjustly. When we are depressed, it is apt to be because we have made the interpretation that someone or something important to our happiness will not be available to us. When we are frightened, it is because we have made the interpretation that something may harm us.

Joy comes when one feels expanded through assimilating new information, resolving inner sources of conflict, or receiving self-fulfilling information.

Emotions are like a weathervane that communicates to the individual or to sensitive observers the status of the self. Emotions differ in kind and level. Different emotions, joy, anger, fear, or remorse, indicate the status of the self system. Within the kind of emotion (for example, anger) the level may range from rage to irritation, depending on how serious the attack on the self is perceived to be.

Staub (1980) pinpoints a very important element regarding the relationship of emotions, self-esteem, and development. Each person strives to maintain a favorable pleasure/pain balance. Exposure to new experiences, challenges, and new self-awareness are threatening because the internal consistency of the self is at risk, and these are thereby potentially pain-inducing situations. Thus, there is a natural resistance to experiences that induce growth since they tend to be disorganizing. On the other hand when new experiences are assimilated, challenges are met and overcome or new insights are achieved, then a sense of exhilaration follows. Thus, there is pain avoidance/pleasure seeking conflict in challenging situations. Secure, successful persons anticipate the exhilaration of an expanded knowledge base and integrated self system and thereby welcome new experiences and challenges. Threatened persons who feel that their self-esteem is endangered tend to focus on protecting the self and thus miss out on growth-inducing experiences. A secure and accepting school atmosphere is especially desirable for students in this latter category.

Rosenberg (1979) offers startling evidence for those of you working with 11- to 14-year-old youngsters. Several studies have established that beginning at age six there is a general decline in self-esteem. However, while interviewing and testing 2000 students from ages 8 to 18 Rosenberg and his associates discovered that dramatic changes occur at about the age of 12. Rosenberg (1979: 229) sums up the finding:

> Self-consciousness, instability of the self-concept, low global self-esteem, high depression, low-valued specific self-traits and negatively perceived selves all rise relatively sharply among the 12-year-olds as compared to the 11-year-olds, although in most cases some rise had begun earlier, particularly the year before.

Anyone working with this age group recognizes that this is an emotionally turbulent period of life. The emotions may or may not be a result of the deteriorating self-concepts but the two do seem to go together. The Rosenberg (1979) data clearly show that depression, self-consciousness, low self-esteem, and instability of the self-image are all hyperelevated during these critical years. We need to also note that during this critical period changes occur in the body chemistry, relationships with peers and parents, physical appearance, and school academic demands. Interestingly, the self-concept disturbances were significantly more severe for those 12-year-olds who attended junior high schools than for those attending elementary schools. Whatever the cause, self-concepts do seem to be radically impaired and emotional outbursts are not uncommon for preadolescents.

Defensive Behavior: Protecting the Self

When a person is emotionally aroused the natural tendency is to act out the emotion. It is difficult to sit still when emotionally aroused. Most often we have to do something with our emotion. Logically, the emotional energy would be used productively to correct the underlying conditions that caused the negative feedback. This only happens when the attack on the self-concept is moderate and the emotional reaction is tempered. The typical initial reaction or impulse is more aggressive. It may come out as an attack on the self that causes further deterioration of behavior. It may be to retreat or it may be to attack other people or property. Behavior that grows out of the emotional reaction to an out-of-kilter self-concept is difficult to predict or understand.

Clinical psychologists refer to this behavior as defense mechanisms. You may recall from your introductory psychology course such examples of defense mechanisms as rationalization, projection, regression, or denial. Berne (1976) calls such defensive behavior "games" and defines them as a series of behaviors that individuals use in interpersonal situations to excuse and protect oneself or otherwise obtain an egocentric end. The games have such euphemisms as "Kick me," "See what you made me do," "Rapo," "Ain't it awful," and "Depter." Berne's book, *The Games People Play,* was a best seller for several years. The games people play are so bizarre and self-serving that they may be funny in retrospect but most often they are serious destructive factors in interpersonal relations. Dreikurs and Grey (1968) noted in analyzing the behaviors of problem youngsters that these defensive behaviors take the form of attention seeking, power struggles, revenge, and passive withdrawal. These "acting out" behaviors are disruptive, offensive, and nonproductive and are thus a problem for both the individual and those around him.

By their nature defensive mechanisms are counterproductive for four notable reasons. First, they are often unconscious in that the person is not cognitively aware of why he is acting as he is. In these cases the behavior is not consciously deliberate and thereby tends to be out of the control of the individual. The following episode illustrates the point. Jon, age 12, was very smitten with his teacher. He didn't completely understand some of the feelings himself. He liked her, but he became confused when she spoke to him. One day, the teacher dropped by his home to see Jon's mother about a church matter and when Jon saw her, he felt an unusual, an unexplainable, sense of excitement. Even more difficult to explain was Jon's behavior. He was all smiles, but blurted out "Oh you, why do people come to your house when they aren't invited?" Jon didn't know why he said that or even what he meant. It just came out. Mother was shocked by this lack of courtesy, but the teacher, though a bit puzzled, passed it off with a knowing smile.

Jon's behavior is only understandable if one recognizes his feelings, his awkwardness in dealing with these feelings, and his inexperience.

Second, in order to protect the self, defense mechanisms distort reality. Thus, the individual's perception of the situation is often inaccurate. For example, if an individual is unable to accept the fact that she has low ability she may rationalize low grades with, "The teacher has it in for me."

Third, since the purpose of the defensive behavior is primarily to protect the self rather than to change the circumstances causing the conflict, the circumstances most often remain unchanged. Thus, further difficulties are likely.

Finally, the defensive behavior is often offensive to other people. The behaviors not only distort reality but are egocentric and self-serving. Thus, although these behaviors may maintain the person's internal integrity and sense of self-worth, they do so at a high cost.

Environmental Reaction: Retaliation

In protecting the self the person in essence denies the messages and mandates of society. In such instances the student appears to ignore admonishments and suggestions. Furthermore, defensive behavior is often destructive. Therefore, we can anticipate that society will respond. As we know, the response of society most often is punitive retaliation. This punitive reaction is likely to lead to further difficulties for the individual's sense of self.

Derogation: A Negative Self-Concept

The feedback from others in terms of reactions to defensive behavior is likely to be interpreted as derogatory. The effects will depend on what the individual has going for himself.

The impressions that one has of himself are a product of a variety of experiences over a long period of time. Information is collected and accumulated from the natural consequences of one's behavior and the feedback that inevitably comes from others. Over a period of time and a number of circumstances, the person generates a sense of competence, acceptance, power, and virtuousness. It is unlikely that a single experience, either positive or negative, could substantially affect one's self-concept unless it was marginal to begin with. The tendency of everything in nature to perpetuate the status quo is too strong.

If a person with high self-esteem comes under attack he is able to constructively deal with it. Everyone, on occasion, receives disappointing information regarding himself. Feelings are hurt, but most of us quickly recover without disturbing others or the environment very much. If the individual has a good reputation people tend to overlook such incidents and very soon everything is back on target. The individual may even profit by the experience, gain special insight from what happened, and adjust his behavior accordingly.

If a person with low self-esteem or a bad reputation experiences difficulties, automatic adjustments are not so probable. The emotional response is more extreme, the defensive behavior is more self-protective and either more isolating or more hostile toward others. The reaction of others tends to be less supportive and more aggressive. Thus, instead of adapting to the incident, the low-esteemed person is apt to aggravate the situation.

To sum up, if an individual receives a message derogatory to the self-concept, he experiences an emotional reaction. The emotional reaction unless otherwise resolved is followed by self-protective defensive behavior. The defensive behavior is often offensive or at least ineffective in resolving the external conditions that undermined the self-concept. Then, people retaliate by being even more disparaging, which causes the individual to be more resentful, sorrowful, and fearful. These emotional responses ignite further unproductive defensive behavior and the cycle continues. The conflict cycle is shown graphically in Figure 3.2.

Explicit professional intervention is possible in four different segments of the conflict cycle. Each will be identified here and then discussed in detail in subsequent chapters.

PROFESSIONAL INTERVENTION

Fortunately, the conflict cycle need not be perpetuated to the point of disaster, although it very often is. The individual may somehow gain in-

Figure 3.2. Conflict cycle.

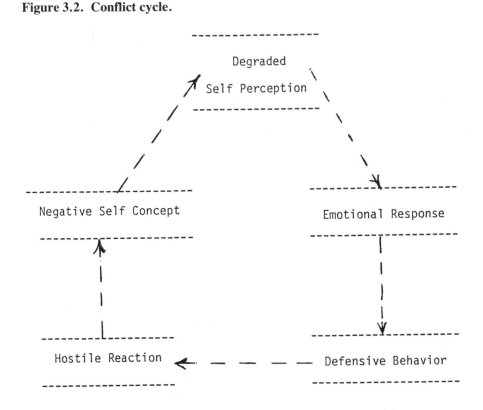

sight into her predicament and with this insight change her behavior accordingly. This insight occurs neither automatically nor easily. It may happen through a dramatic or traumatic experience. It may happen if one experiences a marked change of status, role, or frame of reference such as starting school, going to college, getting married, or other alterations in family structure. In most cases, however, it is going to happen only when an understanding, skilled adult intervenes.

Our task is to develop the necessary skills to enable us to appropriately intervene and thus interrupt the conflict cycle. In the subsequent chapters of Part II we will be studying four explicit strategies.

Dealing with feelings. The cycle may be interrupted if at point A (see Figure 3.3) the individual has an opportunity to explore the significance of his emotions. To do so requires a skillful listener with whom the individual can interact openly and honestly. Chapter 4 identifies and discusses necessary listening skills as well as offering exercises to enable us to develop the necessary competence to intervene.

Figure 3.3. Professional intervention strategies.

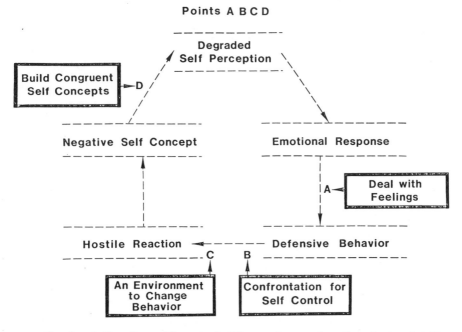

Confrontation for self-control. The cycle can be altered at point B. The task here is to confront the individual with the reality of his behavior. The objective is thereby to help him become aware of the behavior, the circumstances in which it is occurring, and the probable consequences. It is possible for the individual with support to change, to strike out in a more appropriate way to reestablish his dignity. Chapters 5 and 6 will discuss the rationale and the explicit steps for achieving this intervention.

An environment to change behavior. Teachers tend to react negatively to the self-serving, counterproductive behavior of students. However, it is neither inevitable nor beneficial. At point C it is possible to intervene with a family of procedures that deals explicitly with the offensive behaviors. Chapters 7, 8, and 9 will describe each of several alternative techniques for focusing on desired behaviors and thereby increasing the probability of their occurrence.

Building congruent self-concepts. As we have noted those persons who have high self-esteem, a positive congruent sense of self, are able to quickly and inoffensively recover from the various setbacks in life as they occur. People can and do profit from trying and erring and from negative feedback. This occurs, however, only if the individual has a storehouse of success and positive regard communicated from others.

One of the explicit objectives of education should be and is often recognized to be the building of positive self-concepts. Such a goal is not incongruent with our primary task of cognitive education. On the contrary; academic development, physical development, and personal development go together hand in hand. You can hardly have one without the other. Educators have a strong belief in the relationship of positive self-esteem and academic achievement. Even if such a relationship did not exist we are encouraged to build positive self-concepts as the basis for happy, social, constructive, and productive adults. The question of how will be examined in Chapter 10.

The positioning of the respective professional intervention strategies with respect to the different stations of the conflict cycle are presented in Figure 3.3.

RECOMMENDED READINGS

Combs, A. and Snygg, D. *Individual behavior.* New York: Harper, 1959.

Rosenberg, M. *Conceiving the self.* New York: Basic Books, 1979.

Wayson, W.W., and Pinnel, G.S. *Developing discipline with quality schools.* Cleveland, OH: Citizens Council for Ohio Schools, 1978.

4

DEALING WITH FEELINGS:
INTERVENTION STRATEGY A

In most deals one has to play with the cards she receives. However, anyone who plays poker, bridge, or pinochle knows that the perennial winner is the one who knows the finer points of communication. Only in such child games as "war" do the cards alone determine the winners and losers.

REACTING TO EMOTIONAL OUTBURSTS

The children came rushing into the room with the ring of the morning bell. It was a beautiful day and Ms. Austin was refreshed and anticipated a productive day. The second graders quickly quieted and Ms. Austin was about to announce the first activity when she noticed that José was curled up under his seat. She hurriedly walked over, feeling a bit piqued at such nonsense. She asked, "What are you doing, José?" José, choking on his sobs, shouted, "Get away from me! You hate me! My mother hates me! The priest hates me and the police hate me!" With this, José burst into loud crying.

Ms. Austin quickly glanced out the window and noted a teacher was on the playground. She said to the class, "I think that we ought to have an early recess today. Go out to the playground and tell Mr. Smith that I asked him to keep an eye on you. Barra, you and Tonya get the kickball and get a game going."

The children excitedly left the room thankful for their unexpected good fortune. Ms. Austin turned to José, who was still sobbing under the desk. She knelt down so as to be at his level and said quietly and gently, "José, tell me about it." She then waited and in a few minutes José began to talk.

There are a number of alternative ways that a teacher might respond to such a situation. He might react punitively to the obviously inappropriate behavior of crawling under one's desk. Or, he may counterattack José's impudent command "Get away from me!", or the teacher might sympathetically indicate, "I don't hate you, José, and I'm sure the others don't either," or the teacher may simply ignore José because this is neither the place, time, nor circumstances for dealing with an upset child. The teacher tasks this morning are to teach reading, writing, and arithmetic. That's what the class objectives and lesson plans call for on this day. Ms. Austin was not trained for psychological therapy. Furthermore, if left alone, José will certainly recover. In a matter of minutes he probably will be back in his seat and they can go on as if this unfortunate incident had never happened.

Roadblocks to Communication

To be more explicit we can identify at least 12 ways that Ms. Austin may respond:

1. *Ordering.* "Stop that nonsense. Sit up in your seat like you are supposed to."
2. *Warning.* "If you stay under your seat crying you'll not get your work done. Then you will have to stay in during recess."
3. *Moralizing.* "Big boys don't cry every time something doesn't go their way. You have to accept whatever happened, stick out your chin and be tough."
4. *Advising.* "Now dry your tears, sit up straight and start work. Things will look better after you do your work."
5. *Teaching.* "Well, crying won't solve your problem. Let's look at the facts. Priests and policemen are trained to help people."
6. *Labeling.* "José, you are just acting like a baby."
7. *Criticizing.* "You ought not to say that about your mother. Besides, you look silly all scrunched down there under your seat. You'll get all dirty."
8. *Interpreting.* "Oh, you just got out of bed on the wrong side. No matter what happens on some days everything looks bad."
9. *Praising.* "Why, José, you are such a fine boy. No one could hate you. You are one of the nicest children in class."
10. *Reassuring.* "José, I don't hate you and I am sure that the others don't either. Dry your tears and smile, everything will turn out all right."
11. *Questioning.* "Why do you say that? What happened? Did you do something bad? Did your mother say something that upset you?"
12. *Diverting.* "Oh, let's talk about something pleasant. It is too beautiful a morning to be sad. It is so nice today we are going to read a funny story about a boy who found a dog. You can be first reader."

These are logical, common alternatives. In fact, Gordon (1974) points out that such statements are offered by 90 to 95 percent of the teachers when confronted with troubled students. He calls them roadblocks to communication. Although they fit many of our conceptions of the role of the teacher or a kindly adult, they are roadblocks because when used they deflect communication from the real issue.

Furthermore, roadblocks are belittling. As you reread them you will note that each in some way denies José the right to have feelngs, to express his feelings, and to direct his own life. You have no trouble sensing that some of the alternatives are bad: ordering, threatening, humoring, criticizing, labeling. However, there are others that seem right. One would think that either praise or reassurance would always have positive helpful effects. Likewise, it is logical that if we are going to help we need the facts, so what is wrong with questioning? Finally, as educated adults isn't it our task to advise, teach, be logical, and solve student problems? Let's look more closely at the nature of praise, questions, and advice.

Praise

Praise has a better reputation than it deserves. As Farson (1966) points out, praise is believed to induce motivation, improve personal relations, reassure people of their worth, free people to be creative, and open up communication. In fact, however, praise tends to threaten people, separate the participants, differentiate the one who praises as superior, and terminate ongoing communication. Perhaps because people have been "had" by praise so many times it can easily come across as phony and manipulative.

Before considering support for the above contentions let us make certain that we have a common notion of the meaning of the concept, praise. Farson (1966) defined praise as a verbal statement that makes a positive evaluation of an object, event, or person, but otherwise contains little supplementary information. For example, statements like "You are a good boy," or "I like you," or "Excellent paper," fit this definition. Differentiate that from responses like "Good, good! You kept your eye on the ball," or "Okay, that's right, you multiply both sides of the equation by equal values, great!" or "That is better, you quietly formed the line without pushing each other—I appreciate that." These latter responses refer to explicit behaviors, events, or products. They can be used as productive feedback which will be discussed in Chapter 8, under "Selective Reinforcement." Describing a behavior, event, or product with an honest indication of support in contrast to global person-oriented compliments has positive effects.

Does praise backfire? For evidence that it does, observe someone who has been praised or reflect on occasions when you have been praised and you will note something peculiar. The reaction is negative. These are symptoms of anger. The recipient of praise not only becomes uncomfortable but often becomes defensive, denies the value of his contribution and derogates himself: "Aw, it really isn't a big deal." "I was just lucky." or "You are just saying that."

Why the defensiveness? Perhaps we learned at an early age not to trust praise. For example, a colleague was having breakfast one Sunday morning with his wife and five-year-old daughter. The mother said, "How sweet you look, Sherrie." Sherrie clouded up and after a moment hesitantly asked, "But?" Not understanding the mother inquired, "But—what?" Sherrie retorted, "But what? When you say something nice you always say but, and then say something bad."

Another reason for resenting praise is that in accepting praise one takes on the responsibility of being praiseworthy. If one accepts at face value "You are very good at arithmetic," one then has a status that must be carefully maintained. Being "very good at arithmetic" has no boundaries. An error becomes a betrayal of that status. Thus, one is constricted by the praise. Once praised the individual is at risk; errors betray one's praiseworthiness.

In addition, when one is praised it is apparent that he has been evaluated. Most of us don't relish the idea of being judged and graded. It is particularly bad because if for some unknown reason later performances are not praised it leaves open the question of why. Was this latter performance not up to par, not praiseworthy? This has a double bind because we then feel we have to please someone else. It is, thus, potentially degrading, particularly if we find ourselves fishing for praise.

When one person praises another the process implies a hierarchy. For example, when one says, "That is a very good painting" and the artist graciously responds, "Thank you," the implication is that the former is superior, one capable of making a judgment on the artist's work. It implies that the painting isn't good until the critic says it is.

Questions

Doesn't the teacher need to ask questions to get the needed information if she is going to help students? In the case of behavioral problems and in particular with feelings the answer is, No! Our task is to help the student deal with his feelings and his perceptions of the factors behind the feelings.

Questions tend to work at cross purposes with these ends in a number of ways.

First and foremost, questions put the responsibility and control at the wrong place, in the hands of the teacher. If the teacher asks a question and the student replies, he then waits for the next question. Out of this develops undesirable expectations: the teacher is collecting information and when she has it all put together she will provide a solution. Since the teacher is asking the questions and thereby controlling the nature and direction of the communication it becomes the teacher's problem. Thus, questioning leads to dependency and a passing of the problem from the student to the teacher. These are undesirable consequences. We want students to learn to own their feelings and problems and to be responsible for seeking solutions. We can accept student feelings and give support, but we need to take care not to take over student rights and obligations.

Questions tend to work toward closure. Almost by definition questions dictate the topics and the nature of the answers. This restricts the student's input and the range of issues to be considered. Contrariwise, dealing with feelings ought to be an opening up, an awareness of feelings and their antecedents.

When one asks questions it is from his own perspective. The questions seek information that the questioner senses is relevant. In many instances the probes go in the wrong directions, focusing on irrelevant issues while bypassing critical information.

Finally, the exploration of feelings and their antecedents is a rather fragile process. Probing and questioning may touch on sensitive areas that the student is not ready to open up. Questions tend to invade privacy. Thus, instead of helping we may frighten or anger the student, causing her to clam up, become defensive, feign indifference, or deepen the feeling. Questioning is too crude an instrument to use when helping someone sort out feelings.

To sum up, when dealing with feelings the fewer the number of questions the better.

Advice

As teachers, we have a strong propensity to be logical and to impart knowledge and advice. To some extent this is our task in the cognitive domain. However, in the affective domain where we are dealing with personal matters and trying to help students clarify feelings, it is out of place.

First, when one gives someone else information or advice, the implication is that the adviser is knowledgeable, that the recipient is not. In reality that which a teacher can give a student about appropriate behavior, values, and feelings is most often already known. When a teacher tells a student what she already knows, defensiveness and hostility are aroused. The student stops listening because she feels put down. At best, the teacher's views are discarded because "he doesn't understand." The generation gap is nowhere as visible as it is when the issue is behavior and feelings and the elder says, "If I were you I would. . . ." We are not the other person and in no way should we impose our solutions on their problems.

Finally, the solution, ideas, or interpretation may be good but not right for the issue at hand. In the teacher's eagerness to resolve the situation, to explain to students what ought to be, he may easily overlook pertinent aspects of the situation. Thus, the advice, admonishments, or information may be right for some situations but erroneous from the perspective of the student.

Roadblocks in Action

In order to obtain a better perspective let's take a look at another episode. This situation occurred in a secondary school:

Cry for Help

It was some time after school and most of the students and teachers had already left for the day. However, it was not unusual for a few students to be around for special projects or individual conferences with teachers. Therefore, when Mr. Gentle walked out of the office and started toward his room it didn't seem too unusual that Jill should come up and start to walk along. As they walked Mr. Gentle made several perfunctory remarks about the end of the day and the weather and noted to himself that Jill seemed to be jittery. All at once Jill burst out, "Mr. Gentle, I'm worried about drugs." Mr. Gentle stopped, looked quizzically at Jill and remarked, "I don't know what you mean." Jill, who was upset but in control of herself, barely squeaked out, "Well, you know—uh, sometimes me and my friends smoke a little marijuana—sometimes for kicks."

"Um humm."

"Well . . . ah . . . mm . . . well a friend of mine, um . . . her dad is a doctor and she works for him in his office and ah . . . he umm . . . he has some drugs there and my friend well she ah . . . she gets some drugs and she uh or aaa . . . we take them to see what would happen and aa . . . Mr. Gentle; I think that I am hooked . . . that is all I think about." (This last bit comes in a rush with some overtones of panic.)

Suppose that Mr. Gentle had responded in one of the following ways when the first mention of drugs was made:

Mr. G.: That is against the law you know. You kids keep that up and you will have serious trouble. The police are bound to pick you up and then your parents will be very embarrassed. (warning)

Mr. G: You ought not do that. It's bad for your health, but more important it leads to other things—bad company. You might become addicted to heroin or something. Drugs are bad business. (moralizing)

Mr. G: Oh, I can't believe that. You are such a fine girl. Why Jill, you are one of the smartest students I have. You are beautiful and have such a bright future ahead. (praise)

Do you think that such comments would have diverted Jill and her friends from using marijuana? Do you think that if Mr. Gentle had responded as above that Jill would have openly continued with what was really bothering her, with the disclosure of the more serious problem? Is it likely that Jill, and her friends, would continue to confide in Mr. Gentle? Would they feel that he was trying to understand them, to be someone they could trust?

At this point the task is to provide an accepting, open atmosphere to allow and encourage Jill to tell what was on her mind. She is upset. The first thing she needs to do is to share these feelings, to get them out so she can look at them, deal with them. This occurs best under conditions under which she can share feelings with someone she can trust.

Let us assume that Mr. Gentle did respond as indicated in the original scene, that is, "Um-humm," which is just an indication that "I'm listening." Jill, as we noted, then exposed the more serious problem. The question remains—what kind of response might Mr. Gentle now give to help Jill? Before going on to some alternatives not yet discussed, let's continue to inspect the possible effects of Gordon's list of communication roadblocks.

Mr. G: I think that things will be all right. You probably haven't had enough to become addicted. You think about it all of the time because you feel guilty or perhaps that it is exciting. Now, just stop doing it and I'm sure that everything will be okay. (reassurance)

Mr. G: I can't imagine a doctor not keeping better track of his drugs. How does she get away with it? What is your friend's name? What drugs are you using? Are you hallucinating? What other symptoms do you have? (questioning and probing)

Mr. G: I'm glad that you brought this to me. First thing is to stop doing it. If necessary stop seeing your friend. The longer you wait, the worse it becomes. After you stop, if you have any symptoms no matter what time, day or night, call me. Meanwhile I'll try to find out some information. (teaching, advising)

These latter communication alternatives may relieve the anxiety that Jill is feeling about the drugs, but at best she has simply transferred her problem over to Mr. Gentle. With all of his wisdom he has assured Jill that all will be okay. His questioning and suggested remedies carry the implication that now that Mr. Gentle is on the scene, everything is going to be all right. She may feel better, and if he has a strong need to nurture and protect others he may feel some satisfaction. However, a disservice has been performed. The good feelings will be short-lived. Jill has given up her right to control and influence her own life. In accepting Mr. Gentle's reassurance she has subjected herself to a subordinate role and will remain a child. Finally, the probabilities are high that she will continue with the kind of behavior that created the original problem. She has not learned much except that Mr. Gentle is a nice person, someone whom you can go to if you have a problem. If it goes this way, Jill will have a nagging feeling that she is a helpless little girl, quite different from the adult she aspires to be. The feeling of anxiety of an unfulfilled self will return. Unfortunately, such conditions are more likely to result in an increase of drug use, contrary to our wishes.

Mr. Gentle's feeling of gratification for having helped someone in need may also deteriorate as he contemplates the problem for which he is now responsible. Will Jill and her friends kick their interest in drugs? Might they overdose? Should he contact the doctor or the police and protect himself and perhaps save the lives of the youngsters at the risk of betraying their trust? To become involved in other people's problems can be risky. However, the risks can be minimized and the help maximized if the intervention is accomplished with care.

THE RESOLUTION OF PERSONAL PROBLEMS

Since emotions are allegedly aroused by self-concept difficulties, they signify a problem for the individual. That is, a personal problem exists for an individual when his concept of self is jeopardized by perceived events. When the problem is resolved the emotional state will return to normal. If we can help the student solve the problem then the emotional effects will dissolve. The discussion of communication roadblocks suggests that the logical means of sympathy, advising or telling, will not achieve the desired end. Fortunately, alternatives that have proven helpful are available. The alternative strategies will become apparent as we study the nature of problems, the importance of problem ownership, and interpersonal relationships that facilitate problem solving.

The Nature of Problems

Guba and Lincoln (1981) define a problem as a discrepancy between what a person wants and what she has. A problem is manifested by the statement, "I want . . ., but the conditions are such that. . . ." When the desires refer to those qualities on which self-esteem is based (competence, control, acceptance, and virtuousness) the individual's integrity is threatened and she develops an emotional reaction.

The process of solving personal problems is a multiple-phase process. The first step is for the individual to become aware of her feelings and the reason for the feelings. Feelings are a signal that something is wrong— there is a problem. The second step is to develop from this awareness of feelings and their causes an indication of what conditions exist and what is wanted. Third, it is necessary to identify what one can do to get what is wanted. The fourth step is to put the course of action in behavioral terms so that it can be explicitly identified.

In order to put the problem-solving sequence in perspective let's consider a simple situation. A student blurts out the following comment: "I feel terrible; I have to leave this school and my friends and go to Chicago. My dad's got a new job and my ma says we gotta move." Our task is not to comfort him but to help him solve his problem and in so doing help him develop the confidence and skills to control his own life by solving his own problems. If we are going to help this student our first task is to assist him in clarifying his feelings. He may be sorrowful about leaving his friends or the comfort of the school, he may be worried about making new friends, he may be fearful of his physical safety in a city, or he may be angry at his parents for changing residence without consulting him. When the feelings are clarified so that he knows what he is feeling and why then we can address desires. Let's assume that through discussing the issue with you he concludes that he is sad because he anticipates that he will be isolated, friendless in his new residence. Only with this recognition can he now specify what he wants, the kind of friends and activities that he values. Once he knows what he wants he can draw on his experiences to identify some strategies for making friends. Finally, he can specify some places where he will go, and what he might say and do in order to become involved with a new group. As simple as this process is, without experience and help from others, people do not use it.

Unfortunately, most people impulsively act out their emotions. As we noted in Chapter 3 when discussing the conflict cycle, such acting out is often disconcerting to other people and they in turn respond negatively. Acting out short-circuits the logical resolution of personal problems. The process of helping students is to initially focus on their immediate feelings, and as these dissolve, the identification of wishes and actions is more reasonable. Before moving on to the necessary communication skills to achieve these ends, however, the issue of problem ownership must be resolved.

Problem Ownership

Gordon (1974) points out significantly that problem ownership is a critical factor in the helping relationship. Although an individual may suggest or obtain help from others, people should resolve their own problems. In order to clarify ownership let's look at these problem statements:

1. I want students to do their own work, but people are copying answers from others. I become angry when I see cheating.
2. I want to play kickball but the other kids never choose me.
3. It is important that everyone scores well on the achievement tests, but the parents in this district won't give any support at home.
4. I want my daughter to be qualified for college, but you teachers don't make any academic demands on the student.
5. The parents don't care if the kids learn or not.

Number 1 is a teacher problem. Number 2 belongs to the student, but number 3 is an administrative problem. The fourth problem belongs to a parent. Item number 5 isn't a problem because what is wanted from the parents is not stipulated; it is just a statement of a perceived condition.

A rule of thumb suggests the following: A person owns a problem when some condition exists contrary to what is wanted by that person, and the discrepancy arouses feelings. Problem ownership is important because the owner should be the one who stipulates the feeling and what is wanted, and selects the action to be taken to resolve the problem. There are several reasons for this point. First, people tend to resist accepting someone else's solution for their problems. Second, an individual ought not be held responsible for consequences of actions dictated by someone else. Third, if others repeatedly solve a youngster's problems, then she never learns the process of analyzing feelings and wants, and thence planning appropriate action. Learning to solve problems takes practice. Finally, if one person solves another's problems a dependency is developed. Such a dependency inhibits maturity and fosters an undesirable relationship.

To resist the temptation to solve someone else's problems takes self-control. We have powerful motives to advise, moralize, and share our wisdom. Students who are upset come looking for someone to take over. People caught in the web of a problem often seek comfort. Beware of communication roadblocks. The goal of education is maturity and independence. Teachers can facilitate such development through helping relationships.

The Generation Gap

When asked to discuss their relationships with adults, students offer three criticisms:

1. Adults don't listen to us so they don't know what we want and feel. They don't identify our point of view.
2. Adults don't respect our judgment. They don't think our ideas are of any value.
3. Adults are phony. They pretend we are the important ones but it is just a game because in the end they want it their way. They have double standards; one for them and a different one for us.

Much of student behavior is retaliation based on these beliefs.

If we expect students to mature and act responsibly then we must eradicate these criticisms by altering the nature of the relationships on which they are based. The way we respond to their concerns is important to this end.

The Helping Relationship

What kind of teacher is most helpful? It is fair to assume that it is not the teacher who controls by manipulating others through harassment, giving false praise, moralizing, threatening, or even giving advice. It is not the teacher who is judgmental, cajoling, sarcastic, stereotyping, or who knows best what is to be done. Likewise, it is more than just being a nice person. Tender loving care by itself is equally detrimental to development.

Gazda et al. (1984) describe a number of conditions and offer exercises for developing skills critical for helping students deal with their feelings and resolve personal problems. These conditions of positive communication were identified and tested in numerous observations of counselors and teachers as they interacted with students. The five selected conditions by which one can help others to deal with their feelings and resolve problems are warmth, confirmation, empathy, respect, and genuineness.

Experience suggests that you will develop the needed skills for arranging these conditions most readily if you become knowledgeable of their respective characteristics, observe models as they work with students, experience the give and take of such communication through role playing, and receive feedback regarding your own communication with students. Every teacher who wishes to honestly and humanistically interact with students should develop these skills.

The characteristics of the selected five conditions will be presented here. Although the conditions will be described separately, when in operation they blend together and are integrated into a natural relationship. Just as the fundamentals of a proper golf swing seem awkward in the beginning, so too will some of these ways of communicating with a troubled student.

Warmth. Warmth and caring are more easily appreciated and discerned than defined. However, it does embody concern, nonjudgmental acceptance, openness, and reaching out. Warmth is established primarily through such physical moves as gestures, posture, tone of voice, and facial expression. A warm person is affective, responsive, and communicates caring. Warmth is contrasted to indifference, glad-handed salesmanship, disapproval, and sympathy. On a continuum the end points may be summed up thus:

Responses that Reflect Warmth: Degrees of Caring

Coldness or indifference	Warmth
Gestures and facial expression are omitted or coldness is exhibited by frowns, turning and leaning away. Stiff posture	Undivided attention exhibited by a relaxed approaching straight ahead posture. Avoid staring, but face to face eye contact

Coldness or indifference	Warmth
or standing over a student communicates rigid authoritarianism.	facilitates communication. Tender physical touching may be helpful, depending on individuality and emotional situations (e.g., never touch an angry person).

Practice with someone on such situations as the following. Concentrate on generating warmth and caring through physical nonverbal behavior.

Student: I hope that I am in your class next year, you are so nice.

Student who has low grades: I am going to drop out of school when I'm sixteen, join the armed service and get an education there. Then maybe I'll come out and go to college and be a doctor or something.

Student: I hate this school and everybody in it.

A fellow teacher: I'm not going to put up with these brats any longer! They act like animals.

Student: I try and try but I always get bad grades. I'm just dumb or something.

Confirmation. Communication often goes astray because the meaning of the message as intended by the speaker was not the same or even close to the one interpreted by the listener. We have a very complex language in which many words have multiple meanings. In addition, a simple word can change the whole meaning of an expression. Confirmation is simply paraphrasing or in some other way making certain that both the speaker and listener are agreed as to the meaning of the message.

Particularly in disagreements, people tend to concentrate more on what they are going to say than on what the other person is saying. Thus, when feelings are involved there often is an important difference between what one person thinks he said and the other thinks he heard. Disagreements can often be solved if that difference is dissipated through confirmation. If you strive to confirm the other person's message, it will help you as a listener and communicate to others that you are trying to understand.

Confirmation is not repeating verbatim everything the other person says. It is more like an occasional, "As I understand your point, it is . . ." or "Let's see if I can summarize what you are saying"; or an interpretation, "Is it fair to say that you want . . .?" Confirmation is a form of paraphrasing that should be shorter and less frequent than the speaker's statements. It is probably more critical during the beginning and closing phases of a dialogue than during the time that the subject details are being discussed.

See if you can paraphrase and thereby confirm that you understand each of the following:

Student: This school isn't as good as where I went last year. The kids here aren't friendly. I used to have a lot of friends.

Student: Marijuana don't hurt you none. It's no worse then all of the smokin' and drinkin' that grown-ups do. My dad and his friends drink all the time and it don't hurt 'em.

Parent: My daughter needs more discipline. I've just thrown up my hands. We can't do anything with her. It is up to you to make her behave at school. It's your problem. You have my permission to spank her. She just won't listen to me.

Principal: You teachers don't understand the position you put me in. If you foul up, the parents call me. If someone's child is delayed in arriving home, mother calls me. By that time most of the teachers have left. If you are going to keep a student after school you have to let me know.

Empathy. Empathy is a two-step process. First, it involves an awareness or sensitivity to the other person's feelings. Second, it includes a *tentative* communication to the other person of this awareness. Empathy is a difficult but critical tool for communication and problem resolution. Gazda et al. (1984) indicate it as the key condition for developing helpful communication. More than anything else empathy tunes into and thereby helps clarify and relieve the emotional stress felt by others. The continuum of empathy may be characterized by these end points.

Responses that Reflect Empathy: Identifying and Indicating Perceived Feelings

Unempathetic	Empathetic
Judging or criticizing a person without in any way acknowledging even surface feelings. Shifting topic away from that behind the other's feelings. Condemning a person for his feelings (e.g., "You shouldn't be angry just because . . .").	Being aware of nonverbal facial and other cues that indicate emotion. Accurately indicating surface feelings expressed by other person. Tentatively identify inferred feelings underlying behavior.

The task of identifying someone's feelings is not as easy as we might suspect. People seem to learn at a relatively young age to cover over their feelings. By the time students reach high school age, as little as 10 percent of their true feelings are expressed in words. Thus, we need to look for non-verbal cues and contextual information as a basis for inferring feelings and then be tentative in indicating what we perceive. Despite people's learned tendency to cover up feelings they respond positively and are more clear headed when someone helps in a supporting way to clarify the felt emotions. The pain of emotion is eased and people are then better able to re-solve the underlying problems if another person supportively listens and indicates an awareness of the feeling. Empathetic listening releases the energy of emotion and thereby enables troubled people to get at the *I want* and *I will do* aspects of problem solving.

Several examples are presented here to help clarify the properties and processes of empathy. No one, except perhaps the person experiencing the emotion, can indicate with certainty the true feelings, causes, and desires. Therefore, there are no right or wrong answers per se. You are encouraged to compare your own responses to these situations with those given here and with those of others who are reading this material.

Empathy Exercises

In this exercise a situation will be established that ends with a student statement. Illustrative inferences are given regarding the student's feelings and the basis for the feeling followed by an empathetic statement designed to help the student clarify the feelings.

The teacher has just said to Jon, a second-grader who is a very poor reader: "If you don't pay closer attention you will never learn to read."

Jon replies, "I don't care. I don't care if I never learn to read. It makes no difference to me."

a. Inferred feeling: Discouragement.
b. Inferred reason: Repeated failure.
c. Empathetic statement: "You feel pretty discouraged because you don't read well."

The teacher walked into the room and noted its general messy appear-ance, particularly the litter on the floor. He turned to Oscar, one of about a dozen students present, and said: "Oscar, you and some of the other stu-dents pick up the paper and leaves off the floor."

Oscar replied: "I ain't going to do no menial work. That is beneath me."

a. Inferred feelings: Humiliation.
b. Inferred reason: Requested behavior incongruent with perceived status.
c. Empathetic statement: "You feel put down because you think that a boy your age shouldn't have to clean up the floor."

Kris came to the teacher during recess and whined, "Nobody likes me. They call me names and never let me play."

a. Inferred feelings: Loneliness.
b. Inferred reason: Rejection by peers.
c. Empathetic response: "You feel hurt because it seems like the other children don't like you."

In this episode the student had skipped chemistry a total of 60 times out of 76 class meetings. He was given a grade of C. The student's response: "Damn that teacher, she gave me a C! She thinks so little of me that she gave me a C!

a. Inferred feeling: Anger
b. Inferred reason: I should have failed the class. She insulted me by giving me an undeserved C grade.
c. Empathetic response: "It is painful to be passed on, no matter what you do."

Respect. To some extent respect is a measure of trust, but more explicitly, respect embodies believing in the other person's abilities, rights, and responsibility to manage her own affairs. Respect is an attitude that communicates: "I'm here to help you, I care what happens to you but I believe that you are fully capable of controlling your own life." Notice that this use of the term *respect* is contrary to the notion of respect as fear. One cannot demand respect out of power. It is something given to another person as a belief in her ability and responsibility to act correctly on her own behalf. When a teacher says "I respect you," the meaning is synonymous with "I believe in your integrity, willingness, ability, and desire to properly govern your own life. You are worthy and have the potential to do whatever is necessary." Generally speaking, people do not get into difficulties beyond their capabilities of working out solutions and alternative behaviors.

Responses that Reflect Respect: Trusting Others to Care for Themselves

Low respect	High respect
Responder attempts to impose his own values and solutions to student problems. Teacher focuses attention on himself as a model. Teacher dominates conversation by asking questions and giving advice. Teacher ignores or challenges the accuracy of the student's perceptions of the situation.	Being open and supportive to student's ideas. Teacher encourages student to act in his own behalf. Teacher is nonevaluative of student or his behavior and the apparent consequences. Teacher strives not to make prediction with a tone of certainty or superiority.

The following examples are designed to clarify the meaning of respect. As in the case with the empathy examples the situation is established by a student remark. High- and low-respect responses will be given for your consideration. Once more, you are encouraged to discuss these examples and responses with others.

Amy: I'm so mad at my parents. They never listen to me or let me do what I want. I think that I'm going to run away.

High-respect response: You must be finding things pretty tough at home. Would you like to explore some alternatives open to you?

Low-respect response: Oh, the worst thing you can do is run away. Terrible things happen to runaways.

Shawn: The principal says that I gotta apologize to Mr. Brown. I called him a bitch because that is what he is. Besides he did me wrong by saying I'm lazy. He owes me an apology. I shouldn't have to apologize to him.

High-respect response: This sounds like a difficult situation. How do you think that you can best handle it at this point?

Low-respect response: You won't get very far in life if you are disrespectful to your superiors.

Brad: I should be going to high school next year. I'm a year behind just because I had a no-account first grade teacher and I had to take it over. I don't see why I can't go to high school like I'm supposed to.

High-respect response: I think that I understand your view. Let's see if we can develop a plan to help you get what you want.

Low-respect response: Well, look at the bright side of it. You'll be a year older than others in your class and that will give you an advantage.

Ann: I want to be in the best reading group. My mom said that I'm a good reader. My best friend, Kristi, is in that group. So, that is where I should be.

High-respect response: You would like to be in Kristi's reading group. Tell me more about why you would rather be in that group than the one you are in. Then we will look at their materials and see if that would help you be a good reader.

Low-respect response: I started school in the low reading group but because I worked real hard I soon was promoted to the top group. It just takes hard work.

Genuineness. Genuineness involves risk taking, an openness that perhaps is best summed up by the term *honesty.* Thinking has to do with cognition, feelings with values and emotions. To be genuine is to share your feelings, your position. Genuineness has to do with owning and exposing one's own biases, views, and feelings but not imposing them on others.

With respect to discipline problems and interpersonal disagreements the genuine teacher approaches the situation in search of causative factors rather than blame. The focus is toward describing situations rather than the evaluation of student behavior in terms of teacher criteria. Genuineness is the antithesis of pretending. Pretending is saying and doing things because they are proper rather than the way one feels. Genuineness is also the antithesis of using role and status as a defense for behavior (e.g., "I didn't want to do it but since I'm a teacher I had no choice."). When students accuse adults of being phony the essence is that the adults are not perceived as being genuine.

Responses that Reflect Genuineness:

Low genuineness	High genuineness
Hiding one's feelings or using them to hurt others. Phoniness and facade. Responding according to preconceived role in contrast to one's own feelings.	Expression of feelings used to facilitate a positive relationship and to clarify student's goals and feelings.

The following examples are designed to enable you to become more familiar with the nature of genuineness. As before, each episode will be established by a student comment.

Sara: I hate you! I hate you with a passion!

High-genuineness response: I'm sorry to hear you say that. Frankly, it bothers me if students don't like me.

Low-genuineness response: I don't like you either. Unfortunately for you, I'm the teacher and you do as I say or you are in trouble.

Carla: I know that I am supposed to be ready to work. But I always forget my material. Gee, I have a lot of other things I have to do. I'm sorry. I just forgot.

High-genuineness response: You have a lot on your mind but you should know that I'm finding it very difficult to be patient.

Low-genuineness response: You are just making excuses. If you do that once more you will lose one full grade. We'll see if that helps your memory.

Parent: How come my child got a C on his report card? He will never get into a college with C grades. You just gave him a C because you don't like him.

High-genuineness response: I resent the charge that I grade on personal feelings. Let's look at the evidence from Charlie's work.

Low-genuineness response: I don't give low grades, students earn low grades on their own. I would give every student an A if I could.

Student confronted with evidence of cheating: Everybody in this class cheats. Your tests are unfair. If you were a better teacher we wouldn't have to cheat.

High-genuineness response: Don't lay your behavior on me. If the tests and teaching are unfair, I want to correct them, so we'll discuss them in class. Meanwhile, you are responsible for your own misbehavior.

Low-genuineness response: You impudent scoundrel. How dare you accuse me of being unfair.

Summary: A New Role for the Teacher

We have said that feelings and emotions are a product of an incongruency between the self-concept and a situation as experienced by the individual. This set of circumstances constitutes a personal problem for the individual.

A personal problem is a state of affairs in which an individual is confronted with significant evidence that she is different from what she supposed herself to be in terms of competence, control over herself and others, acceptance by others, or her own value system. The discrepancy may become apparent as a result of a message from another person, a reflection of one's own behavior, or some objective information like a test score. Whatever the source of information, if it is significantly at odds with some important aspect of the self-concept, an emotion or feeling will be aroused and the individual will be moved to act.

Acting out of the emotions in the form of defense mechanisms is often disruptive, but with help and learned skills the arousal of emotions can be simply an indication that a problem exists. The emotion is a signal. The energy from that emotion is better used to solve the problem than in defending the ego of the person. Thus, aiding students to confront their feelings, analyze what is wanted, and search for appropriate solutions is the task.

To better understand the nature of problems let's look at current events for three high school students.

Sam is spending a very restless night. He can't sleep because he has a gnawing feeling in his stomach. He knows what it is and as he tosses and turns he tries to divert his mind to more positive thoughts but the feeling keeps coming back. Because he has gotten up several times his parents ask if he is ill or if something else is wrong but he responds, "No, nothing." But something is wrong. Sam did something today, he cheated and although no one else knows, Sam feels terrible and it keeps haunting his mind.

Susan isn't going to the junior prom. *Everybody* is going and this girl wants to go very much but she isn't going. The other girls are all talking about their prospective dates, or the after-dance party, but mostly about the dresses they are buying for this one big dance, the junior prom. It is the biggest event of the school year. A boy Susan liked and hoped would ask her did, but she said no. She didn't have a prom dress. Susan's mother would happily make one but it wouldn't be like the others, so she said no. They would all make fun of her.

Today is report card day. Most of the students are excited, few are indifferent. Gary is depressed. He already knows that he is going to receive the grade of B in mathematics. Gary is a junior and this will be his first non-A grade in high school. His mother will be disappointed. She wanted him to have a perfect record and he is getting a B. Gary belittles himself for being so stupid. He fleetingly thinks of suicide. Gary is getting a B.

These appear to be three completely different episodes. They appear to be unrelated except that all happened to high school juniors. The first issue is cheating and a boy's discomfort for betraying himself. The second concerns a girl's fear of what an elusive "they" will think if she is not appropriately dressed. The third is a boy who is sickened by the thought of disappointing his mother and blemishing his record. None of these conditions is very unusual or particularly serious from the practical view of an outsider. Students do cheat, few of us have all of the material things we want, and a B is a very respectable grade. If unresolved, it is probable that each of these young people will go on and lead respectable, productive lives. It is also probable that each will not forget their respective crises. They may or may not laugh about it later, but such episodes leave a mark. Furthermore, if the feelings are not defused, a variety of near future undesirable behaviors are likely. Instead of glossing over such events and passing them off as typical teenage growing pains, could they be a critical means for personal growth? Let's see if we can identify an appropriate process which a sensitive, problem-oriented teacher might use to help each of these students.

If a teacher is to help a student with a personal problem it would seem that three general objectives ought to prevail:

The student resolves the current dilemma with desired consequences. That is, that the student would achieve his desired ends without trespassing on other's rights.

The student learns the significance of his feelings, and how to read his feelings and use them as the basis for signaling the existence of a problem. Strange as it might seem, the best communication in terms of the nature of problems comes to us via our feelings. It is a big help if one can learn to tune into one's feelings.

The student learns a process for resolving personal problems: (1) to reflectively consider what his feelings are; (2) to seek the basis of these feelings in terms of exactly what he wants; (3) to analyze the situation to discover within the circumstances what can be done to get what he wants; and (4) to put the selected procedures into operation so as to feel better and achieve a better state of affairs.

A dialogue between the respective high school juniors and a teacher might be as follows (bold items in left-hand column display comments by nonparticipating observer):

A continued relationship based on warmth and caring is a necessary requisite.

Sam decided to see his teacher, Ms. Rite, about what he had done. It is likely that he would only do so if he felt comfortable and not threatened by her. He would confide in Ms. Rite only if he perceived her to be generally helpful and trustworthy.

Empathy

Sam: Ms. Rite, I, ah, um . . . I have to talk with you.

Ms. R: (after a brief moment of silence)

You seem to be bothered about something, Sam.

Sam: Well, yes, I, ah, didn't sleep much last night.

Mrs. R: Um-hum.

Sam: I've got to tell you. I, ah, I cheated on the test yesterday.

Genuineness

Ms. R: Well, ah, that surprises me a bit. Can you tell me more?

Rationalization as a defense mechanism.

Sam: I didn't mean to, honest. I mean, well, I've been so busy lately with student council and my other studies and sports. I just didn't have time to study for the test and it was harder than I expected.

Empathy. Note the focus is on feelings and causes.

Ms. R: You have done something you feel is wrong and now you are feeling guilty.

Sam: Well, yeah, it really bothered me to think that I cheated.

Although this is a question it is supportive rather than information seeking. Sharing the issue has made Sam feel better and he is satisfied. He would quit now, but Ms. Rite wants to use this as a learning situation so she once more empathizes. Sam affirms that she is accurately tuned in to his feelings.

Mrs. R: Would you like to tell me more about the way you feel?

Sam: Yeah, I guess I would. I couldn't sleep last night. I felt terrible; gee, I'm not a cheater. I don't think that is right and here I cheated. Boy, I'll never do that again. I felt awful. But now that I told you I feel better.

Ms. R: It really made me feel terrible because you had cheated.

Sam: Yeah, it sure did. I didn't like that.

Respect. Note: this does not mean that Ms. Rite abdicates her involvement as a full partner in this. These last two statements clarify the problem in terms of what is and what is wanted.

Ms. R: You would like to be free of the guilt feelings that come with cheating. Let's see if we can figure out a way to ensure that it doesn't happen again.

Sam: What do you mean? I told you I'm never going to cheat again.

Genuineness and

Ms. R: I know, Sam, you don't expect to.

continued focus on problem solving.	But, in all honesty you didn't plan to this time. What could we do to keep it from happening again?
	Sam: I see what you mean. Well, I did that because ah, I, ah, I wasn't prepared because I had a lot of important things to do.
Confirmation: This is what I heard you say.	*Ms. R:* Time seems to be a critical factor for you.
	Sam: Yeah, I had too much to do. But I want to do all of those things.
Respect	*Ms. R:* You are interested in a number of activities but don't seem to have enough time. Well, what can we figure out here?
	Sam: You know, I waste a lot of time, sometimes. Watching TV, razzing my sister, or just bumming around.
Confirmation with a lead	*Ms. R:* You're suggesting that if you got yourself organized that you might be able to do your school work and still do all the activities you enjoy.
	Sam: Yeah, I'll get organized.
Confirmation, summary of problem solving	*Ms. R:* Sounds good! But I want to make certain that I have it all straight. You cheated on an examination and really felt badly about it. You couldn't sleep and kind of had a tight feeling in your stomach. You had gotten yourself in a bind for time because of so many activities. You want to continue all of the activities and think that you can do so if you get organized.
	Sam: Um-hum. Yeah, that's it.
Problem-solving last step: putting it into operation. Continued concern and warmth. Note the difference between this statement and praise.	*Ms. R:* Okay, but we have one more step. Here let's draw up a schedule. You fill it all in and show what you will be doing at different times. Check back with me on, ah, Thursday, so we can see how it works. (Pause) Thanks for coming in, Sam. It took real courage to share your feelings and tell me about your problem.

Exit Sam. Did he learn anything from this experience? We don't know if he will cheat again or if he would have had he not felt comfortable enough to come and see Ms. Rite. It seems fair to conclude that within this experience he did have a chance to reflect a little about feelings and what they signify, and realized that he can control his feelings and his own destiny. That doesn't come all at once in one lesson, but if we have helped him grow in that direction it is well worth our effort. Now, let's consider Susan's situation.

Susan wants to go to the prom but is fearful that the homemade dress will not measure up to the commercial dresses of her friends and thus she would be subject to ridicule. Susan's fantasy may or may not be true, but to Susan the possibility is real enough to cause her to cut off the opportunity to attend an affair that she highly prizes. She will not take the risk on her own. If we found out about Susan's dilemma it would be tempting to:

Praise.	Oh Susan, you are such a pretty girl and your clothes are always nice. You will be beautiful at the dance.
Coerce.	Oh, that is silly. No one will laugh at you. Everybody will be having too good a time. You go and have a good time or you'll regret it for the rest of your life.
Share our feelings. Moralize and give advice.	I understand how you feel. Once I didn't want to go to a party because I didn't know anyone. I thought everyone would be such snobs and I would just sit over in a corner by myself. I didn't want to go but I did anyway. Do you know what? I had a wonderful time. Everybody was so nice. That is where I met my spouse. You see, if we do things that we think might turn out badly, they often turn out to be the best. You have to take chances.

The evidence is that such responses as these rarely help others develop the assurance and will to overcome fears and to take risks. Let's explore another possibility using the communication skills already described.

Show of warmth and concern.	*Ms. Helper:* Susan, I understand that you have decided not to go to the junior prom this year. *Susan:* No, I'm not going. It's not that important, besides I don't want to put my mother to all of the work to make a dress for one night.

Confirmation, an indication that the teacher listened and tentatively got the message.

Ms. Helper: I think that I understand. You have weighed the question and think the work your mother would put into making the dress would be too much for the enjoyment you would get out of it.

Susan: Yes, that is about it.

Respect. If our original notion of the reason for Susan not going to the dance was correct, she is playing a martyr or some other game. However, it will best serve our educational goals to show respect and accept her statement at face value. Furthermore, we may have been wrong, the explanation given here may be more nearly correct. Many of the statements made when introducing Susan were inferences about her thoughts and feelings. They never can be identified for certain. The door is open either way.

Ms. Helper: Okay, I just thought that if there was something you wanted to discuss we could talk about it.

Gary offers a different issue, although the processes are the same. Try your hand at writing a dialogue between Gary and a teacher who is skilled in dealing with feelings. Better yet, role play the episode with a colleague.

Effects

Does dealing with feeling work? Aspy (1975) summarized a number of studies that indicate a variety of effects of a teacher's use of empathy: Such teachers were rated as more effective by supervisors; students of such teachers functioned at higher cognitive levels and expressed less deviant behavior. Harbach and Asbury (1976) observed the classroom misbehaviors of 11 teachers who developed empathetic skills. Prior to the skill development the observers noted that student negative behavior averaged 3.52 offenses per student per day. Three weeks after the teachers demonstrated the use of the skill, the misbehavior stopped. Only two of 300 students failed to respond. The change did not occur immediately. During the first week the students appeared to be suspicious but by the end of the first week they began to respond.

If feelings are unattended, then as noted in the conflict cycle, defensive behaviors erupt. We see a variety of such behaviors in school. The next two chapters will focus on confrontation for self-control, which is a direct means for teachers to deal with such behaviors. In Chapter 5 we will learn how to promote student responsibility. Chapter 6 will help us to facilitate value-moral development.

RECOMMENDED READINGS

Gazda, George M. *Human relations development.* Boston, MA: Allyn and Bacon, 1983.

Ginnot, Haim. *Teacher and child.* New York: Macmillan, 1972.

Gordon, Thomas. *TET: Teacher Effectiveness Training.* New York: Wyden, 1974.

5

PROMOTING STUDENT RESPONSIBILITY: INTERVENTION STRATEGY B₁

A STUDENT VIOLATES A RULE

One of the frequently mentioned, annoying disruptions is that of pupils straggling into class after the bell has rung. Smitty has such a problem with Mabel.

The bell rang, students moved to their seats, and Smitty began immediately to direct the students to the tasks of the day. After about three minutes, everything was settled—the kids were all on task, the door opened, and Mabel came in, panting for breath. She sort of slid down the wall toward her seat with an apologetic grin. She truly looked sorry for being late. It was the second time this week, last week it had been once, and the week before it was twice.

Tardy students were to either have a written excuse or be sent to the office for a pass. Going to the office normally took about one-half of a period, so sometimes Smitty overlooked the rule. Typically, displeasure would be communicated by a scowl or comment. Smitty had talked with Mabel several times about the tardiness with little apparent effect. Mabel always apologized and offered half-reasonable excuses and promised to do better.

Several questions are pertinent:

1. Why is Mabel late?
2. What might Smitty do to encourage Mabel to get to class on time?
3. What is the probable effect of such action?
4. What principles are exemplified by Smitty's options and their probable consequences?

ONE TEACHER'S SOLUTION

Here is one teacher's solution. (Left-hand column contains side comments by non-participant observer.) Smitty signaled Mabel to a relatively remote part of the room and quietly inquired:

Student is confronted with his/her errant behavior.

It is reasonable, she probably is embarrassed and sorry. However, that won't change her behavior for long. She will be late again and again, each time feeling the pain of sorrow. From the point of view of the students, Mabel in particular, these are legitimate reasons for being late. Note the promise, which often is enough to get one off the hook.

What is happening here?
Mabel: What do you mean?
Smitty: Everybody but you is in their seat.
Mabel: I am late for class—I'm sorry.
Smitty: What happened?
Mabel: I stopped to talk with my friends and then I couldn't get my locker open and my locker is so far away. There isn't enough time between bells, I'm sorry, I won't be late anymore.

Smitty: Did your being late help you?
Mabel (puzzled): No.
Smitty: Does it help me or the rest of the class?

But Smitty is not buying the promise this time.

Mabel (a little more defensively): No.
Smitty: Well, if being late doesn't help anybody, wouldn't it be a good idea to change? What could you do, to make sure you won't be late?

Now Mabel is playing a little blame game. It is the school rules that are at fault. Smitty is not going to argue the point, but is also not accept it.

Mabel: Well, I could run, but that's against school rules.
Smitty: Uh-huh.

Notice that Mabel now has an explicit time limitation. Smitty is not asking her to be good forever. Mabel is happy to get this over. She'll say ok to anything. But Smitty wants to nail it down as tightly as possible.

Mabel: I guess that I could skip talking with my friends. Maybe just say "Hi" and tell them I'll see them after school.

Smitty: That sounds like a good idea. Suppose that you put your idea to work tomorrow and ah, Monday, Tuesday, and Wednesday of next week.

Mabel: "OK." [she started to move toward her seat.]

Smitty: No, Mabel, I want *you* to state your idea in terms of what you are going to do.

Mabel: [Hesitates a moment] I will not talk to my friends, except to say "Hi" and and will hurry so as to get to this room before the bell.

Smitty: Okay, that sounds good, we'll try that through next Wednesday, four days; I know you can make it.

We don't know for sure if Mabel will change, but there is a principle behind Smitty's action: People who publicly commit themselves to a plan that is reasonable and acceptable in terms of action and time will do more to live up to that plan. The meaning and significance of this principle will become more evident as we progress through this chapter.

GLASSER'S REALITY THERAPY (EDUCATION)

Most people conform to established rules as a matter of course but a few always tend to be working around the edges. They are not malicious but seem to repeatedly violate rules. They try, via excuses, promises, bargaining, denial, and blaming, to be free of sin with a fully protected self. Our task here is to consider ways to eliminate these styles, along with unproductive defense mechanisms. A number of strategies have been developed that offer the means for us to achieve this objective and in so doing achieve several other important objectives.

Rationale and Research

Each individual perceives the world uniquely and in some way differently from reality. That is, expectations, motivations, understandings, feelings, wishes, and interpretations vary from one individual to another for each event, and thereby each person perceives differently what is happening. Each person responds not to reality but to her perception of that reality. If we are going to help an individual behave more reasonably we need to do so from within the perspectives of that individual. However, the goal is congruity of individual perspectives and reality.

William Glasser (1975) offers a process for enabling students to become more aware of reality and thus more responsible for their own behavior. The reality of any behavior includes the behavior, its antecedents and its consequences. An awareness of what is happening and the incongruity of the consequence with what is desired enables the individual to behave with more self control.

Glasser is a psychiatrist and thus he views his treatment as therapy. The recommended treatment, however, may be more appropriately called "reality education." First, people do not act irresponsibly because they are ill. If there is a medical analogy, it is more related to deficiency than illness, a deficiency of those experiences that encourage and enable one to become responsible. Second, the treatment is composed of a series of steps that any professional teacher can put into operation. Finally, the objectives of the program can best be achieved in a natural setting such as a school.

The thesis of reality education fits very logically within the conflict cycle model. The four elements of self (competence, affiliation, control of one's life, and virtuousness) are the cornerstones of schools without failure. Glasser explains that those persons with a failure identity have not found sufficient opportunities for success. Without the experience of success on which to build and sustain a positive self-concept, these persons are left angry, frustrated, lonely, and antisocial. Glasser's proposed solution is summarized as follows: "In helping children, we must work to make them understand that they are *responsible* for fulfilling their needs, for behaving so that they can gain a successful identity" (1969: 19).

Glasser conceived the core of reality therapy through his 11 years of work with delinquent girls at the Ventura School within the California Youth Authority. These girls, although institutionalized, were primarily asocial. Just as with many of our school-oriented problems, their behavior seemed to be more counterproductive than antisocial.

Glasser has demonstrated the steps of his theory to thousands of teachers within the school setting. However, despite extensive distribution and many advocates there has been limited empirical research to demonstrate its effects. Its primary support comes from the numerous teachers who have adapted Glasser's schools without failure (SWF) plan and enthusiastically reported a sense of success.

Masters et al. (1976) summarized a number of studies by pointing out that SWF made pupils more task-oriented and more likely to be involved in work activities. Teachers report that pupils more openly participate in both intellectual and problem behavior discussions. As a result of experiences in class meetings teachers become more oriented toward meeting pupil personality needs and less threatened by pupil-proposed innovations. Pupils report that they feel more involved and more responsible for their own behavior, and recognize more strongly the need for academic achievement. One report indicated a 60 percent drop in drug abuse. These are valued achievements, but in each case the contention is based on participant testimony and not on independent observers or hard data.

Masters et al. (1976) used trained classroom observers in their own study, which involved 150 teachers and 3,500 pupils in 10 elementary and middle schools. The study lasted two years, and the observers reported that those teachers with SWF training asked more questions, lectured less, reacted more positively to pupil ideas, and praised and criticized less frequently than did the untrained teachers. Disciplinary referrals to the principals dropped 50 percent, allegedly because teachers felt more capable and confident to deal with behavioral problems. Once again observers, teachers, and administrators seemed pleased with the results.

In summary, Glasser is a valued workshop leader; a large number of schools have adopted the schools without failure plan and enthusiastically report a sense of success. Individual teachers typically react favorably to reality therapy. It offers a positive approach, makes sense, and is readily applicable to a wide variety of behavioral problems. Most important, teachers report that it works.

HUMANITY: A MODEL

Reality education is firmly rooted in Adler's (1964) model of humans. It will help us to put reality education into operation if we comprehend Adler's assumptions. Adler's study of human nature led him to advocate such concepts as the following:

1. Behavior is purposive. People act so as to achieve a goal(s), which may be either explicit or implicit.

2. The major goal is fulfillment, to overcome feelings of inferiority and to become a self-identified, better person. The goal very often is fictional, untested by reality but nevertheless real for the individual. Each wants to eliminate deficiencies, to be in control of his destiny.

3. Reality is uniquely perceived by the individual. Each person reacts, not to the reality of what is happening, but to his perception of who did what to whom. A critical perception is the interpretation of other people's expectations.

4. Social interaction, social support, and social identity are critical. Life problems are mostly social problems: to reckon and to adapt ourselves to others. This social disposition is an innate potential, but the details and skills must be learned. With unfavorable learning conditions the outcome may be underdeveloped or misdirected behavior.

5. People learn what they live. Each individual develops a prototype of a life style out of his experiences. This style is then maintained because of the perceptual bias.

6. Each individual's style of life is controlled by the decisions he makes. People are able to consider alternatives and select the one with the best consequences from their point of view. Behavior is more future-oriented than past-controlled. Each of us actively seeks, interprets, and uses stimuli material for his or her own purposes.

7. Self-evaluation is continuous. Each individual is aware of his harmony or lack of harmony with the universe, particularly with other persons. In this way, we are continually trying to understand the meaning of life, society, and the significance of our own behavior.

Adler's position is epitomized by this quote, which seems particularly relevant for reality education:

> The high degree of cooperation and social culture which man needs for his very existence demands spontaneous social effort, and the dominant purpose of education is to evoke it. Social feeling is not inborn: but it is an innate potentiality which has to be consciously developed (1964: 31).

Adler's assumptions add up to the conclusion that behavior is within the domain of the individual, but that internal control must be learned through experience.

RESPONSIBILITY IN JUXTAPOSITION

Few people would argue with the proposition that one of the primary purposes of school is to help pupils move toward self-responsibility and maturity. A group of teachers listed these qualities for responsible students:

Someone you can depend on.

Gets his work in on time.

A student who does all of his own work, no cheating.

Someone you can trust.

He freely chooses to work and doesn't have to always be reminded to get to work.

A student who initiates actions on his own.

A student who behaves as he should.

A student who knows what he is supposed to do and does it without the teacher supervising him all of the time.

These qualities focus on freely chosen desired behaviors achieved through adult support rather than authoritarian supervision. Responsibility refers to behavior initiated and governed by the individual and not to consequences governed and administered by someone else.

Glasser (1981) points out that whenever the teacher makes the rules, enforces them, and deals out punishments, the students are denied self-monitoring, self-control, and a sense of responsibility. If the teacher is doing everything then the student does not have the opportunity to become responsible. At best, the pupil becomes obedient. Obedience and responsibility are often thought to be synonymous. However, they are quite different.

Responsibility Contrasted to Obedience

The concepts of responsibility and obedience are distinguishable by at least three properties: choice, consequence, and need satisfaction.

A critical factor of responsibility is that the individual acts as a free moral agent capable of determining his own act. On the other hand, obedience replaces choice with submission and compliance to the wishes, restraints, control, and command of authority. Such conformity seems to be the antithesis of maturity, of democracy. Most people are shocked and disappointed when the evidence of Crutchfield's (1955) classic studies of conformity and Milgram's (1963) studies of obedience are presented. Despite our folklore the evidence strongly suggests that Americans tend to conform and obey without too much regard for what they are asked to do. This comment by Virginia Satir (1972: 236) helps to put obedience and responsibility into juxtaposition.

. . . I have control over the choice of whether or not to act and the course of action I take. For this I can be held responsible to myself as well as to others. . . .

In obedience, choice is forsaken. When a person is merely obedient, her responses are determined by someone else.

A person is acting responsibly when she chooses to behave or assume a task to obtain consequences that will not only achieve satisfaction of her own needs but also will not trespass on the rights of others. The realization of the two-way relationship between one's acts and their consequences is important. In obedience one is concerned about consequences in fear of harm and derogation or in pleasing an authority. In responsibility, the concern for consequences is in terms of (a) positive need satisfaction and (b) interference with the rights of others. In obedience, the rights of others is not an issue; only the power of others is important.

Both obedient and responsible behaviors have the potential for satisfying personal needs. However, the needs that obedience satisfies are those of deference and survival. Responsible behavior satisfies needs of power, autonomy, and a sense of controlling one's own destiny.

The demand for obedience is based on the assumption that human beings will not forgo hedonistic behavior unless more powerful aversive consequences in the form of guilt or punishment exist. Reliance on personal responsibility rests on the belief that people strive to maintain internal consistency in their needs, thoughts, behavior, and values.

The Consequences of Responsible Behavior

Martyrdom is the sacrifice of oneself for the good of others. Selfishness is the sacrifice of the needs and rights of others for the sake of oneself. Responsibility is neither of these—it is not a sacrifice but neither is it purely hedonistic. Responsibility is choosing to behave in a way that is careful to protect the rights of others while constructively obtaining satisfaction for oneself. The reasonable person inquires and anticipates: Will this act help me? Will this act help others? Will it derogate either myself or others? Only after consideration of these consequences will the responsible person act. Note, the responsible person is held accountable for his behavior both to himself and to others. Freedom to choose is not a license to act impulsively on one's desires. Responsibility is to behave in ways that obtain what is wanted, with the constraint that other's rights will not be violated.

THE CONDITIONS FOR RESPONSIBLE BEHAVIOR

As noted earlier, Glasser has expressed his views extensively in articles, books, and teacher workshops. The basic conditions of discipline and the proposed steps to enable pupils to become more responsible are adapted from these various sources.

Conditions for Good Discipline

In order to have good discipline six basic conditions must exist. Glasser (1981) identified these six conditions as (1) schools must be a good place; (2) students are trusted; (3) rules are established; (4) students agree to and accept the rules; (5) rules are open to change; and (6) rule violations have consequences.

School must be a good place

A good place is wherever a person can enhance herself. Generally speaking, if a student feels in control of her destiny, finds friends and success in school, it is a good place. To help students experience this, teachers must be supportive and friendly. As the reader knows, in some cases this becomes a very challenging task. However, it is a critical factor. Ideally, each student experiences each day as a good day. At least we should try to have the good experiences outnumber the bad, and focus attention on the good. It helps if we greet students positively with a "What good things are we going to accomplish today?" attitude. More particularly, with problem students start each encounter fresh. No matter what the history or repetition of the problem, act as if today is the first time the misbehavior has occurred. You will be impressed with how pupil attitudes will change as we change our attitude. As we have already noted, such interpersonal teacher behavior as empathy, genuineness, and respect are reflected not only in pupil attitude but increased academic achievement.

For example, Aspy (1975) tells about a group of middle-school teachers who discovered that when they gave positive personal attention to individual problem pupils, about three times an hour, behavior noticeably improved. With the improvement in behavior came an increase in academic achievement. Each attention episode only took from 5 to 20 seconds. All it takes is a smile, a wink, a positive comment.

School is a trying experience for many students. They have no choice but to attend. To reach the age of six in the United States is to be sentenced to 12,000 hours in an institution. In this institution, school, the individual is subordinate to an apparently all-powerful adult. Space is limited in that 25–40 people are crowded in a single room. Movement is restricted, as is communication with others. As many as 40 percent of the high school students in a typical school are unaffiliated, without any friends. One can take care of personal needs only during short, specified times. The furniture is uncomfortable and restrictive. For most, a message is frequently communicated that you are inferior to others in one way or another.

If you were given the task of improving morale in your school with a reasonably free hand to make changes, what are some possibilities? Think of at least five ideas and two ways each might be put into operation.

You may now wish to compare your ideas with those offered by other teachers and administrators.

- **Make certain that everyone is aware that school is a good place to be is a schoolwide goal.**
  - (a) Handouts, posters
  - (b) Form several committees to work on improving school conditions.

- **Involve parents, strengthen and use PTA.**
  - (a) Send home regular positive newsletters, with pupil names and activities identified.
  - (b) Use parents as volunteer aides.
  - (c) Have a parent's room with a hot pot of coffee.

- **Principal open to input**
  - (a) Pipeline board for suggestions and gripes.
  - (b) Principal meets 1 hour per week with a *real* cross section of pupils.
  - (c) Open rap sessions.

- **Support from teacher's unions.**
  - (a) Include demand for appropriate facilities in grievance and annual negotiations.

- **Make school look "welcome" and relaxed.**
  - (a) Murals on the walls
  - (b) "Proud walls." Students decorate areas with personal achievements, possessions.
  - (c) Photo boards.
  - (d) Fix up own room with easy chairs, area carpets, conversation areas.

- **Recognition days or certificates of achievement.**
  - (a) Birthday announcements.
  - (b) Certificates of merit (e.g., attendance, popularity, helpfulness to others). Everyone gets at least one a year.

- **Pay off for taking care of school.**
  - (a) Share financial savings for drop in vandalism.
- **Emphasize friendship and esprit de corp.**
  - (a) Introduction days. Everybody wears a personalized name tag.
  - (b) Multicultural picnics.
  - (c) Intramural competition in academics, art, athletics, and dancing.
- **Develop strong bond with parents.**
  - (a) Make school a family learning–recreation place.
  - (b) Offer one-night help programs for parents.

Vary classroom assignments and routines. Sameness is tiresome and monotonous.

Be businesslike, crisp in establishing class activities. If students sense confusion, they feel rejected and become demoralized.

Work up a slogan for your room. Include the pupils in developing a theme, thought, and wording. Perhaps a creed.

Recognize special days (in addition to Christian and Western holidays) with programs, exercises, bulletin-board notices, and so on.

Organize a student self-government program or at least an advisory board and make it legitimate by giving it power, tasks, and evidence that its reflections will be utilized.

Join in activities that the pupils perceive to be important.

Students are trusted

Trust has two meaning here. (a) We trust the students to neither betray us nor abuse our property. (b) We trust the students to do the right thing in their own behalf and not to violate the rights of others. The latter point is closely allied with *respect* as discussed in Chapter 3. Trust in this sense means that you believe that people, including students, are capable and willing to govern their own behavior. Trust and respect are self-fulfilling prophesies. If teachers expect students to fail, to be dependent, to act immaturely, and to only obey when closely monitored, then that is what will happen. If, on the other hand, teachers indicate through word and action that students are to act maturely and make responsible decisions, then they will. Educational literature is replete with examples like the miracle of Helen Keller and the variety of "Pygmalion in the classroom" studies which demonstrate that support and positive expectation are powerful forces for influencing behavior.

Rules are established

The teacher's behavioral expectations must be clearly communicated to the pupils. Preferably the accent will be on positive desired behavior. If one knows what is expected it is easier to know how to behave than when one only hears what one ought not do. An interesting example comes from a study of written instructions for airline passenger safety procedures. The message of about 200 words included 25 details. Half of the passengers received only affirmative statements such as: Extinguish cigarettes, fasten seat belts, remove all sharp objects from your purse. Other passengers received negative directions such as: do not leave cigarettes lighted; do not leave seat buckles unbuckled; and do not leave sharp objects on your person. Performance of the adult passengers was significantly better when the instructions were positive (e.g., "Do . . ."). Admonishments, such as "don't do . . .," come off as nagging. Furthermore, some people have an overwhelming urge to test and challenge admonishments of "thou shalt not."

Rule making will be discussed in some detail in Chapter 7.

Students agree to and accept the rules

Even the most recalcitrant student understands the need for rules. No game or organization can exist without rules. If rules are presented early in the relationship, in a reasonable fashion, with some rationale beyond "because I said so," then we can expect that most pupils will abide, at least temporarily.

Rules are open to change

Classroom situations change and the rules ought to change accordingly. Each class is unique as to personnel and objectives, and the guiding rules ought to reflect this uniqueness. Most important, it is desirable that the students perceive that they are participants in rule making and instrumental in changing unproductive rules. We are not suggesting that rule making be turned over to students. It is just that students' views are important if the rules are to be just and achievable. Moreover, the evidence throughout industry as well as schools is clear-cut: If workers are involved in establishing a standard, the result is an increase of productivity and on-task behavior, with a corresponding decrease in off-task behavior.

Rule violations have consequences

Students must realize that there are consequences to all behavior and that rule violations are not to be ignored. However, the consequences need not be authoritatively induced punishment. The offender is confronted with the behavior and its consequences in terms of personal need satisfaction and the deprivation of others' needs and rights. Note, if the only apparent consequence to rule violations is authoritative punishment, then the appropriateness of the rule is in question and we are back to the previous item, rule change.

Consequences Defined

Dreikurs et al. (1982) clarified the differences between natural, logical, and punitive consequences. Natural consequences occur because of the nature of the universe. No interpretation or action is required beyond the causative act. If someone stubs a toe or touches something that is very hot it just naturally hurts; no explanation is needed. Natural consequences inevitably follow the act. Logical consequences, like punishment, do not happen inevitably and they must be arranged. Logical consequences, like natural consequences, must be *experienced* by the student as a natural phenomenon. To help us better understand logical consequences Dreikurs and Grey distinguish it from punishment in five ways.

a. "Logical consequences express the reality of the social order, not of the person; punishment, the power of a personal authority" (1968: 71). For example, a family may have a social rule that all members eat dinner together unless there are unusual circumstances. If a child is playing and forgets to come in for dinner until after others have finished and the table has been cleared, he doesn't get any dinner. A classroom example would be a student who dawdles over his seat work and thereby doesn't finish before the next task. He might then be required to complete the work during recess or after school.

b. "The logical consequence is logically related to the behavior; punishment rarely is" (1968: 73). Punishment is usually arbitrarily administered for reasons best known to the authority. To be effective the student must connect the act with the consequence. For example, during a ballgame two students continually interrupt the game by arguing, scuffling, or fooling around. The teacher might scold them and tell them to sit on the bench as punishment. On the other hand the teacher might logically point out, "Your behavior is ruining the game and you therefore have to sit on the bench until you feel you are ready to play properly."

c. "Logical consequence involves no element of moral judgment; punishment inevitably does" (1968: 74). Punishment is awarded to bad people. Logical consequences do not connote sin. Logical consequences do not judge people, they simply convey an intolerance of some behaviors because others' rights are violated.

d. "Logical consequences are concerned only with what will happen now; punishment dwells on the past" (1968: 76). Punishment follows the undesired behavior, thereby it is retroactive. That is one reason that it doesn't work. Punishment is applied as a payment for misbehavior. The payee often resents it; at best he accepts it as atonement which frees him to repeat the act. Logical consequences are in force whenever the student disregards the incongruence of his behavior and the rights of others.

e. "The voice is friendly when logical consequences are invoked; there is anger in punishment, either open or concealed" (1969: 77). Retaliation underlies punishment. A harsh tone connotes demands, anger, derogation. It is important in logical consequences that they be administered in genuine friendliness. If the teacher is personally involved and thereby emotionally aroused, the feelings should be genuinely shared. The teacher owns the feelings rather than acting on them.

Dreikurs and Grey (1969) elaborate on these five principles by indicating four conditions to guide our use of logical consequences.

a. *Give the student a choice.* Offending students should be asked to choose between continuing the misbehavior and behaving in ways consistent with rules. If he elects to continue the misbehavior then certain conditions and consequences should be stipulated. Dreikurs and Grey (1968) offer this example: A fourth-grade boy habitually tipped his chair back so as to sit precariously on the two back legs. The teacher pointed out, "I am concerned for several reasons: you might fall, other students are distracted, and it is destructive to the chair since the weight and angle of the two back legs weaken the joints." The boy responded, "I forgot, besides it's fun." The teacher said, "I'm going to do something to help you remember." She then put two old books under each of the two front legs so the chair was tipped back enough to be uncomfortable but not enough to tip over. The boy was then directed to sit in the chair as it was adjusted and to do so "until you can sit properly." Before long with no more attention from the teacher the boy removed the books and there was no more tipping back of chairs.

b. *Identify and understand the student's goal.* The goal of much mischievous behavior is to interact with either the teacher or other students. Dreikurs and Grey contend that most misbehavior is directed toward obtaining attention, getting revenge, or trying to influence others. We allow ourselves to be trapped into rewarding the behavior by giving attention and otherwise reacting. If the teacher and other students did not respond and thus satisfy the goal-seeking behavior, it would be changed.

c. *Beware of dangerous situations.* There are times when we cannot risk natural or logical consequences. The classic examples are the young child who wanders into the street or the student who brings a lethal weapon to school. The procedure for these types of situations is clear. They cannot be tolerated. If a child won't stay out of the street he must be locked in the yard or house. Likewise, if a student insists on a dangerous behavior then he is denied participation in the social milieu.

d. *Be patient when nonpunitive consequences fail.* We try a tactic and the misbehavior persists. Our typical reaction is to discard the tactic as useless and revert to punishment. The teacher is advised to keep the following notions in mind. Nothing works every time, so we should not expect continual success. Spasmodic success is particularly likely during the period in which we are learning the skill and its application. We must be patient. These techniques will work for us, but not automatically. We need to practice, to adapt them to fit our circumstances and style. Finally, if something doesn't work, reanalyze. What happened? What did you say or do? Since the teacher is the most important element in a discipline program, if it fails the missing link is most likely the teacher's behavior.

STEPS FOR DEVELOPING
RESPONSIBLE BEHAVIOR

The strategy as presented here is an adaptation of Glasser's reality therapy. Although all elements of the procedure need to be included to help develop responsible behavior, you may find paying more attention to one element and less to another is most appropriate for you when working with a given individual.

The point of reality education is to use incidents of deviant behavior as opportunities to develop responsibility. If a student is continuing to violate rules, to be unproductive, to act irresponsibly, then *stop* the way you typically respond. Apparently your response is not obtaining the desired effects. What is effective with one student, at one time, may not be effective in other instances. The recommended alternative steps are:

1. Confront students with their counterproductive behavior. Wait and have a confrontation regarding explicit, obvious, well-defined behavior. Focus on what is happening here and now. The task is to have the offending student become explicitly aware of what she is doing, to identify overt acts. It is desirable, especially at the beginning, to focus on behaviors that are so apparent that admission is simple and straightforward. Most important, concentrate on the reality of the present. Dwelling on the past is a diversion, an opportunity to justify the behavior. Focusing on the past will not encourage the student to change behavior. Recall that when Smitty confronted Mabel she tried to offer reasons and blame others for her tardiness. General statements like, "This is the third time this week" or "You have been fooling around all hour" are counterproductive. The point is not to make the pupil ashamed or defensive, just openly aware of what she is doing.

2. *Student evaluates the consequence of the behavior.* When Smitty asked Mabel, "Did your being late help you?" "Does it help me or the rest of the class?" he was asking Mabel to critically judge her behavior not in terms of whether it was good or bad, but in terms of its effects. The criteria for such judgments are twofold: the individual's values and the natural consequence of the acts or conditions created by the student. If students are to act responsibly they must consider and anticipate the appropriateness of the consequences of their behavior. The emphasis on the effects of one's behavior here is directly related to the task-centeredness of reality education. It is better to say, "Could you tell me what happened here?" rather than, "Why did you . . .?" because the question invites the student to rationalize his action. It is also important that the teacher refrain from evaluating the behavior. Evaluation by others invites defensiveness. The student alone is responsible for his behavior. Therefore, let him evaluate the effects of it.

3. *Plan an alternative behavior.* Now that the student has identified and evaluated his behavior the question remains, how should he act in the future? The student must recognize that he is not locked into his previous behavior. There is room for choice. The choice must take into consideration his own needs, the rights of others, a variety of alternatives, and their respective consequences. In addition, the selected alternative behavior must be such that the student can put it into operation. The student develops the plan. However, if it has unacceptable elements, the teacher has the responsibility to say so and to ask for another alternative. Plans must be manageable for the student, have time limits, and be tentative. It is not a good strategy if the student only says: "I will try to . . . ." That is too easily excused. Proposed plans should be stated in terms of explicit conditions and

behavior. For example, "When Jeri insults me (condition) I will walk away" (behavior), or "when I have completed my work I will go to the reading shelf and select a book to read."

4. *Paraphrase or restate the selected plan* so as to make certain that everybody understands and agrees to the details.

"As I understand it, you are going to make it a point to bring your math book and a pencil to math class tomorrow and every day next week." Note the stipulation of time. Particularly in the beginning we ought not expect students to commit themselves forever. Begin modestly; limit plans to two or three days. You may wish to include an escape valve, such as: "Okay, for the rest of this week you are going to take a deep breath and say such words as geez, gross, or nertz when you get frustrated and angry. I know Tuesday's a bad day for you, so how about stopping by before the test and we'll try to put together a special strategy."

5. *Student publicly commits himself to the plan.* A commitment is an oral or a written statement made by the student regarding the conditions, behaviors, and timing of his acts. It is insufficient, not a true indication of responsibility, for the pupil to just say okay to your suggestion. Whether they are six or sixteen years old, pupils will hesitate, and resist making a verbal statement, "I will . . .," because they sense that it is more binding. However, that is the point. A more or less public commitment to a plan of action makes it a matter of integrity and considerably increases the probability that it will be adhered to.

It is relatively easy for a student to bow his head and say, "I'm sorry," or to say, "okay, I'll try" when the teacher or administrator lists the expected behaviors. The pinch occurs when the student explicitly stipulates in the form of a contract what he will do.

6. *Follow-up.* It is up to the pupil to live up to his commitment, but most often he needs help. Let him know that you are with him. For example, "Hey, I've been noticing from time to time how well you have been doing on your commitment, nice going, two days and no fights." Pupils must know that you support them and that you are taking their commitments seriously. That is only known if you communicate it. It takes less time, and congratulating appropriate behavior pays off much better than reprimanding undesired behavior.

7. *Renegotiated broken plans.* If the behavior holds up through the duration of a plan, make a point of it and perhaps renegotiate an extended plan. If the contingencies of the plan are violated, *do not punish* or *accept excuses.* Both are counterproductive. Accept the explanation, acknowledge the failure and difficulty at face value, and repeat steps 2–7.

The failure suggests that the original plan was faulty. It is desirable to put the emphasis on the plan rather than fault the student.

8. *Don't give up.* Don't expect instantaneous success. You are changing life styles, both yours and the students'. Perceptions, expectations, and habits are not easily forsaken. Try and retry; in the beginning you may only be able to focus on partial success. For example, "You went under only once this morning; I know it's hard—let's see how it goes this afternoon."

9. *Give thinking time.* Frequently, the pupil needs time beyond what you can give for steps 2, 3, and 4. If he is mute, unable to identify what he is doing or the consequence of his behavior, for himself and others, or can't identify alternative ways to behave, he may need some thinking time in a quiet, out-of-the-way place. Notice you are not banishing him as punishment. You are just recognizing that sometimes it takes a little time to let off steam, to get over feeling abused and to think up alternatives. Select a place without diversion, remote from public attention. It is not a punishment, but it can't be a reward place either. For additional ideas about this point see "Time Out" in Chapter 9.

10. *Use in class.* Classroom meetings involving all or a portion of the class can be conducted within the same framework as that given for individuals. Such meetings, if focused on ongoing behaviors, are reality group education. If the topics are broader and not specifically relevant to rule or social violations they might be termed value clarifications. Values are the next topic under consideration. In both cases it is best for the class to sit in a circle so everyone can see and communicate directly with everyone else. Each student ought to be encouraged to voice his or her own point of view. No one should fault another's perceptions. The questions in reality-group education are essentially the same as they are for individuals. The exemplar episode that follows is a good example of how the strategy was applied to a group.

An Exemplar: Responsibility

A basketball team reacts to defeat

This situation, told by Barbara Sizemoor, principal of a hard-core ghetto school, illustrates the class meeting strategy for developing responsibility. The primary participants were a group of boys with a long record of impulsive antisocial behavior.

As it happened these boys constituted the high school basketball team. The episode focuses around a particular game that they had wanted very much to win. Their confidence was increased considerably just before the game started when they found out that one of the game referees was a close friend of the coach. They assumed that the friendship would result in favored officiating for them. The game was lost. The referee at best had been fair to both sides, and in the view of the boys a couple of calls that could have gone either way favored the other team. In their frustration after the game the boys tipped over their coach's automobile.

Why the coach's car? They blamed the officiating for the loss, and since the coach and official were friends it was a "natural" way of getting back at the referee. Finally, the boys decided that the coach had asked the referee to call fouls against the team to punish them for goofing off in practice.

The coach had a number of alternatives: (1) he could have kicked the boys off the team or canceled the rest of the schedule; (2) he could demand that the boys' parents pay the service charge for righting and repairing the car; (3) he could have turned the whole matter over to the police; (4) he could have used the incident as a basis for recommending school suspension or expulsion. Any of these actions would seem to be a legitimate retribution.

The coach elected a different alternative. He called a team meeting to find out what happened. He had asked Ms. Sizemoor, the school principal, to come to the meeting about 15 minutes late and play ignorant about the game and the car incident. The coach confronted the boys, but mostly received garbled messages—clowning, blaming, accusations, and "I don't know."

As prearranged, Ms. Sizemoor came in and simply stated that she didn't know anything about basketball but had heard that the team lost. "What happened?" she asked. As the boys explained their interpretation of the game, Ms. Sizemoor asked simple, concrete questions about baskets scored, passes thrown wild, and the game in general. The boys' explanations became more concrete and specific. Finally one of them recognized the obvious. "You don't think we play very well?" Ms. Sizemoor replied, "Well, they did score more points." "Yeah, we lost it, it was our fault." "It wasn't the referee or the coach. We play sh——y. That's why we lost."

Ms. Sizemoor then asked, "Wasn't there something about a car being tipped over?" These boys don't often show shame but they did this time. She pressed on, "What are you going to do about it?" After several false starts the boys not only concluded that they were at fault, but initiated a plan for playing for the damages by getting jobs.

The boys' decision to pay restitution was based on their decision that it was the right thing to do rather than under coercion or personal payoff to them—a giant step toward responsibility.

TRY YOUR HAND

Try your hand with the following situation. Outline in some detail what you would say and do, along with your interpretation of what students might do and say in response. Include Glasser's initial six steps. After you have completed the exercise compare your procedures with another reader.

The Disruptive Class

Pat had just completed a workshop on the management of classroom behavior. Some of the ideas sounded like they might help, so Pat was looking forward to a chance to put them into operation. One of the several techniques, a process of making the students responsible for their own behavior and its consequences, seemed particularly potent. Pat generally taught homeroom, English, and social studies. One of the classes, which also was the homeroom group, although generally nice kids, tended to be a bit raucous at times. Therefore, it was not too surprising that when the class arrived for social studies, one of the students had a note from the music teacher who worked with them the previous period: "Do something about these monsters, descriptive words escape me other than to say that they are rude, uncontrollable, and lazy. I have given the whole class F's for the last two days."

Pat knew it to be a difficult class, but not monsters, and decided that this might be a good group to confront with the issue of responsibility. The steps that she, and you, should follow are:

1. Confront the students with a question about the nature of the behavior
2. Ask the students to identify the value of the behavior and its consequences
3. Make a plan for alternative ways to behave in music
4. Identify the explicit details of the plan
5. Ask each student to sign or otherwise commit himself to the plan
6. Follow up

RECOMMENDED READINGS

Alschuler, A.S. *School Discipline: A socially literate solution.* New York: McGraw-Hill, 1980.

Glasser, N. (Ed.) *What are you doing?: How people are helped through reality therapy.* New York: Harper and Row, 1980.

6

FACILITATING VALUE-MORAL DEVELOPMENT: INTERVENTION STRATEGY B₂

THE IMPORTANCE OF VALUES

The third step of Glasser's reality education asks the students to evaluate the effects of their behavior. Evaluation is based on criteria. The ultimate criteria of the appropriateness of behavior are one's values. If an individual is to assume responsibility for controlling his behavior he must be aware of a guiding structure of values.

A short anecdote regarding a middle-school boy named Bo may help to make the point.

Bo was very upset because someone had stolen some of his personal belongings. Because theft was an unfortunate condition in the school, everyone had been advised to bring a wooden box with a lock to protect anything of value. When questioned about the whereabouts of his box, Bo gave the following explanation.

"Well, you know where I live, there are no stores or places to get a box 'cept a lumber yard about four blocks from my house. The only way I could get wood for a box would be to go down to that lumber yard at night, crawl over the back fence, steal the wood, and bring it home."

In order to clarify the explanation the teacher paraphrased, "Bo, it would bother you to steal the wood from the lumber yard?"

To which Bo responded, "Hell, no, but who wants to carry all that wood four blocks?"

From this incident and others it was evident that Bo's notion of right and wrong included statements like, "Ripping other people off is a way of life," "Only stupid people work," "Everybody in this world is for himself," and "You get what you can get away with." If Bo were confronted in reality education with the question, "Did this behavior help you and others?" his reply would be based on the value system ascribed by the above statements. So we ask ourselves, what do we do with Bo? Our impulses are to:

(a) Punish him. A few swats will let him know that society won't tolerate such attitudes.
(b) Write him off. If at the age of fourteen he doesn't know right from wrong there isn't much the school can do.
(c) Moralize. Explain to him that good people don't live that way.

Unfortunately, the record of success with such alternatives as these isn't very good. Our prisons are full of people who have been punished, written off, and moralized. Bo needs a prosocial set of values.

Dreikurs, a noted child psychiatrist, sums up the importance of values for discipline with this comment (Dreikurs et al. 1982: 80):

> Discipline, as love, as respect, or as the acceptance of responsibilities is not a subject that can be taught out of a book or that can be obtained by sheer demand. All aspects of discipline grow out of social relationships. Discipline is an inner process; an integrated part of one's values. Therefore, we cannot discuss discipline without emphasis on the importance of values.

THE NATURE OF VALUES

Before we can identify more explicit means for helping pupils to develop useful values, let's explore the nature of values in the context of other constructs. Although a number of psychologists, philosophers, sociologists, and social psychologists have defined, described, and studied values, we will limit our discussion to Rokeach's (1973) thoughts. He provides the following definition:

> A value is an enduring belief that a specific mode of conduct or end-state of existence is personally or socially preferable to an opposite or converse mode of conduct or end-state of existence. A value system is an enduring organization of beliefs concerning preferable means of conduct or end-states of existence along a continuum of relative importance (p. 5).

As Beliefs

Note that Rokeach indicated that values are beliefs held to be true. Values as beliefs are distinguished from other beliefs in that the latter are descriptive statements of fact that can be tested as true or false. Values are beliefs of goodness that are held to be true but are not directly testable. The beliefs of goodness may pertain to processes or means (e.g., honesty, hard work) or to ends (e.g., personal freedom, knowledge). Since values as beliefs of goodness differ from the descriptive beliefs that make up the bulk of our academic curriculum, it is likely that a different teaching approach will be necessary. More on this later.

Durability

Values are not absolute or rigid because they do change over time and circumstance, but there is continuity. The values held by a person at different age levels or circumstances are not independent, random, or whimsical. Value change is more apt to resemble the flow of molasses than leaps from one set of values to another.

Prioritization

Values are arranged in a system of priorities along a continuum of relative importance. The issue for an individual may be whether or not a given behavior violates or reflects a given value. More often, however, the dilemma is that a given behavior involves at least two values. Thus when confronted with a student who is lying or cheating or is disrespectful we need to consider the probability that a dilemma is involved in that behavior: to lie or jeopardize a friend's reputation; to cheat or fail an examination and thereby disappoint a parent; and to challenge a teacher's authority rather than to lose face with one's peers. Contrary to the teacher's opinion that some pupils are without values, it is more likely that the value in question simply has a lower priority than some other value. For all individuals, value systems are such that some values are more dominant than others. It is a matter of priority. At different age levels and different circumstances there are shifts in the hierarchy so that different values become more or less dominant; however, valuing continues to be a matter of choosing between desired or undesired valued states. Value education is a process whereby learners redefine and reprioritize their values.

Interrelatedness of Values, Needs, and Rules

Values and needs are closely allied but they differ. Rokeach (1973) suggests that values are cognitive representations or transformations of needs. Values are not just wanton expressions of needs but embody the constraints of societal and institutional demands. When we establish classroom rules we are placing constraints on the way the students express their needs. Thus values, needs, and rules are interrelated. The rules become the meeting ground of the teachers' and students' respective need-value systems. In establishing rules it would seem reasonable, educational, and just that the ground be mutual. Unilaterally adopted rules without rationale and open discussions would seem to miss an opportunity for value sharing and education.

The transformation of the self-esteem needs of power, affiliation, and competence into values is ameliorated by social desirability. For example, aggressive power is transformed into ambition, athletic prowess, and so on. Our pupils have needs. The channeling of these needs into socially desired behavior is within the task of all teaching, elementary and secondary. Any time that we reward a particular behavior (e.g., a pat on the back or an "A" for a pupil who is striving to be competent in mathematics) we are strengthening a need-value relationship.

In conclusion, values are *beliefs about what is desired as end-states of existence and the appropriate means of achieving them.* As such, values reflect the psychological needs of the individual and society. Thus values, needs, and rules are interlocked and cannot be considered independently.

Multidimensionality

A value is more than a simple belief that A leads to B. Values have added dimensions of behavior, affect, and expectations.

Values are best known by what a person does rather than what is said. One's value system acts as a guide to behavior, and thus behavior becomes the best measure of the underlying values.

Values have an affective dimension. If values are challenged, one becomes defensive. Rokeach puts this succinctly in terms of maintaining and enhancing self-esteem:

> . . . all of a person's attitudes can be conceived as being value-expressive, and all of a person's values are conceived to maintain and enhance the master sentiment of self-regard—by helping a person adjust to his society, defend his ego against threat and to test reality (1973: 15).

Moreover, he continues to suggest that emphasis on such values as cleanliness, politeness, and national security serve ego-defensive functions. It seems likely that toughness, resisting authority, and being cool and sexy also serve.

Values Represent Various Morés

Values may represent at least three different meanings: personal preferences, social conventions, and moral prescriptions.

Some values are simply adhered to and prized by an individual and they may or may not be held by others. Whereas one person may favor being outdoors, vacationing in the mountains, and bird watching, others are attracted to people and visiting crowded cities.

Social conventions are also arbitrary, but they are determined by social consensus. Dress codes and sexual morés are good examples. Moral prescriptions (e.g., hurting others) are neither arbitrary nor determined by social regulations. The rightfulness or wrongness of moral issues is not contingent on a stated rule but stems from the intrinsic effects of the event on the victim. Whereas social conventions are established by written or unwritten regulations (rules and morés) within particular social contexts, morals are held more universally and are intuitively recognized. Nucci (1982) points out that such behaviors as calling teachers by their first name, chewing gum in class, dressing in particular ways, swearing, using the opposite sex's bathroom, or publicly exposing oneself are instances of deviancy from social conventions. Behaviors such as stealing from individuals, telling a harmful lie, malicious destruction of property, not sharing abundant goods with the needy, or allowing someone else to be blamed for one's own misdeeds are listed as moral transgressions. Nucci reports that children as young as three years of age recognize that moral transgressions are inherently wrong while social conventions are only wrong because adults set up rules. Young children also realize that violations of moral issues are more serious. Schoolchildren recognize that some school rules are arbitrary social conventions and thus alterable. Older students are more sensitive and may feel that such rules are an infringement on their moral rights of freedom and equality.

This discussion is not to imply that social conventions are unimportant or that violations are trivial. However, Nucci's (1982) summary does offer three major implications of value differentiation.

First, we need not be particularly concerned about establishing rules to govern moral issues. Most students readily accept their validity. We may only need to help students recognize where such values apply.

Second, the internalization or acceptance of social conventions appears to be cyclic. Allegedly, development progresses through four sets of stages, in each of which conventions are rejected and then accepted. In successive stages the conventions become more abstract and internalized. In each stage the rejection segment is a necessary requisite for progress to the next acceptance level. The rejection and argumentation of rules is normal and healthy. Hang in there. It is all part of growing up.

Third, Nucci believes that teachers need to respond differently, depending on whether student behavior pertains to moral issues or social conventions. Nucci points out

> Our research suggests that teachers' responses to students' moral transgressions should focus on the harmful or unjust effects of actions on others, and on considerations of others' feelings and needs. In contrast, responses in the context of social conventional transgressions should focus on aspects of social order and normative expectations. Stated differently, our suggestion is that teachers' attempt to moralize about acts students view as conventional issues or responses to the impropriety of moral transgressions in terms of social organization (e.g., school rules) would be domain inappropriate and therefore unlikely to stimulate development. (1982: 115)

Teachers ought not respond in the same way to such adverse behaviors as poor academic work, running in the hall, hitting other students, stealing, ignoring a directive, and destroying property. Violations of social conventions are different from moral transgressions. Social conventions are learned in a manner distinct from that of moral issues. The difference must be maintained.

PROGRAMS FOR VALUES EDUCATION

Historical Community Experience

In the past values education has been broad and both implicit and explicit. However, sources and opportunities for values education have radically changed.

Until the end of World War II communities were more or less stable. When people did move, it was usually either local or included a large segment of the community. Typically, grandparents, uncles, aunts, and cousins were in the neighborhood. Those who didn't live within the same house, lived nearby. People tended to have roots in neighborhoods, so that each had the same set of friends and acquaintances over extended periods of time. Interhome visits were common, and staying over for dinner was natural and informal.

Everyone knew everyone else's business: where they went, what they did, and with whom. The result wasn't surveillance as much as open conversations—exchange of views of why this is important, that is proper, or the other is improper. Although limited in geography, the range of issues was broad because youngsters had the run of the community. One could wander down to the lumberyard and the owner would explain what scrap wood was available and why; at the local store an uncle or friend of the family let the children watch as he unpacked boxes, kept records, and perhaps discussed writing off losses. At the newspaper office one could overhear discussions of what was fit to print as well as what was accepted or rejected as truth according to the evidence. The gossip at the barbershop, or overheard at church or over the back fence was about known people and events. The community ne'er-do-wells were equally accessible. On a given day a youngster could see and hear a wide range of attitudes and interpretations of events.

Out of all of this came an awareness of what different people felt and thought, of the basis for making decisions, of the natural consequence of behavior, and an awareness of one's own feelings, reasons, and goals, because caring, interested people asked for explanations.

Formal Education

During the nineteenth century moral education was blended into the regular curriculum. The McGuffey *Eclectic Readers* were universally adopted to teach children to learn to read. The *Readers* were not only designed to develop reading skills; each story also pointed out the virtue of such morals as nationalism, truth, honesty, kindness, and loyalty. Toward the turn of the century attention was given to personal heroism, and the history and literature textbooks regularly featured in detail the Horatio Alger success stories of such folks as John D. Rockefeller or Leland Stanford. Clean living, dedication, and hard work were shown to pay off.

Probably from the beginning of time people have been telling each other how to behave and what to believe. More specifically, in American education, morality was a key part of schooling in the early years of the republic. Teachers were to develop habits of piety and obedience. As Hersh et al. (1980: 16, 17) note, the content and processes were little short of catechism. For example, as late as 1850, teachers' manuals recommended this exercise:

> T: You must obey your parents.
> S: I must obey my parents. (The pupils, at each repetition, place the right hand, opened, upon the breast.)
> T: You must obey your teachers.
> S: I must obey my teachers.

The litany contained injunctions against lying, stealing, swearing, and so on. Then "lowly and in a soft tone,"

> T: God always sees you.
> S: God always sees me.
> T: God hears all you say.
> S: God hears all I say.
> T: God knows all you do.
> S: God knows all I do.

Control was external. Parents and teachers established the rules and God monitored all behavior. We may still be using this external control for our very young children, as evidenced by this story related by a mother:

> I was working in the kitchen and suddenly realized that there was an ominous quiet throughout the house. From my experience I knew that when Billie was quiet the consequence tended to be disastrous. So, I called out, "Billie, are you doing anything bad?" To which Billie responded, "How can I do anything bad with you, Jesus, and Santa Claus watching me all of the time?"

The Effects of Life in the 1980s

Life has drastically changed. People are transient. An astonishing number of children move to different neighborhoods, away from all acquaintances, except for visits of immediate family every year or so. Extended families are uncommon, and even parents are more or less unavailable for the children. In 1950 the typical family unit was composed of a working adult, a home adult, and the children. Currently, fewer than ten percent of U.S. families live by this pattern. Adults are isolated from children.

In the past most children watched and often worked side by side with parents. Now, most often places of the parents' employment are physically and psychologically removed from the growing child. Even socializing is likely to be segregated by age levels. Children spend more waking hours watching TV than anything else, including formal education. There is very little talk time (sharing feelings, ideals, and thoughts) while watching TV. Recreation is often in such adult-controlled activities as Little League, dancing school, and tennis lessons, where the rules are preestablished with minimum opportunity for discussion. Allegedly, American children typically spend less than 20 minutes a day in conversation with their parents. Most of that time is spent on reprimands for rule violation.

In the spring of 1980, President Carter indicated that in his view the threat to the United States was not Communism, the shortage of oil, or inflation. Rather it was the demoralization, lack of integrity, and responsibility by the American people. He might have pointed out in support of his contention that vandalism cost U.S. education more money in 1979 than did books. He may have legitimately pointed out that in time of disasters, tornado wipeouts, floods, or electrical black-out, looting and pillage is so common that the police are virtually helpless. He may have pointed out the apparent ease with which our congressional representatives are bribed and then forgiven by their colleagues and the public upon proof of guilt. However, our need for value education need not be documented. Upgrading of morals and values is very high in the public's current mandate to the schools. A national Gallup poll in 1980 showed that 79 percent of the adult population favors an increased emphasis on moral education.

Before outlining possible procedures for value education it is important that we note two additional factors: (a) Our value system is changing very rapidly. Many of those values considered stable and true a decade ago are no longer accepted by most people. The details of values are in flux. (b) The mass media bombards individuals with a wide variety of divergent messages: Exposés within the business and political world, national and international confrontations with seemingly unresolvable problems, and the soap opera fiction entertainment in which virtually all possible behaviors are portrayed as being natural and normal.

Perhaps the only certainty is that we in the schools cannot be laissez-faire about value development.

The traditionalists claim that values education is outside of the school's function, and the true and natural place for such learning is in the home and church. However, we see that values education has a long history in our schools. The need is compounded now with recent shifts in the Western manner of living. Schools ought to recognize our heritage and heed the wishes of the majority of the adult population and boldly include values education. Ideas, programs, and theories are abundant.

We will briefly consider two programs that are currently advocated as consistent with our needs and what is known about the nature of values and the way people learn. The respective programs are values clarification (VC) and moral development (MD).

Educational Programs

Values clarification (VC) and moral development (MD) are the two most currently advocated strategies for changing values. Both are curriculum-type strategies in that activities are planned, scheduled, and repeated. Contrary to many people's expectations neither of these strategies intends to teach specific values. VC focuses on the process of valuing, whereas the purpose of MD is to enable students to develop moral maturity through a series of principled stages. The educational task in each case is to arrange experiences whereby the learners can freely express their views and hear those of others. Although both strategies are criticized as being too free, too nondirective, and contentless, neither is contrary to the thesis of academic discipline. Historians, physicists, and psychologists assume that knowledge is open-ended and that part of the inquiring process for extending what is believed is open dialogues among interested persons.

The rationale for focusing on valuing processes and the development of moral principles is most often based on the findings of the classical Harshorne and May (1928) *Studies in Deceit.* Although there are a variety of more recent studies and interpretations of observed behavior that confirm the Hartshorne and May conclusions, the original studies of deceit continue to be the most legitimate reference. The sum of the Hartshorne and May conclusions is that behavior depends more on the situation or a person's perception of the situation than on persistent traits of integrity or deceit.

Admonishments of "thou shalt not" are not sustained over a variety of circumstances. Some children who would never cheat in mathematics do so quite willingly in history. Few people never lie and likewise few people consistently lie in order to promote their own position. Perhaps the most damaging evidence is that as the young become older and more intellectually mature, they seem to be governed less by moral dictation and their behavior becomes less predictable. Adolescents are more apt to cheat, lie, steal, and so on, in the same circumstances than would their younger counterparts. It is thereby concluded that moral behavior is not governed by the early understanding of specific commandments. Moral conduct is governed by both interpretation of circumstances and personal disposition. Thus, the task of education is to help students to be aware of their respective beliefs and know how they apply to a variety of circumstances.

Teachers agree that it is professionally unethical to encourage students to adopt a given moral code. However, most of us admonish our students to work hard, and not to cheat, lie, steal, treat others harshly, mistreat property, or use drugs. Neither VC nor MD attempts to teach a moral code. Yet each offers the teacher an opportunity to enrich the values of students and to work toward moral maturity.

Values Clarification

Values clarification (VC) was designed to alleviate the overdissenting, overconforming, apathetic, indecisive, purposeless, inconsistent types of behavior that allegedly all too often typify many of our youth. The advocates of VC claim that the cause of such behaviors is the general uncertainty of what is valued, how to select values, and how one can and ought to express his or her values.

The human dilemma is that each individual has a variety of needs and desires that she wishes to fulfill. At the same time she lives in a society that places restrictions on her behavior and demands on her time while allegedly offering a wide latitude of freedom in the selection of religion, occupation, friendship, and residency. The individual's values mediate and balance these forces. If this is true, then it is apparent that values and subsequent behavior would be more appropriate if each individual clearly understood herself, her wants and needs as well as the contingencies of society. The purpose of VC is to promote this understanding and thereby move people from those behaviors on the left to those on the right (as shown in the diagram on page 121).

Values are generated out of social experience, and many of today's youth have little opportunity for such experience in an open give-and-take atmosphere. Raths et al. (1966) introduced and popularized the particulars of VC, while several other authors have designed exercises to encourage students to reflect on their roles, beliefs, behaviors, and what they prize.

The general process is for the teacher to establish and maintain a supportive, nonjudgmental atmosphere, and within this environment to prod students to examine their lives, actions, feelings, ideas, perceptions, expectations, and aspirations. Raths et al. (1966) recommend that values clarification programs include the following in some shape or form:

Degree of Clarity of One's Relationship to Society

Unclear behaviors   Clear behaviors

    Apathy   Enthusiasm
    Overconformity   Positive attitude
    Overdissension   Pride
    Vascillation   Purposefulness

Expected effects of value clarification

1. A means whereby students make choices freely.
2. When students are faced with alternatives, help them identify and examine several options.
3. Encourage them to consider the consequence of the respective options when making decisions.
4. Give students frequent opportunities to identify what it is that they prize and cherish.
5. Afford students the opportunity to publicly affirm their choices.
6. Encourage students to live and otherwise behave according to their choices.
7. Help students examine their behavioral patterns and styles in terms of underlying values.

A teacher may work toward values clarification in three ways: incidental learning, planned exercises and curriculum concomitants.

Incidental learning

A student, Gary Goodrich, announces in class, "Our family is going to Washington, D.C., for our vacation." The teacher or a classmate may respond, "Oh, lucky you," or "You will have an opportunity to see how the government works. When you return you can tell us all about it." At best, such responses unwittingly reflect the speaker's values. Most likely, the comments are simply passing the time.

As an alternative the teacher might have responded by asking, "What new experiences do you think you will have in Washington?" or "Why do you feel that going to Washington will be a good vacation?" Such inquiry will encourage the student to reflect on what he wants and the need for a plan. The process opens up the possibility for the student to consider alternative feelings and the factors behind the feelings.

The following student–teacher exchanges are presented to further illustrate how incidents may be converted to opportunities for student contemplation.

Student comments/questions	Teacher response
1. "How long should our papers be?"	1. To encourage choosing: "Your topic is important; how many pages do you think will be necessary to express your ideas?"
2. "He hit me first, so I just hit him back."	2. To examine alternatives: "I understand, but what are some other ways you could act after you have been hit?"
3. "The president should have declared martial law."	3. To weigh alternatives: "What assumptions are involved in that conclusion?"
4. "... that is why I think that we need more governmental control."	4. To identify what is prized: "In either case we are giving up something. Which would be most important to you?"
5. "Chemicals like that should be banned."	5. To publicly affirm choice: "Would you sign a petition in support of that idea?"
6. "The kids in this school should be allowed to do that."	6. To act out choices: "What is the first thing you need to do to get started?"
7. "I liked doing our spelling that way."	7. To examine life patterns: "How could we arrange our schedule so we could do that more often?"

The atmosphere for VC is described by such terms as *nonjudgmental, warmth, caring, sharing, genuineness, openness.* However, the process is not merely nurturant, tender loving care. Students are confronted with difficult real-life decisions and asked to indicate their choices, to prize these choices by openly expressing them, and then to show how they might be acted out.

Planned exercises

The valuing process may be initiated through simple exercises, such as asking students to rank-order a list of conditions. For example, what priority would you place the following ideal for yourself?

To be the most popular student in class
To be the smartest student in class
To be very good in sports
To make all of your own decisions
To be treated fairly by everyone

In such exercises the teacher emphasizes that there is no right or wrong order. Students are then asked to share their list and tell why they put one or another state of affairs ahead of others. Caution is taken here to make certain that everybody's choices are uncritically accepted. Finally, students are asked to indicate what conditions would have to exist for the order to be as desired and what one could do to arrange such conditions.

Exercises such as this are one phase of a curriculum for clarifying and operationalizing one's values. Simon et al. (1972) have put together 79 exercises that can easily be used in the classroom by any teacher. Some of the exercises are geared for elementary school, some for middle school, others for high school, while many may be more appropriate for adults. Simon et al. are among the leading authorities of VC, and it would therefore be instructive to review the purposes they give for the respective exercises. Several exercises attempt to achieve variations of the same purposes. The objectives of the exercises are such that students will

Become aware of conflicting values
Identify resources and the basis of personal pride
Learn how to express feelings and concerns
Compare and contrast values with others
Bring everyday behavior consistently into harmony with feelings/values
Search out alternative ways of behaving
Identify alternative consequences of each alternative behavior
Undertaking appropriate actions to bring about desired change
Commit themselves to plans of action
Learn to help others to clarify their values

Although the emphasis is on process it would seem from these purposes that VC is designed to help students become more aware, understanding, and tolerant of other people. In addition, with more emphasis, a major element of VC is for students to become more aware of the importance of values and how they ought to be used for living, planning, and enjoying life.

Simon et al. (1972) contend that people

frequently find themselves acting one way in a situation and later regretting it or wishing they had behaved differently. The clearer people are about their values, the more congruent their actions are with their feelings and beliefs, and therefore the less often they later regret their actions (p. 198).

The point of VC is to reduce impetuous behavior by helping students to be more conscious of what they value. If you agree that life is more satisfying when one's behavior is congruent with one's feelings, awareness, and values, or if you accept the proposition that managing classroom behavior includes the clarification of student values, then you may find the book by Simon et al. worth exploring.

Curricula concomitants

A third vehicle for VC is through the subject matter. Kirschenbaum and Simon (1973) offer suggestions as to how to incorporate VC into such subjects as English, history, mathematics, foreign language, and science. The contention here is that value-laden questions enrich subject matter, which helps student cognitive understanding and makes the content more relevant. The value dimension helps to personalize the content. Students will become more involved and thereby not only achieve the objectives of VC, but the added motivation will increase academic achievement and reduce off-task behavior. The following examples are offered:

1. When the United States constitution is studied, factual questions such as "Where and when was the Constitution signed?" or conceptual questions such as "What is the meaning of justice as determined by the Bill of Rights?" may be supplemented by questions regarding values. For instance: "What rights and obligations does each of us have in this class? in this school? with our friends? or at home?" or "Should anyone, if he can meet the financial requirements, be allowed to live anywhere he wishes?" In other words, bring the content into the here-and-now lives of the students.

2. As a supplement to the factual and conceptual curricula in Hamlet, the literature teacher might encourage VC by asking: "King Claudius allegedly killed for his own advantages. What do you do to get what you want?"

3. In mathematics those horrific word problems can be made more personal and meaningful by building in a value issue. For instance, Joe paid $72.00 for a bicycle and used it for three years before deciding to sell it. He took the bike to a shop for appraisal and was told the bike is now worth $36.00. However, it had a hidden hairline crack in the handlebar that could

break at.any time. If it broke when someone was riding, the result could be a serious injury. New handlebars cost $11.00. Joe wanted to know the prorated cost of owning the bike for three years. Show what the cost would be for each year if he sold it as is. What would be the cost for each year if he replaced the handlebars? If you were Joe, would you buy new handlebars before selling it even if you still could only get $36.00 for it?

In a different way the teacher can help students clarify values in informal situations and conversations. For example, the teacher probes a student to go beyond what is said; for example, a student says: "Democracy is the best form of government." The teacher responds by saying, "Your point will have more meaning if you could tell us what you mean by 'best.' " Or a student says, "I like coming to this class, it is the best class I have." Teacher probe: "It is nice of you to say that. Can you tell me some of the things that make this class enjoyable for you?" A multitude of possibilities exist that enable the teacher to translate content into personal experience. Dramatic representation of significant incidents or simply a question such as, "If you had been _____, how would you have responded (felt or thought)?" "What would you have hoped to accomplish?" "What made you feel that way?"

In my work at the university I frequently find that students cannot address their own feelings about issues, situations in history, or other persons. When asked, "How did you feel when he _____?" A surprising number respond, "I think he _____." We have come to substitute thinking for feeling and thereby isolate ourselves from personal involvement. Students often indicate that they have never been asked "How do you feel about _____?" while in school.

Values clarification suggests that the work of scientists, characters in literature, and episodes in history will have more meaning and simultaneously serve to broaden the personal experience of learners if emotional identification is made. It behooves the teacher to broaden that experience, to clarify values as part of the daily curriculum.

Critique of values clarification

If we are alert to the possibilities we can easily integrate the processes of VC into our regular program. To allow students to express and act on their values seems risky, but in the long run it ought to pay off in more responsible behavior.

Lockwood (1978) criticizes values clarification on three counts. First, the emphasis of VC is on process, leaving the value itself up to the student. The teacher is nonjudgmental. The critics point out that a society cannot exist if everyone has his own notion of right and wrong. Some folks feel that education ought to give direct guidance as to what values students should have. It is, however, a moot question.

The second criticism focuses on the lack of rigorous research to identify the effects of values clarification. Lockwood (1978), in an excellent review of the research, concludes that there is now little legitimate data to support the conclusion that VC either effectively helps students to clarify their values or change behavior. The lack of results, however, may be attributed to poorly designed experiments rather than the ineffectiveness of the program.

Third, the emphasis in values clarification is on feeling. The teacher's role is to create a supportive, nonthreatening atmosphere in which the student feels safe and trusting and therefore is willing to express his views. It is said that too much emphasis is placed on student feelings. The focus is on helping students to get in touch with their values rather than urging them to view situations in new and multiple ways. Since the emphasis is on liking and disliking rather than right versus wrong, the critics see values clarification more as a movement to achieve more purposeful and secure self-concepts than as a means for developing a set of directing values.

MORAL DEVELOPMENT

Morality tends to be defined as behaving in the appropriate way, guided by conscience and sanctions from society. However, Kohlberg's (1984) summary of his extensive research suggests that morality is a cognitive process, a form of reasoning based on an identifiable set of principled assumptions. The assumptions are reflections of stages of moral development. The moral stage in which people function depends on the level of their cognitive development, as defined by Piaget, and their social perspective. Thus, the process of moral development requires both cognitive and social education.

The Piagetian cognitive development processes are well known and are thoroughly described elsewhere in the literature. However, we need to become more aware of the nature and development of both moral stages and their underlying social perspectives. Just as in cognitive development, moral and social development progress through a series of stages as a function of maturation and learning experiences. Maturational development prepares the mind to examine input for logical consistency and congruency. This preparation, when applied to one's own assumptions, produces new assumptions through encounters with experiences that jolt the mind to use the matured capacities.

Selman (1980) studied social perception development by interviewing 245 people ranging in age from three to forty. Forty-eight of these subjects were interviewed three times over a five-year period. The evidence from these many interviews indicates that the capacity to view one's own thoughts, feelings, and behaviors in terms of human relationships progresses through an orderly sequence of stages. Initially, a child assumes that others see events in the same way that she does. However, about the time she enters school the typical child is able to differentiate between her own perspective and those of others. Following this, during elementary school years the child develops the capacity to see interpersonal relations as reciprocal, so that others' perspectives can be taken into consideration. During early adolescence the youngster is able to step outside of given relationships and take a third-person perspective. This involves a shift from seeing relationships as reciprocal cooperation for the respective participants' self-interests to seeing them as collaboration for mutual and common interests. During the fifth and final stage of development the individual recognizes that people have many needs, including dependency and autonomy. In good relationships each partner offers strong emotional and psychological support, but allows the other to develop independent interests and friendships. Thus, both interdependency and autonomy are incorporated into relationships. In mature social perspectives people become deeply involved with one another but remain aware of their respective individuality and need for freedom to move into other relationships.

Kohlberg's (1984) summary of research on moral development and behavior indicates the importance of both social interaction and cognitive development. Therefore, the Selman (1980) findings add an important dimension to our understanding of both the nature and facilitation of moral development. Kohlberg (1984) reports that when people are presented with dilemmas they do not act capriciously. Behaviors are based on a set of assumptions about the nature of morality. Kohlberg presented scenarios to persons from a wide variety of cultures from all over the world and asked them to indicate what action would be appropriate and why the selected action is right. Regardless of social mores he found the following principles to be constant: (a) Six stages of moral reasoning within three major levels were apparent from the participants' responses. (b) The nature of the stages are universal; they are virtually interchangeable from one culture to another. (c) Development is sequential and unidirectional. Although only a few people in each culture are found to be at stage six, everybody begins at stage one. (d) People do not seem to skip stages. (e) Each person is primarily in one stage, although each may show evidence of reasoning in one stage up or down from his or her primary stage. (f) The primary motivation for morality comes from the self-esteem needs to be accepted, competent, in control, and virtuous, rather than from fear and anxiety. (g) Moral norms and principled assumptions arise out of experiences of social interaction, role taking, and situations that require moral integration rather than the internalization of rules generated by authority. (h) Moral development occurs as a consequence of cognitive and social stimulation instead of by punishment and reward.

The order of the stages is substantiated by noting that persons who reason at the higher levels recall having at one time reasoned at lower levels, and can understand the lower levels but now reject them as incomplete. Those at the lower levels seldom use the higher-level principles, do not understand their relevance for given issues, and tend to reject them as possible guidelines.

Kohlberg's notion that MD progresses through a series of stages is confirmed by other independent studies. For instance, Peck and Havighurst (1960) identified in their longitudinal studies of youth that growth seems to follow these sequential steps:

1. A moral behavior guided by whim and impulse.
2. An expediency that is self-centered. Other people's welfare only considered as a means to one's own personal gain.
3. Conformity, in that right is determined by what others are doing.
4. Irrational conscientiousness in which one blindly follows internalized rules, ignoring that they are man-made.
5. Rational altruistic morality in which one functions by a stable set of principles but is concerned about the consequence for others as well as oneself.

Stages of Moral Development

Inasmuch as stages are the cornerstone of moral development, we will describe them in some detail.

1. The most basic stage of morality is to obey the rules in order to avoid punishment by powerful people. Good and bad are not determined by the effects on others but by the consequences for oneself. People in stage 1 seem to assume that the weak are to be punished at the displeasure of the strong.

Power, social order, and respect depend primarily on external signs like age, position, and material wealth. Rules and control are established by others. One is praised for goodness, punished for badness. What is bad is punished, therefore what is punished is bad.

In stage 1 the person is not responsible for his behavior. That is, he only does what he is told to do. In our recent history some notable tragedies seem to be traceable to stage 1 morality. From 1939 to 1945 Adolf Eichmann engineered the death of millions of Jews on behalf of the Nazis. He could not understand the anger and lack of appreciation of the world, including the Israeli court, for his defense that he was only doing what the Führer had asked him to do. The followers of Charles Manson wantonly and cruelly murdered his chosen targets simply because he ordered them to do it. Perhaps the most bizarre event in our history happened in 1978 when several hundred adult American members of the People's Temple in Guyana not only committed suicide but murdered their own children at the bidding of their ascribed leader, James Jones. In all of these instances the people were "educated" in the sense that they had completed public school and in many instances were university graduates. Education would appear to be amoral.

2. Stage 2 morality is a matter of each satisfying his own needs and not interfering with others. The motto "You be good to me and I'll be good to you" prevails. People work together by mutually agreeing to exchange favors. Like stage 1, stage 2 is marked by egocentricism, but here the emphasis is to obtain need satisfaction via an exchange rather than protecting oneself through obedience. A person need not blindly follow rules if there is a personal reason not to. However, stage 2 persons generally obey rules because it is inconvenient if caught. Although we may offer other explanations it is probably stage 2 thinking when we ignore the danger and increased gasoline consumption and drive 70 mph on the highway except when police surveillance is present or threatened.

3. Stage 3 represents a view that acknowledges other's views and attempts to live up to the rules and morals defined by significant other people. Being a good person is important. A stereotyped notion of goodness is used as a guide. One's reputation and the expectations of others are important. Being good is synonymous with being proper: good motives, loyalty, respect for authority, and showing gratitude.

Peers exert powerful forces for ascribed behavior. Group solidarity is important. Groups tend to isolate and reject those persons who disagree or don't go along with the group's opinion, behaviors, or mores. Reputation and popularity are important factors for stage 3 morality.

Stage 3 attributes (loyalty, friendship, commitment to the group) have the potential to achieve much good. It is apparent in our society that church, fraternal, neighborhood, and informal groups not only satisfy affiliation needs but serve the society. Groups within the classroom could be used to generate cooperation, peer help, mutual support, and productive behavior just as it helps to promote informal dress code, language usage, and some forms of abberant behavior. Stage 3 morality can also be detrimental. Let's look at three examples.

Scapegoating

"Ya, Ya, squinty eyes," the kids chanted. Geoffrey Feingold was one of those people who didn't fit in. Most of his problems come from the fact that he was smaller than his classmates, who were generally a year older. He wore thick glasses, read a lot, and used words that many others didn't understand. He was nonathletic, and striking out in recess baseball without even moving the bat was the basis for the jeering. Geoffrey was different. Geoffrey was socially isolated and rejected. The other students didn't want to work with him. To be closely affiliated with Geoffrey was the kiss of death. He was the class scapegoat.

Scapegoating, including listening to and laughing at ethnic jokes, is complex, with more than one possible explanation, but stage 3 morality is part of it. If there is to be an in group to which one belongs and is loyal, it must have an identity. The simplest way to do this is to attribute some qualities to it, designate some outs, and then clearly communicate that the outs are undesirable because they do not have these qualities. One way to identify, strengthen, and perpetuate group quality and solidarity is to ridicule outs who don't have the qualities.

Most people have such a strong need for affiliation, to be liked and to belong, that when someone is pointed out to be different, the way is open to assert the "we, the in-group feeling" by rejecting the one who doesn't fit. The need for affiliation keeps the respective members from vetoing the treatment of the scapegoat for fear of being cast out themselves. Groups typically do not tolerate much dissension.

Use of drugs

The rationale for illegally and irrationally smoking and drinking is often that others are doing it—Stage 3 morality. Initially it tastes bad, but adolescents, in particular, put up with the bad taste and ignore the alleged dangers. If one is in a crowd and others are doing it (whatever "it" is), disavowing interest or willingness to try it is too risky for stage 3 morality.

Sex in the balcony

Jamie, an eighth-grade girl, liked Scott very much. She openly told her friends that they were going to be married and passed many notes during class with amorous drawings that were went to Scott. One Saturday Jamie and her friends went to the movie. As it happened Scott and his friends were also there. With some goading from the others Jamie and Scott went up to the empty balcony. Although they hadn't done anything but hold hands, Scott told Jamie that he wanted to do it. When Jamie rejected the idea Scott told her, "If you don't do it, I'll tell everybody we did but if you let me I won't tell anybody." Jamie was afraid about what others would say, so she did. Meanwhile two other boys came up to the balcony to see what was happening. They observed Scott and Jamie and they too said, "If you don't let us do it, we'll tell."

Jamie's stage 3 concern for her reputation with a little help from the boys with stage 2 morality generated a very bad reputation.

4.   Whereas in stage 3 the person is guided by goodness as defined and agreed to by significant others, in stage 4 the loyalty is toward the social system. The rules of society dominate. Duties, laws, obligations become the guidelines. A contribution to uphold the institutions of society is important. The status quo is protected because that is the heart of the structure. Concern is shown for possible breakdown of the system (e.g., "We couldn't do that because if everyone did it then . . ."). Mutual trust, honesty, and dependability are important because if we can't depend on and trust one another, then the whole system would falter.

In stage 4, individualism is subverted to the system. An individual's status and role are determined by his position within the system. The soldier's motto, often given in jest, exemplifies stage 4 morality: "It is not ours to question why, it is ours to do or die."

Lande and Slade (1979) point out that stage 4 commits us to two equations: (a) morality equals legality—anything that is legal is moral and also if it is illegal it is immoral. (b) Morality equals patriotism—Within a 60-year period of the twentieth century, 120,000,000 people have died in wars that have strong patriotic bases. In each of the combatant nations the people support killing as part of their patriotism. In World War II a popular song, allegedly written by a priest, was *Praise the Lord and Pass the Ammunition.*

Here is an example of a driver who was frozen by a stage 4 dilemma. The incident occurred at an intersection of two divided highways whch was congested but controlled by a traffic light. A driver appropriately stopped for a red light. Almost immediately an ambulance with siren blasting appeared behind him. The siren was urgent and all traffic at the intersection was stopped. The driver glanced at the rear view mirror, up at the red light and in horror in other directions. In a flash of insight that makes heroes I stuck my head in the window and said, "You can legally make a right hand turn after you have stopped." The driver's face immediately brightened and with a smile of relief and gratitude he turned, clearing the way for the ambulance.

This driver was so locked into obeying the law that when accidently confronted with two opposing laws he was unable to resolve the dilemma by establishing a priority. A law is a law. This rigidity is not uncommon at stage 4.

5. Stage 5 persons reason that rules are desirable for the welfare and protection of all people's rights. Therefore, a sense of need to abide by the law comes out of an obligation to people. Laws are perceived as a contract, a rational agreement regarding the greatest good for the greatest number. However, one keeps in mind that rules are made by people.

Persons in stage 5 recognize that ethical and legal points of view may be in conflict and therein lies a difficult dilemma. Some rights such as life and liberty supersede agreements, the law, and popular opinion, and therefore must be protected at the cost of violating generally upheld commitments. Concerns are repeated in clashes between the interests of the group and the independence of the individual, between order and progress, and between the conforming bonds of habit and thinking for oneself. Through such dilemmas the stage 5 person is continually seeking new interpretations of moral issues. As John Dewey (1897) put it, "conflict is the gadfly of thought."

The contract for stage 5 is: When you live in a society you respect and uphold the rights of others. The appropriateness of society is judged by its holding that the rights and welfare of individuals, rather than rules, are appropriate if they support the society. The Constitution postulates universal human rights and the concept of government as a social contract, freely chosen and committed to protecting the right of all individuals who are party to that contract. Stage 5 reminds us that the people who devised and signed that document did so out of principles contrary to the law and order of the land at that time. The morality is exemplified by Emerson in his lecture "Man the Reformer":

> Nothing can bring you peace but yourself. Nothing can bring you peace
> but the triumph of principles. . . . Whoever would be a man must be a

nonconformist, unhindered by the name of goodness, exploring for himself whether or not it is goodness.

6. A person in stage 6 recognizes that certain ethical principles are the fundamental guidelines. Laws and rules are derived from these principles, and in those instances where the principles are in conflict with the law, the principles prevail. The primary principle is that of justice. Other principles, such as equality of human rights and respect for the dignity of human beings as individuals, are subsumed under the primary principle.

All human beings have an equal, valid claim on freedom, dignity, and justice. No one's life is less or more worthy than another. If two want it and only one can have it, the decision is settled by negotiation. Few of us are able to consistently resolve value dilemmas with stage 6 reasoning.

In moral development, behavior is not the critical factor. Rather it is reasoning, the explanation offered by the individual to either justify or decide on an action. People at different stages may respond to a situation in exactly the same way but their reasons would probably be different. For the sake of illustration let's consider a brief and oversimplified situation. Two different individuals are stopped by the police for driving 80 mph. Person A says: "I can't talk to you know. I have a sick person here whom I am rushing to the hospital." This may be an example of stage 5 moral reasoning. Person B says: "I'm sorry officer, I am really a safe driver and seldom exceed the speed limit. I won't do it again. I would appreciate it if you would let me go. I have a sick person here whom I'm taking to the hospital." This may best represent a stage 3 rationale. Both are speeding, breaking the law, allegedly to achieve the same end. Is there a moral difference? Most certainly in reasoning and response to authority.

For purposes of clarification let's summarize the moral development stages in a slightly different way. Kohlberg and his associates have found that there are six discrete stages of moral development. The first two stages are essentially egocentric. Behavior is guided by concern for oneself and those people who are closest. In the middle two stages the respondents are society oriented; the individual solicits social approval, demonstrates loyalty to persons and authority as well as concern about the welfare of others and the society. The needs of the individual are subordinated to the good of the society. In the final two stages the concern is once more for individuals but not the me and mine. The individual of stage 5 and stage 6 is the universal individual. The stage 5–6 person is concerned about rights, not just his own but everyone's rights and he may be willing to challenge the social order to protect those rights. The directives of right and wrong do not come from society but from the principles of trust, freedom, and human rights. In stage 5–6 the person commits himself, not to the society, but to a just and moral society.

Most adults are found to function primarily in stages 3 and 4. However, Kohlberg (1984) suggests that about 25 percent of the adult population functions at least part of the time in stages 5 and 6.

All people at times behave inappropriately, so immoral acts may occur by persons at stage 6 as well as at stage 1. However, the consequence for those in stage 1 is fear of punishment by a powerful external force, while those persons in stage 6 are concerned out of recognition that they have not been true to their own principles.

A critic could justifiably ask, since behavior is reputedly independent of the different moral stages, what difference does it make if a person is in stage 1, 2, 3, 4, 5 or 6? That is, why should we educate students to function at the higher stages of morality? Kohlberg (1975) reports three findings that suggest that the level of stage development does make a difference. In one study of college student cheating it was found that while 70 percent of those at stage 2 cheat as compared to 55 percent of those in stage 3 and 4, only 15 percent of those at stage 5 and 6 cheat. In the Milgram studies of obedience, people were told to severely shock others as part of an experiment. Whereas 65 percent of the general adult population typically obey the directive, only 15 percent of those at stage 5 or 6 do so. Finally, convicts who participated in Just Community programs, which incorporate a variety of moral development experiences, have shown a recidivism rate of about 15 percent, as compared to 75 percent for the nonparticipants.

Table 6.1 will help put the respective stages of cognitive development, social perspective, and moral reasoning in perspective.

Female moral development

Females may progress through parallel but different sets of stages. Kohlberg worked almost exclusively with males. Gilligan (1979), working with adolescent females, has found that females reason from a perspective different from that of males. Whereas males tend to see dilemmas from the perspective of power, order, rules, and the protection of human rights, females apparently sense human relationships in terms of caretaking, responsibilities, protection, and caring.

Gilligan (1979) has identified three levels, with each comparable to two Kohlberg stages. In level 1 the focus is on survival and self-gratification. Deference is given to powerful others, but the motive is self-preserva-

Table 6.1. Cognitive, Social, and Moral Development Stages

Requisite cognitive development	*Social perspectives*	*Assumptions for moral reasoning*
1. Preoperational	Egocentricity. No apparent awareness of other's views.	Avoid punishment. Authority has power and therefore is right.
2. Concrete operations	Individualistic. To each his own.	Each serves own interests. Trade on other's needs.
3. Concrete operations	Individuals relate to other individuals. Share feelings, expectations, agreements.	Golden rule. Good persons are loyal, trustworthy respectful and grateful.
4. Concrete operations	Member of society. System defines rules and roles.	Protect the system. Responsibility is to contribute to social order and live by rules.
5. Formal operations	Rational individualism. Aware of values and rights within social order. Concern for due process.	Rules are relative. Aware that people differ in values and opinions and that rules are relative.
6. Formal operations	Each person is an end in himself/herself and must be treated as such.	Universal moral principles of justice, equality, rights, and human dignity are basic commitments.

Source: Adapted from Kohlberg (1984).

tion and self-satisfaction. Just as in the original moral development stages 1 and 2, this level reflects selfishness and self-protection.

As the individual becomes more aware of the social value of acceptance by others, the notion of classic feminine goodness is adopted. Level 2 focuses on connectedness and care for others. Ideas about the need to nurture, protect, and serve the dependent and disadvantaged predominate. The wife as subordinate and helpmate to the husband would be a good example of level 2 morality. Likewise, the woman who dedicates herself to the welfare of her children and sacrifices herself to their service is at level 2. This deference to others is similar to the commitment to social mores in Kohlberg stages 3 and 4. Committing oneself to the service of others sometimes leads to feelings of being manipulated and used. The resulting sense of dissatisfaction can lead either to apathy or to a growth surge to level 3.

The way the individual handles the ambivalence of feeling morally responsible to serve others but simultaneously resentful depends on the quality of self-concept. Gilligan notes if the individual feels unworthy then she cannot claim equality and her assertions for rights fall prey to charges of selfishness. Thus, many people are arrested at level 2 with moral commitments to serve others mixed with a sense of martyrdom. This dilemma is a classic case of a need for supportive professional help which enables the individual to deal with the feelings and thereby resolve the underlying problem. Such help as that discussed in Chapter 4 enables the individual to move to level 3.

In level 3 the individual recognizes and serves the rights and obligations to the self. Unlike level 1, however, in which self-gratification is the primary concern, in level 3 the individual considers the satisfaction of one's own needs as critical for mental health and appropriate relations with others. An individual may insist that her wants, needs, and feelings be gratified as a matter of open honesty in the name of fairness. Whereas in level 2 the individual is concerned with "what others will think" if I do or don't, in level 3 the consideration is a broader perspective in which intentions and the consequence of actions for me and others is the primary factor. The nature of level 3 is epitomized by assertiveness, which is discussed in some detail in Chapter 11.

Rather than thinking of male morality and female morality it would be more realistic to conceive morality two-dimensionally. One dimension deals with power, rule orientation, and human rights in the sense of property and commercial relationships. The second dimension refers to relationships as connections, compassion, and caring. The critical issue for us is the process by which student experiences for moral development can be arranged.

PROCESSES OF MORAL DEVELOPMENT

Harsh punishment is not unusual in school, particularly for students of minority background with lower socioeconomic status. Teachers tend to defend this treatment by noting, "They will not obey without the threat of harsh punishment. That is what they get at home and that is the only thing they understand." That may or may not be the case. However, if control by the threat of punishment is the primary experience one has, then we can expect the individual to remain at stage 1. He will be as he is. If our goal in education is self-regulation, trust, social responsibility, future orientation, and prosocial rather than egocentric morality, then we need to seek an alternative.

The vehicle for moral development is experience. If we as teachers note that our pupils do not have the appropriate values, then it behooves us to arrange the right experiences so that they may develop the morality we long for them to have. If we ignore them, talk about them, or punish them for improper values, this does not change them. We need to recognize that many children experience such a restricted, isolated family and social life that they have little opportunity to compare their views with those of others. Education needs to arrange these experiences.

Research on MD has identified three kinds of experiences that move people to higher stages. The first is role playing, the second is open discussion of critical social issues, and the third is participatory democracy in the school as a community.

Role Playing as a Mechanism for Moral Development

The primary objective of role playing is to help individuals become more aware of the feelings and perceptions of others. This ability to feel or recognize what others are feeling in a given situation is a critical factor of morality. If an individual is to anticipate and heed the consequence of his actions he must recognize what it would be like to be the recipient of those actions. If an individual is to care what happens to others then he must feel what others must be experiencing. This feeling of what others are experiencing is called *empathy*. In Chapter 3 we discussed ways that we could use empathy to help students resolve feeling problems. Here we are discussing the teaching of empathy.

Developing empathy through role playing can be a powerful strategy. Feshbach (1978) related how she was able to significantly reduce the antisocial behavior of a group of incorrigible third-grade delinquent boys by training them to be more aware of what others experience when they are hit, robbed, cheated, and cursed.

In addition to training in empathy, role playing offers several potential advantages over other forms of education. It can be realistic in that situations can be selected from current issues. It is nonthreatening in that everyone realizes that it is acting and not real. It allows for comparing and contrasting alternatives in that at any given point the teacher can say, "Okay, that is one way that it could happen, now, let's start over and do it differently," or "Thank you Jake, now we want to see how someone else might handle this situation. Mary, would you take Jake's role and show us how you would handle it?" Finally, it is integrative in that role playing involves behavior, thoughts, and feelings.

Robert Hawley (1975) suggests this format:

(a) Focus on a specific situation. For instance, Rick and Susan are very good friends and both do quite well in school. Rick is quite busy with athletics and several clubs, so he sometimes gets behind in school work. He has had particular trouble with algebra and realizes the night before a big test that he knows little about the current material. Susan knows the material and it seems likely that she will do well on the test. Rick asks, "Susan, I'm in a real jam and I'm panicked about the test tomorrow. If I get stuck will you pass me some answers?"

(b) Begin with a five-minute brainstorm on the issue. Ask everyone to think of as many different responses as possible. All ideas are acceptable as possibilities. The teacher copies them on the board. Don't worry about quality—include all possibilities without any negative comments about anybody's ideas.

(c) Select one of the alternatives. You might let the students vote or the teacher may combine two or three possibilities.

(d) Establish a role-playing situation. It may be a straight one-to-one situation involving two people, but here is a different approach that enables you to involve several people and thereby involve more sharing of ideas. Place two chairs facing one another. Ask three students to collectively take the role of each of the mythical persons sitting in each chair. The scene should look like the drawing below, in which a_1, a_2, and so on represent students.

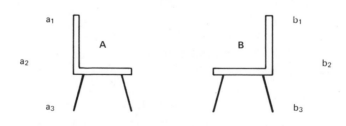

At any time, a_1, a_2, or a_3 may confer or individually speak for A, and likewise b_1, b_2, or b_3 for B.

(e) Establish a simple set of rules. Set a time limit. Role playing is to start with the signal "begin" and stop with "end." Anyone wishing to step out of role momentarily may request a "break." Neither acting nor script may be criticized.

(f) Debrief the participants. Immediately after the role playing has ended, the students are asked about their experience: What did you feel? What were the consequences when . . .? What are some of the assumptions we made about Rick, Mary, or the teacher? What values and concerns are involved here?

(g) If deadlocked, try reversing the roles.

Hawley (1975) believes that several lessons are learned as a consequence of such role playing: Each student, observer as well as participant, becomes more aware of his own value frame of reference. Students see that real problems can be worked out, that behavior is purposeful when it has explicit goals, that one's beliefs and values are expressed in behavior, and perhaps most important that decisions and behaviors have consequences. Students are helped to consider alternatives, to confront and evaluate the way different people handle a given situation. These are the ingredients of responsible moral behavior.

Schmuck and Schmuck (1984) report that role playing increased the morale and cohesion of classes. After role playing the class has a stronger sense of community and this is reflected in better behavior and improved academic achievement.

Selman (1975) points out that such role playing increases student awareness of other persons and the society's point of view. It increases the likelihood that a student will shift his or her perception from "what will happen to me" to the possible consequences for others. The behavior in role playing is reportedly representative of at least the stage in which the person is functioning and often reflects principles of the next higher level. Selman developed two filmstrips (*First Things: Values* and *First Things: Social Reasoning*) of episodes that can be used for elementary school youngsters. These are available through Guidance Associates, New York City.

Discussion of Issues for Moral Development

The second and most commonly recognized means of moral development is via issue discussion. The point of issue discussion is to involve students in taking a position, defending it, listening to feedback from others, as well as listening and responding to other positions. This process encourages students to think through their beliefs and commitments in increasingly complex ways. The basic assumption is that human beings are active processors of information, that is, people seek to achieve order, stability, and congruence between what is believed to be true and input information. When someone challenges a person's position or logically presents a more comprehensive and consistent argument for a given position, then cognitive disequilibrium results. If explanations are at a lower stage of thinking, the person is able to comprehend the meaning, but given his higher level of thought he perceives the moral to be inconsistent or incomplete and rejects it. When presented with arguments much higher than his own, the individual doesn't comprehend the reasoning and so it too is rejected. The growth occurs when the moral reasoning is not only different from his own but at about his own level or the next higher stage. A disequilibrium results because the more adequate logic cannot be rejected and the need for balance motivates the person to think through to a more comprehensive, consistent position.

Rokeach (1975) conducted a series of studies that illustrate the effect when a person realizes an inconsistency in his thinking.

A randomly selected group of university students was asked to individually rank-order 18 valued conditions (e.g., true friendship, inner harmony, freedom, equality, a world at peace). Each student was then asked to indicate his or her views and contributions to civil rights movements. Finally, each was confronted with the incongruencies within the rankings and alleged inactivity in organizations for resolving social inequality.

All students tend to become more liberal during the freshman year of college. However, Rokeach (1971) reported that those students who participated in this activity changed much more than did those who had not been confronted with the incongruency of their thinking. These changes and the differences were still evident 15 months later.

Moral change is most likely to occur in those situations in which discussions succeed in arousing cognitive conflict among the participants. Individuals express their respective views, interpret the reasoning of others, and weigh what is being said for consistency and logic. If other people's arguments are different but reasonable, and if the emotional quality of the discussion is such that degradation is minimal, then each participant explores the merits of alternate views.

Three points need to be clarified regarding the nature of moral development. First, development is not a matter of rejecting one's own views and switching to someone else's. Moral development is more like reconsidering and reconstructing one's own reasoning when inconsistencies become apparent. Second, although much is made about vertical development from one level to the next highest in the stage hierarchy, perhaps most development is lateral. That is, most growth is in the form of generalizing old principles and ways of reasoning to a wide variety of situations. The implications of a given stage must be applied to many different issues and circumstances. Third, few of us are purely in one stage or another. More likely our thinking on issues ranges over two or three stages because the exposure and generalization noted in the second point have not been completed.

The change in vertical development was rather dramatically illustrated by a teacher in one of my classes. The teacher had taken a rather strong position and during the discussion was defending a point. In the middle of a sentence she stopped, looked troubled, and said, "Wait a minute, something is wrong here. I have to think about this for a minute." We went on and in about 15 minutes she jumped back in beaming, "I still think they [the persons in the issue] were right but my reasons were wrong. It was right because. . . ." Her reconsidered position, although defending the same behavior, was a full stage above that offered in the earlier part of the discussion. As it happens such dramatic changes are rare. However, change does occur.

Blatt and Kohlberg (1975) report from a series of studies involving sixth- and tenth-grade students that gains averaged one full stage of moral development. The student groups met twice a week for three months and discussed specific moral dilemmas. The differences between the participating students and control groups who were otherwise occupied during the moral development meetings were maintained in a follow-up test one year later. The procedures Blatt and Kohlberg used are not different from those within the realm of most teachers.

The teacher's role is fivefold:

(a) To select and present a moral dilemma to which students will react. By definition a moral dilemma is controversial, such as when two or more morals are at cross purposes. The moral dilemma is imbedded in an episode. Episodes may involve such competing issues as the desire to protect a friend at the expense of someone else being falsely accused, or living up to particular family values at the risk of losing one's standing among peers. Particularly in the beginning there may be advantages in focusing on relatively remote dilemmas, such as sustaining the life of a person who is experiencing severe untreatable pain or police shooting a fleeing person suspected of theft.

(b) To ensure that students understand the dilemma faced by the persons caught up in the situation. Students need to be reassured that there is no right or wrong response. Students are directed to give two responses: Indicate "yes" or "no" as to the appropriateness of whatever action was taken in the situation. Explain the basis for your "yes" or "no" response.

(c) To help students conform to the moral principles at issue, for example, "The question here is, should Mary help her friend, who she knows is in trouble without her help, or should she live up to her obligations to the others in class who would be unjustly cheated by his actions?" In order to highlight the moral issue the questions usually contain an "ought" or "should" or an "Is it right or wrong" connotation.

(d) To elicit and encourage all students to share their respective judgments. Active participation is a necessary condition. Mere exposure to other's views is insufficient. For moral development the individual must express his view, challenge, and be challenged. He must clarify his hazy feelings by putting them into words, by owning them. The teacher probes responses with "why" questions (e.g., Why do you think it is wrong for Julie to . . .?")

(e) To encourage students with different interpretations and different rationales to interact with one another. One of the many ways the teacher does this is by contrasting the views of different students. Example: "It is my understanding that Norma is saying many people might be injured, but Cindy believes that that is a necessary risk, because otherwise Mr. Rogers' whole reason for being would be lost."

In order to clarify, to challenge, to encourage, or to support one or another, the teacher may find it necessary to complicate or simplify the original situation, for example, "Suppose the boy's mother had asked him to lie—would that make a difference?"

After the students are involved in sharing, challenging, and explaining, the teacher needs to shift to in-depth questions to force students to grapple with competing claims, rationales, interpretations, and conclusions. Hersh et al. (1980) list four general in-depth strategies: refining questions, clarifying and summarizing, highlighting contiguous-stage arguments, and role playing.

The refining questions are designed to probe points of view in order to expose all possible innuendos and meanings in order to maximize awareness of different views. Don't hesitate to get at the particulars of student thinking. Ask for examples. Ask students to defend one another's positions, including those antagonistic to their own. In confronting one another's ideas students need not be adversaries. We probe to make certain that everyone, including the advocate, understands the consequences of a given moral act.

Highlighting contiguous-stage arguments is necessary because it is the higher-stage reasoning that stimulates a person's moral development. The task is to compare and contrast arguments ("Both Bruce and Pedro say that it is wrong for the government to lie to the people. However, Bruce suggested that it is wrong because lying is wrong and no one should ever lie, while Pedro is suggesting that to lie is betraying the trust of the people. Are these really different reasons, and if so why?") Some students will of course be at the highest stage for the group. In this case, hopefully the teacher will be sufficiently aware of higher-stage interpretations and will play devil's advocate to stimulate thought slightly beyond everyone's moral reasoning level.

Clarifying and summarizing are necessary teacher moves. First, it is necessary to occasionally summarize positions in order to establish a base for more discussion. The point is to periodically get things organized in some sort of order, otherwise some students will get lost in the argument. Chaos is not the only danger. It is easy to move too far out on tangents. It therefore behooves the teacher to be wary for the need to pull things together. Another aspect of this function is to link together certain critical elements! (E.g., "In what ways are we in agreement and in what ways do we differ?")

As we previously noted, role playing is a potent way to enable students to reason their way to higher stages of moral thinking. Perhaps the most important advantage of role playing is that the process enables the participants to sense what it is like to be someone else, to experience other perspectives. One of the most critical variables in morality is to be aware of the consequences for others of one's actions. Many of our students are very egocentric and therefore need opportunities to experience what it is like to be in someone else's shoes.

In summary, Hersh et al. (1980) point out that the value-oriented person cares, makes judgments, and acts in ways consistent with his values. Value-moral education should focus on these three elements.

Caring involves support for oneself as well as concern for the welfare of others. Caring involves intellectual understanding of the needs and wishes of oneself and of others. It involves empathy—knowing and communicating to others that one senses what it is like to be in that position. Caring includes an emotional valuing, attachment, and affiliation with oneself and others. Finally, caring means nurturance, a need to help others in distress.

Judgment is critical since moral dilemmas require deliberation and decision-making. It is not enough to simply take a position (e.g., taking the life of a human being is wrong). Few would argue with that as a proposition. The issue remains as to circumstances: Save one at the risk of many? How about self-defense or the defense of an innocent bystander? Considered thought requires an evaluation of conflicting interests in view of particular situations.

Acting in a moral way in the final analysis is the critical variable. However, behavior in itself is neither moral nor immoral. If a person's motives and reasoning are set aside, then his actions have no moral status. Pushing someone aside is amoral until the question of why the pusher did it is answered (To injure the recipient or to save the recipient from being hit by a fast-moving vehicle?). The former motive makes it an immoral act, whereas the latter is a commendable moral act, particularly if in doing so the pusher endangers himself. If the push were an accident, nonintentional, then the contact would be amoral. Despite the cautions on judging given acts as reflecting a particular morality, it is apparent that morality, like education, can be truly reflected only in behavior.

Participatory Democracy in the School as a Community

In most schools the authorities impose a number of rules regarding such behaviors as attendance, movement about the school, dress codes, the use of property, and student communication. When authority imposes rules with power, the students have four options: (a) to ignore the rules and do as they please, (b) to subtly undermine the rules, (c) to passively obey the rules, or (d) to actively challenge those rules perceived to be unfair. Options (a) and (b) would seem to be counterproductive. The third option may please the authorities, but if students obey the rules to avoid punishment we are locking them into stage 1 and stage 2 morality. Some educators logically argue that (d) has much merit, although most of us don't value haggling with students over the appropriateness of our rules.

School operations are complex. (1) Student behavior is governed by standards imposed by student norms as well as school rules. The two sets of rules are often in conflict. (2) Each teacher interprets and enforces school rules differently. (3) Every school has several subgroups of students, each with its own set of norms. (4) Both peer-group norms and many school rules are established and maintained with limited discussion or conscious agreement. (5) The task of the school is twofold: (a) to establish an orderly, comfortable setting in which people can work without threat, disturbance, or interference; and (b) to educate students to become self-directed, but rule-governed citizens.

A number of schools in all parts of the United States recognize this complexity and its potential. The most visible of such schools are the alternative high schools. They have few rules and strive to openly discuss and amend the rules through some form of participatory democracy.

Although alternative schools are public, students normally attend them by choice rather than geographic mandate. Furthermore, programs are often distinct from those found in comprehensive high schools. However, the major distinction is in the student–teacher relationship, which focuses on mutual trust and interdependence rather than adversity.

Gregory and Smith (1982) compared student and teacher need satisfaction in 15 alternative high schools with that in 12 conventional high schools. The measures dealt with four types of needs: (a) Security: a stable, orderly and controlled environment; (b) Affiliation: belonging and friendship; (c) Self-esteem: achievement, success, and status; and (d) Self-actualization: becoming a fully integrated person. The schools were samples from four states. One of the alternative schools had a back-to-basics orientation. The students in four of the alternative schools were youngsters who had experienced behavioral and academic problems in conventional schools.

The findings of the Gregory and Smith survey are enlightening. In all four need areas the alternative schools were found to be superior to such a degree that there was virtually no overlap with the conventional schools. Both the teachers and the students in the alternative schools indicated that they were more secure, more social, possessed a higher sense of self-esteem, and experienced more opportunity for self-actualization than did the teachers and students in conventional high schools. Gregory and Smith contend that the remarkable differences in satisfaction are due to the difference in prosocial attitudes.

The alternative schools have fewer rules, but in other respects are no more permissive than the conventional schools. The minor difference between the schools seems to be the matter of freedom to choose and more opportunity for self-governance.

A report by Power et al. (1982) will help us gain insight into the effects of freedom to choose. High school students from Cluster, an alternative school administered with a major objective of moral development, were compared with students from two nearby conventional high schools. All three schools are located in Boston. Students were interviewed with respect to four dilemmas such as the following:

1. An unpopular student needs a ride to a college for an important interview early on Saturday morning. His family has no automobile and the sponsoring teacher's car is being repaired. Your family car is available. Would you or other students in your high school be inclined to help this student by getting up early Saturday morning and driving him to his appointment?

The responses of the students from the alternative school are clearly different from those who attend the regular high schools on two closely related accounts: (a) a collective norm and (b) the valuing of the school as a community. The meaning of these respective factors can be best understood by typical responses of students from the respective schools.

Collective Norms

A conventional school student said, "I don't have an obligation, especially if I don't know them. You are more responsible to yourself and your own actions." Clearly, a live-and-let-live position. In the alternative school the students expressed an obligation to other students. For instance, "You have a responsibility to all the kids in the school, even if you don't like them all that much . . . because everyone is supposed to be one, it is our school, it is not a school that all these separate people go to that don't care about each other." Responsibility extends beyond oneself to members of the whole group. At the conventional school behavior is based on whether a rule existed which stipulated how one should behave. If there were no such rule there was no obligation. At Cluster the responses reflected an attitude that we care, help, and protect each other on all occasions because we are all together.

Valuing the School as a Community

A typical student comment from one of the regular high schools was: "The school lacks togetherness. Nobody really takes pride in the school except a few who are good students or very good athletes. Where people don't take pride in something or go out of their way to help each other, the community doesn't really benefit. It doesn't promote the welfare of the school. Kids go [sic] vandalize a lot. There is no sense of caring, helping each other." In contrast, a student from the alternative school said, "Stealing affects the community more than the individual because that is what we are.

We are not just a group of individuals." Group commitments and ideals are valued and the school is perceived as an organic whole composed of inter-related systems that represent the total group.

Developing the School as a Community

The alternative schools tend to be small, democratic schools. Although Gregory and Smith found that within the limits of their study, size was not a factor, small schools have a distinct advantage with respect to this issue. Power et al. (1982) are instituting their program in a large urban high school by establishing school-within-school clusters of 125 students and incorporating direct participatory democracy for rule making and governance within these units. We will have to wait and see if a large, bureaucratic urban high school can adapt to a sense of community and shared responsibility.

The community feeling of Cluster School took four years to develop. In the beginning, meetings were chaotic and students took advantage of the situation. For instance, the first vote was to eliminate compulsory school attendance. This is to be expected. If behavior control has been traditionally by coercion, then when the lid comes off we should expect a burst of uncontrolled demands for freedom. Students are accustomed to thinking of rules as something that carries enforceable punishment for violation. When adult dominance and punishment are withdrawn there will be temporary disarray.

In the case of Cluster, the majority soon reasoned that if you don't have to come to school there would be no school. The rules that were then established by the student-dominated meetings and the means to enforce them were very liberal. It wasn't until the third year that students began to collectively face the issues and govern themselves as a responsible community. At that time the students voted for an absolute no-cut policy. As one graduating senior said,

> If you have a certain amount of cuts [allowed] . . . it gives you excuses.
> . . . But if you have an obligation to fulfill, then you have to face up to it
> and if you don't after a certain amount of time, then I guess you don't be-
> long there. (Power et al. 1982)

Some students complained that the no-cut rule was unfair because of the boring classes. However, others argued that was just an excuse and that cutting was a form of nonparticipation and an offense against the community. In the fourth year the no-cut rule was again ratified by the students, except that its title became the 100 Percent Participation Rule. School attendance as an issue had shifted from a disciplinary problem to community responsibility. Compliance changed from fear or avoidance of punishment to a self-consciously chosen commitment to live up to one's obligations as a community member. Considering the background of some of these students, such changes constituted a growth of two or three moral development stages.

This change occurred allegedly because issues (including the expulsion of some students) and school policies were openly discussed among student–teacher groups. Rules were generated within the boundaries of state law, but student, teacher, and administrator votes were weighted equally. Meetings were not tranquil. Teachers pushed their views by reason, not power, and often lost the battle. However, in the long run, astonishing educational objectives were achieved.

Cluster students proposed strengthening the curriculum by adding fundamentals: drills in grammar, reading, and writing for students who needed them. Students recognized that such fundamentals were tedious, but a coalition of the highest and lowest academic achievers championed the proposal. It won nearly unanimous approval.

About 40 percent of the students who enrolled at Cluster had a previous history of truancy and other disciplinary problems. For a number of the students this was to be a last chance to complete high school. It is rather remarkable that such students came to vote in favor of a no-cut policy and support a whole community-based set of norms. For instance, during the first year stealing was a serious problem, but by the middle of the third year theft within the school had completely stopped. Another indicator of program success was the fact that over 90 percent of the graduates from Cluster went to college, as compared to less than 50 percent of the graduates from other Boston public high schools.

Thus far we have focused our attention on the intangible personal factors that influence behavior. Next we will consider more explicit, direct ways to change behavior by directly controlling the environment.

The conflict cycle stipulates that people evaluate themselves in terms of perceived competency, power, acceptance, and virtue. If the person perceives himself to be inadequate in any one or a combination of these criteria, he responds emotionally. The individual then acts so as to protect the self. Unfortunately, this acting-out behavior often is disruptive or otherwise incongruent with social mores. Other people, particularly authorities, tend to punish such behavior, and the feedback causes further deterioration of the individual's self-esteem. The consequence is further emotional reaction and the conflict cycle is perpetuated.

As we have noted professional intervention may intervene at points A, B, C or D. Chapters 7, 8, and 9 focus on C, an environment to change behavior. As we shall see there are a variety of alternative ways that one might respond to a student's acting-out misbehavior and interrupt the cycle by replacing misbehavior with desired behavior.

RECOMMENDED READINGS

Curwin, R.L. and Mendler, A.N. *The discipline book.* Reston, VA: Reston, 1980.

Ginott, H. *Teacher and child.* New York: Macmillan, 1972.

Gordon, T. *TET: Teacher effectiveness training.* New York: Weyden, 1975.

Sheban, J., ed. *The wisdom of Gibran.* New York: Bantam, 1973.

7

ENVIRONMENTAL CONTROL
OF BEHAVIOR

THE INCORRIGIBLE STUDENT

Mickey Trobol is a new student at Lincoln High School. Mickey is not here because of a change of home address. He has been transferred here as an incorrigible. His behavior at Washington High School, and all of his preceding schools, was such that the administration and teachers alike were happy to see him go. The principal accurately pointed out to Mickey that this is his last chance. If he is expelled from Lincoln his next transfer will be to the reform school.

What is an incorrigible? Webster's *Third New International Dictionary: Unabridged* (1971) notes that to be incorrigible is to be "incapable of being corrected or amended as (a) bad beyond the possibility of correction or rehabilitation . . . (e) unwilling to change or to give something up" (p. 1145).

Whether or not Mickey is incorrigible remains to be seen. His behavior is intolerable. Except when he is with his friends Mickey tends to be grim. He has a hard look on his face that communicates, "Keep your distance, this is my territory and I don't like trespassers." He has a long record of fighting, destruction of property, profanity, and challenging authority. He and his friends were intoxicated by alcohol and drugs while in school on more than one occasion.

The teachers and administrators at Washington had done everything they could think of to shape Mickey into decent, rule-abiding behavior. They clearly communicated rules and pointed out the consequences for rule violations. The teachers warned, scolded, isolated, and referred Mickey to the principal for his misbehavior. Over an extended period of time the principal gave Mickey several chances to change. He was repeatedly told that he was in trouble. His parents were repeatedly notified. In addition to the reprimands he was paddled, and suspended for one day, then twice for three days before the final recommendation for transfer. The alternative to the transfer was reform school.

The apparent conditions at home are not ideal. The father is only occasionally employed. He has a drinking problem and periodically beats his wife and the kids. An older brother quit school at age fifteen and has been in trouble with the law. Over the years the parents have received innumerable messages from the schools in terms of the boys' bad behavior. Neither parent responds as far as the school knows, but the parents do reprimand the boys at home and do admonish them to change. The parents don't approve of the sons' behavior, but have no idea about how to straighten them out other than haranguing them and on occasion using corporal punishment.

The administration at Washington High School recognized that part of the problem was the contagion of behavior among Mickey's friends. Therefore, when Mickey was referred to Lincoln the others were sent to other schools in an attempt to break up the gang. This unilateral decision angered Mickey more than anything else. The idea of going to a new school for a fresh start was okay. In fact, Mickey fantasized that maybe everything would work out well, that he would get passing grades and wouldn't get into trouble. He didn't want to go to reform school.

Mickey felt that the teachers at the new school wouldn't know him, so they would be fair. He hoped that they wouldn't know of his bad reputation, which (a) Mickey believed to be unfair and (b) meant that teachers at Washington had it in for him and overreacted to every little behavior, so that he never had a chance. Nevertheless, Mickey resented the administration separating him from his friends; they were all he had. He knows no one at Lincoln High.

What are the prospects for Mickey? Given what we know, what is your bet as to Mickey's behavior in six months?

Mickey's Prospects

He won't change	New school
He will smoke, drink, be truant, fight, swear, and mouth off here just as he has always done.	New friends
	New chance. He knows the consequences of another expulsion. He's smart enough to shape up and behave.

Mickey's behavior in six months will depend primarily on the teachers and administrators of Lincoln High School. This is true because the immediate environment is a major factor in determining behavior, and more than anyone else the faculty controls the school environment.

Moos (1975) demonstrated that about 30 percent of the variance of such feelings as hostility, anxiety, and empathy can be attributed to other persons, the particular setting, and mode of response interactions. To put this percent figure in perspective: 30 percent of variance is about as powerful as any single variable, such as intellect or previous academic performance, in predicting future grades. With respect to students like Mickey, Moos offers the following conclusion from his review of studies on person-environment: "Thus, evidence indicates that behavior settings, social and organizational climates, reinforcement variables and so on, all have important impacts on aggressive and violent behavior." Problem behavior is not solely a function of the personality of the person.

BEHAVIOR: AN INTERACTION OF PERSONAL CHARACTERISTICS AND ENVIRONMENT

It is the student's behavior that is the problem rather than the student himself. Most often the disruptive student is not abnormal. The behavior is not strangely unique but different in frequency, intensity, timing, and place. Most of us sometimes interrupt others, become angry and glare at others, are tardy, procrastinate, and perhaps even lie. Most of the behaviors normally prohibited in school are tolerated and accepted in other circumstances. Therefore, it seems reasonable to conclude that the student is not bad, but just that his behavior is inappropriate in timing, frequency, and intensity.

Bandura (1977) interprets the relationship between behavior (B), the individual's personal characteristics (P), and the environment (E) as a reciprocal interaction. Pictorially the relationships would be

An individual's behavior is not only aroused and changed by the environment, but individuals through their behavior have an impact on the environment. Likewise, personal characteristics are partial determinants of behavior, and in turn, through learning, are shaped by the behavior and the environmental reactions to that behavior. This reciprocal interaction offers us a viable means of influencing the immediate behavior of students and in addition those personal qualities that will ensure continued appropriate future behavior. Control of the current environment is thus a critical factor for influencing both current and future behavior.

The Behaviorist Point of View

A large number of psychologists (generally known as *behaviorists*) believe that it is nearly impossible to know how various personal characteristics interact and collectively influence behavior. Therefore, they argue that it is more advantageous to focus attention on the environment. The simplest, most precise, and most certain way to influence behavior is to control selected elements in the environment.

Two views contrasted

Two short scenarios regarding a student named Scott are presented to contrast the personal characteristics orientation with that of the behaviorist. This scenario depicts two teachers discussing Scott, his behavior and his problems.

Teacher No. 1: How are you getting along with Scott?

Teacher No. 2: Poor Scott. He can't sit still, he's out of his seat more than he's in it. He hits the other students and yells. He's really hyperactive. I spend half my time yelling at him to sit down, to return to his seat. I humor him, I yell at him, I tried paddling him twice, but that didn't help. I'm at the end of my rope.

Teacher No. 1: I agree; I had all kinds of problems with him last year. He is mentally slow. He just couldn't keep up with the reading group. I requested testing to see if we could officially declare him as mentally retarded. They couldn't take him, though.

Teacher No. 2: He is not reading well at all. I think he has a learning disability. His answers to questions are so bizarre that I think he might be brain-damaged.

Teacher No. 1: You know, his parents can hardly speak English. The other students tease him all the time and he is always trying to get attention. I'll bet he has a low self-concept.

Teacher No. 2: Yes, I should build his self-concept.

From this conversation we could conclude the following:

Behavior: Out of seat, yells and hits others, no reading skills, bizarre answers to questions, others tease him.
Problem: Hyperactive, mental retardation, learning disability, low self-concept.
Current treatment: Humor, punishment.
Recommendation: Testing, build self-concept.

The next scenario depicts two other teachers discussing Scott's behavior:

Teacher No. 2:	Scott is driving me crazy. He is always out of his seat. He talks out of turn and interrupts me when I'm working with others. He wants attention so badly.
Teacher No. 1:	What do you do with him?
Teacher No. 2:	I scold him constantly. I've tried everything. "Sit down! Stop interrupting! Get to work!" I sent him to the principal, called his parents, and punished him, but nothing works very long.
Teacher No. 1:	Hmm. He is continually misbehaving and you always react by punishing him and telling him what to do. Could all of that attention be rewarding the misbehavior?
Teacher No. 2:	How could punishment and attention be rewarding?
Teacher No. 1:	Beats me, but you punish him and he keeps coming back for more. I wonder how it would work if you paid attention to him only when he is doing something good. You know, smile at him and praise him only when he is in his seat working or raises his hand before speaking.
Teacher No. 2:	What do I do when he's bad?
Teacher No. 1:	Well, if he's doing it to get attention, try ignoring it.
Teacher No. 2:	Do you think he is brain-damaged or hyperactive?
Teacher No. 1:	Who knows? The first thing is to get him to work. Once he starts to spend his time doing his lessons, we can analyze his responses and academic work, then we can see what needs to be changed. We can't tell much until you get him to spend some time on task.
Teacher No. 2:	I feel better now. I have something positive to focus on.

From this conversation we could conclude the following:

Behavior: Student out of seat, talks out of turn, interrupts and bothers others.
Problem: Teacher "going crazy."

Current treatment: Scold, punish, refer to others.
Recommendation: Attention contingent upon proper behavior. Ignore improper behavior. Focus on one behavior at a time.

Behaviorists point out that in working with Scott, teachers need to focus attention on his behavior and the immediate environmental conditions that are maintaining that behavior. Behaviorists do not deny that Scott has various personal characteristics that are a factor in his behavior. But these personal characteristics are complex, difficult to measure, and perhaps impossible to control. Therefore, teachers ought to concentrate on the observed behavior and the immediate environment, which is also a critical factor in determining behavior.

The teachers at Washington High School might have described Mickey Trobol in the same terms as the teachers did in the first scenario. If they did, the description of Mickey might be as follows:

Mickey's Malady

Behaviors	*Problems*	*Past treatment*
Fighting, profanity. Destroys property.	Incorrigible	Strict rule enforcement. Punishment.
Belligerent to authority.	Disrespectful.	Punishment.
Parents on welfare, heavy drinkers and unresponsive to school notices.	Parents don't care. No moral training at home.	Write off parents or tell them to teach morality and enforce proper school behavior.
Drug and alcohol consumption.	Weak character, immoral.	Suspend and refer to reform school.

The transfer from Washington to Lincoln High School is evidence enough that such an analysis and treatment of Mickey was unproductive. If Mickey's behavior is to change, a different strategy will be necessary. Before identifying the ways that the teachers at Lincoln High School might respond to Mickey, we need to better understand behavior as defined by behaviorists.

BEHAVIOR FROM THE BEHAVIORIST POINT OF VIEW

For behaviorists, behavior is the critical issue. It is not perceived as a symptom but rather as the target of treatment. The behaviorists contend that it is of little help for the teacher to interpret given behavior as "He just wants attention," or "He is acting out the anger that he feels toward authority figures." Rather, the emphasis is on increasing the frequency and variety of desired behavior while decreasing the frequency of undesired behavior.

The teacher will not be able to help Mickey or other students if they simply try to change him from a troublemaker into a good person. Teachers will be more consistent and successful if they identify specific target misbehaviors and focus their efforts to change them.

Critical Factors, Re: Behavior

In order to accurately identify behavior, four criteria need to be considered:

(1) *Specificity.* Behaviors need to be identified in precise, observable, countable forms. For example, hitting fellow students, lying, tardiness, and immediate responses to teacher directives are readily observable. However laziness or a desire for attention is at best inferred from behavior and is not specific in any sense of the term. The immediate target of classroom management is to identify and change specific observable behavior.

(2) *Frequency.* How often does the behavior occur during a unit of time? Teachers are sometimes amazed to find that some behaviors, although irritating, in reality do not occur very often. We may feel that a student is *always* interrupting, but when we record the occasions on which it happens we may find that over several days it occurs only once every few hours.

For example, a very passive first grader reportedly never did anything. On closer observation, however, it was found that over a three-hour period he did pick up a book or pencil and paper four times. Total on-task time was only about 17 minutes, so it was easy to understand the teacher's conclusions. However, he was on-task 1.3 times per hour. That is not much, but it is something with which the teacher can work.

A second reason for noting frequency is that it enables the teacher to compare post-treatment behavior with that of pre-treatment behavior. In that way we have an explicit measure of success.

(3) *Desirability*. If we are to change the behaviors of the students it is important that we differentiate between those behaviors that we want to occur from those we wish to extinguish for the particular setting. If behavior is to be changed, the undesired behavior must be replaced by specific desired behavior. If we wish to eliminate impulsive speaking out in class, we need to identify and emphasize raising one's hand and waiting to be called on before asking questions or expressing a view.

In using behavior modification we need to focus attention on the behavior we want. As opposed to saying, "You are not to be tardy again," we ought to say, "You are to be in your seat when the bell rings." Rather than focusing on the *Don'ts* of behavior, it behooves us to respond positively to those behaviors that are desired. Recall the Kounin (1970) findings that desist messages do little to change on-going behavior.

(4) *Priority*. Among the behaviors to be encouraged, some are more critical than others. Change and success are more likely to occur if the teacher focuses initially on one or two behaviors. The question is, which ones? One criterion would be those behaviors that are most consistent with our objectives. However, we need to also consider the probability of success, ease of identification, and possible negative consequences. In order to get the momentum in the desired direction, the teacher may wish to initially select an obvious simple behavior for which the chances of success are fairly high. For example, staying in one's seat is more likely to succeed than is not talking to anyone. Raising your hand is more easily controlled than is waiting until others have had a chance to finish before you talk.

With these criteria in mind let's take a closer look at some of the desired and undesired behaviors you perceive to occur in your classroom.

Behaviors Differentiated

Four different categories of behavior can be identified: desired (valued and to be increased in frequency), tolerable (not particularly valued but of low priority for change), undesired (behavior that is incompatible with educational goals), and replacements (desired behavior that is incongruent with undesired behavior, and if increased would subvert undesired behavior). For instance: speaking only when called on, slouching in seat with head in hand, walking around during seat work, and sitting in seat except when permission to leave is granted, are respective examples of desired, tolerable, undesired intolerable, and replacement behaviors. Note, the replacement and undesired intolerable behaviors are matched and are incompatible. Each behavior is also stated in observable terms. Each can be tallied and placed in a priority order with other behaviors. If you can do this with five sets of behavior you are well on your way to a well-managed classroom.

ENVIRONMENT FROM THE BEHAVIORIST POINT OF VIEW

The behavior of students cannot be changed directly. As noted earlier, behavior is the outcome of the interaction between personal qualities and the environment. The teacher can only control segments of the environment. The student enters the classroom with the personal characteristics. If we are to influence behavior we can do so only by arranging the environment.

The question regarding Mickey Trobol's incorrigibility needs to be rephrased. Given his habits, expectations, and other personal qualities, the teachers at Lincoln High School must create a new environment for Mickey if his behaviors are to change. The environment at Washington High School was such as to maintain Mickey's misbehavior. What kind of environment will it take at Lincoln High School to rehabilitate Mickey?

Two parts of the environment are of particular importance: (1) the stimuli that are signals or cues for behavior, and (2) the effects that occur immediately following the behavior.

One category of effects is punishment, which we noted in Part I only irregularly and under rather precise conditions significantly reduces the reoccurrence of the behavior. In contrast to punishment, a family of positive effects, generally known as *reinforcers,* more consistently and directly influences behavior. The stimuli elicit specific behaviors that have become habituated or conditioned by repeated reinforcement.

The following scenario may clarify the significance of differential effects.

The First Day of School

Jones decided to start this semester off by establishing a friendly but businesslike, on-task atmosphere. On the first day of school Jones was at the door and greeted each student as he or she entered: Jones identified himself by name, offered a genuine smile, and inquired about the name of the student. Following this Jones said, "Please select a seat and read the material which is on your desk. The paper will give you an orientation to some of the things we will study this semester. I want you to sit right down and begin reading." All of this was said with a warm but firm tone.

By the time the bell rang to signal the beginning of the period, all of the students were in the room and Jones left the door to attend the activities of the class. A glance around the room showed about one-half of the group sitting quietly in seats, apparently reading the assigned material. Several students were sitting, but not reading; they were either curiously looking about the room or just watching Jones. Two or three other pairs of students were quietly whispering. Two separate small groups, one boys and the other girls, were chatting and playfully laughing in the back of the room. A student was at the pencil sharpener. A girl was sitting at a desk, rhythmically and noisily hitting various objects with pencils simulating a drum player. A boy was walking down an aisle, rapping others on the head.

What might Jones do at this moment to move the class toward the desired atmosphere? Whatever Jones does now will be an important factor in determining patterns of student behavior for the whole semester.

A Thought for Jones

An on-task atmosphere as a condition will exist only if the participants find being on-task rewarding. If being on-task leads nowhere or if it is more rewarding to be off-task, then we can expect that few people will be on-task. So, what is rewarding? What is rewarding to one person may not be to others. What is rewarding at one time may not be at other times. Reward (which hereafter will be called *reinforcement*) is anything that follows behavior and tends to increase the probability that the behavior will be repeated. Strangely enough, as O'Leary and Becker (1968), among others, have noted, a negative reaction to a student's behavior may have this effect. This apparent paradox may be explained by the nature of human needs or motives. Murray (1938) identified 28 needs, any one or a combination of which motivates human behavior. The following are among the most common needs expressed by today's youth:

Need for affiliation as evidenced by socializing, wanting to belong and be accepted by others.
Need for activity as revealed by the walking, playing around, running, shoving, and the apparent endless energy of youth.
Need for power as manifested by bossing others, giving directions, and trying to influence others.

Need for achievement as expressed when a person strives to win, to overcome obstacles, and to accomplish difficult tasks.

Curiosity drives people to explore unique stimuli, incongruencies, and irregularities.

Need for competence is the basis for striving to master tasks, to generate skills, to become knowledgeable.

Need to nurture is expressed by helping and assisting others.

Need for deference is reflected in obedience, respect, and seeking advice or encouragement from persons in authority.

A given behavior will persist if it is reinforced. It will occur less frequently and become extinguished if it is not reinforced. Given the variety of human needs, any reaction from anybody to a given overt behavior may be reinforcing, depending on student motives.

Jones No. 1 responds: "Okay, boys and girls, it's time to go to work. You folks standing back there, get into your seats and stop talking. Stop looking out the window. Now, you two back there whispering—stop that and start reading." Turning in the other direction, he continues: "No pencil sharpening without permission. Don't just sit there and watch me, let's get on with the job."

Jones No. 1 smiles triumphantly because all of the students obediently move toward their seats and pick up their papers. What did the students learn? That is, what behavior was rewarded by teacher attention?

Jones No. 2 responds differently: "I am pleased to see so many of you reading as I asked. I appreciate that." Jones No. 2 moves unhurriedly around the room, commenting to those individuals on-task. "Very good, ah Mary, isn't it?" To another student, "Glad to see you at work." "Good going," as she touches the shoulder of another student. "Juan, I'll be interested in your views on this article." Surprisingly, all of the students are soon at their desks, reading. What is your prediction about future student behavior in Jones' No. 2 class?

Recall the various studies discussed in Student Responses to Teacher Directives. It was reported in these studies that the teacher reprimands actually increased the frequency of the punished behavior. That is what will happen with Jones No. 1. Everston et al. (1984) reported classroom observations in which three weeks after the first day of school a teacher, whose behavior was much like that described for Jones No. 1, repeatedly had to go around the classroom telling students to sit down, get to work, stop talking, *ad infinitum, ad nauseam.* The behaviorist explains this apparent paradox by saying that Jones No. 1 is reinforcing and thus perpetuating the behavior that he wishes to eliminate. Jones No. 2 is likewise responding to student behavior. Both teachers arranged the original stimuli so as to encourage immediate on-task appropriate behavior. In both instances although several students complied, some students did not. The teachers differed not only in the way they responded but also to what they responded. The teacher response to student behavior was different in the two classrooms and the consequences in terms of student behavior were different. Everston et al. (1984) reported that the students of teachers following the Jones No. 2 pattern were primarily on-task within three days and thereafter.

The behaviorist position can be briefly stated as follows: In a classroom, as in most settings, there are innumerable stimuli. One of the tasks of teaching is to arrange for students to attend to and respond to selected stimuli while ignoring others. Students might respond to given stimuli in a multitude of ways. Therefore, another task of teaching is to encourage students to respond to the selected stimuli in a particular manner. The most direct means for a teacher to have students attend to the desired stimuli and respond appropriately is to make it satisfying. If a student finds that behaving in a given way under particular circumstances is more satisfying than behaving in alternative ways, then it is reasonable to expect that he will behave in that way again.

What is satisfying? To some extent that is a personal matter. As suggested in the note to Jones above, there are a number of personal human needs. If a person is characterized by one or a combination of such needs, then he will feel satisfied when those needs are met. He will also tend to repeat those behaviors that preceded the need satisfaction.

The professional staff and students at Lincoln High School can help Mickey survive, become productive, and behave in ways congruent with the rules of the school. They can do so by arranging the environment so that when Mickey behaves appropriately the effects will be satisfying. Note that the change from Washington to Lincoln school is not by itself a significant change for Mickey. If the students at Lincoln High School reject Mickey, if the faculty punishes him, then it is likely that he will perceive that Lincoln High School and Washington High School are the same and he will behave accordingly. We will now consider a number of related strategies that will enable the people at Lincoln High School to help Mickey.

Strategies for Modifying Behavior

Environmental control of behavior focuses on three factors: the ABCs of discipline. There is an antecedent (A) for each behavior (B) as well as consequences (C). The behavior can be controlled or influenced through either its antecedents or its consequences. Five strategies for controlling the antecedents and five for using consequences to influence behavior will be considered. We will understand the antecedents better if we consider consequences first. Therefore, the order will be reversed.

The five strategies for controlling the consequences are:

Selective reinforcement: The frequency of a behavior is increased or maintained if it is followed by a reaction.

Extinction: Misbehavior is frequently perpetuated by the attention it gets. The behavior is extinguished if ignored.

Token economy: If tokens are offered immediately after the desired behavior the effects are the same as with selective reinforcement.

Contingency contracting: An agreement is established whereby the individual receives a valued payoff for desirable behavior over an agreed-to-period of time.

Self-management: The student is given the task of monitoring his own behavior and rewarding himself for agreed-to behavior.

The five strategies for antecedent controls are:

Stimulus control: The stimulation that arouses the misbehavior is pinpointed and eliminated.

Time out: The alert teacher can sense when a problem student is losing control or otherwise profit from a brief (three to five minute) period of isolation.

Negative reinforcement: If an aversive condition is established prior to behavior and then relieved following the behavior, the frequency of the behavior will increase.

Desensitization: Stimuli that tend to arouse inappropriate behavior due to fear are neutralized by pairing them with neutral or pleasant conditions.

Modeling: Behavior of respected kindred persons will tend to be imitated.

The ten strategies for controlling the environment all have the expressed purpose of increasing specified desired behaviors while decreasing undesired behaviors. Therefore the identification of behaviors to be maintained or changed is the critical first step for each strategy. On the other hand the process for controlling the environment is unique for each. Therefore, we will consider the details of what is to be done for each strategy. The five strategies for controlling the consequences will be discussed in

Chapter 8. Chapter 9 will focus on means for influencing behaviors by controlling the stimuli for appropriate behavior.

RECOMMENDED READINGS

Clarizio, H.F. *Toward positive classroom discipline.* New York: John Wiley, 1980.

Epstein, C. *Classroom management and teaching.* Reston, VA: Reston, 1979.

Long, J.D. and Frye, V.H. *Making it till Friday.* Princeton, NJ: Princeton Books, 1981.

8

REINFORCING DESIRED STUDENT BEHAVIOR: INTERVENTION STRATEGY C₁

Each of the five strategies discussed in this chapter is based on the psychological principle: Behavior is maintained by its consequences. That is, if a given behavior is followed by a reinforcer, the tendency to behave that way again is increased.

SELECTIVE REINFORCEMENT

Kounin (1970) found in a variety of classrooms at all grade levels that negative teacher reaction to misbehavior has little effect in reducing that behavior. However, a wide variety of in-school experiments have clearly demonstrated that the frequency of behavior can be increased by what follows it. That is, behavior that is reinforced will reoccur. As we shall note there are several ways to arrange the reinforcement and thereby obtain the behavior we desire. Let's look at a typical classroom scene.

Mr. Gun, as usual after recitation, referred the students to the assignment on the board and asked that they take out workbooks and proceed as directed. Most students immediately complied. Bett was an exception. As was often the case, Bett was quietly tapping her feet in rhythm with the pencil she was tapping on the desk. Mr. Gun quietly said, "Bett, will you please stop the drumming and get to work." Bett continued with only a slight glance toward Mr. Gun, which indicated that she had heard the directive. Mr. Gun, after a short pause, repeated his admonishment with more force. "Bett! Stop that nonsense and get to work." The no change in Bett's behavior stimulated Mr. Gun to state with more authority, "Bett, I'm warning you! If you don't stop that drumming I'm going to send you to the office!" Mr. Gun took two or three menacing steps toward Bett. She immediately responded by opening her book to the assigned page and began to do the exercise. Mr. Gun smiled, and said "Thank you," and with some warmth continued, "Bett, why didn't you do that when I first asked you?" Bett replied, "I dunno."

Is it possible that Bett is ignorant about the connection between teacher directives and her behavior? There are at least three possible explanations for Bett's behavior. (1) She may be consciously defiant, maliciously manipulating the situation for her own pleasures. (2) There may be no connection in her mind between her behavior and the teacher's directives and responses. (3) She has learned to respond only to the third type of teacher directive, the hostile, threatening one. If either of the latter two explanations is right, then Mr. Gun has two choices: He can continue the threat, with its concomitant disturbance for the rest of the class and the cost to his own sanity, or he can arrange for Bett to respond to the original directive as she did to the hostile threat. How can Mr. Gun achieve this change?

Reinforcement Procedures

Martin and Pear (1978) offer this set of procedures for selective reinforcement as one way to get others to do the right thing at the right time and place.

1. Select the behavior to be changed. The identification of behaviors should be based on four criteria: specificity, frequency, desirability, and priority. Select *one* specific behavior as the primary target.

2. Identify or establish distinct signals for the behavior. Since behavior is tied to the environment it will be adapted faster if the signals are clear.

3. Select an appropriate reinforcement. With some forethought and consultation with the respective students appropriate reinforcements are easily identified. Table 8.1 offers some possibilities. For selective reinforcement the consequences should be:

    a. readily available.

    b. presentable immediately following the desired behavior.

    c. such that they can be used repeatedly without satiation.

    d. such that execution is neither time-consuming nor otherwise disturbing.

e. desired by the respective students and acceptable to you. Thus, for selective reinforcement such consequences as consumables, possessions, and social reinforcers may be most appropriate.

Table 8.1.
Examples of consequences as reinforcers

Consumable reinforcers
    Health foods like dried fruit, popcorn, nuts, cereals.
    Sweets such as candies, cookies, soft drinks.
Activity reinforcers
    Quiet, in-class activities such as reading, working puzzles.
    Audiovisual activities such as previewing films, listening to records.
    Recreational activities like extended recess, calisthenics, painting.
    Privileges such as helping the teacher with chores or running errands.
    Out of school field trips.
Possessions
    Recreational objects like games, toys, balloons, puzzles, books.
    Personal belongings such as combs, jewelry, hair clips.
Social reinforcers
    Oral comments, including "super," "good try," "beautiful idea."
    Written comments, like "I appreciate your efforts," "bravo," "double plus idea," "A + job," and the universal smiling face.
    Physical expressions can be as simple as a smile, raised eyebrow, thumbs up, affirmatively shaking one's head, or applauding.
Awards
    Citations, letters to parents, good-deed charts.
Relax time
    Behaviors which normally would be unacceptable in class may be allowed within controlled circumstances: arm wrestling, standing and stretching.

Source: Compiled by the author.

A general clue as to what will be reinforcing for an individual is what he does, particularly during free time.

A bit of trivia will help put reinforcement in a historical perspective. The first recorded use of reinforcers occurred during the seventh century, when a monk took pieces of leftover oven bread dough, folded them in the form of children with their arms crossed in prayer, and baked them. These miniature biscuit figures were then awarded to the children for correctly learning and reciting their prayers. The monk referred to the biscuits as *petriolas,* which in Latin means "reward." The word and tradition of *pretzel* were thus derived.

4. Apply positive reinforcement.

a. Discuss the plan with the student(s) prior to beginning. Identify the undesired behavior and why it is offensive. Also indicate the precise desired behavior and the strategy for increasing its frequency.

b. Reinforce *immediately* following the desired behavior. The sooner reinforcement is administered the better. Just as with punishment, a delay significantly reduces the effect.

c. Particularly in the beginning supplement the reinforcement with verbally precise statements of the desired behavior, such as "Thank you for raising your hand before speaking out." Do *not* be vague, as in "You are a very good boy."

d. Pair the reinforcer with personal praise, and if appropriate, physical contact. As for the physical contact—some people like it, some don't. You need to know yourself and the recipient on this issue. Note, if you are using verbal praise either as a supplement or as the primary reinforcer you must use variety. Repetition of the same comment is satiating and will cease to have an effect. Instead of repeatedly saying "okay" or "good," mix in a healthy dose of alternatives such as "fantastic," "great," "nice," "right on."

5. Wean the student(s) from the program.

a. After the desired behavior begins to occur with some regularity (which may take as many as a dozen repetitions) shift to an intermittent schedule.

Figure 8.1 illustrates a hypothetical situation in which a teacher initially observes and counts the frequency of a given undesired behavior. Treatment is begun by reinforcing a replacement behavior. As the replacement behavior increases in frequency (as a result of reinforcement) the misbehavior decreases. If, after the replacement behavior is occurring with a desired frequency the teacher ceases the reinforcement, the behavior pattern will gradually return to its pretreatment status. One might conclude at this point that to maintain the desired condition of minimal misbehavior, the teacher would need to forever offer a continuous stream of reinforcements for each expression of the replacement behavior. This is impossible. Fortunately, the reinforcement schedule can be phased out through intermittent reinforcement.

Intermittent reinforcement is a process by which the teacher gradually reduces in an unpredictable pattern the reinforcers. When this is done the behavioral patterns established through treatment are maintained, although reinforcements are only occasionally awarded.

Examples of the effects of intermittent reinforcement are plentiful. Gamblers, like fishermen, continue despite only occasional payoffs. TV viewers and athletic fans sit through many boring "plays" and are only occasionally reinforced by outstanding performances. We can use this phenomenon to wean students from reinforcement and our continued attention without losing the desired behavior.

b. Gradually eliminate tangible reinforcers and substitute social reinforcers. Likewise, the social reinforcers, although never eliminated, ought to be reduced and replaced by natural reinforcers. Good behavior ought to pay off naturally in positive reactions from others and in achievement. Our task here is to pair positive social comments and a sense of success on the part of the student with concrete reinforcements.

c. Monitor the behavior by counting its frequency or intensity to make certain the desired behavior is being maintained. An occasional booster shot of treatment may be necessary.

Figure 8.1. An illustration of the typical pattern of behavior as an effect of reinforcement

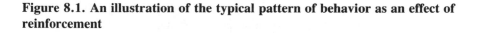

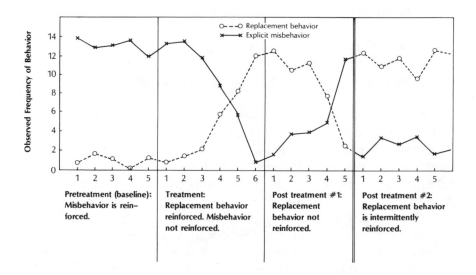

In summary, let us see if we can apply what has been learned about selective reinforcement by advising Mr. Gun in his response to Bett. As we observed, Mr. Gun is responding to explicit behavior and it seems regrettable that in so doing he is reinforcing the behavior he wishes to eliminate. That is, Bett overtly ignores his directive to get to work and he immediately responds. When the signal became powerful she obeyed and he reinforced her for responding to the harsh signal. It would appear that at best he increased the probability that in the future she will ignore the initial directive and respond to the harsh command. What can Mr. Gun do?

Bett's rhythmic drumming does not seem to be a particularly bad behavior, except that it is counterproductive to the assignment so it is best to ignore it and focus on the desired behavior. The behavior to be increased is to initially pick up the tools (paper, pencil, and book) necessary for working on the assignment, then to do as assigned by focusing attention on additional directions. Mr. Gun should develop explicit signals: an assignment written on the board and the statement, "Okay, we will now turn to our workbooks and proceed on page 79 as directed on the blackboard." To increase the probability that Bett responds to this signal it would help to do two things: (a) Discuss with Bett beforehand his wishes and explain that he will set up a reinforcement program and how it will work. (b) Be at her side and use her workbook as a signal to the rest of the class to turn to page 79. His proximity and handling of her book are powerful stimuli for her to respond as directed. She can hardly miss or ignore the signal. A conforming response is most likely.

Any positive response by Bett toward doing the assignment when Mr. Gun hands her the workbook open to page 79 must be reinforced. If the reinforcement is concrete it should be supplemented by a social reinforcement, such as a touch on the shoulder, or an approving smile and comment ("good going"). He will need to experiment some to identify a reinforcement that works. In the beginning Mr. Gun should be close to Bett and be lavish with reinforcers. As her work time is extended, so should the space between reinforcements. If he begins with concrete reinforcers, they should be paired and gradually replaced by social responses, and these in turn by the natural reinforcements of increased achievement. It is important that Bett make the connection between the behavior of responding as directed and the respective payoffs.

Teachers sometimes feel that such payoffs are inherently bad because they are a form of bribery. Bribery connotes immorality. Bribery is immoral, not because of an agreement or payoff, but because typically it is used to elicit illegal or unethical behavior. The behavior that we wish from students is obviously not immoral. If our objection to reinforcement is that we want students to do things "because I tell them to do it, rather than for a payoff," then we are expecting youth to function in ways contrary to our societal mores. The free enterprise system is based on the notion that good performance pays dividends.

If our students are to behave well and to value education, they must learn to do so. Reinforcement procedures are a powerful means to this end.

EXTINCTION

Extinction/Reinforcement/Punishment

When an individual emits a response that heretofore has been reinforced, but is no longer reinforced, then she is less likely to respond in that way again when she next encounters a similar situation. Simply put, if nothing in the environment reacts to a behavior, then the behavior will go away. This phenomenon, which has been frequently studied and confirmed in both controlled laboratory and practical settings, is known as *extinction*.

In a classical series of experiments with animals, Estes (1944) demonstrated that behavior that has been established by reinforcement may be reduced by either punishment or extinction. The respective effects of punishment and extinction are shown in Figure 8.2. Let's assume that a

Figure 8.2
Comparison of extinction and punishment on frequency of behavior

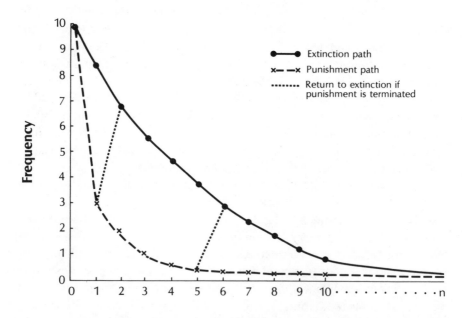

Source: Adapted from Estes (1944) to illustrate the respective effects of extinction and punishment of the frequency of behavior.

given behavior has been reinforced and occurs at a rate of ten responses per hour. If over the next ten sessions reinforcement is withheld, the frequency of behavior will decrease by extinction to a point approaching zero. Note the continuous line. On the other hand, if the behavior is punished it will be temporarily suppressed, as noted by the discontinuous line. If the behavior is punished every time it occurs then the suppression will continue and after ten trials will virtually disappear. If after the first punishment is administered no further punishment or reinforcement is given, then we note the frequency of that behavior will follow the path of extinction. If the behavior is reinforced during any of these succeeding trials, it will return to a higher or the original rate of occurrence. Unless punishment is repeated on every occurrence of the behavior, the effect will be the same as it would with extinction. Note, even after five punishments, if the punishment is missed the frequency rate will return to that of extinction.

Principles of Extinction

The following points sum up what we know of extinction:

1. Extinction is most effective when combined with selective reinforcement. This principle is particularly robust if the target behavior is replacement behavior, incongruent with the behavior to be eliminated.

2. If a behavior has been continuously reinforced it is more easily extinguished than if it has been intermittently reinforced. This principle is a reaffirmation of the previously discussed weaning process.

3. Extinction applies to all behavior, desired and undesired. We often unwittingly contribute to the extinguishment of good behavior by ignoring students when they are on-task, and contrariwise, reinforce bad behavior by "hassling" students when they are off-task.

4. If reinforcement is withheld for a given behavior, that behavior will extinguish, but an equally noxious behavior may replace it. The need behind the behavior still exists for the individual, particularly if it is a need for attention. This phenomenon increases the necessity and potency of selective reinforcement to focus on replacement behavior and simultaneously satisfy student needs.

5. Behavior, if ignored, may temporarily increase in frequency or intensity before it diminishes. The old adage, "if at first you don't succeed, try harder" seems to be in effect here. That is, if a student is snapping his fingers to get your attention and you do not respond, he is apt to do it more vigorously or shout. If we keep our cool and continue to ignore such behaviors they will disappear. Paradoxically, the increase is a sign that the extinction is taking hold. Hang on, for if you respond in any way it may reinforce and thus increase the probability that the new behavior will continue.

6. Extinction initially is frustrating to the student and he in turn may respond with mild aggression. The phenomenon is not unlike occasions when an individual puts money in a vending machine and nothing comes out. The customer then responds by kicking the machine.

7. Reduction in the specified behavior is gradual with extinction.

8. Extinct behavior occasionally spontaneously reappears. This spontaneous rearousal will be short-lived and disappear if left unreinforced.

TOKEN ECONOMY

Overcoming Selective Reinforcement Problems

Selective reinforcement has several shortcomings: (1) To administer the reinforcement the teacher often needs to interrupt the ongoing desired behavior. If a student is on-task you do not wish to distract him. (2) The payoff is immediate and this seems to perpetuate the characteristic of working only for immediate gratification. A valid objective of education is to encourage students to work for future, delayed rewards. (3) The process seems to be juvenile, somehow beneath the dignity of adolescents. (4) Many of the reinforcers listed in Table 8.1 and valued by students are bulky and too extravagant to be immediately administered. (5) It is difficult and time-consuming to identify the particular reinforcers for a variety of students in a typical classroom. (6) Different kinds of behavior ought to be worth different valued payoffs. For example, an approximation of a desired behavior ought to be rewarded, but less so than if the behavior itself had occurred. Flexibility in weighting different behaviors would be desirable. The token technique, an extension of selective reinforcement, relieves these problems.

Our paychecks, more token than most of us would prefer, and the grades awarded to students are illustrative of the token economy process. A token is an otherwise worthless marker given as a reinforcer. The token, like money, can then be exchanged for valued things such as those listed on page 166. The token economy allows the teacher to unobtrusively, selectively reinforce target student behavior.

Operationalizing the Token Economy

Tanaka (1979), a successful consultant for teachers, offers an excellent and detailed summary of procedures for putting the token economy into operation. His recommendations are based on repeated experiences with teachers in their classrooms. We will do well to adapt his procedures for our purposes. Teacher responses to his program are realistic and positive.

Tanaka's goals for classroom management are:

1. Teachers will cue and reinforce proper behavior.
2. Students will spend an optimum amount of time on-task.
3. Students will exhibit self-management skills.

Establishing the Program

Establishing a program to achieve the objectives involves four steps. The first two are the same as those for selective reinforcement.

Step one is to ascertain the nature, frequency, and sequence of student and teacher behavior as they are exhibited in the classroom. The best procedure is to invite an outside observer to record the behavior. A third-party observer is desirable since the teacher is preoccupied with directing student activities and therefore can only estimate what happened. Observers ought to refrain from making judgments or from interacting with either the teacher or the students.

Observations may be made for the whole class, if that is the teacher's concern, or for a limited number of designated students. Both teacher and student behavior should be systematically recorded on a form. The form should have squares such as on graph paper. The rows represent the individual students, identified by name or a seating code. The columns represent time slots. A typical observation schedule includes several 20-minute periods at various times over a week or so. The time slots each represent a specified bit of time, perhaps two minutes during which the observer surveys the class and notes and records everyone's behavior according to a code. Symbols are used for critical behaviors: for example, on-task (+), disruptive noise (N), out of seat (O), verbal interaction (V), physical interaction (P), talking without permission (T), sitting off-task but not disruptive (S), and (*) intense behavior such as (N*). With respect to the teacher, location is important, so it should also be recorded. The simplest way is to use the same code as is used for student seats. Teacher behavior selected at the beginning of each two-minute slot is recorded as structuring as directing (S), questioning, or explaining; giving approval (+); giving disapproval (-); ignoring (I).

The record not only allows us to count behaviors but also to note reciprocal interaction between the teacher and the students. Teachers respond to students and, likewise, students respond to teacher behavior and location. An analysis of student–teacher behavior interaction in sequence ought to furnish the teacher with valuable information regarding the maintenance of student behavior.

Step two is to analyze the ongoing behaviors from the record sheets in order to identify those student behaviors to be maintained, tolerated, eliminated, or substituted. The teacher will want to maintain the desired behaviors by selective social reinforcement. Remember the substitute behaviors will have these qualities: (a) desired and incompatible with the behaviors to be eliminated; (b) observable, such as raising hands and speaking only when called on.

Step three is to explain the program to students. All reinforcement programs will be most effective if the whole program is explained to the target students and to the rest of the class. Everyone should know that tokens or reinforcements will be distributed on an agreed-to schedule for specified behaviors. The teacher needs to take a few minutes to note the behavioral problems and the kind of behavior that is needed so the whole class can go to achieve its objectives. Identify the desired behaviors and indicate that some students will be getting tokens to help them function better in class. The procedure of paying some students and not others is not unique, as the well-behaved students are already receiving tokens in the form of good grades and other special privileges. Don't resist taking students into your confidence. Don't worry about temporarily giving some of your target students extra payoffs for doing what others are already doing. If the process is open and public, then others, especially if they are making it themselves, will accept the special treatment.

Step four is used to specify the trade-in value of the tokens. The point is to stipulate a contingency (if, then). Every student must understand the connection between his behavior and the token rewards. Specify the time, place, and conditions under which tokens will be awarded and how they in turn may be traded for desired articles and events.

In addition to those procedures discussed in selective reinforcement there are two critical elements unique to token economy: the tokens and their distribution, and a trading post so that tokens may be exchanged for selected payoff items.

The Nature of Tokens

To put the token economy into operation after the procedure has been explained to the students the room must be arranged for efficient and immediate implementation. The aisles and desks should be arranged so that you can easily and immediately navigate about the room. Second, the room and your activities need to be arranged so that the majority of students are within your eyesight at all times. These are good teaching practices under any circumstances and are a positive factor in good discipline with any strategy.

The tokens must be attractive, light-weight, portable, small, not easily counterfeited, and easily stored and counted. Homemade stamps, stickers, poker chips, or seashore shells are good examples. Tickets that can be punched or marked are handy. In one classroom that was near chaos (the teacher couldn't even get the students quiet long enough to explain the program) he simply wrote everyone's name in the corner of the chalkboard and began putting checkmarks behind the names of those students who at the moment were sitting in their seats and being quiet. It worked remarkably well and in a few minutes everyone was quietly seated and watching the teacher. He then explained the program. The token may be almost anything that is convenient, countable, and tangible. However, some students respond better to concrete tokens, which they can hold in their hands or in a personal container. If the tokens are objects, the bank should have a reserve of about one hundred for each participating student because some students will hoard their tokens.

The Exchange of Tokens

A process is needed for exchanging the tokens for desired privileges or items. In one form or another this becomes a trading post. The trading post functions in a variety of ways:

1. *Item display.* A variety of items, with different values, ought to be available for purchases. A number of the reinforcers listed in Table 8.1 are good examples. McLaughlin and Malaby (1972) reported the results of a series of studies involving fifth- and sixth-graders. The students distinguished the payoff activities from those opportunities naturally available in the classroom. For illustrative purposes here is the list and the devised values that one sixth-grade class selected:

Time for sports	60 tokens
Looking at animals	30 tokens
Serving on a committee	30 tokens
Working on special projects	25 tokens
Special maintenance jobs	25 tokens

Sharpening pencils	20 tokens
Special writing on the chalkboard	20 tokens
Coming in the room early	10 tokens
Listening to records	5 tokens
Carrying playground equipment outside	5 tokens
Looking in the teacher's gradebook	5 tokens

Experienced teachers advise us to begin with a number of low-valued items that can be purchased with just a few tokens. As the idea catches on, more expensive items will be sought. A major problem is pricing. If items are too expensive, the students become disenchanted because it takes so long to accumulate the price. One teacher solved this by xeroxing a book of judo, and instead of handing a price of 1000 on the book she sold the pages one, two, or three at a time for 20 tokens each.

Such items as the use of the tape recorder are always popular. One teacher rented out blackboard and bulletin board space. Book rentals do surprisingly well. One of my colleagues charged tokens to read articles and pamphlets on the subject matter he was teaching and found the work effort increased significantly, as did the number of articles read, compared to levels when he assigned them and used them as bases for tests.

Good merchandising, unusual items, and sales keep interest up and good behavior in fashion. The greater the turnover in stock the better. The trading post should be open frequently in the beginning, perhaps twice a day for the first week and progressively less frequently thereafter.

The final step is to administer the program. Although the provisions specified here are for a self-contained classroom, the procedures are the same for one-period classes. Modifications are of course necessary for individual use. The provisions are offered here as checkmarks.

The day is divided into four periods, with a point tally scheduled at 10:30, 12:00, 2:00, and 3:15. Each student has a record card placed on the corner of his desk. Each card, as illustrated in Table 8.2, has a list of abbreviated rules and a tally for the respective periods.

At two or three random times during each period the teacher surveys the class to note and record those who are behaving according to the stated rules. At the designated time the teacher circulates and awards points on the cards of those students who have obeyed the rules.

Bonus points, one possible for each half day, are awarded to students who either show great improvement or perform a special act of prosocial behavior. Thus, for each day the possible point total is 22.

Tanaka suggests that if students act out serious disruptive behaviors that cannot be ignored, such as fighting, throwing objects, leaving the

Table 8.2
Student point record card

	10:30	12:00	2:00	3:15	Points
In seat (S)					Sum (S,Q, + ,H,I)
Quiet (Q)					+ bonus
On-task (+)					- fines
Raises hand (H)					
Ignores other's misbehavior　(I)					Daily total

Source: Compiled by the author.

room without permission, or destroying property, then a fine of two points should be immediately levied. Of course, students need to be informed beforehand that such fines will be levied. Repeated disruptions might also be fined. This finding process is called *response cost.*

Response Cost: Tokens Tied to Behavior

Some programs, for instance one reported by Phillips et al. (1973), have found that the effects of the token economy are more powerful if tokens are not only awarded for stipulated desired behaviors but also retrieved for contrary behaviors. Response-cost programs usually begin by awarding each individual a set number of tokens, which can be protected by not misbehaving and supplemented by behaving in prescribed ways. A good example of the response-cost process would be a teacher who awards a token for every five minutes of in-seat on-task behavior, but subtracts a token for each instance of being out of seat. The evidence shows that response-cost tends to be more effective and more powerful than the straight token economy programs. However, there is a tradeoff.

Teachers who elect the response-cost program should recall the stringencies we noted in our considerations of punishment. Also, McLaughlin and Malaby (1972) observed that in the programs with response-cost elements, both the teachers and students were less prosocial in their interactions. Sulzer and Mayer (1972), after reviewing the evidence noted that although response-cost can be a powerful technique, it ought to be used sparingly because of side effects.

At the end of each day (week for those functioning on a one period day) awards are given to those students who have a sufficient number of points. The teacher collects the cards and calls the qualified students to come up and select their reward. Students are called in the order of their point total, so the better behaved obtain the better selection. When paying off, the teacher ought to be laudatory with social reinforcement and emphasize expectations for the next day. These verbal and nonverbal spontaneous reinforcements are critical. In the end they are the heart of managing classroom behavior.

In some programs students are allowed to accumulate tokens for more valued awards. Tanaka prefers to operate on a day-to-day basis—every day begins with a new record with no carry-over. The choice is up to the individual teacher. In the Tanaka plan a minimum number of points are established for payoff. He recommends that the minimum point total be such that about two-thirds of the students qualify. Whatever the cut-off is, it must be announced at the beginning of the day and then adjusted downward to include the optimum number of students. Remember, your goal is a well-behaved class of students in which most come to believe that good behavior pays off.

Problems and Suggested Solutions

The token economy, like most other programs, has some problems. Let's look at a number of potential drawbacks and some possible ways of lessening their impact.

(a) Awarding 25–50 tokens per person per day to large numbers of students can be taxing. It would seem best, particularly in the beginning, to start out with just a few students.

(b) Focusing on the tokens will be confusing and distracting. This distraction may occur, but in two or three days it passes and things return to normal.

(c) When tokens are distributed, students tend to play with them, count them, and mostly drop them. Teachers report that this tapers off if ignored.

(d) Some students will try to play a con game, claiming they have tokens coming or promised. Be precise in explaining the program. Indicate the behaviors involved, when and how tokens can be earned and spent.

(e) The more troublesome students may accumulate tokens by some unauthorized means either by gambling, stealing, or shaking down the weaker students. Code some students' tokens by color or some other means.

(f) Some students will behave only for tokens. Students who normally behave in prescribed ways for intrinsic reasons will learn to do so only for tokens if they're so reinforced. Caution is necessary here. Students can learn to shift from natural, intrinsic motivation to external token reinforcement. The procedures we have been discussing are for students not normally on-task. Therefore, those students who are already behaving as desired should not be put on a reinforcement schedule. It will backfire. Individualize your program and use it to change behavior and not merely to maintain good behavior if it is already in operation. Second, your program must include a weaning segment. Gradually reduce the use of tokens and replace the process with social and natural intrinsic rewards of success. Decrease the number of behaviors being reinforced externally, increase the delay between the behavior and the reinforcement, award the tokens more intermittently, and gradually decrease the value of tokens by raising the cost of payoffs.

(g) All of this takes time, which is already in scarce supply. However, in the long run the program will give you more time. In addition, we should seek more help. Help in the form of teacher's aides is often closer than we think. Parents, students from the local university, or even high school drop-outs may be relatively cost-free because they are seeking experience or a means to help society. Cross-peer tutoring and help are available to all parties.

(h) Reinforcement forever is too demanding. As in all other programs deliberate weaning is part of the process. Tanaka (1979) offers an excellent program for those readers who wish elaboration.

(i) Organizing the program could get out of hand. Records of earnings and expenditures is demanding. It helps if the teacher enjoys record keeping. If not, turn it over to one of the aides. You may be pleasantly surprised to find that some of your most troublesome students will respond very positively to such responsible tasks.

As an alternative to the token economy, some teachers find a contracting program to be more manageable and effective.

CONTINGENCY CONTRACTING

The following case study, reported by Clement (1973), is enlightening.

Ralph was a very imaginative student when it came to ways for getting into trouble. He hit other children both in class and on the playground. In class he disturbed others by whistling, blowing on them, touching them, taking their belongings, insulting them, and otherwise being a nuisance. He was constantly in motion—walking or running up and down the aisles, crawling on the floor, scooting the desks around, and occasionally just leaving the room. If he did stay at his desk he either did nothing or played with toys, doodled, or just fooled around. He often talked out of turn. Altogether, he spent little time on-task. Ralph's major school accomplishment was that he drove the teacher up the wall.

The school personnel considered Ralph to be emotionally disturbed. However, he was mainstreamed. His background was unpleasant: broken home, rejection, repeated physical abuse, irregular sleeping and eating patterns. Given all of this Ralph is not unlike a few students in every school.

Of particular interest to us was Ralph's response to three questions:

1. List the things you do at school that other people do not like. Ralph's list was as follows: Talking, fighting, standing up, spitting, flying airplanes, saying bad things, bossing other kids, and moving my desk.

2. List those things you do not do but others want you to do. His list was: Do homework, mind the teacher, cooperate, stay in line, be nice to other children, work with others, and obey the principal.

3. List those things you do at school that others seem to like. Ralph's list included only two items: Don't cheat at games and pick up trays in the cafeteria.

Three conclusions are warranted. First, Ralph is very aware of his behavior and the variety of ways available to him to disturb other people, particularly school officials. Second, the don'ts are much more explicit and behaviorally stated than the dos. Third, he knew many more things regarding his misbehavior (questions 1 and 2) than his good behavior (question 3). At best authorities have communicated to him the general ways that he displeases them. For his own salvation Ralph needs to know ways of gaining valued favors.

Ralph agreed to a self-control contract, with talking out of turn as the target behavior. He gave himself a point for every five-minute period in which he didn't speak without permission. He agreed to accumulate 200 points in exchange for an airplane ride. He reached his target in three weeks.

His fellow students would not believe that he had gone for an airplane ride, so he set 450 points as the basis for taking a witness with him. After four weeks it was noted that his time on task had tripled, although this was not part of the contract. The contract was rewritten so that one point was awarded for each uninterrupted five-minute period on-task. By the end of May Ralph had accumulated his 450 points. It took two months to accumulate 37.5 hours of studying. By most standards this isn't much, but in comparison to his prior record it was about 37 hours more than could otherwise be expected.

Note, Ralph arranged the conditions of the contract by himself. He is an incorrigible, seriously maladjusted child who recognizes the negative effects of his behavior but has little notion of what to do right. He is not without goals, and given the opportunity to earn them, he performs. In doing so, he had no specific help from school officials. It is reasonable to conclude that Ralph learned something of himself and the ways of the world from this experience and that if given the opportunity, he will continue to learn. The procedures used with Ralph were like the token economy in that points were accumulated to be exchanged for a valued commodity.

Payoff Provisions

Contingency contracting is a deceptively simple logical arrangement. The student gets something he wants after doing something that the teacher wants him to do. The idea of a contract is not unusual. However, in many classrooms and homes the contract may be summed up as: If you do X, then you will be punished. The contract is imposed by an authoritarian adult and is negative.

In most life situations, except in the courts, which are primary punitive, contracts are positive. In shopping, employment, and within the system of intercorporate operations, contracts are usually a positive exchange of desired payoffs.

To be effective the payoff for the student needs to be something currently valued. Promises for the distant future, such as college attendance or a good job, are generally inappropriate. You may have to check and rewrite the contract periodically because desires and conditions change.

Second, the desired payoff ought to be something *not* easily obtained from another source.

Contracting Procedures

Homme (1970) offers the following ten rules, based on findings of laboratory and classroom studies, for organizing and operating a contingency contract program:

1. The contract payoff should be immediate. This is of particular importance in the beginning.
2. Initial contracts should call for and reward small approximations of the desired end behavior. In the beginning we need to focus on explicit small tasks that have a high probability of success. We are not only trying to achieve the task but to have the student learn that working and being on task, pay off.
3. Reward frequency with small amounts. As we know from token economies, once students learn the value of the exchange they are able to delay gratification, and desire larger packages, but we need to begin with small ones.
4. Contracts should call for and reward accomplishment rather than obedience. It is better to say, "If you do X then you will get Y," rather than "If you do as I say you will get Y."
5. Payoff comes after performance. Particularly in the beginning students are apt to say: "Let us play such-and-such a game and then we will do the vocabulary words." Thus, the pay precedes the performances, which is a bad contract. Second, note that the performance was not specified, also a serious omission.
6. The contract must be fair. Each side of the contract ought to be reasonable in terms of the other.
7. The terms of the contract must be clear. Be explicit in terms of what and how much is to be done in exchange for what and how much payoff. We may intuitively feel that students ought to do the work for intrinsic reasons. However, many students have not experienced and thereby learned to value academic effort or positive interpersonal relations. Therefore, the concrete contract makes sense to them and they will perform as needed. Students under contract, like those using tokens and other reinforcement agreements, can be weaned to social and intrinsic motivations.
8. Contracts must be honest. To ensure honesty they should be consummated immediately and meet the details of the contract. Contracts should be established so that the students receive payoffs. If they are never paid the system will fail.
9. Contracts must be positive. "We will listen to a record of your choosing after we read and answer the question of chapter 9," is much bet-

ter than "If you don't read chapter 9 we will not be able to listen to the records."

10. If used, a contract should be used systematically. Set it up as a program rather than using it spasmodically when things get out of hand.

Copper et al. (1980) offer an example in the use of contingency contracts for resolving a problem in the Dade County schools that we as teachers can appreciate. Despite admonishments and directives from central administration the cost of utilities and teacher absenteeism was soaring. The administration changed its tactics, and this simple contract was offered: Eighty cents will be returned to the school for each dollar saved by husbanding utilities and limiting the use of substitute teachers. The principal and teachers of each school then could use that money for anything they wished. In the first year of this contract the schools had an extra $735,039.00 in their budget for savings in utilities. The teachers in one elementary school received over $25,000.00 to use at their discretion. In the second year the schools shared another $546,400.00 from savings in substitute teachers. Everybody seemingly profited. The public saved tax dollars, administrators reached their goals, and the students got a better education because their regular teachers were present more often—an increase of 18 percent. The schools had more funds for those important "extra" items necessary for educational excellence. Morale increased because the right people had the power to control the effects.

Contingency contracting involves trust, promotes independence, and increases the probability of responsible student behavior. If properly arranged everyone wins. We will now consider self-management, which calls for greater trust on the part of the teacher and more responsibility on the part of the learner.

SELF-MANAGEMENT

Student as the Disciplining Agent

Self-control is most often thought of as a restraint, an ability to resist temptation. "If I had more will power I wouldn't eat so much, smoke so much, procrastinate so much, talk so much. . . ." Many or most of us reproach ourselves and blame will power for behavior we later regret. How about crediting self-power for good behavior or more precisely, promoting the development of good behavior through the development of self-control.

Self-control, self-management, or self-power is a condition in which a person behaves appropriately, but in an unexpected fashion, rather than in a highly probable, but inappropriate way to a situation. Let's look at a couple of examples. A child comes over and grabs a toy from another and begins to play with it. The high-probability response for the second child is to scream to authority or hit the first child or grab the toy back or just sit and whimper. A child in self-control on the other hand might say, "I was playing with that toy and would like to play with it some more. I do not like to have someone else grab something that I am using. I want it back." Or a teenager who is being goaded into doing something he feels is inappropriate, such as consuming toxics, might with self-control respond, "Look, you may do that if you like and that's okay; I don't feel comfortable about doing it, so I am not. There are other fun things that we can do." These are low-probability responses, but in each case we would judge them to be mature reactions. The purpose of school discipline is to encourage mature, self-controlled behavior.

The essence of this chapter is controlling the environment and thus far we have discussed ways the teacher might achieve this through contracts, withholding reinforcement, and token and selective reinforcement. Now, we will explore shifting the control and responsibility to the student. Self-control is a process whereby the person himself is the agent of his own change in behavior. The principles are very much like those we have been discussing, except the student will do the monitoring and reinforcing. It does require two things of the teacher: trust and help.

The desirability of self-management need not be sold. A major characteristic of a free society is that therein the citizens direct, coordinate, and maintain individual activities without external coercion. Thomas (1980) notes two additional important advantages of self-control:

(a) The effects are more likely to be generalized to a variety of situations. Whereas externally reinforced behavior is apt to be situation-specific, the effects of internal control will be naturally generalized to a variety of situations. The student will have learned a strategy that he can utilize whenever he finds that his behavior is not leading to desired ends. It is likely that such self-controlled strategies may be more resistant to extinction than may be the case with externally regulated behaviors.

(b) The process helps students develop a feeling that they are in control of their own destiny. Thoresen and Mahoney (1974) show that opportunity to choose is a powerful motivator. People have a preference for activities in which a choice is possible. For example, students were given the choice of selecting option 1 or 2. (1) "You may begin now to do task A for which you will be given this candy bar." The experimenter held up a candy bar, which had been randomly selected from those on a table. Or (2) "You may select to do Task B and then you will be allowed to select whatever candy bar you wish to earn by doing Task A." The second option was the popular choice by a significant margin. Thus, the majority expressed a willingness to do an extra task in exchange for the privilege of choosing their own candy.

Two isues are critical for us: Will the process of self-control work to influence critical school behavior, and if it does work, how can we arrange it?

The procedures for self-control have been found to be effective for both students and adults for such changes in behavior as reducing the consumption of food, tobacco, and alcohol; increasing study time; controlling fears, anger, and anxiety; reducing sexual deviancy and time spent on sexual fantasies; increasing persistence on tasks and substituting long-range goals for immediate gratification. Although self-control research has been limited within the school setting, there have been some findings and these, along with the success in other settings, offer a sound basis for including self-control as a feasible classroom strategy. We will describe various findings as we focus attention on specific process techniques.

Procedures for Self-Control

Self-management procedures may be used to control behavior in three ways: monitoring on-going behavior, self-reinforcement, and stimulus control.

Monitoring ongoing behavior

Self-observation seems to have an effect in its own right. That is, sometimes when an individual gathers information about his own behavior, that information in itself seems to affect the behavior. Put another way, when an individual knows that he knows, it has an effect. The knowing would seem to involve four steps: (a) An awareness that something is happening. For example, "I'm talking loudly and everyone is watching me with a funny look on their faces." (b) Noting the frequency with which the behavior and its consequences occur (e.g., "This is the third time this week that I have been late for history."). (c) An evaluation of the behavior ("If I continue to do this, I am really going to get it."). (d) Setting goals ("I'm not going to talk with anyone this afternoon, just study for the history test.").

A case reported by Broden et al. (1971) illustrates the four conditions. Lisa, an eighth-grader, was concerned enough about failing history to ask for help. In discussing the problem with her counselor, she quickly indicated an awareness that she was failing because she wasn't attending to the class activities. She recognized that she was bored, her mind wandered, and she rarely did the assignments. She also recognized that if she continued such behavior, it would result in failure. Despite discussing all of this with her counselor and promising to work harder, Lisa's classroom behavior did not change. An outside observer noted that over a seven-day period she was on-task only about 30 percent of the time. Awareness in itself did not change behavior.

Lisa was instructed to record if she were on-task or off-task every few minutes by placing a plus or minus sign on a record sheet furnished by the counselor and placed on her desk. On-task was defined as attending to the teacher-assigned task, facing the teacher, taking notes about what the teacher was saying, reading assignments, facing any student who was responding to teacher questions, and reciting when called on. Off-task behavior was defined as being out of seat without permission, talking without being recognized by the teacher, facing the window, playing with nonacademic materials such as a comb or purse, and working on tasks other than history. On-task was specifically defined and set as the goal. The effects were immediate as demonstrated by an on-task behavior increase to 78 percent of the time. However, after seven days the counselor said that he was out of recording forms, so Lisa did no recording for five days. She did little work and her time on-task dropped to 27 percent. The self-recording was renewed and over an eight-day period the on-task time averaged 80 percent, except for two separate days for which no recording forms were available. On those two days work on-task dipped below the 30 percent level.

During all of this time, beginning with the baseline, it had been noted that the teacher reacted specifically to Lisa on an average of less than two times per period. As Lisa continued to record her own behavior, the teacher was asked to deliberately increase attention in the form of praise. He did so and the observer noted that the praise frequency was now about 3.5 times per period. Lisa's on-task time increased to 88 percent over the next eight class meetings. Lisa was then weaned away from the self-recording by withholding the recording sheets, although the teacher continued the excessive praise for five additional days. The on-task behavior continued at a 77 percent rate. Thereafter, the frequency of praise returned to the normal rate, but Lisa continued to be on-task about 80 percent of the time. This work level probably was being partially maintained by success, since Lisa had now raised her grade from D- to a C.

Lisa had three sources of feedback that she could use to evaluate her progress toward her goal. She found that she was on task more, behaving more appropriately by her own records. The teacher reacted positively to her behavior by praising her about every ten minutes. Finally, she was getting tangible results in terms of academic achievement. The self-monitoring in itself had a definite impact on Lisa's in-class behavior. The reinforcement was an added effect. In addition, weaning was facilitated by the reinforcement.

Broden et al. (1971) also reported a second case that contrasted with Lisa's in several important ways. Another eighth-grader, Stu, was referred by a teacher who requested, "Find some way to shut Stu up." An observer established that Stu talked out of turn on an average of 1.1 times per minute. He was instructed to self-record his behavior, defined in much the same way as Lisa had been instructed. Talking out of turn dropped to about 30 percent of its previous rate. After 23 days of self-recording, Stu was not given any more recording forms. Talking out of turn immediately increased in frequency, slightly in excess of its original level.

Stu's case was different in several aspects. Whereas Lisa was concerned about failing, we do not know what Stu wanted, but we can infer that he was striving for social need satisfaction rather than achievement needs. No doubt Stu had a goal, but we have no reason to believe that he perceived his behavior to be incongruent with his goal. Self-monitoring did alter Stu's behavior, but he apparently was not supported and helped to connect his behavior with goals and was not reinforced for the new behavior. Just as with most strategies, self-monitoring will not work if the process is either incomplete or ineptly applied.

Reinforcing students is somewhat of a chore and is underused by most teachers. Wouldn't it be nice if students could learn to reinforce themselves?

Self-reinforcement for self-control

Reinforcement is considered to be the most critical element of behavior modification. In self-management, the procedure requires that the individual select and administer the reinforcement at appropriate times.

The student at any age would need help to learn to do this effectively. The payoff, however, in both immediate and future behavior, is well worth the effort.

As we might expect, McLaughlin (1976) found that students who had previous experience with selective or token reinforcement programs are most adaptable to self-management procedures. However, the steps for self-reinforcement are the same as they are for other reinforcement programs. First, students are asked to identify the frequency or duration of specified undesired behaviors in particular circumstances over a number of days. Then, productive alternatives to such behaviors are identified. Third, a system is arranged for the student to record the number of tokens earned according to some agreed-to schedule. Setting up a schedule so that students will know when to record themselves on-task can be a problem. The system works best if the signal is random and simultaneous for all students who are in a self-reinforcement program. Some teachers use beeps on an audiotape, others use wristwatch alarms, or just randomly call out, "record." The signal ought to go off about every five minutes in the beginning, and slowly the time is increased between recordings until weaning is complete. Finally, an exchange system is organized. Students help to identify payoff articles or events. The respective token values for the payoff are agreed on, and times are arranged for exchanging tokens for rewards.

Students have to be taught the procedures, but the four steps are such that first-graders as well as high school students quickly catch on. The experience of teachers who use the self-management program is that students are fairly accurate and honest in recording on-task behavior. If this is a problem, you can add extra rewards on a random basis for those who are in agreement with your own estimate of their behavior. You can use this quality control, but teachers find it is best to trust the students, because most often it works. Students may tend to be more generous than teachers with tokens, but this tends to balance because they often overprice the payoff items.

Self-management programs have been found to be just as effective as other reinforcement programs, and they have a very big benefit in that the student learns that he is in control of his own behavior and the consequences. Knowing that has a powerful impact on the individual's sense of self.

The environment is a powerful factor in influencing the way people and animals behave. The procedures discussed thus far have specified how to use selective reinforcement, extinction, the token economy, contingency contracting, and self-reinforcement. All of these techniques are important direct procedures by which teachers can induce students to behave in desired ways. These procedures not only help us to keep students on task, but benefit the students in teaching self-control and result in more positive self-esteem.

Behavior is not only controlled by its consequences, but it is also aroused and directly by antecedents. We will next study the ways that we can use this principle to our advantage.

Stimulus control

The third procedure in self-management is stimulus control. Habitual responses to given stimuli are at least some portion of everybody's behavior. A familiar example is people who smoke only in given situations: when sitting down or drinking coffee or talking to someone or watching TV. When these smokers are in such situations they automatically, and seemingly unconsciously, reach for a cigarette. One easy way to regulate one's behavior is to set aside the stimuli or antecedents that arouse that behavior. The Greek maxim "Know thyself" perhaps would be better stated as "Know thy controlling variables"—the variables being that which stimulates and reinforces our behavior.

An age-old teaching ploy is to move students' seats so they are not sitting near friends or in particular parts of the room that encourage misbehavior. There are two drawbacks to such action. It is usually punitive, at least in the eyes of the student, so he becomes resentful, and, as we have noted, the positive effects are negligible. It is an action by the teacher, thus depriving the student of the opportunity to govern himself. Most of us would like our students to learn to be self-governing. Therefore, it is a good idea to teach the student to control the change in stimuli.

For example, Ben not only doesn't do well in history, but he sits in the back of the room and frequently disrupts the class with loud talking and laughter. During an in-class seat exercise, Mr. Reason asked Ben to step to a remote part of the room and said, "Ben, I sometimes become irritated. You often just seem to be sitting back there wisecracking, talking, and laughing. What seems to be the problem?" Ben responds, "Aw, I dunno Mr. Reason, I try to do my work, but well, sometimes I can't hear or see what is going on very well, and ah, Jack just breaks me up. He don't do anything, but when I just look at him I have to laugh." Mr. Reason sums up Ben's statement, "You would like to do better but the conditions seem to work against you. What could you do about that?" "I could just not look at Jack." Mr. Reason responds, "Um-humm." Ben continues, "I could change my seat." He offers this last suggestion with hesitancy and a slight grimace. Mr. Reason, "Changing your seat would be a little distasteful for you, but it has the best chance of succeeding. That is a mature idea and I'm pleased to hear you make it. Where do you think you could sit to maximize your hearing and seeing and at the same time minimize your being distracted by Jack?" Ben: "Well, how would it be if I sat up there at the front of the room next to ah, what's her name, ah Nancy?" "Super suggestion, Ben."

Is this a naive situation? It only took two or three minutes, less time than the typical teacher spends repeatedly admonishing students like Ben. It takes understanding, patience, and trust of the student. It is a reasonable, professional attitude—an expectation that students want to succeed and get along. There is a good reason for this assumption, although we need to recognize that for many students this desire is deeply buried under hostility for the system, fear of failure from years of failing, and distrust of teachers because of the years of not being respected.

Thoresen and Mahoney (1974) shared this rather humorous but true anecdote, which clearly depicts the process of self-managed stimulus control. A pack-a-day cigarette smoker tried unsuccessfully to kick the habit on several occasions. Finally, he tried this self-control strategy. First he noted that he mostly smoked when drinking coffee or beer, when he was alone without anything in particular on his mind, or when he was with friends. These were all valued events that he did not want to eliminate. Contrary to his previous unsuccessful attempts to quit smoking, he decided this time that he would continue to smoke whenever he wanted a cigarette, but only when alone in a bathroom. If he had the urge to smoke when driving, he held off until he found a service station or a restaurant, went to the restroom and smoked. When with friends and unable to refrain from smoking, he excused himself and went to the bathroom. He drank his beer and coffee in the bathroom so he could smoke. Within two weeks he found himself putting off the smoking because it had become inconvenient and not particularly satisfying. He found that he lost interest in smoking. He did report, however, that whenever he was around people who were smoking, he frequently had an urge to urinate.

The point to be made here is that behavior is stimulated by the immediate environment. One means of managing students is to wall off the specific stimuli that are arousing the inappropriate behavior. If the student, rather than the teacher, identifies and controls the stimuli, the effects are greater and more positive than would be the case had the teacher manipulated the change.

RECOMMENDED READINGS

Jones, V.F. and Jones, L.S. *Responsible classroom discipline.* Boston, MA: Allyn and Bacon, 1981.

Macht, J. *Teacher/teachum, the toughest game in town.* New York: John Wiley, 1975.

Tanaka, J. *Classroom management: A guide for the school consultant.* Springfield, IL: Charles C. Thomas, 1979.

9

BEHAVIORAL CONTROL THROUGH ANTECEDENT CONTROL: INTERVENTION STRATEGY C₂

We have found that a teacher might control the environment through selectively responding to a student's behavior and thereby influencing the probability of the reoccurrence of the behavior. In addition, since the environment arouses motives, triggers certain behaviors, and signals directions, still another dimension of behavior control is possible.

In studies of motivation, for example, Atkinson and Raynor (1978) found that even among persons with high needs for achievement or power or affiliation, a warm-up activity that stimulates the given needs causes more potent responses as expressions of the need than would be the case without the warm-up. When students competed in an anagram contest for 30 seconds as a prelude to a task, they demonstrated a higher need to perform the task well than they did without the anagram challenge. It would behoove teachers to have warm-up exercises in cooperation or competitiveness to stimulate whatever motives are needed for a given activity.

A number of processes can be used to influence behavior before it occurs. We will consider the following: stimulus control, time-out, negative reinforcement, stress control, diet and stimulation, and modeling.

STIMULUS CONTROL

If doing the right thing at the right time and place is a reasonable way to describe discipline, then attending to the right time/right place signals is critical. These signals are stimuli.

Most of the behavior that we desire in school is within the repertoire of our students. They can sit still to watch television for periods exceeding 20 minutes. Most are able to persist in games. It follows that most youngsters do not need to learn correct behavior, but what stimuli to attend to and connections between stimuli and particular behaviors. Teachers can facilitate such learning in two ways: stimulus discrimination and signal learning.

Stimulus Discrimination

The following dialogue occasionally occurs in the principal's office. John, who seems to have frequent problems, enters and hands the secretary a hall pass. The secretary guesses why John is there but asks, "John, you are supposed to be in Mr. Smith's class. What seems to be the trouble?" John replies, "I dunno, I was just sittin' there and ol' Mr. Smith just told me to get down to the principal's office. Honest, I wasn't doing nothing." A likely story? It sounds like a con game. Perhaps so, but perhaps not.

When people are angry, afraid, sad, or joyful, they express their emotions by means of a number of universal cues: frowning, smiling, curling the lips, and focusing the eyes, for example. However, some observers either don't notice these cues or falsely interpret them. We all have met people who have to be "hit on the head" before they realize that others are bored, angry, or disgusted by what is going on.

Dil (1971) showed 32 still pictures, each of which illustrated one of eight emotions to students, and asked the students to identify the emotion depicted in each picture. Dil found a high correlation between discipline problems and insensitivity to emotional facial expressions. Those students who were insensitive to emotional cues tended to be the same students whom teachers identified as behavioral problems.

Perhaps John is not trying to con the secretary. Suppose that John had done something like spontaneously saying something really funny to which others, including the teacher, had positively responded. John picks up on this positive response, and having been positively reinforced, he repeats the behavior. This time the response from others is tolerance, but hardly encouraging. Most people back off at this point and go on to other activities. However, if John happened to be one of those who doesn't discriminate others' feelings by facial expressions or other nonverbal signals, then he may continue his "not so funny" behavior. As he repeats the behavior, the signals become more negative, but he misses them until the fatal, "Out! Out!" Since he missed the signals, he is bewildered by the hostile reaction to the behavior that had heretofore been rewarded.

Students like John are considered to be deviant in behavior—deviant liars and poor social learners, since they do not learn from repeated punishment. Guilford (1967) defines this social discrimination as a particular kind of intellect, independent of other kinds of intelligence. Dil (1971) found the phenomena to be independent of sex, socioeconomic status, and I.Q. scores.

We can do two things to help students who seem to lack the natural ability to discriminate among social signals. First, we can use more explicit signals. For example, one junior high school teacher found success with a pair of small lights. One light was red, the other green. He explained that when the red light was on the students were to be in their seats on-task, with movement or talking permitted only by specific permission. With the green light students were permitted greater latitude. He likened the red-green class lights with the stop-go traffic signals. Students understood these simple signals, and since all were eager to drive a car in the future, they rather liked the signals. Second, we can teach students to discriminate between more complex stimuli.

Signal Learning

Learning to discriminate among the various social signals would seem to be an important task. The student would need to learn to become aware of the signal, code it, and respond to it in prescribed ways. It seems clear that simply sending the signal and then punishing the student who doesn't respond properly will *not* help him learn this discrimination. We want the student to connect the appropriate behavior (getting on task) to the signal, and that can best be done through reinforcement. The task is to present the signal in such a form that it is difficult to miss and under circumstances in which the right behavior is most likely to occur, and then reinforce.

Let's go back to John. Instead of grimly scowling from across the room, let's begin with, "John, it's time to return to the assignment," with the teacher standing close by. Because of the proximity and verbal message John is most likely to comply. When John does so, he needs to be reinforced. A simple positive statement ought to work very nicely. After the appropriate pattern of behavior has been established, John can slowly be weaned by shortening or modifying the signal to "John, it's time," and then "John." Likewise, the weaning can occur with respect to proximity so that the message can be sent from across the room as well as from within arm's reach. Meanwhile, we ought to be pairing nonverbal stimuli with the verbal directives, so that the former are learned as signals. While we are teaching John to respond to explicit signals, we ought to make them pleasant. Pleasant or neutral signals will not only foster a more congenial relationship and a positive general classroom atmosphere, but they will also be easier on the teacher's nerves. All of that frowning and scowling causes wrinkles. Signals just have to deliver the message; they need not be harsh.

In conclusion, John's nature can be changed from *con* to *can*: Use distinct signals. Use the particular stimuli only to signal particular behavior. The teacher who is frowning all of the time can not use a frown to signal students to sit down and open their books. In the beginning, use signals under circumstances in which the probability for conformance is high. Reinforce the desired response. Do not use the selected signal in situations in which the probability is high for inappropriate behavior. Be careful of undesired by-products. A shout may get attention but may also startle students, cause giggling, and arouse a number of other undesired behaviors.

TIME OUT

An alternative to changing stimuli to control student behavior is to move the student to a neutral environment. In this instance we are not referring to suspension, which is a last-resort treatment of exclusion.

Time out is more like a short-time cooling-off period. Redl and Wattenberg (1959) referred to this treatment as antiseptic isolation. The process and purpose are nonpunitive. It is a means of removing an individual for a few minutes from a situation that he seemingly can't handle. A simple example would be to excuse a student who is coughing to step outside for a few minutes to get a drink of water and relax. In a like manner a student with the giggles or another who is showing extreme test anxiety may regain his composure if allowed to momentarily step away from the causative stimuli. Time out can be as simple as a first-grade teacher directing students to cradle their heads in their arms on the desks for a few moments. Meditation is a helpful way of removing oneself from the hubbub of the ongoing environment. Athletes and other performers sometimes find it helpful to momentarily isolate themselves in order to "pull my head together."

Thus far, time out has been described as isolation from distracting stimuli long enough for the individual to reorient himself. Time out also is used to remove an individual from the positive reinforcement that is maintaining undesired behavior. Recall that if behavior is reinforced, it will be repeated. Thus, one way to stop the behavior is to remove or isolate the student from the setting of reinforcers. The individual is placed in a space or position free of stimulation, in which reinforcement is nonexistent. The idea is not punishment. Explanation to the student is matter of fact (e.g., "You seem not to be able to stop laughing. I think that it would be helpful if you were to go to the time out space for three minutes while the rest of us do. . . ."

Time out is quick and easy to implement. Typically, there are few, if any, emotional side effects. Time out offers an opportunity to explicitly identify undesired acts, and finally, it rapidly reduces misbehavior. Let's now consider the ways and means of using time out procedures.

Time out works best if students can be sent to an isolated spot. Ideally it would be close by. The identified space need not be, but could be in the classroom, perhaps a chair in a corner cut off by a low screen. Note, it must *not* be a place of ridicule, like the old dunce chair where students were sent to wear a dunce hat for misbehavior. A closet is inappropriate. We are not punishing the student and we don't want to make him a martyr. Some students, such as a withdrawn child probably ought not be isolated. It could turn out to reinforce behavior we wish to eradicate.

The duration of time out should be short—from three to five minutes. If it is too long, the enterprising individual will invent a rewarding activity within the time-out area. Furthermore, we don't want the student to miss important on-task time. The simplest way to control time is to place a small timer, such as that used in a kitchen, in the time-out area, and allow the student to set it and automatically return to the class when the buzzer sounds.

Timing may be an important issue. Time out during an examination or an activity that the student perceives to be unpleasant may increase the aberrant behavior we are striving to eliminate. Time out will only work in classrooms in which students enjoy and are reinforced for participation. Isolation must be less satisfying than being in class with friends and ongoing activities. If classroom conditions are aversive, time out could be a relief that induces repetition of the escape behavior. This process is called *negative reinforcement,* our next topic.

NEGATIVE REINFORCEMENT (ESCAPE–AVOIDANCE BEHAVIOR)

Mr. Smith has a dilemma. His classroom is on the west side of the building, and the glass windows let in the sunlight during the afternoon, making his room intolerably hot. During one particular hot spell, he opened the windows, but there was so little air stirring that it didn't help. The next day he brought a large fan from home and placed it in the open doorway so the fan could pull the cool air from the halls into the room. That helped considerably.

However, there was a problem. This was a particularly noisy class (uncontrollable would be a better description). The inevitable happened. The class was so noisy that teachers up and down the hall complained. The principal left Mr. Smith a note, indicating that if he couldn't keep the noise down the door to his room would have to be closed. Any advice for Mr. Smith?

Possible Solution

Mr. Smith started out with the door closed, windows open, and fan on. The room soon became stifling because the fan only circulated warm air. The students began to complain and requested that the door be opened. Mr. Smith explained the dilemma, read the note from the principal, then suggested the following: "We will divide the class time into five-minute segments. If we are quiet for five minutes, the door will be opened. If the noise goes up during any five-minute period, the door will have to be closed immediately and will stay closed until we are quiet for five minutes. It is all up to us." The class immediately went to work quietly and Mr. Smith opened the door after five minutes, to everyone's relief.

The door stayed open for about 15 minutes before the noise went up to its standard level. Mr. Smith immediately closed the door and explained, "I'm sorry, we will have to start a new five-minute quiet period before the door can be reopened." Mr. Smith ignored the groans, begging to open the door, promises to be quiet, and the angry shushing. In a few moments it became quiet and Mr. Smith said, "We can begin our five-minute quiet time now." He wrote the time on the board. In five minutes, since all had been quiet, he again opened the door and there was no need to reclose it that day.

In a few days the weather changed for the better but the door stayed open and the class remained reasonably quiet. One of the students commented with pride, "This is a good class. We can have the door open and not get complaints from other classes." The new quiet, businesslike attitude of the class must have been satisfying and conducive to work, but there was a new concept illustrated by the episode—negative reinforcement.

The principle of negative reinforcement may be summed up as follows: If a mild aversive situation is terminated by a given behavior then that behavior will tend to be continued or repeated. In Mr. Smith's class the hot, oppressive atmosphere was the aversive condition. Five minutes of good behavior terminated the discomfort. The fact caused the good behavior to be repeated. Timing is important; the relief from the aversive condition must occur immediately following the desired behavior. In some respects, this procedure may seem to be punitive, but there are several significant differences.

Punishment Contrasted

In negative reinforcement, the aversion precedes and is terminated by desired behavior. By contrast, in punishment the aversive conditions follow undesirable behavior. Thus, there are two significant differences: timing and type of behavior to be emphasized. Whereas punishment at best represses behavior, negative reinforcement increases the probability of the repetition of desired behavior. Furthermore, in negative reinforcement the teacher is able to naturally and logically indicate how the desired behavior relieves the aversive condition. Finally, the teacher can be a good guy. He is watching for good behavior, which then can be the basis for relieving an aversive condition.

Although negative reinforcement is a viable alternative and may be useful under selected circumstances, it is risky if the teacher is the source of the aversive condition. Escape and avoidance behaviors may not always be desirable, but may be learned because they reduce the discomfort. Examples of escape behaviors include daydreaming, cheating, dropping out of school, or passively sitting in class as a nonparticipant. Furthermore, the aversive feeling can easily be generalized to schooling, authority, or subject matter. Aversive conditions turn people off.

We need to consider methods for helping those who tend to fearfully back off from activities. Stress control will be our next topic.

STRESS CONTROL

One of the simple exercises I arrange in class to bring forth an issue is to ask for volunteers. I repeat several times without further disclosure a need for people to stand up and come forward. After about five minutes of requesting and cajoling I usually have about 50 percent of the class as volunteers. I then ask the volunteers and nonvolunteers to jot down why they behaved as they did. Those who volunteer typically report that they do so because "I am curious"; "I find that it is the best way to learn"; "Being involved is just fun, I would rather participate anytime than just sit and watch"; or "I feel it is my responsibility as a class member to help out in any way that I can."

The nonvolunteers indicate as their reasons such things as: "It is too risky, I won't do anything unless I know what is going to happen"; "I might make a mistake in front of the whole class, then what would they think?" "Too frightening, I want to but I just get nervous in front of people."

Approach behavior is explained in terms of curiosity, enjoyment, responsibility, and learning. Avoidance is explained as fear, shame, or distrust. Withdrawing, isolation, diminished participation, and other avoidance behaviors are as deviant and undesired as is interrupting, rowdyism, and other interfering behaviors.

Most teachers could identify several bright, energetic students who tend to contribute very little to projects and class discussions. Studies of test anxiety report that at least 20 percent of our students are dehabilitated and therefore perform less adequately than they might because of fear. Fright takes a heavy toll in class recitation and oral reading. Finally, many people are socially crippled for lack of courage to meet and mix with others.

Southern and Smith (1980) point out that stress is a two-sided coin. On one hand it is a factor in life and to some degree a necessary motivation for getting people out of bed and into a productive day. Moderate stress can arouse and direct energy to productive ends.

However, in many instances (particularly in school for both teachers and students), the level of stress exceeds not only the optimum motivational level but the tolerance level as well. In these instances we have a situation in which the demands of the environment exceed the response capabilities of the individual. Some students are repeatedly asked to perform under conditions in which they do not understand the directions, do not possess the necessary skills, have not attained the cognitive development levels required for the task, or are distracted by emotional hang-ups carried over from past experiences or home conditions. When unresolved stress is experienced over an extended period or to an overwhelming degree, then it becomes devastating, chronic, or inundating. Excessive stress leads to learning impediments, problems in communication, physical and mental exhaustion, as well as expressions of anger and aggression.

A number of procedures are available for teachers who wish to either help others or relieve themselves of such stress problems. The procedures include selective reinforcement, rigorous structuring of activities, relaxation, desensitization, role playing, and stress inoculation training.

Identification of Stressed Students

The initial step for all of the procedures is to identify students who may be encumbered by emotional responses to a variety of situations. Although we need to be cautious about labeling students, the following symptoms are definite signals:

(a) Depression lethargy, apathy as indicated by slow movements, disinterest, low energy, lack of facial expression or color.
(b) Easily stimulated, overreaction to pain, minimally provoked expressions of anger, guilt, sadness. In some instances, hyperactivity.
(c) Rebelliousness and uncooperativeness. Overcritical of others.
(d) Fantasy as a means of retreating from the real world and achieving the feeling of success without productivity.
(e) Overly compliant so as to make certain that others are never displeased.
(f) Shy, withdrawn, and severely inhibited or controlled behavior.
(g) A number of classic indicators of emotions such as rapid breathing, sweaty palms, flushed face, grimaces, stiff movements, and trembling.

Every one of these "symptoms" is exhibited by most people occasionally. Drawing a line regarding frequency or degree beyond which a teacher ought to be concerned is difficult. There is a continuum between being free of such behaviors to being overwhelmed. People move up and down this continuum, but some tend toward the overwhelmed end and are there more often than not. These are the kinds of students to whom we need to be alert.

The cause of the felt stress is usually apparent (for example, the presence of an authority figure or having to present something to a group). However, for the most part it takes close teacher observation and listening to students in order to identify the disturbing stimuli. Moreover, sometimes the student himself has no clear notion of why he acts as he does. Anxiety in particular is amorphous and the exact cause is illusive. Relaxation, one of the procedures to be studied, offers one means to identify sources.

Let us now move to the specifics of the respective procedures for relieving excessive stress.

Selective Reinforcement

We have already discussed selective reinforcement and need to note only that it is applicable here. In the case of encouraging appropriate responses to fear, it is probable that reinforcement of close approximations as a means of shaping behavior will be necessary rather than waiting for the desired behavior to occur before applying reinforcement. Stress-relieving behaviors to be reinforced vary from breathing deeply before making a presentation to organizing one's life so as to have necessary work completed long before deadlines.

Rigorous Structuring

Anxiety is more common in open, unstructured, complex, new situations. The task here is to help anxious people feel more comfortable and confident. Productivity will increase if such people know exactly what, when, and in what form their efforts are to be conducted. The details of establishing performance objectives, the sequencing events, and organizing tasks are beyond the scope of this discussion, but there are a number of excellent sources. We might note in passing that many educators feel that extensive structuring is dangerous in that it invites overdependence.

Hunt and Sullivan (1974) offer an excellent, well-researched process for establishing structured programs and thence weaning students to independence.

Systematic Relaxation

Relaxation is a powerful tool that can serve diverse ends. Sometimes just a few minutes of relaxation prior to bed enables people to fall asleep more readily and sleep more soundly. At other times 20 minutes of relaxation is often rejuvenating. Most of us recognize that if in a tense situation we are able to take just two or three deep breaths we feel calmer, have better control of our muscles, are better able to analyze the situation, and feel in better control.

Jacobson (1964) describes a simple method by which anyone can quickly obtain a state of relaxation by alternately tensing and releasing muscles. A number of authors have modified the Jacobson model, but Martin and Pear (1978) offer the most useful adaptation for training students in the techniques of relaxation. Relaxation is not only a powerful instrument for stress-weary students, but those readers who suffer from the symptoms of burnout will find the relaxation exercises helpful. The routine is neither difficult nor complex, but too extensive to detail here. An overview will give the reader an idea of the task.

The ideal place to practice relaxation is in a quiet, dimly lit setting with few distracting stimuli. Begin by taking a deep breath, hold it for about five seconds and then completely exhale. Repeat the inhale-hold-exhale cycle twice more. Next, in sequence, the muscle systems identified here are tensed, held, and relaxed. The noted muscle systems are the fists; biceps; forehead and eyes; lips, chin, and jaw; neck; shoulders; stomach and thighs. As you go through this series think and feel the relaxation, freedom to breathe and the warmth that permeates the body. Occasionally tense, hold, and relax all muscles simultaneously.

Persons wearing contact lenses should remove them before doing this exercise.

The goal of the exercises is to learn near instantaneous relaxation. If the Martin and Pear process is repeated several times over two or three days, a weaning process can begin.

Desensitization

The individual can become immune to given stimuli and thereby be less stressed. The basic procedure is to pair up the stress-inducing event with a stimulus that produces a response incompatible with the feelings of anxiety. That is, the stress is neutralized if a comforting or positive event occurs simultaneously. The process is relatively simple but takes some time and effort.

The process involves three steps: identification of a neutralizing stimulus, identification and ordering of the stress-inducing situations, and pairing of the neutralizer with the stressful stimuli.

A state of relaxation is one of several stimuli that could be used to neutralize the stress. Ideally, a security blanket would be handy. In the absence of that close a friend, eating favorite food or the proximity of a supportive teacher are possible stimuli. Anything that normally arouses positive feelings can be used to desensitize given events so that students can function without being overwhelmed by emotion.

Next, the individual needs to identify the target situation, such as presenting an idea in front of the class. Second, he identifies a series of related segments of the event, such as standing in front of the class with everyone watching, walking up to the front of the class, raising one's hand, or being called on by the teacher. Third, he rates the respective segments as to their stress-inducing capacity. For instance, being asked to read the assignment is less arousing than is standing in front of the class to recite. Finally, he places the segments in a graduated order from least to most threatening.

The desensitizing process begins by pairing the neutralizing agent with the segment most remote from the core of the stress situation. In each succeeding step, when the individual is able to remain calm or tolerate the formerly stressful stimuli, the pairing shifts up to the next most threatening segment. In this way the person soon finds that he is able to remain calm and in control of the situation even when confronted with a previously terrifying event.

Role-playing

Role-playing, like desensitization, is a means by which one can gradually move toward feeling comfortable or in control of a situation that is otherwise threatening. The process seems almost innate to the species since infants without instruction often repeat and rehearse fearful and difficult behaviors as a means of developing competence. Much of young children's play is role-playing. Another example is the almost universal tendency for people to reduce anxiety about a pending or past threatening confrontation with another person by rehearsing in fantasy what we did or said or will say and do.

Role-playing is establishing a potentially threatening or difficult situation in such a way that participants can freely exhibit their feelings and behavior without suffering the consequences. It is learning by trial in which the errors can be observed, and understood as cues for change rather than as fearful consequences. Role-playing is a means to learn about interpersonal relations just as simulation is a means to learn specific skills, such as how to fly an airplane. Thus participants can experience and learn about challenging events with minimal risk. Involvement is high.

You will recall that we discussed role-playing in Chapter 6 as a mechanism for moral development. Since the processes are similar, the reader is advised to review the recommended procedures described earlier.

Stress Inoculation

Meichenbaum (1977) developed a system that resembles a miniature conflict cycle to explain student behavior. The intervention process incorporates many of the procedures we have been discussing.

Students often act inappropriately because they find themselves in frustrating circumstances without the necessary skills to perform as required. They then act out their emotion by being disruptive or hurtful to others. As we noted in the conflict cycle a sequence of events such as the following occurs: a frustrating or degenerating event occurs that arouses an emotional reaction such as anger. The emotion, in turn, generates a defensive behavior. The behavior is often antagonistic, although it may also be withdrawal or sulking, depending on the particular feeling and the style of the individual. The cycle is completed and self-perpetuating when other people respond punitively to the maladaptive behavior.

Stress inoculation training (SIT) has been used successfully in classrooms where stress and anger are the basis of impulsive and acting-out behaviors.

The point of SIT is for the student to learn to intervene in this sequence with verbal, cognitive cues so that the trouble-inducing behavior does not automatically follow the emotion. In stress inoculation, the individual directs himself with a self-talk through potentially difficult situations, ranging from overzealous body contact on the playground to confrontations with teachers.

The first task is for the individual to understand the nature of his emotions, what causes them, what they feel like, what the consequences typically are, and what alternatives exist. Students need to experience, identify, and attribute the meanings of sudden hot flashes, facial tension, perspiration, and clenched fists and realize that these are signals of a condition but do not necessarily call for aggressive action. These feelings need to be consciously connected with environmental conditions or events that arouse them. Therefore, it is necessary for each individual to establish a list of connections: When _____ (happens) I feel _____ (e.g., When *people look at me* I feel *flustered.*). Thus, the individual will become able to anticipate the physiological feeling of his emotions. He also needs to recognize that if his behavior is unchecked, particular consequences will ensue. If SIT is to work, he must come to realize that the consequences are bad. So the first step is for the student(s) to fully understand the antecedent-behavior-consequence of emotion.

After the individual understands his emotions and the effects, he is ready to learn a set of coping skills. The coping skills include recognition of bodily messages as signals of impending danger; relaxing and staying calm, as heretofore discussed; and confronting adversary events. The confrontation involves deciding what to say and assertively saying it. Assertiveness means expressing one's feelings and desires, but doing so without aggressiveness. The details of assertiveness are discussed in Chapter 11. Finally, the individual must learn to verbally reinforce himself.

To sum up, SIT is verbal self-control. The individual learns to talk to himself about emotion, its cause, control, and verbal expression. He talks to others in terms of how he feels, why he feels that way, and what he will do about it. Finally he talks to himself about how well he performed. Everybody converses with himself. SIT just organizes the self-talk so that it is cognitive and self-controlling.

Let's illustrate how a teacher might use this process to inoculate himself from some of the stress he has been experiencing with a group of youngsters. Formerly, when students hid behind those in front of them and made distracting noises or ethnic slurs to other students, the teacher would lash out at the culprit. This inevitably was followed by a dialogue of accusations, denials, more profanity, and distraught emotions. The effects of all of this are teacher burnout, antagonistic feelings throughout the classroom, and a promise of future repetitions.

Meichenbaum (1977) suggests four steps for inoculating oneself from stress by controlling emotions: prepare for the stressors, confront and handle the stress when it arrives, cope with overwhelming feelings, and reinforce oneself for controlling actions. To put the steps in operation, the teacher begins by anticipating the stress: "Sixth period already, it's Friday so they'll be raucous"; "Okay, I can feel the pressure building, relax, take a couple of deep breaths and let all the air out"; "I'm not going to let them get to me today"; "I'm not attacking anyone today." Second: "There, it started, relax, you are in control"; "I'm not going to be aroused, I can manage these feelings"; "One step at a time, calmly move to the windows and then to the back of the room." Next, the need to cope with feelings: "Period is half over"; "Relax now and feel your stress decline"; "Keep moving, focus on the lesson." Finally, despite some taunting, the teacher suddenly realizes: "I did it"; "It feels great when I, rather than the situation, control my feelings"; "With my moving around—not shouting or reprimanding them— nothing bad happened"; "Okay, I really did it."

DIET AND STIMULATION

Millman et al. (1980) summarize a number of studies on hyperactive youngsters. The conclusion from these studies is that hyperactivity is not a simple phenomenon and that too many students are so labeled and too often drugs are arbitrarily prescribed. There appears to be considerable disagreement among experts as to who is and who is not hyperactive. Nevertheless, studies consistently estimate that between 5 and 10 percent of the students are hyperactive, and about 40 percent of those referred to mental health clinics are so labeled. Furthermore, the symptoms are not outgrown, so it is best to attend to such children early in the schooling years. Incidently, the ratio of boys to girls is seven to one.

A number of treatments including the following have been found useful: stimulating drugs, selective reinforcement, token reinforcement, self-instruction, time out, relaxation, diet, and physical stimulation. Drugs are used at the discretion of physicians, but at best their use is controversial. Also, the available evidence suggests that they are most beneficial if supplemented by teacher treatment utilizing some combination of the techniques above. The effects of controlled environments are often found to be equal to or better than that of drugs. Since we have not discussed either diet or physical stimulation, a brief summary of each shall be presented.

Although experimental studies are reportedly flawed, the effect of types of material commonly found in our food is impressive. Salicylates are contained in such foods as apples, berries, pork, and tomatoes. When these foods have been removed from the diets of hyperactive children, the effect in improved behavior has been dramatic. Food coloring and artificial flavoring have been shown to be equally stimulating. The consumption of foods on the current market containing such additives is prevalent. Two children who had been on an additive-free diet for a year were given cookies with food coloring. At home their motor activity and patterns of sleep reflected the change, as did their in-school, out-of-seat behavior and duration of on-task behavior. The evidence suggests that the elimination of certain soft drinks and other foods from the diet of at least some children is warranted. You may wish to discuss this with selected parents and school officials. A book by B.F. Feingold (1975), *Why Your Child is Hyperactive,* is an excellent source for further study.

Although the effects have been inconclusive, it has generally been assumed that the reduction of environmental stimulation would reduce hyperactivity. One could logically conclude that overstimulating surroundings cause some children to overreact. However, as paradoxical as it seems, stimulant drugs have been often found to be more effective in reducing hyperactivity than are depressants. Zentall (1977) argues that people need and seek stimulation. He hypothesizes that hyperactive youngsters filter out stimuli so that in normal environments they receive very little stimulation. Such children allegedly seek out stimulation by increasing their activity, socialization, and poking into things. The proposed cure: place such children in stimulating environments. Zentall points out that when hyperactive youngsters are placed in highly stimulating environments their behavior is not unlike that of "normal" children. As an alternative to isolating hyperactive children in the quiet corner, particularly when such moves are ineffective, the teacher may wish to try some combination of the following strategies:

1. Place the student near bright colors and varied patterns such as we sometimes have on bulletin boards. Distant visual stimuli have also been shown to reduce activity.
2. Increase nearby movement. Desks might be turned to face a street or animals in the classroom. A mechanical device may be utilized.
3. Task variation ought to help. Frequent activity change is needed for some students. Observation of people deeply engrossed in a film will show that despite their total involvement, considerable movement over time is evident.
4. Novelty is a powerful motivator. If the teacher is able to introduce unusual, unexpected, incongruent stimuli before and after tasks we might expect more concentrated effort on the task itself.
5. Select tasks that can successfully be completed. Hyperactive students tend to be overwhelmed by internal frustration.
6. Long periods of waiting are disastrous for hyperactive students. Therefore, large group activities in which individuals perform in turn ought to be bypassed.
7. Self-paced activities are more apt to keep the hyperkinetic person on-task. Waiting periods don't exist and the student can consume his energy through multiple tasks.
8. Active participation, movement, and manipulation are also desirable. Isometric exercises between tasks may help.
9. If reinforcements are used they ought to be stimulating or consumable. It would seem that tokens or teacher records would be less stimulating than something the hyperactive student could hold or see.

MODELING

Teaching by modeling is a recognized potent means for influencing behavior. Commercial advertisement, in particular, uses models as the prime means to encourage us to buy and use a product that otherwise may have little to commend it. If in a group one person yawns, begins to speak in a whisper, peers intently at the ceiling, or starts to tiptoe, soon others are yawning, whispering, quizzically peering upward, or tiptoeing. More germane to our purpose is that much natural teaching is achieved through modeling. Language, cultural morés, the rules of games, trade skills, and most rituals are learned by observing real-life models. "Let me show you" is a natural and generally successful teaching technique. It is only reasonable that we should use it as a means for helping students learn appropriate school behavior.

Bad Effects

Largely ignored by the television industry, if children watch violent behavior and are then presented with similar stimuli, the observed behavior will be replicated. For example, Bandura et al. (1963) arranged for one of two groups of youngsters to observe an adult abuse a "Bozo" clown in a variety of ways with different instruments. The viewers, male and female children, observed the assaulting behavior. The findings, as summed up by the authors, were conclusive:

> The results of the present study provide strong evidence that exposure to filmed aggression heightens aggressive reactions in children. Subjects who viewed the aggressive human and cartoon models on film exhibited nearly twice as much aggression than did subjects in the control group who were not exposed to the aggressive film content (1963, p. 9).

We need to remind ourselves that Kounin (1970) found that the primary effect of witnessing a teacher's angry punitive reaction to other students was an increase in distress and aggressive behavior.

Good Effects

O'Connor (1969) found television models could be used for positive effects. Nine teachers in nursery schools were asked to identify isolated, asocial children who were least likely to participate with other children in any activity. Thirty-two children so identified were closely observed, and 13 of these who consistently were nonparticipants were finally selected for further study. Six of these children were randomly chosen to individually watch a 23-minute film on TV in which 11 episodes were shown of a child approaching and becoming involved with other children. In the film the other children responded positively to the newcomer. A female narrator commented on the children's social behavior, pointing out the particular prosocial acts. Meanwhile, each of the seven control children observed a film of acrobatic dolphins, accompanied by a musical soundtrack.

The effects were marked. The six children who had observed the social film immediately demonstrated social behavior, and post-treatment observers were unable to distinguish them from other normally social children. No change was evident in the social behavior of the seven children who had see the dolphin film. As a group the socially trained children engaged in social interactions five times more frequently after than before seeing the film. At the end of the school year the teachers were once more asked to identify isolated children. The teachers allegedly did not know about the film treatment. However, only one of the six treated students was listed as an isolate, while four of the seven nontreated children were still considered to be isolates.

Modeling Conditions

A variety of studies have identified conditions to increase the probability that desired behaviors will be imitated.

1. The more similar the model is to the learner, the more likely the behavior will be imitated. For example, age, sex, dress, and other apparent bases for the learners to sense a likeness with the model, help identification.
2. Models with status, that is, persons who are admired and valued, are most likely to be imitated. If the model is skilled or powerful, the credibility and effects are increased.
3. Models, particularly if they are adults, are more powerful if they are warm and caring while attempting to influence the destiny of the learner.
4. Narration by the model or commentary by others, which clearly identifies cues or specific behaviors, increases the probability that behavior will be copied.
5. If the behavior is complex or involves a sequence, it first should be demonstrated, then separated into explicit moves, and finally synthesized back into the integrated behavior.
6. The effects of modeling are increased if the model is reinforced for the behavior.
7. The modeled behavior will most likely become part of the learner's mode of behavior if the learner is reinforced for exhibiting the behavior. The reinforcement is particularly powerful if the model is the reinforcing agent.

Imitative learning is not the result of any single factor. It involves the same elements that we have identified in other behavior modification strategies: identification of the desired behavior, cues to indicate how to behave, and show evidence that the behavior pays. The use of models enables us to clearly define and illustrate the cues, the behavior, and the consequence. Furthermore, the models may initially arouse and direct the attention of the would-be learner.

The process is flexible in that the model may be live or on film. Heroes such as historic figures or celebrities can be utilized if the teacher incorporates the appropriate conditions.

We need to be aware that undesirable as well as desirable behavior may be imitated. If the conditions are right the behavior will be learned, intentionally or unintentionally. A case in point was recently reported in the news. A mother noticed one day that her young son was limping and dragging one of his feet. She asked if he were feeling well or had hurt his leg. He replied, "No." After a few days she became alarmed and took her son to the doctor. The boy was examined and no problems were discovered. Still, the limping continued, and perhaps even worsened a bit. On the doctor's advice the boy was taken to a bone specialist several hundred miles away. Once more a thorough examination was unable to identify a cause. The puzzled specialist finally asked the boy, "Can you think of any reason why you are limping and dragging your foot?" The boy replied, "I dunno, but maybe it is because Grandpa walks that way." After a brief discussion the boy walked as he had prior to his grandfather's visit.

It may be that imitation itself is a learned behavior. For example, in most families considerable attention is paid to the young. When the infant is babbling and the mother, father, or sibling says, "Mama," "Dada," or whatever, and the child responds in kind, there is not only reinforcement for talking, the child also learns that imitation is a valued behavior. This reinforcement for imitation must occur innumerable times in the typical home—thus the child learns to imitate. However, for a variety of reasons it is likely that some children never learn to imitate. If this is the case we may wish to reinforce and thus establish imitative as well as imitated behavior.

Reader's task: Design a modeling program to induce an elementary school student to hang his coat up in the closet or a high school student to submit neat papers with proper margins and paragraph indentations. Do not forget to incorporate a number of the conditions above.

The use of a unique model to help a boy who seemed destined for serious trouble was described by Davis (1979). Eric, an 11-year-old fourth-grader, was a ferocious fighter and often verbally attacked teachers. Various procedures such as paddling, loss of privileges, suspension, and token economies had failed. The school authorities were ready to give up and expel Eric.

A videotape recorder was brought to the classroom so that various playlets enacted by the students could be recorded. In scene i of one of the vignettes Eric and two boys acted out a specially written script. The two boys called Eric a variety of names and shoved him around. The climax came when one of the boys pushed Eric hard up against the wall and said, "I'm going to beat you up." Eric, as directed by the script, responded, "I don't fight anymore," and walked away. In scene ii of this episode, Eric reports the incident to a teacher, who commends Eric, "That was very mature of you Eric. It was a tough thing for you to do and I'm proud of you."

In another vignette Eric is seated at a desk with his head down ignoring the work piled on his desk. A teacher comes along and crossly states, "Get busy! You haven't done anything all morning." Eric responds by picking up the books and simulating work. The teacher gives him a pat on the back and praises him.

The videotapes of 11 episodes were shown to the class and all were applauded. Following this experience Eric's behavior remained unchanged. One shot, even on TV, does not win a war. Behavioral rehearsal or role playing may not suffice with problems like Eric's, especially if it occurs only once.

The school psychologist persisted. For two weeks the peer aggression episode was shown to Eric every day, with various suggestions to the effect that, "This is the way that you should act." The frequency of fighting dropped to one incident per week. For the next two weeks the work scene was shown, with comments regarding proper behavior. The frequency of hostile responses to authority figures dropped to about five a week, which was far from desirable but tolerable, and much better than his prior record. This illustrates a modest success, a start that must be pursued with other strategies. This is costly, but the alternatives for people like Eric and society are enormously more expensive.

Stephen Judy, who spent most of his life in prison and was executed in the state of Indiana on March 9, 1981, for raping a mother, killing her, and then brutally murdering her three children, summed it up very poignantly: "You knew that I was a problem when I was six years old. You told me over and over again since then that I am a bad person, but you never did anything to change me. You just punished me. You had better kill me now, because you won't try to change me and I'll just kill again."

Fortunately, we do have a variety of ways to control the environment and thereby change behavior. We don't have to give up on the Mickey Trobols and the Erics or repeatedly jail and release the Stephen Judys until one day they commit a crime so hideous that we feel justified in eliminating them.

SUMMARY

The teachers and others at Lincoln High or any other school are not without resources for helping Mickey Trobol. It is incorrect to say that someone like Mickey is incorrigible. It is more precise to say that an individual will not change if the environment does not change. However, if the environment were unchanging none of us would learn. A basic tenet of all psychology is that changing environments are a necessary requisite for cognitive and personal development. We confront infants with one kind of environment, children with a completely different one, and adolescents with still another. These changes in stimuli, demands, and rewards help people to mature. Control of the environment is critical as a means to influence behavior.

Some of our students seem to prosper under all circumstances. They respond to the environment and the environment responds to them in such ways as to foster maturity. On the other hand, some of our students need designed environments. Mickey, with his perception, attitudes, and habits, needs a specially designed environment. If Mickey is to become a credit to our society, it will occur only if his teachers use alternatives to punishment. One set of alternatives includes some combination of such consequences as selective reinforcement, extinction, a token economy, self-management strategies, and contingency contracts. If, on the other hand, the teacher wishes he may establish the environment in such a way as to induce different behaviors. This may be achieved by teaching students through selected stimuli, time-out procedures, negative reinforcement, desensitization, and establishing models of desired behavior. If you are the teacher, it will not be sufficient for you simply to learn the names of these procedures. You need to be able to put them into operation. Practice and feedback in each step of each technique are necessary, and then we can still expect something less than 100 percent success.

Despite these limitations control of the environment via behavior modification has been used successfully for a wide variety of students from preschool through adult education. A review of the publications summarized in *Psychological Abstracts* and the *Educational Retrieval of Information Centers System* between 1975 and 1981 shows 180 independent reports of changing student behavior by means of reinforcing desired behaviors or controlling the antecedents and thus the behavior. Ninety-two of these reports deal with normal students and 73 refer to treatment in grades one through nine. The other 19 were directed toward changing high school students.

The Effects of Student-Controlled Environments

Who controls the environment? Common sense and research indicate that student behavior influences teacher behavior just as teacher behavior influences student behavior. We have discussed the issue from the perspective that the teacher arranges the antecedents and consequences, but there may be value in considering the interaction when the students control the environment.

Gray, Graubard, and Rosenberg (1974) reported a series of episodes in which the students learned to use selective reinforcement, extinction, and stimulus control. The students then used these skills to stimulate behavior from others that was mutually satisfying. The details of the program, known as the Visalia Project, are noteworthy. In Visalia Junior High School about ten percent of the students were considered to be incorrigible. The school had the highest suspension and expulsion rate in the district. Seven students, aged 12 to 15, were selected from the incorrigibles to be participants. The students understood that they are participating in an experiment and that they would therefore need to keep accurate records. It was found that accurate record keeping by the students was a critical variable in the success of the program. The students were told that they would learn to respond to teachers and fellow students in such a way as to influence target behaviors.

For two weeks students learned to specify desired behavior and the behavior to be eliminated and to identify appropriate replacement behavior. The first serious problem emerged when the students began to record others' behavior in order to establish baseline conditions. The students had no difficulty identifying and scoring negative behaviors. Independent record keepers found that although teachers frequently responded positively to the students, the students often did not pick it up. For example, an observing aide reported that a teacher had praised a student, but the student reported that "The teacher chewed me out." Recall Ralph, and the Dil (1971) study. Some, perhaps most, of our serious troublemakers are not able to properly understand and interpret other people's feelings and messages. This factor and its implications are critical, and we as teachers must include sensitivity to others' communication as part of the school discipline program.

The directors of the Visalia Project taught the students the critical cues and how to identify the positive teacher behaviors by role playing and analyses of videotapes. The students learned and were finally able to accurately record others' behavior.

The students were then taught how to reinforce other people. Interestingly, the misbehaving students also had problems with this task. They had to learn how and when to smile, make eye contact, and offer praise (e.g., "I like to work in this room when people are nice to each other."). One of the seven students was not able to smile. When he tried the appearance was a menacing leer. It took practice before a videotape camera and feedback before he developed a smile which communicated positive regard.

Learning to respond to teachers was particularly difficult for these students. It took practice for them to be able to respond to a teacher's negative communications (e.g., "It is hard for me to do good work when you are cross with me"). That kind of message is difficult for most of us. However, these boys and girls also had difficulty sincerely praising teachers. The students were awkward and embarrassed at first and tended to mouth the words, but did not include the all-important nonverbal cues. Many of us need to work on this. These students became quite skilled with practice.

With effort and patience the students were able to fill out behavior identification tables and from this establish baselines and set up selective reinforcement, extinction, and stimulus controls. The results? The data for the original seven students shows that prior to the program negative student–teacher confrontations averaged about 20 per week. Positive student–teacher interactions averaged about eight per week. At the end of six weeks of the program the negative confrontations were down to about two per week, and the positive interactions were up to 32. The change indicated by this data was not immediate or sudden. Changes of this nature are gradual.

Visalia has since expanded the program to include several different groups, including gifted students who were having some interpersonal behavioral problems. The teachers are reportedly pleased with the program. Although it was generally successful, some students were never able to achieve their goals.

We are reminded that some folks have difficulty observing and correctly interpreting others' feelings, behaviors, and intentions. Some find it difficult to respond positively to other people. These are learned phenomena that are very important for prosocial interaction. If a student is without such skills, where else but school is he going to develop them?

Perhaps the most important outcome of teaching students to control stimuli and use selective reinforcement is the reported change in self-concept. Gray et al. (1974: 45) noted that many children often suffer feelings of impotence when they encounter the school environment. The program apparently was able to alter that perception.

As a result of their training the students reported feeling more powerful in their relationships with their teachers and the school than ever before. And with that feeling of power came a new feeling of self-confidence.

Building of self-confidence is a critical task that we will consider in detail in the next chapter.

10

BUILDING CONGRUENT SELF-CONCEPTS: INTERVENTION STRATEGY D

AN IDEAL (?) SCHOOL

Weinstein and Fantini (1970: 72–73) described a program in an upgraded demonstration school. The students were highly articulate strivers conversant with current world events and social issues.

> Their parents were faculty members of the university or graduate or undergraduate students. It was obvious that all the students were from upwardly mobile families, although their family incomes may have been low at the time. . . .
>
> The students' interests and abilities seemed to be consistent with the school's purposes; they enjoyed and were involved in doing the things that they were expected to do at school, such as writing, discussing, and reading. Their families strongly supported and enriched the school activities. School life and home life were complementary and harmonious, since the same values, skills, attitudes were rewarded in both places.

Sounds good? Read on!

> Most of the students indicated a concern for a positive self-image. "To be somebody, you have to make the rest of the kids look up to you," was a widely held sentiment. One child said, "You have to be independent and not do what everyone else is doing." Another said, "To stand out I take the opposite side of every issue—I'm very individualistic."
>
> A concern for power or some kind of control over people and events seemed pervasive. "In this class you have to be a controller—cool and

tough—and be able to take control of any group and run it" was a typical attitude. "You have to fight, squabble, gossip your way to the top." "You have to be secluded and not get involved unless you can be in control." Teachers who imposed control were resented: "He's always making me do things when I don't want to."

The verbal cues of the students in this school seemed to indicate that the two major concerns were in the areas of self-concept and power. Most of them manifested both concerns by competing to make the cleverest, brightest remarks, not only to attract attention of teachers and classmates, but also to "put down" other students in a kind of one-upsmanship game.

In one of the class activities students were asked to wear special glasses to represent specific frames of reference: "pride," "suspicious," "cool-tough," "controller," "humorous," "independent," "studious." When asked to identify the glasses most natural to them (easiest to wear when regarding the world), the most frequently mentioned alternative was "suspicious." From the discussion regarding choice of glasses, Weinstein and Fantini concluded that most of these youngsters were possessed by an underlying fear of being exposed or depreciated—being made to feel worthless, small, or helpless. Suspiciousness was articulated as: "Are they going to make fun of me?" or "Will she flunk me?"

The point to be made here is that students from all sorts of schools—inner city, suburban, and even those that appear to be highly successful—are marked by a search for identity. The concern for self is epidemic among adolescents, but the concern begins early in our schooling and is a factor throughout life.

IMPORTANCE OF SELF-CONCEPT

The multitude of studies of self-concept among educational, psychological, and social scientists is testimony of the importance of self. Perhaps most pertinent for us is a study reported by Coopersmith and Feldman (1974). The teachers of 42 elementary schools and the parents of 200 schoolchildren were asked to rank 36 educational goals. The schools were selected from diverse locations throughout California. Care was taken to include parents from the full range of socioeconomic levels.

Parents ranked reading comprehension as the most important goal, but significantly, self-concept was ranked second. Put into perspective, computation was ranked seventh, spelling sixteenth, history twenty-sixth, and physical education thirtieth. Self-concept was rated by the teachers as the most important of all goals.

Most authorities on adolescents agree with Erikson's contention that identity formation, the reassessment and reformation of the self-image into a personal identity, is the crux of adolescence. From a slightly different perspective, Biehler and Snowman (1982) contend that depression, self-depreciation based on feelings of having little control over one's life, is the most common emotional disorder during adolescence.

Self-concept is important in its own right, but in addition it is generally believed to be the key to decision making, social relations, and all other aspects of life. The evidence is not very pervasive, but most educators accept Purkey's (1984) conclusion that self-esteem is a major factor in academic achievement.

Paradoxically, Coopersmith and Feldman (1974: 197) cogently argue that the schools are a major factor in depressing self-concept.

> In traditional elementary classrooms verbal intelligence has generally been recognized as the major, if not the sole, basis for determining who is capable and likely to succeed. Teachers in these classrooms have generally failed to teach children to recognize, utilize, and value their other skills and abilities. Consequently, many children who are not in the top quarter in verbal intelligence feel that they are incapable and are virtually doomed to fail. Many traditional schools have also favored the use of grades, competition between children, and fear of failure as means of motivating children. The schools have, thus, set up a system for generating negative self-concepts and low self-esteem—a system that virtually guarantees that a great many children will feel they are incapable and have not succeeded. It should, therefore, come as no surprise that there is a regular and consistent decline in children's self-esteem between the second and seventh grades.

DISCIPLINE AND SELF-CONCEPT IN PERSPECTIVE

Either directly or indirectly we have made the self the cornerstone of each of the strategies for helping students to behave appropriately. Emotions and feelings were identified as a manifestation of incongruency between self-concept and messages from the environment. Thus, in dealing with feelings a fundamental goal is to communicate to the person that "I care about you," "I trust you," and "I respect your judgment and integrity." The outcome of such a relationship is not only a restoration of emotional balance and a resolution of problems, but a move toward a more positive, substantive sense of self on the part of the student.

In reality education, the student is confronted with his behavior and its consequences. The individual is asked to plan, coordinate, evaluate, and thereby govern his own behavior according to a self-appropriated value system. The purpose of this program is not only to improve behavior but to make individuals more self-responsible. An important product of such self-governed behavior will be a more resolute sense of an autonomous self.

The original advocates of controlling the environment to induce desired behavior did not deny the existence of a person's inner world. Rather, because the individual's inner world was considered to be complex, abstract, difficult to conceptualize, and not directly measurable, the behaviorist elected to focus attention on the behavior. Hypotheses were generated, and as we have noted, researchers found that behavior can be changed by controlling the environment. In summarizing the effects of social reinforcements, Sulzer and Mayer (1972) and Krumboltz and Krumboltz (1972) conclude that the recipient's self-esteem is directly enhanced. In contrast they note that punitive actions tend to create adverse conditions, which are reflected in students' negative comments about the self ("I am a bad person."). They continue by noting that such self-deprecating statements have a negative impact on school achievement. Becker, Engelmann, and Thomas (1975), who are among the most avid behaviorists, report that self-confidence and self-esteem are natural by-products of effective teaching, which inevitably includes frequent reinforcement.

Thus, it is fair to conclude that each of the strategies we have studied not only increases the probability of more appropriate socialized behavior, but increases the likelihood of positive perceptions of the self as a by-product. For some students more direct approaches to build positive self-concepts are needed. As a core concept of human personality, self is a complex and elaborate phenomenon. Therefore, we will begin by discussing in more detail the nature of self. We will then note the significance of self-congruence to behavior and finally identify the means by which teachers can influence collective and individual self-concepts.

NATURE OF THE SELF SYSTEM

Few psychologies fail to note or include a sense of self as an important concept of human personality. The history of self psychology dates back to the ancient philosophers. More recently, William James wrote an all-encompassing and thorough treatise on the topic in 1890, at the dawning of modern psychology. During the two decades prior to 1970, over 2000 studies were conducted on the concept of self. The rate of such studies has not decreased.

In spite of (or more realistically, because of) the relatively long history of the self-concept and its importance to such a variety of theories, the term has widely proliferated and has thereby almost lost a specified meaning. Bonjean et al. (1976) reported that during one decade, sociologists alone published 84 articles in four journals and used 55 different instruments to measure the self-concept. The varieties of instruments comprise a problem for us, because in interpreting findings about the self-concept we must ask, "By what measure?" Regardless of what the construct is called, its meaning must be derived in terms of its measurement. If 55 different instruments are used it is apparent that different phenomena are being measured.

Furthermore, an assortment of names has been attached to what are apparently the same phenomenon. Wells and Marwell (1976) point out that self-esteem is often undifferentiated from such terms as self-confidence, self-respect, self-acceptance, self-satisfaction, self-regard, self-worth, a sense of adequacy, a sense of competence, self-ideal, congruence, and ego strength.

In order to establish meaning and continuity for our reference to the self-system, we need to establish a set of meanings and relationships of different aspects of self. Figure 10.1 is a representation of relationships that differentiates awareness and perception of self from non-self.

Self-concept is one of several constructs that characterizes and governs the behavior of each individual. Intelligence, motivation, and cognitive style are other factors that determine the nature of each person. Each person not only acts so as to maintain, enhance, and protect the self-concept, but also evaluates himself. This evaluation generates a sense of goodness and self-esteem and feelings or emotions about the self.

If we are to help our students become prouder and more confident, and in general have a more positive sense of self, we need a clear understanding of some of the components of the self-concept. As already noted, much has been written from diverse points of view about self-concept. We will paraphrase Rosenberg's (1979) interpretation.

COMPONENTS OF SELF-CONCEPT

Each individual gathers information about himself from two mirrored images. One of the images is the product of his behavior. Skills, thoughts,

Figure 10.1. Self-concept as a subordinate and superordinate construct.

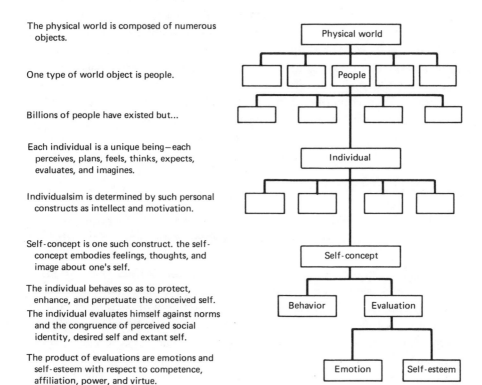

The physical world is composed of numerous objects.

One type of world object is people.

Billions of people have existed but...

Each individual is a unique being—each perceives, plans, feels, thinks, expects, evaluates, and imagines.

Individualsim is determined by such personal constructs as intellect and motivation.

Self-concept is one such construct. the self-concept embodies feelings, thoughts, and image about one's self.

The individual behaves so as to protect, enhance, and perpetuate the conceived self.

The individual evaluates himself against norms and the congruence of perceived social identity, desired self and extant self.

The product of evaluations are emotions and self-esteem with respect to competence, affiliation, power, and virtue.

and actions are reflected in the quality of the products. Thus, one can learn about himself by noting accomplishments. A second image is formulated through feedback from other people. Others react to an individual's acts and products. The reaction is noted and becomes information for knowing and judging the self. Feedback from others is so common and important that most psychologists include perception of other people's perception as one of the three primary components of self-concept. The other components are the person as he would describe himself and as he would like to be. The content of each of these three components is descriptors (e.g., "I think that he sees me as being tall"; "I am tall"; "Tall is a good way to be."). A collection of such self-referent statements constitutes the self-concept. Each of the three components (the perceived social identity, the extant self, and the desired self) will be discussed in some detail.

Perceived Social Identity

People are born with identities that have profound effects on how they live and on their self-concept. At birth each person is quickly classified in such terms as sex, race, nationality, religion, socioeconomic status, place in family, and name. Age is also a perennial marker. Thus, the individual automatically becomes a member of designated groups and is labeled as such. The labels and significance of this grouping will become important parts of the self-concept and remain so throughout life. In the United States to be born a white, male, Anglo-Saxon, Protestant, middle-class person turns out to be fortunate. First, many opportunities and tasks important to society are matched to qualities most often found in such people. Second, the reaction of others is differentiated and favorable to this group. As one example, such a person's identity is heralded in history books, so that he has a ready-made positive identity within his heritage. In contrast, in many areas to be a female and a minority is to have a bad reputation. For example, in California a physically mature 13-year-old girl of minority descent indicated a reticence to appear in public because whenever she went downtown somebody inevitably propositioned her. She was stereotyped as a prostitute independent of her own behavior.

Such labels as "the baby in the family," "Jew," "Italian," and "female" are not only used by others to describe the person but are used extensively, with meaning by the person to define himself. Thus, the labels are important in whatever ways that self-concept is important.

Another aspect of social identity is reputation, allegedly derived from observable behavior. Reputations are labels such as "responsible," "kind," and "good worker," as well as "thief," "lazy," "sexually deviant," and "drug addict." The label may be ascribed from extensive patterns of behavior, one episode, or even rumors without an original behavioral basis. Nevertheless, once labeled, the effects are potent, particularly if the status is deviancy.

Reputations based on behaviors are an important aspect of self-concept. To be a nonidentity, without reputation, is nearly fatal. Each person must feel that he is known to others for something if he is to maintain a sense of completeness.

Self-concept is an immediate phenomenon ("I am"). However, plans and hopes for the future make us feel good in the present. A person can enhance present reputation by including the future ("I am a premed student"). Likewise, through others' expectations, an individual's identity tends to be a product of his past. Once a youngster establishes himself as a good student, a loyal friend, reliable, or a fun guy, things go easier and the general sense of well-being is reflected in his feelings and expectations about himself as well as his behavior. On the other hand if a person has been apprehended for stealing, cheating, or other examples of deviancy, he may develop a reputation as a clown, cheat, liar, or whatever. As these roles become integrated into the self-concept, they tend to be perpetuated through behavior.

Gold (1970) reported that nearly all adolescents at one time or another are guilty of felonious behavior. However, the ones who are apprehended and charged are most apt to be repeaters. This conclusion is based on interviews with 522 males and females between the ages of 13 and 16. The interviewees had been randomly selected from a population of 13,200 adolescents in a large midwestern city.

The findings include the following: Eighty-three percent of the sample were confessed delinquents, that is, they had committed chargeable offenses such as illegal drinking, truancy, running away, fornication, trespassing, entering, false identification and fraud, extortion, robbery, stealing cars, assault, and petty theft. About one-half of the youngsters admitted to four separate offenses.

Such behaviors cannot be ignored. However, the evidence strongly suggests that apprehension and threat or derogation have detrimental behavioral effects. Gold (1970: 106) concludes, "Getting caught by the police had no deterrent effect on youngsters. On the contrary, youngsters who were caught went on to commit more offenses than youngsters who were not caught, no matter what the police did." When the adolescent is caught, he becomes resentful, not remorseful. He doesn't expect to be caught. He knows that others are doing the same thing and getting away with it. The message that seems to come across is not "You are a good person who has done something wrong and therefore you must repent." Rather, it seems to be, "You are a bad person and you had better change or you will be in serious trouble." The threat is contrary to rehabilitation. The shoplifter who is caught and punished is most likely to repeat the act. It seems strange, but recall the evidence in Part I regarding the effects of punishment. Also recall that Glasser (1972) strongly recommended that with problem students we need to begin each day as a new lease on life, ignoring reputation and past deeds. Moving Micky Trobol (see Chapter 7) to Lincoln High School will have rehabilitative potential only if the teachers, other students, and Micky himself can ignore the past and establish a new reputation. Unfortunately, this will not happen automatically and special care will be needed to enable Micky to be "born again." First, his expectancy and habits are pressures for perpetuating old behavioral patterns. He will feel most comfortable continuing with past behaviors and friendships similar to those he established at Washington High School. Also, others will think of him in the present in terms of his past. We tend to label people in the present according to the past as we refer to ex-convicts, high school graduates, war veterans, or divorcees, and then treat the person accordingly.

The presentation of oneself to others is very important, perhaps because of the wish to have friends and lovers to satisfy affiliational needs but also to establish and protect reputations. Regardless of motive a good deal of human behavior seems to be impression management. For example, some teachers present themselves as authorities to be respected and obeyed, while others strive to be "nice guys." Thus, we assume roles that are reflected in our behavior and others' reaction to us. Likewise, some of our troublesome students assume such roles as the swearing, swaggering tough, or the clown who suddenly awakens in the middle of a lesson to the need to make everyone laugh, or the young adolescent who struts and shuffles to display new-found sexuality.

The presentation of self is more than just putting on an act. One of its purposes is self-enhancement—to be liked, accepted, respected and perhaps to keep others from knowing one's feelings about shortcomings. Thus, people assume roles, conform to others' suggestions, and bend to social pressure. A second purpose is to confirm working hypotheses as to who or what one is. The reactions of other people are an important source of information for validating self-images. Adults are confirming the notion of who they are and their qualifications, but youth utilizes the process to test, establish, and shape a developing self-concept.

Much of our student's behavior is thus testing various reflections of identity. In development, the identity is tentative, varied, and sometimes inconsistent. Thus, in a given situation a student may believe himself to be defenseless and act out helplessness. Shortly thereafter, the behavior may shift to represent a betrayed victim of external circumstances who despite the odds will tough it out. Still another time the same student may respond in a carefree manner. It is as if the selves are tried on like clothes in a store, brought out to see how they fit and enhance one's image. In the case of self, the reflecting mirror is the response of others. Thus, the developing person learns who he is by acting out different roles: the fun guy, the intellectual, the tough, the princess, or whatever else seems right. The hardening of particular concepts of self and the respective behavioral manifestations depends on the reaction of others. This feedback from others is not so much reinforcement for behavior management as it is a confirmation of "You are the type of person who . . ." The learner's behavior as such may be less indicative of self-concept than is the reaction of others in formulating the nature of future self-concepts.

Finally, presented behavior may be interpreted as living up to expected social roles. Thus behavior is conforming to the norms established for the person. As already noted, some of these are culturally prescribed by such factors as age, race, sex, and socioeconomic status. Others are more universal, like loyalty to country or loving care for the young. Specific norms are established for particular groups. The society has certain expectations for medical doctors, others for teachers, and different ones for politicians. Within groups, individuals are assigned roles with prescribed behaviors. Thus, in families the youngest child is expected to behave in one way and the eldest in quite another.

Likewise, social groups set up circumstances that seem to force individuals into such roles as wit, scapegoat, source of new ideas, and the enforcer. The individual may resist, feel that such behavior "isn't like me," but then act it out. Thus, the behavior may or may not reflect fundamental self-perceptions, but with confirmation become more integrated with or without satisfaction for the individual.

In concluding these notes on the importance of one's self-presentation, it is worth noting that Dale Carnegie's book, *How to Win Friends and Influence People* (1937), is still in print, has sold nearly seven million copies, and has been translated into virtually every major language. People all over the world are very concerned about creating the right image of themselves in the minds of other people. In so doing, through feedback the right image is also established and confirmed in the first person.

The Extant Self

The term *extant self* refers to the way an individual would describe himself independent of his perception of others' views. Extant self refers to the "I am" responses to such questions as Who are you? What are you? and How are you? or to directives such as "Describe yourself." In addition to the varieties of social identities already listed, individuals describe themselves in terms of competencies, moods, achievements, affiliations, virtues, social behaviors, and physical appearance. The potential list included in such a range of categories could be quite extensive, although for one reason or another students seem to quickly exhaust themselves.

After two or three social identities most pre- and early adolescents focus many of their self-descriptors on physical properties, which strongly suggests that physical image is important to them. It is reasonable to assume that physical characteristics are very important to everyone beyond a relatively early age. Americans allegedly spend more dollars on cosmetics than on education. More than half of plastic surgery is devoted to improving physical appearance. Several studies have shown that five- and six-year-old ethnic minority children show a preference for the physical characteristics of white Anglo Saxons. Moreover, the great majority of people are unhappy about some aspect of their respective physical appearance and would change some physical attribute if given the chance.

Students in the early grades tend to focus on particular competencies ("I am a good runner"; "I can read"; "I don't do so good in cursive writing"). Adolescents often include future education and occupational plans in their self-descriptions.

Teachers are often advised to respond to student misbehavior by differentiating the student from the deed. For example, "I like you, but laughing at other children when they fall is bad." It seems logical that we could thus protest behavior but protect the individual's self-esteem. However, Rosenberg (1979) found that for two-thirds of the students a comment about such things as poor academic performance is not differentiated from comments directly derogatory for the whole person. The sense of self (I, me, mine) is extended to include phenomena beyond the physical self, so that anything said about one's family, bike, clothes, performance, friends, or nationality is a reflection about the person himself. All of the feelings and behavioral reactions that would occur regarding the self are likely to occur when the extended self is involved.

On the other hand, going back to Rosenberg's (1979) finding, one-third of the students did not seem to perceive comments about their school work as comments about themselves. Apparently for these youngsters academic work was not part of the extended self, or at least it had little weight or importance for the self. People differ in what is valued in the self.

An individual might make and believe a wide variety of statements about himself. As noted earlier the dictionary lists about 20,000 adjectives that could be used as self-descriptors. Each of the statements or descriptors differs in importance from others in a variety of ways. Rosenberg (1979) lists nine dimensions that determine the meaning and significance of a given self-reflected statement, "I am . . .":

1. Content refers to whatever aspect of the self he is referring to (e.g., tall, intelligent, or male).

2. Favorable and unfavorable suggest positive or negative feelings regarding given content.

3. Intensity is reflected in the choice of wording. An individual who says "I am a bit shorter than average" doesn't seem to be reflecting the same concern about himself as the person who says "I am just a sawed-off, little shrimp of a person."

4. Salience is a direct indicator of importance of given phenomena. Some elements are at the core of feelings about oneself while others are of minor importance.

5. Consistency refers to internal congruence of feelings, awareness, behavior, and outcomes. That is, optimally the individual consciously acts so as to achieve desired consequences. If desires, behavior, perceptions, and feelings are askew, the effect on the sense of self is confusion.

6. Stability enables the person to know who he is over time and within a variety of circumstances. The stable person possesses a core of views of himself that remain unchanged despite incidental happenings.

7. Clarity indicates the sharpness and degree to which the individual differentiates himself from other phenomena. The use of "sort of" and "kind of" reflects a blurred notion of who and what one is.

8. Accuracy expresses the degree to which the person acknowledges himself. Some distortion about oneself is common and necessary for self-acceptance. However, some persons maintain themselves with a variety of absolute and consistent false impressions.

9. Verifiability is more possible for some elements, such as height and weight, than others, such as morality and likability. Much of our behavior is to verify or confirm our sense of identity. Concrete, specific feedback is needed to build positive self-concepts.

If we are to understand, interpret, or attempt to enhance the self-concept of our students, we must function within the framework of these nine dimensions. In fully reflecting on the meaning of an individual's self-descriptions it is necessary to do so with respect to each of these factors.

The Desired Self

The third component of self-concept is a sense of what "I desire to be." The desired aspect of self-concept in turn is composed of three images: a moral image, an ideal image, and a committed image.

The moral image is the internalization of the cultural mandates of what the good person must, ought, or should be. The content of the moral system as a set of standards is derived from religious training, family morés, peer pressures, and formal education. Although there are common elements, (thou shalt or shalt not), morality is also somewhat idiosyncratic. In addition to not being universal, the moral image is not always logical or consistent. The special significance of the moral image is that when it is violated, the consequence is self-condemnation accompanied by feelings of guilt, depression, and shame. The development of the moral image begins with mandates of "you must . . ." and matures into feelings of obligation "I ought . . ." For some persons the moral image is not clarified. If the mandates were "Be nice," or "Always do the right thing," or "Do as you are told," then the individual is more apt to have generalized anxiety and feel remorseful for falling short.

The idealized self-image is conjured up to free the individual of what he is. He fantasizes himself to be the kindest, the strongest, most beautiful, or the most intelligent person of all. The idealized image represents the ultimate in terms of what the individual would like to be. Each of us has a Walter Mitty within our self-concept. The fantasies provide a break from the humdrum of life, generate good feelings, and establish optimism for the future. The danger comes if the person either spends too much time in the fantasies of ideal self-images or rigidly uses them as standards for judging himself and others.

Both the moral and the ideal self-images are too demanding for realistic, day-to-day functioning. Therefore, most people moderate the desires for self with a more reasonable committed self-image. The committed self-image is best represented by what one expects of himself or seriously hopes to achieve. A ninth-grader might respond with "medical doctor" to the question, "What would you like to be when you are an adult?" If questioned further about what he expects to be, he may then say, "I hope to graduate from high school and get a job at Jones Industry." It is healthier for him to strive and judge himself in terms of committed expectations rather than the fantasies. The healthy personality recognizes this difference early in life, perhaps before starting school. However, some folks never differentiate the three types of desired self and are haunted by the excessive demands of the moral and idealized self.

In conclusion, self-concept is a very personal, complex, and significant perception of a critical object in the lives of all people. The self-concept has three components; the perceived social self, the extant self, and the desired self. The self-concept as defined by these three components is used by the individual as a guide for behavior.

The three components are interrelated in such a way that they must be in balance, congruent with one another. If any of the three components is significantly out of kilter with the other two, the self-system is degenerated.

IMPORTANCE OF INTERNAL CONGRUENCY

Good feelings depend on the congruence of the three elements. If they are significantly disparate or unclarified, then the individual feels shame and disappointment. If they are congruent, then the individual feels pride and joy and will behave accordingly. The task of education is to create conditions that will increase the probability that our students will develop positive, congruent self-concepts.

The issue of congruence is inevitable. Human beings have a strong propensity to evaluate, to judge the goodness of all that is beheld. The most critical target of evaluation is the self.

A person is thought to have a positive self-concept if he makes a preponderance of positive statements about himself. This is the basis of many of the published self-concept measures and studies. However, as we have noted, Rosenburg (1979) pointed out that the significance of a self-referent statement depends on nine distinct factors. Moreover, the degree of congruence within the self may not be reflected in flat statements about the self. Teachers, therefore, would do better to attend to the relationship of the three components of the self-concept. The importance of the internal congruence is emphasized by Fitts and Hammer (1969) in an extensive study of juvenile delinquents.

Although Fitts and Hammer worked primarily with youngsters more deviant than most students, the conclusions are noteworthy. For some of our students the distance between school behavior problems and punishable social deviancy is a short step. Selected relevant findings from the Fitts and Hammer (1969) study are summarized here:

The unique self-concept of the typical public offender can be summarized as follows:

a. His self-concept is negative. He does not like, value, or respect himself, particularly in terms of his basic identity, his own behavior, and his adequacy from a moral-ethical standpoint or as a family member.
b. He is apt to be rather uncertain in his picture of himself.
c. He has difficulty defining himself and is easily influenced by external suggestion. In this sense he is easily influenced by his environment and tends to turn outward for control and evaluation of his own behavior.
d. He does not defensively distort the self-concept he reports. On the contrary, he is often lacking in the kinds of psychological defenses that would enable him to maintain normal self-esteem.
e. His self-concept is confused and characterized by many conflicting and contradictory perceptions of himself.
f. His self-concept is variable and internally inconsistent across the different areas of self-regard.
g. He is markedly lacking in the kind of personality integration, or strength, that would enable him to function effectively in the face of stress, frustration, or external pressure.
h. His self-concept in general indicates much inner tension, dissonance, and discomfort. This is especially true in terms of his self-satisfaction, and his feeling that he is a "bad" person and a poor family member.
i. He is very much at odds with himself and thus it is no surprise that he is also at odds with the world around him. He sees himself as bad and worthless, and he acts accordingly.

The implications include:

Since delinquents do not like, value, respect, or trust themselves, then demeaning, degrading, and overly punitive treatment by society tends to reinforce their self-concepts and perpetuate their antisocial behavior.

Delinquents need firm but fair external controls, but they also need to be treated as individuals of worth and value.

Correctional programs must provide effective behavioral controls but, even more important, delinquents must be helped to discover new, more positive behaviors which will earn more favorable reactions from others and especially from themselves.

Active participation and responsibility by delinquents in the planning and operation of treatment programs is probably essential to the success of the treatment (Fitts and Hammer 1969: Preface, iii).

THE SELF SYSTEM RESISTS CHANGE

One of the prominent characteristics of self-conception is the tendency toward perpetuating stability. Deviations from the ongoing perceptions of self tend to be short-lived. The congruency among the components has an elasticity that tends to maintain the sense of self-identity. If something occurs that would seem to be contrary to one or more of the components of the self-concept, one of several alternatives occurs. The incident may be distorted or explained away (e.g., "It was just a lucky shot" or "You are just saying that"). The veracity of the evidence is tested. We are particularly aware of the troublesome youngster who immediately follows a success or compliment by doing something dumb or antisocial. It is as if he were challenging our tolerance but more often it is just testing to see if what previously happened is real and trustworthy. At any rate there is a strong tendency to revert back to the self-conceptions as they previously existed. For those persons with positive self-esteem who happen to have a bad experience, the rapid return to normalcy is good fortune. For the individual who labors with a poor self-esteem the tendency to revert back to negative behavior shortly after the ecstasy of success is unfortunately discouraging but predictable.

Weiner (1980) reports that students in the same class given feedback of success and failure respond differently. Those with ongoing high self-esteem take credit for successes, thus using it to affirm their competence. If they fail in an exercise, they explain they didn't study hard enough, the teacher goofed, or they were unlucky. Thus, the failure tends to be brushed off. The students with low self-esteem responded to success and failure differently. The failure was accepted as an indication of the lack of ability or a typical pattern of poor preparation, while success was accepted as a fortunate piece of luck or just an easy test.

The point here is that we cannot expect either easy or quick success. Building positive self-esteem requires a multitude of experiences over an extended period of time. Coopersmith and Feldman (1974: 197) sum up the situation:

> Telling children that they are successful, encouraging them to persist, or flattering or rewarding them are all unlikely to increase feelings of self-esteem. Nor do educational innovations that focus on the open classroom or allowing the child complete expressiveness or exploration necessarily foster a positive self-concept or high self-esteem.

Consistent development of positive self-concepts will occur only when teachers establish programs to this particular end.

FACILITATING SELF-ESTEEM

The target is to develop in each student substantive self-esteem. The task is no less momentous than the teaching of reading. For many students a momentum toward positive self-esteem has been established and much of what happens both in and out of school supports the ongoing level of purposeful behavior, positive expectations, persistence, and the resultant pride in self. For others the antithesis of self-esteem exists. The behaviors and expectations that are being perpetuated are self-defeating. It is not an accident that many of those students who experience academic difficulty also exhibit behavioral problems and manifest low self-esteem. A number of studies demonstrate a substantial relationship. Success and positive self-esteem feed and complement one another. Covington and Berry (1976) offer an excellent explanation of success and how failure effects self-esteem. This is a short but well-written exposition of how and why schools enhance and derogate self-worth.

Teachers need to make a concerted effort to enhance both academic achievement and self-esteem. The means for increasing academic achievement can be found in other sources. We will focus our attention on building self-esteem.

Self-esteem is a function of the congruence of the three components of self-concept: the desired self, the perceived social identity, and the extant self. The individual will regard himself negatively if either a wide discrepancy or incongruity exists among the components or if the various components are negative. For a person to have high self-esteem it is necessary that both conditions, congruency and high self-regard, exist. The teacher will ideally arrange experiences whereby each student's desires for self are maintained at a high level, achievement is explicit, and feedback from others is consistent and positive. Our immediate task is to identify means for enhancing self-esteem from the perspective of each of these components. The initial target will be the desired self.

The Establishment of an Operational Desired Self

You will recall that there are three categories within the desired self. The ideal self is composed of the fantasized "wouldn't it be nice" goals. If taken seriously, these far-out ideals would tyrannize the person because they are beyond reason and are insatiable. Likewise, the healthy person tolerates the fact that he does not always live up to the moral self. Whereas the ideal self is derived from fantasy, the moral self is incorporated from parents and religious training. The moral image represents a set of standards, a system of required behavior. If violated, the consequence is self-condemnation. The motive is guilt and shame. The ideal and moral self-image is most apt to be personal and not easily changed. The committed image is a more viable and pertinent target for education.

Richard deCharms (1976: 4) demonstrated in a classic study that the commitment of students is changeable. His assumptions about human nature and the labels he uses are fundamental to both his goals and procedures.

> Man at his best must be active, not reactive; he must strive rather than submit as a puppet. Man must author his own behavior, rather than have it dictated by authority. Man is not a pawn to the dictates of others; at his best man is the origin of his actions. The objective antecedents of a person's behavior may be external events, but to the person *he* is the cause of his behavior when he decides to act from personal commitment. This is *personal causation* and it is our fundamental assumption about motivation. "Man's primary motivational propensity is to be effective in producing changes in his environment. Man strives to be a causal agent, to be the primary locus of causation for, or the Origin of, his behavior; he strives for personal causation."

The dimension of personal causation ranges from feeling that one is the origin of his life, behavior, and the consequences to feeling that he is a pawn manipulated by others at their whim. Whereas the Origin feels that he is in control of his fate, a Pawn feels that he is a puppet and others are pulling the strings. Coleman et al. (1966) found that a sense of destiny control is more powerful in predicting academic success than is any other single personal factor including I.Q., socioeconomic status, race, or sex. DeCharms has shown that Origins are positively motivated, optimistic, confident, and accepting of challenge. Contrariwise, a Pawn is negatively motivated, defensive, irresolute, and avoids challenge. The difference is the feeling of power to control the environment and thereby one's own destiny. The critical difference is that Origins act with commitment and competence.

In constructing an atmosphere conducive to educating Origins, deCharms is not advocating permissiveness, relaxed teacher guidance, or indulgence of student whims. The teachers do not become Pawns in order that students be Origins. The task is for teachers to be Origins while acknowledging and treating students as Origins. The absence of all constraints does not produce freedom, commitment, achievement, or satisfaction—all of which are critical ingredients for becoming an Origin.

DeCharm's underlying concept is *personal causation*. A prison is epitomized by a convict swinging a sledgehammer to break up rocks in a meaningless exercise. Being in prison is devastating not only because of the physical restrictions but because life in prison is purposeless. For many students, particularly those who are behavioral problems, school is a purposeless, meaningless prison. Many students are just there. If assignments are completed it is because teachers force it. An answer is right or wrong because the teacher designated it so. These are examples of external accountability. Arbitrary rules without explanations, busy work that does not require thinking, and motivation by threat of aversive consequences are additional examples of teacher choice and control. Students in all such cases become Pawns because they are treated like Pawns. Pawns typically respond in one of three ways: passive acceptance and conformity, passive resistance, or open rebellion. In any case neither the teacher nor the student feels much joy, satisfaction, commitment, or success.

In contrast, some students attend school with purpose and meaning. These students are committed to well-defined goals and standards. These students are Origins in control of their lives. DeCharms (1976) described a project that enabled a large number of students to become Origins.

DeCharms' project lasted four years. The school was an inner-city junior high. When the project began the teachers spent more time and effort on behavior management than on teaching subject matter. The students came from large families; the average size was more than five children. The homes were not in a slum area but represented low income. About half of the families included two parents.

The first year of the project was spent becoming acquainted with the school, testing the students who were then in the fifth grade, and conducting workshops for teachers. The workshops, which lasted five days, are described in detail by deCharms (1976: ch. 4). They included 21 separate exercises designed to acquaint teachers with various meanings of teacher–student interaction. Real-life problems were discussed and role played along with specially designed exercises. Within some of the exercises teachers were directed and treated in ways not unlike some teachers treat students. In such instances, as expected, the teachers began by carefully following instructions. However, soon many became frustrated, passive, or rebellious. The teachers universally rejected being Pawns.

How can a teacher help students to become Origins? DeCharms (1976: 64–65) offers this thought:

> The fundamental step in helping a person to change is to get him to change himself for reasons that are important to him. If the change is to be genuine and to have lasting effects, the impetus for change must come

from within the person, not be imposed from the outside. To affect a real and lasting change the teacher must nurture the child's desire to improve himself. This process does not happen suddenly.

McClelland (1965: 327), a foremost authority on achievement motivation, adds the following:

> The more an individual can perceive and experience the newly conceptualized motive as an improvement in his self-image, the more the motive is likely to influence his future thoughts and actions.
>
> Changes in motives are more likely to occur in an interpersonal atmosphere in which the individual feels warmly but honestly supported and respected by others as a person capable of guiding and directing his own future behavior.

The deCharms project alerts us to the conclusion that altering self-concepts and motives is not an offhand task. Just as the study of reading, mathematics, history, and science requires extensive and varied experiences, so does the rehabilitation of self-concept. The deCharms project included five curricular units that extended over parts of two years. The respective units were called "The Real Me," "Stories of Success and Achievement," "The Spelling Game," "Person Perception Training," and "The Origin Manual."

The "Real Me" unit was designed to help each student define himself as a unique, valuable person. Each student created a book in which the hero or heroine was himself. Each week for 11 weeks a given topic, such as "The Kind of Person I Want To Be" or "The Ways I'm Different," was discussed daily and then on Friday everyone wrote a chapter based on personal experience. The written content was supplemented by photos, self-portraits, poems, and personal artifacts that illustrated the focus of the particular chapter.

The objective of "Stories of Success and Achievement" was to describe success as the product of planning, perseverance, and overcoming obstacles. In order to orient students they were encouraged to read and create stories that emphasized competition, unique accomplishments, and long-term involvement. The stories emphasized meeting standards of excellence and the pleasure of achievement. Achievement was not only stressed in the plots, but stories were evaluated against student-developed criteria and then rewritten to meet the criteria. When the criteria were met the author was applauded by student judges. In addition, 15 achievement-oriented words were suggested, defined, and discussed by the students each week.

"The Spelling Game" utilized the ongoing curriculum. In addition to improving spelling practices this unit encouraged students to establish clear, realistic goals. Atkinson and Raynor (1974) report several studies that demonstrate that the academic goal of many students is simply to avoid failure. This phenomenon is particularly true of those students who have a history of school failure. Fear of failure is the antithesis of achievement. Students avoid failure by clowning around, forgetting work materials, not understanding the assignment, and otherwise avoiding the task.

The objective of this unit is for students to set reasonable goals that reflect a good but not absolute probability of success. The achievement of the goal ought to be a self-imposed challenge. Goals for students are too often set by parents and teachers.

The weekly spelling lessons were selected from a standard sixth-grade spelling book. The lessons were taught within a standard procedure except that a spelling bee was substituted for the weekly test. Each student was a member of one of two standing teams. Spelling words were in three categories. Category 1 was composed of words previously spelled correctly. Category 2 contained the words from the current list. Category 3 was composed of difficult words from advanced lists. When a student spelled a word correctly, his team received a number of points depending on the chosen category. Each student selected a category (goal) from which he wanted his week's spelling words to be drawn. If the goal was too easy, the team did not sufficiently benefit. Likewise, if the goal was beyond the student's success, the team suffered. Within a few weeks all students were selecting goals appropriate to their spelling skills. Once the activity objectives were achieved, however, the game continued because the students were enthusiastic about spelling, and teachers did not want to lose the effect. Students continued to tutor one another and spelling achievement increased, a happy consequence for everyone.

The purpose of the Person Perception Training Unit was to enable students to identify their own and others' feelings and motives in a variety of situations. Students were asked to respond to open-ended questions, role play situations, write stories, create a person based on some sketchy information, and present opposing points of view in vignettes. Stories searched to find examples of interacting people who were mutually responsible and caring for one another.

The Origin Manual was a personal daily record maintained by each student of how he behaved as an Origin. Twenty-five exercises, one for each day, were included to guide the students' thinking and to focus attention on different aspects of origin behavior. Both students and teachers valued this experience, so it was also continued after the project ended. Many students took the manual home to work on it after school, and one boy who had been expelled took the manual with him and later returned to show the teacher how well he was progressing toward being an Origin.

The most dramatic consequence of this systematic curriculum for personal growth was a sharp increase in behaviors and scale scores that reflected that students felt in control of their fate, that the cause of their behavior is within themselves. The origin scores for those who participated for one year doubled, for those who participated for two years the score tripled, while scores for nonparticipants remained unchanged. This factor of personal responsibility is not only critical for self-esteem as defined by Coopersmith (1981), but foremost in our goals of discipline. Although the academic results were not as dramatic, those who participated in the program were significantly superior in basic skills as compared to the control group. The typical regression in achievement scores was reversed, although the students did not attain grade equivalence. Most important perhaps, attendance, attitude toward school, and teacher–student relations all significantly improved.

The Enhancement of the Perceived Social Identity

One of the cornerstones of self-concept theory is the proposition that a person more or less unconsciously sees himself as he thinks others see him. The proposition needs clarification with respect to who "others" refers to, and what determines the "more or less" potency. Obviously, some persons' views are more important than others. Likewise, some feedback would have more effect than others.

Rosenberg (1979) and his associates interviewed 1917 students from Baltimore schools in order to clarify these and other issues. The students were selected randomly, except that care was taken to appropriately represent students with respect to race, economic status, and grade level.

First, the interviews did confirm the notion that the self-esteem of a person reflects whether or not he cares what others think of him. Although some students indicated they didn't care what others thought, these students tended to have lower self-esteem. Second, parents were found to be the most significant "other" people. While 84 percent of the students indicated that they cared very much what their mothers thought of them, only 30 percent indicated that they cared as much about what the other kids in class thought of them. The relative importance of "my parents care for me" is not limited to elementary students but extends to those in secondary schools as well. Other studies have shown that junior high school students indicate a comparable level of concern. From a slightly different perspective Englander (1965) asked 229 high school students to rank order the persons they would most likely confer with if confronted with a variety of problems. Parents ranked number one over peers, clergy, teachers, counselors, and other people in the neighborhood for such problems as making a personal decision; getting out of trouble; learning to do the right thing; understanding religion; and understand oneself. Only in the case of specific problems, such as finding out about school activities, or getting a better grade in a class one is failing, did peers and teaches surface as more popular sources.

An important factor that moderates the importance of what others think is whether the student believes that others' opinions are positive or negative. The importance of mothers' opinions ranged from 64 to 91 percent, depending on whether the opinion was unfavorable or favorable. In the same categories the range was 38 to 81 percent for teachers and 13 to 52 percent for classmates. This data offers a good basis for establishing a program for raising self-esteem.

To summarize, parents, particularly mothers, are valuable educational allies. Students highly valued their mother's views and concerns. Feedback from parents is most likely to be incorporated into self-concepts. In addition, feedback is more potent if positive. Apparently, corrective messages or unfavorable comments are discounted as unimportant by the self-protecting perceptions of the individual. Feedback from others is more valued, and more likely to be incorporated into the self if it is favorable and from significant people.

Contrary to common assumptions, feedback from peers may not be as potent as is positive information from parents and teachers. Of course social acceptance and friendship are important—it is more fun to do things with peers. But adults remain the most valid source for "How am I doing?" The Rosenberg data confirms the notion that peers help satisfy the need for affiliation and thereby influence interests and social behavior. However, inner qualities are worked out by the individual, and feedback from valued adults plays a prominent role. Teachers would do well if they sent positive messages to parents and let the parents deliver the "You are a good person and I am proud of you because you . . ." messages. For some students a selected teacher or counselor could best serve this role.

One of the questions Rosenberg asked students was, "What is it, that the person(s) who know you best know that others do not know?" The 8–9-year-olds predominantly responded in terms of external observable phenomena: behaviors, achievements, preferred activities, and physical characteristics. However, the 14 and older adolescents most often identified inner feelings and thoughts, interpersonal attitudes and interests. Rosenberg concluded that the younger child's self-concept is composed of concrete external visible characteristics while the adolescent thinks of himself in terms of a variety of internal personality traits. If a teacher is to be a significant source for strengthening self-esteem, care must be taken to focus on those elements critical to the individual. The elementary teacher may be of the most help with such statements as, "Your cursive writing has improved so much and your papers are neat and clean." However, the secondary teacher needs to focus on the more complex and abstract inner dispositions. The focus needs to shift toward such reference as, "You seem to be aware of people's feelings. I've noticed that you focus on that very often." Moreover, the task for adolescents becomes one of sorting out and integrating thoughts, feelings, wishes, fantasies, interpersonal feelings and attitudes, aspirations, concerns, and secrets. Feedback is optimal when it is nondirective, resonating with the student's expressed inner experience. The secondary teacher needs to be an acute interpersonal communicater. In Chapter 4, a number of communication roadblocks were contrasted with the trust-building communication processes. Feedback for enhancing self-esteem will most likely be effective if couched in trust-building communication.

From a different perspective Staines (1958) observed teachers interacting with their students. The teachers were categorized as positive or negative, depending on the way they responded to students regarding performance, status, values, desires, and overt behavior. For example, in an instance where one teacher might say, "Frankie, you can't do that, you're too small," another teacher would say, "Frankie, you have such a good reach that I'll bet if you stood on that box you could get the books off of the top shelf." The positive teachers on the average gave five positive statements for each negative one, while the negative teachers gave an equal number of positive and negative statements. The positive teachers focused on self-direction about six times more frequently than did the negative teachers. The negative teachers gave three times as many desist messages as did the positive teachers. Finally, the positive teachers focused on positive student values and aspirations significantly more frequently than did the negative teachers.

The effect of the positive teachers on their students was notable. Students described themselves more positively, perceived themselves as more honest, more willing to try more difficult tasks, and more self-directive. The students of the positive teachers not only described themselves more positively but indicated more precisely who they were.

All teachers can utilize the curriculum and special projects to upgrade self-esteem as noted in the values clarification section of Chapter 6. Several sources are also available for elementary teachers, such as Canfield and Wells (1974), Bessel and Palomares (1970), and Ginott (1972).

A good example of an elementary teacher acting so as to build positive self-esteem is illustrated by this case. Nicola Long noted that three of her second-graders were continually excluded by other students. The three isolates were slow, unskilled, socially shy, and often described themselves negatively, starting many sentences with "I can't." Nicola found two or three games that required some unique although not-too-difficult foot movements. While the other students were busily playing social games at recess, Nicola took the three isolates back into the classroom and taught them the footwork necessary to play the games. After the three students had mastered the skills, the games were introduced to the rest of the class. Immediately some of the bolder students volunteered to show how the game should be played. Just as Nicola had anticipated, the footwork was unique enough so that even the better students had some difficulty. The isolates were then asked to demonstrate the game, and much to everyone's surprise they played the game very well. The isolates beamed with pride and the other children responded positively. That was the beginning, and after several such engineered victories Nicola long concluded that she had significantly improved three lives.

Long's strategy would be inappropriate for older students. However, Rosenberg (1979) reported that 73 percent of the 16 year-old and older respondents indicated that they valued interpersonal traits above all else, and another 18 percent indicated that such traits were the most important qualities that they lacked. People need people, and the adolescent is fully aware of this. The specified traits include friendliness and liking people, as well as attractiveness, likability, and pleasant and pleasing attitude. Teachers can best help students develop a sense of social acceptance by helping them to feel liked and likable. Skill development in the art of self-presentation would be appreciated, serve our purposes of more appropriate classroom behavior, and probably result in more positive self-concepts.

Try your hand. Respond as did the teacher of the untouchable and share your ideas with others.

THE UNTOUCHABLE

The bus pulled up to the lane to the run-down house that was visible in the distance. Two or three children boarded, but attention focused on Virginia, a 15-year-old girl. As she sat down in a seat that seemed reserved for her, someone yelled, "Untouchable." The driver frowned and raised his eyebrows, his mouth showed disgust, but he said nothing and he drove on. At the next stop, several children boarded, but no one sat next to Virginia.

That afternoon in math class the students were asked to go to the board by rows and demonstrate the solutions to assigned math problems. After Virginia's row finished and the next group approached, one of the girls advised the rest of the group, "Don't touch that eraser or chalk—she touched them." Earlier in the day Virginia had told a boy, "Don't touch that, it's untouchable," with regard to a library book she had read and laid down.

To better understand what is happening, perhaps we ought to read the math teacher's description of Virginia: "She is perhaps the most disdainful person I have ever seen. It is not just that she is homely. She is filthy—she wears her clothes until they fall off of her. No doubt she sleeps in them; they are never washed. One can just see the stains pile up on one another. Her hair is not only unwashed but never combed. She smells (stinks is more appropriate). She not only has body odor, but with garlic and no tooth brushing, she often has very bad mouth odor as well. Finally, her language is foul—profane and seemingly unaffected by punishment."

The situation came to a head when in the math class one of the students started to pick up a pencil from the desk. Ms. Carriage said, "Don't touch that, it . . ." She then gasped, realizing that she had almost said "because it belongs to the Untouchable." She had frequently reprimanded the pupils for saying such things and here she almost did it herself.

At that moment Ms. Carriage decided to change Virginia's life style. The question is, how? (Referrals to the school nurse or counselor are inappropriate. The task is yours to achieve.)

Sharpening the Focus of the Extant Self

When people refer to the self-concept they tend to refer to the self as if it were a global identity. To think of the self as a collection of specific subselves is more appropriate. For example Weinstein and Fantini (1970: 114) suggest: "The self can be thought of as a cast of characters, all playing different roles, whose interaction with one another constitutes a unified self-image."

We have already established the principle of a three-component self-concept made up of the desired self, the perceived social identity, and the extant self. Within and across these three components are a number of sub-categories, developed around roles and tasks. Thus, a person respectively may have self-concepts as a student, member of a family, athlete, church member, club member, friend, and employee. For each of these subselves the individual has the desired, perceived social, and extant selves. Depending on the dominance of a given role in the life of a person, the respective subself may or may not be a significant part of the global self. The significance of subselves is twofold: (a) Different people may have positive self-concepts based on completely different subself concepts. All students need not compete in the same arena. We can build positive self-concepts for different people in different arenas. (b) If we are to measure or build positive self-concepts we need to do so with respect to the dominant or unique combinations of self-concepts for the individual. This would suggest that for each person with whom we are targeting self-concept development, we would need to ascertain the status of different subself concepts with respect to each of the nine dimensions listed earlier in this chapter.

In the extant self-component the teacher ought to strive to encourage students to view themselves as a composite of subselves, with special attention to increasing the favorability, intensity, salience, consistency, stability, clarity, accuracy, and verifiability of each. The critical elements in each case are feelings of power, competence, belonging, and virtue.

We should probably begin with those elements in which the individual has natural strengths. As the individual becomes more confident in those areas, the impact will generalize to other areas, those more highly valued by the institutions of education. We don't have to do this for everyone and we don't have to do it alone. If each teacher focuses on three students, as did Nicola Long, and enlists the aid of other teachers and the parents, the task becomes more reasonable.

Weinstein and Fantini (1970: 75) describe a program designed to alter the plight of the 10–11-year-old students described at the beginning of the chapter. The process and the results are enlightening.

> It was our conviction that a sense of connectedness [a sense of belonging] was prerequisite for the development of stronger feelings of potency in these children. In classrooms where there is little connectedness and much competition, only a few children—the leaders—can ever gain a feeling of potency; the rest of the class feel powerless. However, even the few leaders in the class under observation did not seem to feel powerful. The tenuousness of their position, their need for connectedness, and their narrow definition of power precluded this.

We hypothesized that a connected classroom situation would encourage the development of a positive self-concept and a sure sense of power in each of the students.

The task was to encourage each student to become aware of the strategies he was using that may in fact have limited his potency and self-identity. Second, students were to identify and develop or expand strategies for the purpose of gaining power and identity.

Weinstein and Fantini offer a number of excellent, proven strategies to improve identity for students of all age levels. It is a worthwhile sourcebook.

Several studies have demonstrated that student self-concept progressively deteriorates as the students move from one grade level to the next. The grades four through eight seem to be particularly devastating. It is tempting to blame the schools and dehumanizing treatment for this common trend. No doubt, some students do suffer from school-related experiences. However, it is quite probable that the general decline in self-esteem is attributable to more natural events.

The Rosenberg (1979) study enables us to pinpoint some elements of these changes in self-concept. Students were asked to identify those characteristics they deemed to be important: Smart, good-looking, good at sports, well-behaved, hard-working, helpful, and honest were listed. Each student then rated himself with respect to his identified list of good characteristics. The difference between "valued" and "I am" was notable and increased with age through adolescence.

Between the ages of 11 and 15, favorable ratings of self dropped 21 percent, 16 percent, 32 percent, and 14 percent, respectively, in smartness, truthfulness, level of effort in school work, and helpfulness. Rosenberg (1979) also found sharp changes between these ages with respect to increased self-consciousness, low global self-esteem, depression, and instability of self-image. Rosenberg notes that during puberty, adolescents undergo rapid, radical changes in physical appearance, muscle and bone development, the nature and quantity of the body's biochemistry, intellect, and social expectations. Since the person changes so dramatically it is no wonder that self-concept should also be diffused and uncertain. Those of us working with students must be sensitive and tolerant of this breakdown, which is natural and nearly universal. An adversary position can only cause these conditions to worsen. During this period more than any other, trust and communication are imperative. Furthermore, we need to offer a curriculum that includes clear, positive feedback, opportunities to clarify the various aspects of the desired self, and experiences on which positive extant self-description can be based.

Self-efficacy, the Expectation of Success

When we observe another person behaving in ways contrary to achieving the common goals of friendship, good grades, the favor of authorities, or other accomplishments, we tend to assume disinterest in goals. Bandura (1977) points out that most often the goals are valued, but that the individuals don't strive to develop and utilize the behavioral skills for affiliation and achievement because they don't believe they are able to perform in the necessary manner. That is, one of the necessary requisites for any performance is the expectation that one can perform effectively. Bandura calls this an *efficacy expectation.* This expectation is closely tied to self-esteem. If an individual believes that he is unable to behave in whatever ways necessary to obtain his goals, then he feels powerless. The individual anticipates failure and is inhibited from putting forth effort. Thus, efficacy expectations determine how much effort people will expend and how much they will persist to attain their desired goals. In this sense, then, the task of building self-esteem is one of enabling the individual to expect that he can behave in ways that will achieve what he wants.

Bandura and others have examined four ways in which a teacher might alter the efficacy expectations (and thereby achievements) of individuals, as a way of building more positive self-concepts. The four means are through performance accomplishments, the vicarious experiences of seeing others perform, verbal persuasion (such as "Give it a try," or "I know you can do it"), and emotional arousal. Direct performance accomplishment is by far the most successful in developing a sense of "I can." Repeated success is a critical vehicle for building the underlying expectations that lead to a more positive self-esteem.

SUMMARY

The terms with which an individual perceives and describes himself are critical determinants for his overt behavior, achievements, interpersonal relations, and sense of happiness. Success, in any sense of the word, depends on the quality of one's self-concept.

The foundations of self-concept are established before youngsters begin formal education. However, the processes of schooling have much to contribute. (a) Self-esteem, the judgment of worth of oneself, is based on the individual's perception of his virtues, his competence, his belonging, his power to control his own destiny, and other behaviors. Each of these is powerfully influenced by the environment arranged by teachers. (b) The criterion by which the individual judges himself is his desired self. The desired self is composed of an idealized self, a moral self, and a committed self. The committed self, composed of expectations, is to a great degree dependent on achievements within the school setting. Reasonable, positive expectations with respect to behavior, achievement, and personal relationships develop out of experience. Furthermore, we learn to value those things in which we are successful. (c) Adults, parents, and teachers are valued sources of feedback by which students know themselves. The most productive process is to accentuate explicit achievements and then generalize expectations of the positive "I can" and "I am" type to broader areas. (d) Radical changes due to natural causes occur in the self-concept during the school years. Changes in cognition, the biochemical balance within the body, physical changes, a more demanding curricula, and changing morés are disruptive forces. These forces can be utilized for greater insight, increased competence, and more power for controlling consequences, or they can be overwhelming.

The changes are inevitable and fortunate because they are critical for the maturing process. Whether the effects will be positive or negative for the individual depends on the quality of experience we arrange.

RECOMMENDED READINGS

Canfield, J. and Wells, J. *100 ways to build self concept in the classroom.* Englewood Cliffs, NJ: Prentice Hall, 1976.

de Charms, R. *Enhancing motivation.* New York: Irvington, 1976.

Felker, D.W. *Building positive self concepts.* Minneapolis, MN: Burgess, 1974.

Purkey, W. *Inviting school success: A self concept approach to teaching and learning.* Belmont, CA: Wadsworth, 1984.

PART III

POTPOURRI

Each of the five major strategies studied thus far has focused on the student and his behavior. The alternatives to punishment offer explicit means for intervening in the conflict cycle. The purpose of each is twofold: to increase appropriate student behavior and to enhance student self-esteem.

Two important aspects of discipline do not naturally fit in the conflict cycle because they are external to the individual. However, knowledge and skills with respect to each will contribute to our ability to successfully conduct our educational program. Both will help us with potential discipline problems. Assertiveness, the key concept of Chapter 11, focuses on teacher power and the judicious means for attaining and preserving the rights of both teachers and students. Organization, as it relates to the school, the community, and the classroom, offers important means for helping students to focus their energies on productive activities. Chapter 12 details the means for incorporating important organizational strategies into educational activities.

Chapter 13 illustrates that the many strategies discussed in this text really do work in schools.

11

ASSERTIVENESS: INSISTING ON THE RIGHT TO TEACH

THE TEACHER'S PERSPECTIVE

Teachers can neither achieve their educational goals nor maintain a sense of sanity unless they possess the power to appropriately control and influence the educational environment. The sense of power rests on the teacher's claim to certain personal rights and establishing the conditions to guarantee these rights. The process is assertiveness.

The Teacher's Charge

Each teacher is responsible for the destiny of his classroom. This destiny must not be controlled by the impulses of students or the mandates of others. Being a teacher does not give an individual wanton power to do whatever he pleases. The teacher, like everyone else, functions within parameters. However, in commissioning a teacher, society gives a charge to help the young generation develop a number of designated skills, become socially adept, understand the nature of the universe, and solidify a direction in life. Along with this amorphous charge the teacher is given considerable autonomy. The teacher is expected to achieve the ends and is given considerable freedom to do so. The point of academic freedom and tenure is to protect teacher rights so that he can properly fulfill his obligations. The freedom is not only a guard against intrusion from outside the classroom, but from student dissipation of time and energy within the classroom. The freedom, however, is only maintained if teachers assertively demand it as a right.

Assertiveness: The Means for Taking Charge

Assertiveness was initially suggested by Wolpe (1969) as a behavior modification technique for reducing anxiety. People complained that they often felt anguish following interactions with others. Self-recrimination seemed to follow episodes in which the individual either felt that he gave in to the demands of others and thus subjugated himself to their will, or contrariwise, berated and thus alienated others.

Although there are few references to assertiveness prior to 1969, the 1970s, with its strong feminist movement, spawned a number of books. The titles are indicative of the flavor of assertiveness: *Your Perfect Right; How to Become an Assertive (Not Aggressive) Woman in Life, in Love and on the Job; Stand Up, Speak Up, Talk Back; Don't Say Yes when You Want to Say No; I Can if I Want To.* The antithesis of assertiveness is illustrated by the title *Winning through Intimidation,* which was popularized during the same era.

Counselors and psychotherapists have been the strongest advocates of assertiveness. However, Canter and Canter (1976) and Silberman and Wheelan (1980) have been widely acclaimed for their materials to assist teachers to become more assertive.

Teacher assertiveness pays off. Fiordaliso et al. (1978) observed the classrooms of 12 elementary teachers and 13 middle-school teachers. The percentage of student time on-task was ascertained for each teacher. In addition, each teacher completed a questionnaire that measured the degree to which the teacher acted so as to maintain his rights. Student time on-task and the scores on the Teacher Assertiveness Scale correlated at 0.43. Although 0.43 is not a perfect cause–effect reflection, there are few specific things that a teacher can do that offer better probabilities. Although only testimonials are offered as evidence, Canter and Canter (1976) alleged that 20,000 teachers have undertaken their program, and illicit student behavior reportedly decreased by 80 percent.

TEACHER RIGHTS

The overriding task of assertive discipline is the pursuit of the following teacher rights (Canter and Canter 1976: 2):

1. The right to establish a classroom structure and routine that provides the optimal learning environment in light of your own strengths and weaknesses.

2. The right to determine and request appropriate behavior from the students which meets your needs and encourages the positive social and educational development of the child.

3. The right to ask for help from parents, the principal, etc., when you need assistance with a child.

The noted teacher rights are simple and reasonable. The complex nature of teaching requires the support of other teachers, school administrators, and parents. The purpose of this chapter is to develop the skills to enable us to obtain that support.

ASSERTIVENESS CONTRASTED

Behaviors are typically classified along a bipolar continuum. A teacher has good or poor discipline. Classrooms are permissive or authoritarian. The continuum is acknowledged, but even so events and judgments tend to occur at the ends of the scale. The nature of assertiveness is tripolar. A teacher may establish situations or respond to others by being nonassertive, hostile, or assertive. Each of the three modes of behavior is distinct, with differentiating properties. We are primarily interested in assertiveness, but its characteristics will be better understood and practiced if we consider it in juxtaposition to the other two poles.

Nonassertiveness

In being nonassertive the teacher abdicates his rights. For example, on the first of October Mr. Bane set the due date and the criteria for a major project to be completed by Friday, October 28. Class time was devoted to the project, and intermittent reminders were given. However, just before class on October 28 two students requested extra time to finish their projects. Mr. Bane responded, "Well, I don't think I should do that. It wouldn't be fair to the other students." The two students looked hurt and stomped off. Mr. Bane felt uncomfortable, as if he had been overly harsh and unreasonable. Just as soon as everyone was seated, several hands were raised. When called on, one of the students apologetically asked, "Mr. Bane, can we please hand in our papers Monday? We had a basketball game last night and I just couldn't finish my paper." Another student chipped in, "I could hand my project in now, but if I have until Monday I could do a much better job. You want us to do a good job, don't you, Mr. Bane?"

It seemed that 8 to 10 students were asking for a delay. Although it put Mr. Bane behind schedule, he acquiesced. "Okay, Monday is the absolute deadline." Later Mr. Bane complained to a colleague about student irresponsibilities. "They always push for something extra. They just count on the teachers giving in. They make me so angry."

Mr. Bane was nonassertive on four accounts. First, although he took a reasonable position he felt uncomfortable because the students reacted emotionally. He turned their feelings on himself. Second, he copped out by saying, "It wouldn't be fair to other students." Late papers are a violation of the teacher's rights. It has nothing to do with the other students. Third, he submerged his rights for the convenience of others. The students were manipulative and he reinforced them. He not only cheated himself but the students as well when he failed to force them to manage their own affairs within the parameter of the assignment contract. Finally, in griping to a colleague he expressed his feelings to the wrong person. Moreover, he blamed the students for his acts of abdicating responsibility for his rights. If the colleague agrees, "Yes, students aren't what they used to be," Mr. Bane will feel okay again because the colleague's response assures Mr. Bane that it is the students, not he, who are weak and irresponsible.

Hostility

Hostility is not a right. When a teacher is hostile, no one wins. Let's assume that Mr. Cane had given the same assignment with identical detail and opportunities as did Mr. Bane. However, when the students asked for extra time to finish the project he curtly replied, "Absolutely not! The papers are due today and that is that." The students moved meekly to their seats. When the tardy bell rang Mr. Cane said, "Mary and Sam wanted more time to finish the project because they goofed around instead of doing their work. There is no place in this world for irresponsible people. Those of you who have completed your work as scheduled pass your projects forward." (pause) "Anyone who has not passed their papers in will automatically be docked one full grade for each day or part thereof that the project is late. Now let's get on with our work." It is most likely that at least Mary and Sam will spend much of the hour sulking.

How was Mr. Cane hostile? Anyone has a right to express his needs and wants, but Mr. Cane abused those of the students, particularly Sam and Mary's. By publicly degrading them Mr. Cane denied them their rights. Second, he in no way acknowledged the proper behavior of those students who complied and did as required. Third, the consequence, "lose one grade for each day or part thereof" seemed an arbitrary and after-the-fact penalty. If we want students to make decisions to act one way or another based on positive and negative consequences, then it is better if they know the nature of the consequences beforehand. Finally, it did not appear that Mr. Cane allowed the students to express their needs and desires. A teacher has not acquiesced if he listens when students make requests or express desires. However, if he refuses to listen or does not encourage students to express their views he is being hostile. Each person, no matter his status or age, has both the right and obligation to indicate his views and needs.

Student Rights

To clarify the rights of others Canter and Canter (1976) list the following as student rights:

1. Have a teacher who is in a position to and will help the child limit his inappropriate self-disruptive behavior,
2. Have a teacher who is in the position to and will provide the child with positive support for his appropriate behavior, and
3. Choose how to behave and know the consequences that will follow.

A fourth condition is warranted.

4. Have a right to open, honest communication during which both students and teacher have an opportunity to express their respective feelings, thoughts, desires, and needs.

Assertiveness

The appropriate alternative to nonassertive permissiveness and hostile authoritarianism is assertiveness. Let's assume that Mr. Sane was also confronted with the request of two students before class. He replied, "I am very willing to listen to your thoughts on this, but I want to remind you that the criteria and due dates have been set for two weeks. I plan to evaluate your projects and give your feedback Monday so we can move on to new work Tuesday."

Mary: Most of the students do not have their projects completed.
Mr. Sane: I'll be collecting the papers in just a moment.

Sam: We just didn't have enough time. That was a very tough project.
Mr. Sane: Um-hum.

The bell rang and Mr. Sane said to the class, "Our projects are due today and from past experience I know that it is best to collect them now, before we begin today's work. Will you please pass your papers forward." As he collected the papers Mr. Sane continued, "I know this was a challenging project. I want you to know that I'm pleased that you finished it. I'm looking forward to reading and reacting to your work." Several students raised their hands and Mr. Sane nodded to Jon.

Jon hesitated. "Uh-huh, like you said, Mr. Sane, this is a challenging project and I want to do a good job on it, so, ah, could I have until Monday so that I can really do my best?"

Mr. Sane: The papers are due today, I don't understand.
Jon: I want to work some more on my project and hand it in Monday.
Mr. Sane: I understand what you want, Jon. I don't understand why you aren't meeting the due date.
Jon: I want to do an extra special job on this project.
Mr. Sane: I am pleased to hear that. I want students to do as well as possible on all of their work, but that is not a matter of extra time. We have had two weeks on this project.
Jon: Well, ah, there was a very important basketball game last night and we just had to go.
Mr. Sane: Your paper wasn't completed, but you decided to go to the game rather than finish the project?
Jon: Well, yes. What is the penalty if we hand it in Monday?
Mr. Sane: It is not a matter of penalty. I want to read and return the projects Monday. That is why we set the deadline. You have to do the project and I do not want to wait until Monday. I can drop by the school tomorrow. I will pick up your work at noon tomorrow. It is up to you to get it in the school mailbox by that time.
Jon: Gee, tomorrow is Saturday. Who wants to do school work on Saturday?
Mr. Sane: Jon, it would seem that you made that decision last night. It is understood that everyone who did not complete and hand in the project must put it in the school mailbox by noon tomorrow. [Mr. Sane paused] Jon, I want to make certain that we understand one another, what are you and I going to do about the papers?
Jon: We have to finish the projects and get them to the school mailbox by noon Saturday so you can pick them up.
Mr. Sane (smiles and nods): Okay, let's get on with today's work.

It is not likely that Jon and the others are happy. However, they know that they have been treated fairly, reasonably, and honestly.

Principles of Assertiveness

Assertiveness differs from nonassertiveness and hostility in a number of ways. Mr. Sane did the following:

1. He established what he wanted and needed and why this was important to him.
2. He backed up what he wanted by action. He stipulated what he was going to do.
3. He set limits clearly and explicitly by indicating what he wanted students to do.
4. He resisted student manipulation.
5. He responded positively to those students who had behaved appropriately.
6. He did not blame students for their errant behavior.
7. He listened to the students. He made it clear that he heard them and what he understood to be the situation.
8. He was consistent without being rigid.
9. He was nonpunitive in the sense of retribution. The stipulation of turning the papers in on Saturday at noon was based on reason. Students having to do school work on Friday night and Saturday morning was a natural consequence of their not working Thursday night.
10. He made certain that the students understood what he wanted, what he would do, and what they were to do.

The assertive teacher clearly communicates what he feels, why he feels that way, what he wants, and what he will do. He makes certain that students understand his communication. He also strives to encourage and listen to student-expressed needs and takes care to support their rights. An abbreviated definition of assertiveness is the old adage, say what you mean and mean what you say, but do not be mean.

The assertive teacher is not rigid; sometimes he must alter or revise rules to accommodate realistic counter-conditions. Nevertheless, as a rule of thumb the teacher ought to be explicit, firm, and consistent. On occasion the teacher's wants and needs may be incongruent with those of others. If the respective wants are incompatible then one or the other must compromise his position. This is necessary and understandable. It must also be understood that the decision is bilateral and reciprocal. In an apparent stalemate situation the assertive teacher might respond as follows when he discovered that he and two colleagues have scheduled important tests on the same day: "Our respective wants are incompatible. We have all planned major examinations on the same day. Three tests on the same day is not fair to the students, so I'll change mine. However, if this happens in the future I assume that a different arrangement will be made."

The Assertive Message

To sum up, assertiveness is the process by which a teacher communicates the following messages:

I care too much for you as a person to ignore the things you are doing that are self-destructive and that will lead to an unhappy and unproductive life.

I care too much for the ideals, objectives, and processes of education to allow you to disrupt our activities and thereby deny others the chance to learn.

I care too much for civilized society based on the protection of individual rights and government by rules to ignore abuse of these rights and rules.

I care too much for myself to sacrifice my desires and needs or to subjugate myself to either the system or other peoples' desires.

The task is to learn to convey these attitudes through our actions and words. The teacher does not unilaterally control all that happens in the classroom. However, teachers are the nominal leaders and it behooves us to establish and communicate the rules and conditions that give meaning to these messages.

Table 11.1 puts nonassertiveness, assertiveness, and hostility in juxtaposition so that we may better understand their respective natures.

SCHOOL AS A RULE-GOVERNED SOCIETY

Every aspect of society is governed by rules. Each organization, game, group, and activity has its own idiosyncratic set of rules. In no instance are we totally free of constraints. If an individual loses control in a blind rage, the ongoing processes are suspended until the individual returns to sanity or is removed. In most instances the rules are understood by the participants and it is unnecessary to specify the *dos* and *don'ts*. Through natural home experiences, play with peers, and observations most children learn that rules are a necessary basis for fairness and that activities are more enjoyable with rules. They understand the nature of rules. The students who come to our schools are experienced at abiding by rules and recognize that schools, like everything else, function according to rules. Furthermore, by their occasional appropriate behavior they demonstrate they understand the prevailing rules and can abide by them. However, some students have learned to be manipulative, think that they are exceptions or that rules are only to be followed as a last resort, or don't understand the particular rules in a given situation—thus the need for assertive teachers.

Table 11.1. A Framework for classifying assertive behaviors, feelings and reactions

	Nonassertive	*Assertive*	*Hostile*
Teacher behavior	Inhibited, self-denying, submissive, quiet, retreating. Denies feelings. Placating.	Honest, firm, clear. Respect for others and self. Task-oriented.	Macho, belligerent, belittling, exploitative, denying, explosive.
Consequent teacher feelings	Loneliness, shame-resistant anxiety which may turn to anger.	Confidence, self-respect, closeness.	Scorn, pity, righteousness, superiority.
Student perception of teacher	Soft, afraid, wishy-washy, incompetent.	Trustworthy, cooperative, knows what he wants.	Nasty, unfair, bossy.
Student feelings about self	Winning, powerful, perhaps cheated.	Valued, respected.	Intimidated, hurt, angry, rejected, shame.
Student reaction	Ignores teacher. Manipulative, exploitative.	Congenial, open. Listening or sometimes aggressive.	Submissive. Diversion or retaliatory violence.

Source: Adapted from similar chart in Alberti and Emmons (1978, p. 14).

Several factors inhibit natural rule making in school.

1. Participation is mandated. On the street if an individual does not like the governing rules of a group or game he can choose not to play. At home he can retreat to his room. At school about the only escape is passive resistance.

2. Unlike in other settings, obedience to rules in school does not have a natural payoff. At home, living within the rules is tuned to affection and caring. In groups, a sense of belonging depends on abiding by the rules. In games, the rules enable participants a chance to win, to be active, and to be accepted. In school the rules deny natural need satisfaction for activity and

affiliation. The majority of students learn they can't even win academically (get good grades) if they abide by the rules. Thus, the classroom teacher doesn't have much leverage.

3. Rules in school seem arbitrary and are often incongruent with needs. For instance, rules often stipulate that students can't run when they are in a hurry, talk to friends, sharpen broken pencils, rest when they're tired, or take whatever time is necessary in the bathroom.

4. Schools are governed by a superordinate line of power. The traditional military establishment is the closest facsimile to schools. Obedience to authority is revered.

5. Teacher authority is easily undermined by parents and the administration. The teacher is in charge in the classroom, but parents are more important to the child, and if the parent downgrades the teacher at home it has a potent effect in the classroom. Furthermore, the principal can easily overrule the teacher.

6. Teacher–student contact is limited. Most often the relationship is over within ten months. Thus, it has a limited future and little opportunity to establish lasting goodwill or closeness. Likewise, the teacher does not have a backlog of intimacy, sharing, or love to trade on.

7. Schools are fast-paced and the teacher must simultaneously deal with a multitude of people. Teachers are in almost continuous communication with someone. Classroom observations show that teachers may send out as many as 500 separate messages during a school day.

8. There is little privacy within classrooms where a teacher and a student could exchange views without an audience. Furthermore, emotion and behavior are contagious, so that an individual student–teacher confrontation can easily spread to the entire class.

9. Each school, each teacher functions within a unique interpretation of rules (recall from Chapter 1, teacher reactions to rule violations). We found great variance in the ways teachers respond to explicit rule violations. Furthermore, the rules are frequently not stipulated. Hargreaves et al. (1975) found through close observations that the majority of school rules are never verbalized. Thus, the only way that students can learn the rules and their meaning is by testing and observing.

The question remains: How can teachers best decide on a set of rules, establish them within the context of ongoing classroom activities, and enforce them? We have already discussed reality education as a valued process for student self-governance and a variety of environmental controls for influencing student behavior. We will now consider assertiveness as a means to govern student behavior by establishing and maintaining rules.

A teacher governs by assertion when he properly identifies his wants and needs, communicates what he wants in the form of rules to the students, enforces the rules, and seeks support and assistance from outside sources.

Translating Rights and Wants Into Rules

The teacher must identify his needs and desires in order to achieve his goals. If a history teacher's goal is academic achievement, then the following conditions are necessary: Students know what they should be doing, students are on task, teacher is able to give honest and frequent feedback. These conditions will exist if students:

(a) Are quiet and attentive when directions are given
(b) Raise their hands and ask questions to clarify the task
(c) Have the necessary materials to do the assigned task
(d) Stay in seats and work on assigned tasks
(e) Meet mastery level competence by incorporating feedback into tasks and redoing erroneous work.

These student behaviors become the rules for that activity in that class. To determine his wants and needs the teacher must first identify his goals, the necessary conditions, and the required student behaviors. Each teacher, class, and activity will have its own set of goals, conditions, and behaviors. Therefore it is necessary for each teacher to specify his own rules. Here are some illustrative classroom rules that you may consider. Students will: make certain that their hands do not touch others as they move about the room; raise hands when they want to ask or answer a question or talk to a fellow student; take turns for getting equipment for recess; keep all four legs of the chairs on the floor; wait until a speaker has completed his statements before offering their own views. Note: The rules are better if stated in behavioral terms and are as explicit as possible. "Students will be nice" or "Respect others" or "Do not bother others" is too vague and abstract to be of much guidance. Furthermore, wherever possible, rules should be stated in the positive. Limit the number of rules. Probably five for a given activity is sufficient for starters. Different activities, seat work, recess, transition periods, and recitation may need special rules.

Try your hand. Write down your goals (Needs and Desires) for a given class. Identify the conditions necessary for the achievement of these goals and the rules you would establish.

Establishing a Set of Rules with Students

The teacher must communicate the rules to the students. Timing is critical. In some respects it seems natural to develop rules as we go along. Teachers do not wish to burden the students with a lot of rules the first few days. However, classroom observations have established two points. Orderly, businesslike classrooms are the most productive. The more successful teachers seem to concentrate on getting things moving in the right direction within the first two or three meetings. Second, the rhythm and rules of given classrooms do not change much after the first three days. About 80 percent of the rules for a class have allegedly been established within that period.

In communicating the rules two points need to be established. The first is the rationale for each rule. Rules ought not be arbitrary from the point of view of the students. Share with the students your principles, your goals, and your needs as a basis for rules.

Students must know what is expected. Rules are a necessary segment of any social organization or activity. The teacher should be as matter of fact, firm, and rigorous in establishing classroom rules as one would be in explaining the rules of a game to a newcomer. Given our goals and statements of rights, there is a reasonable set of behaviors that must be followed. Rather than emphasize the consequences for violations it would seem more appropriate to emphasize agreements and acceptance based on mutual rights. Introduce rules as a Bill of Rights and then briefly discuss each one in terms of student and teacher behaviors. The bulk of the discussion should focus on student interpretation of how they are to behave.

Silberman and Wheelan (1980) caution teachers with these suggestions regarding the establishment of rules:

1. Rules must be acceptable and reasonable from the point of view of the constituents if they are to be willingly obeyed.
2. Wherever possible state rules positively. It is better to say, "Walk in the halls" rather than "Don't run in the halls." In the latter case someone is going to test the rule by skipping to see how broad the meaning of "running" is.
3. Be succinct and to the point so that interpretation is straightforward.
4. Focus on observable behavior. "Be nice" or "Be kind to other students" doesn't translate very easily.
5. Make your rules public and before the fact. That is, rules must apply equally to everyone unless an acceptable explanation is given beforehand.
6. Rules should be enforceable. "Desks must be clear of all notes and papers during a test" is enforceable, while "Everyone must have a clean mind" is not.

The second point to be established when making and enforcing rules is the expectation that everyone will abide by them. Two contrasting points of view will be identified here. My bias will be readily apparent, but each reader must come to his own conclusions.

Predetermined Preventative Consequences Ought to be Published

Canter and Canter (1976) strongly advocate that teachers clearly indicate what the consequence will be if and when the rules are disobeyed. Lee Canter feels that consistency is the key to consequences. Identical negative consequences must be administered for every student at every time for rule violations. He believes that students, parents, and the administration must all be advised as to the rules and the consequences. As an example, the letter below was sent to the parents of the students attending Juanita School in Oxnard, California.

Figure 11.1. Letter to parents stipulating conditions of assertive discipline.

Dear Parents:

Parents throughout the country are concerned about discipline in public schools. Several members of the Juanita School staff were fortunate in participating in a workshop on assertive discipline. It was taught by Lee Canter, an educator and researcher who wrote the program and book *Assertive Discipline*. The teachers have been trained in the technique and are putting it into action in their classes.

We believe:

1. No child may behave in a way that prevents the teacher from teaching or another student from learning.
2. No child may behave in a way that might injure himself or another student.

Each teacher will select five rules for the classroom. The children will be taught these rules. If any child breaks the rules, an established series of consequences will occur:

1. First episode: 10 minutes of "time out"
2. Second episode: 15 minutes of detention after school
3. Third episode: 30 minutes of detention and 30 minutes of "time out" in another classroom

    4. Fourth episode: parents will be called and a note will go to the principal

    5. Fifth episode: child will be sent to the principal

A child sent to the principal three times will be suspended from class. For these severe misbehaviors a child will be immediately sent to the principal and suspended from his class for a half-day:

1. refusal to work
2. causing physical harm to another
3. destruction of property
4. stopping the entire class from functioning

As we work to eliminate these negative behaviors, we will be rewarding positive behavior daily. Each day each teacher will send at least three positive notes home with children. Every teacher will verbally praise each child at least once a day. There will be many positive activities used to reinforce appropriate behavior. When your child receives these notes, praise him and display his reward. It will make him feel great. It is in the children's best interest that we all cooperate to eliminate problem behavior. Your child needs to know that home and school are working together.

We want parents to be informed about our policies. Please complete and return the form below. Returning the form indicates only that you have received and read our plan.

. . . .-

    I have read the Juanita School plan for school discipline.

_____

Signature

_____

Date

    The Juanita School letter to parents includes most of Canter's (1979) recommendations. Parents are notified beforehand of the consequences. The plan applies equally to all students. The consequences become progressively more severe. Offenses are not forgiven for follow-up good behavior. That is, if a student violates the rules twice in the first 15 minutes of school, he is detained after school even though his prior record has been spotless and he is a model student the rest of the day. Notice, the last resort is referral to the principal. The principal's action is predetermined by principal–teacher agreement. Although the Juanita School letter does not designate time limits, Canter recommends that each day be started anew. However, if several students violate a given rule or if an individual student continues to violate a rule over a three-day period, the consequences ought to be made more severe.

Canter (1979) says his experience and research have shown that these advanced warnings of explicit consequences are necessary. His position is valued by teachers; however, support data is unreported. In order to discover if any effects of the program were known I wrote to the principal of Juanita Elementary School. Mr. Baumgartner's reply regarding the letter, is very enlightening. Reinforcement programs are strongly supported. "We are in our fourth year [of the Lee Canter Assertive Discipline Program] and we are finding it highly successful. . . . I find it is the first program we have tried which stresses positive reinforcement for correct behavior. We have made modifications to the program. . . . we no longer need to use the 'marbles in the jar' techniques or any of the group techniques. Instead we work completely on the individual plan where each student is responsible for his own behavior. . . . Parent response has been very supportive. I believe this is the result of the parents receiving notes, awards, etc. of a positive nature which far exceeds any of the negative kinds of reports."

Research, particularly that pertaining to punishment, strongly suggests that warnings and the inevitable punishment for violations as directed by Canter are not successful. Even if students were to function without violating five rules, one wonders about other behaviors and side effects. However, the most critical question pertains to what the students might be learning other than obedience from the behavior management domain of their education.

Furthermore, it would seem that in establishing the rules and consequences for rule violation the teacher is indicating that he anticipates that the rules will be violated.

The Canters (1976: 92) make the point that threats are detrimental: "Assertive teachers 'promise' rather than 'threaten' to follow through on their verbal requests. A 'promise' is a vow of affirmative action. A 'threat' is a statement or expression of intention to hurt or punish."

Canter and Canter contend that such consequences as those listed in the letter are promises, not threats, because students have a choice to function within the imposed limits or face the identified consequences. However, students perceive detention, referrals to the principal, and calls to parents as unilaterally determined punishments.

Focus on Positive Behavior

In contrast to the potential of teacher as adversary that is established by identifying the consequences for rule violations, an alternative is to focus on the positive. Each of the strategies discussed in Part II emphasized trust, support, and positive payoff for abiding by rules, and downplayed punishment. Each of these strategies strongly advocated rule conformity, but the belief is communicated to students that they want and will live up to the agreements they have made.

The Canters recommend that the daily record of student offenses be kept in one portion of the chalkboard. That is, on the first violation a student's name is written on the board. Checkmarks are placed after the student's name for subsequent rule violations. Hopefully, this reminds the student throughout the day of the pending consequences and this thought encourages rule conformity. In contrast, the names of those students who are on-task can be written on the board and occasionally reinforced to remind students that such behavior is valued.

Enforcing the Rules

Rules must be enforced. Perhaps the most critical moment of truth that differentiates nonassertive, hostile, and assertive teachers is the reaction to rule violations. Differences are evident in both verbal and nonverbal messages.

To discern the differences in verbal messages let us assume that during a seat work assignment a student has not done anything constructive other than to place a book on the desk. He has been chatting with nearby students, twisting around to see what others are doing, and idly doodling. The categories of possible teacher responses given below were adapted from Canter and Canter (1976).

The nonassertive teacher responds in such ways as the following:

(a) Ask the student to focus on a subsidiary task rather than the desired one.
Make an effort: "I know this is boring but won't you at least try?"
Think about behavior: "You had better think about how you use your time."
Worry about the future: "You will be sorry that you wasted this time."
Don't get caught: "Don't let me catch you goofing off again!"
(b) Focus on undesired behavior rather than on what is wanted.
Past behavior: "You are always wasting your time."
What is happening: "You haven't even started yet."

Questioning student: "What are you doing?"

Questioning intentions: "Are you interested in passing?"

(c) Sends "I want" message but fails to follow through.

Short attention: "Get out your pencil and start to work right now." Student half-heartedly picks up pencil and teacher returns to other tasks. Student puts pencil down again.

No follow-up: "It is important that you read this chapter and answer the questions. Student picks up book and lazily gazes at it but doesn't make an effort to read. Teacher does not respond.

(d) Threatens the student but fails to follow through.

Teacher: If you don't get busy you will sit here through recess and lunch. [Student picks up pencil but does no more.]

Teacher: I mean it, no work, no recess. [Student picks up papers, shuffles them around, but no real effort.]

Teacher: I mean it now. You keep goofing around and you'll miss lunch. [Student grimaces and makes a face.]

Teacher (angrily): I don't have to put up with that. You are going to flunk. See if I care.

(e) The student and his behavior are ignored. Some teachers have a number of students who are just "sit-ins." The teacher and the student have a tacit agreement, "I won't bother you and you don't bother me." However, both are really bothered because they know it is not supposed to be that way. Student gives excuses: "I don't have the right paper" or "You never explain the stuff right" or "I'll do it in a minute, I'm just resting." The teacher responds, "Do as you wish, I'm tired of arguing with you."

The hostile teacher maintains his position by authoritarian behavior. He violates the rights of students and others. He projects blame and his feelings. He tends to view relationships with students in terms of "we" versus "they." He tends to be suspicious of student motives and believes that their basic desire is to get away with whatever they can. Therefore students must be watched and subdued. Here are five ways that hostile teachers typically respond:

(a) Sends a "you-" message in which the student is blamed for problems, rather than communicating an "I want" message.

"You never listen so you won't know what to do."

"Your attitude is disgusting."

"You haven't done anything all week."

(b) Expresses negative value judgments about the student and his behavior.

"You act like a kindergartener."

"You are lazy and don't care if you learn anything."

"Your kind always makes excuses."

 (c) Acts out emotions aroused by student behavior.

Menacingly approaches student as if to attack him.

Sends a hostile glare.

Says, "I'll sure be glad when I get rid of you."

 (d) Uses overly severe or extended punishment.

"So—no work, no recess for three weeks."

"Let's see if doing 25 pushups will get some energy into you."

 (e) Physical attack with intent to cause pain.

Yanking the slumping student up and turning him around by an ear or the hair.

Paddling a student so hard he can't sit down.

The assertive teacher indicates the behavior to be stopped and more explicitly what is to be done. The secret is to do so immediately and stay with it until the student complies. If the teacher is going to take the time and effort to send a "do" message, he must take the time and effort to make certain that it is done.

 (a) Be explicit.

"Turn to page 222 and begin the exercises right now."

"The rule is, if you want to speak you raise your hand and I shall call on you."

 (b) Use warmth and support.

"John, I want to make certain you have the idea. Do the first problem and I'll check your answer."

"Keith, I can't always see and hear you back there. Come up here so that we can communicate better."

 (c) Examines your own feelings in response to student misbehavior.

"I feel discouraged when students are not interested in school."

"I become angry when I ask somebody to do something and they ignore me."

"I had hoped that everyone would get an 'A' on this assignment and it frustrates me when students don't try."

 (d) Persist in the insistence that directives will be fulfilled. Students sometimes stall by either going on endlessly with excuses, alternative plans, blaming the teacher or other students, dawdling, or just putting the teacher off. They have learned that when they do so the teacher gives up and moves on, angrily blows up, shifts to pleas and bribes, argues back, or shifts to other students. Note that this learned behavior and expectation may not be malicious or even conscious. It is just a pattern of behavior. The proper teacher reaction is persistence.

Persistence is tunnel vision. The teacher does not allow himself to become sidetracked. Instead of responding to the students' manipulative signals, the teacher focuses on his own request. One such procedure is the broken record, repetition of the request. It is very important that the teacher does not show any irritation or impatience. The voice should be firm, insistent, but not intense. Don't be distracted by student comments or excuses. An example may help.

T: John, I want you to begin this exercise right now.
J: I will, I will. I'm just getting my stuff together.
T: I'm waiting, I want you to start now.
J: I was just asking Bo what the assignment is.
T: John, open up the book to page 222 and start.

Teachers report that three times is usually sufficient. If it isn't, then change to a different strategy.

An alternative to the broken record is silent persistence. The students have learned that through a variety of delay tactics they can wait the teacher out, start an argument, distract him, or obtain a better deal. The student will learn otherwise and change his behavior if the teacher doesn't go for the bait. If the teacher stands by patiently, maintaining eye contact but sending no other message than "I'm waiting," the student typically will get on task.

Feedback may be requested. The teacher may say, "I want to make certain that you understand my request. What do you understand me to be asking you to do?"

e. Control the nonverbal messages.

Eye contact. If the teacher wants a student to do something, it is very important to stand in front of him, face to face, and gaze into his eyes. The nonassertive person tends to look down or past others or perhaps to look at them sideways. The hostile person is apt to stare or fix the other person in their eyes. The assertive eye contact is not a stare, locked eyeball to eyeball, but looking at the other person face to face in a natural open way. Blinks occur and the gaze may shift to other facial features.

Posture. When one is relaxed, leaning forward slightly or erect, then interest is communicated. Stiffness denotes anger or anxiety. When one leans back it suggests fear, and slumping is a signal of indifference. The assertive teacher wants to move toward students, neither against them nor withdrawing from them.

Distance. The ideal normal space for person-to-person communication is from one to three feet. Closer than one foot is an invasion of privacy that is either a hostile action or, if invited, one of intimacy. A distance in excess of three feet becomes public. If the teacher wishes to speak with a student the distance between them should be slowly closed. The teacher ought to walk slowly, not menacingly, toward the student as they talk.

Latency. When people are hostile the time between messages tends to be short or nonexistent as each strives to attack the other. Delay often communicates passiveness. Rules of thumb are difficult to establish except to note that latency matters.

f. Penalize rule violations. In discussing persistence we noted that if the student failed to respond within two or three requests an alternative strategy must be employed. Punishment, the typical teacher reaction, is complex and unpredictable. Silberman and Wheelan (1980) offer a variety of ways for the teacher or parent to assertively respond.

Student choice. The point of assertiveness is to let the students know exactly what is wanted and why it is wanted. Given this information the student then decides to conform to the wishes or to disregard them. A better alternative to punishment for disobedience is a legitimate choice. For example,

Teacher: I cannot allow you to miss the opportunity to learn this material. You will either do the exercises here and now or in the principal's office at 3:30. The choice is yours.
John: But I have to catch the bus at 3:30.
Teacher: The choice is yours. You can either do the work now or in the office at 3:30.

A legitimate choice must be just that. The choice cannot be to do the task or to skip it. Likewise, it ought not be to choose between two punishments. Since we prefer that the student stay and do the task as we construct it, the alternative ought to be something the student would naturally reject.

Time out. For a variety of reasons students sometimes need an immediate change in environment, or an escape valve. This temporary change is called "time out." The reader may recall that the technique was discussed in Chapter 9. Canter and Canter (1976) suggest an excellent possibility. Arrange for a student to be sent to another teacher's room for a short period of time. In a strange room, with an unfamiliar teacher, and among unknown older students an individual is much more apt to work on-task. Referrals to another room ought not be done as punishment, but rather as an alternative to continued off-task behavior.

The Canters report that after one or two such experiences students choose to stay and work in their own home classroom. Arrangements, of course, have to be made with colleagues beforehand. The process is simple. Two teachers agree that if the need arises individual students from either class will be sent to the other's room. A chair is set aside in an out-of-the-way location. The student will bring seat work and is directed to take the seat and do his work. The referral is made matter of factly, not punitively: "John, you are having a lot of trouble sticking to your work. Please take your workbook and pencil and go to Ms. Snow's room, number 36. You will stay there until 10:30." As always, the assertive teacher sticks to the directive and does not back down when the student apologizes or promises to be good.

The penalty should fit the behavior. Penalties assessed in athletics are usually assessed to fit the offensive behavior. Thus, for pass interference in football the would-be receiver gets the ball at the point of the infraction. In baseball, a strike is called if the batter fails to swing at a pitch over home plate. In the same way it is natural and logical that anyone destroying property ought to replace or refurbish it. Time lost in class because of forbidden off-task behavior should be made up elsewhere at other times. It would seem more logical to have youngsters come to school on Saturday or holidays to make up time lost through unexcused absences than to suspend the errant student for three school days. The message of the former is, we think, that school is important and one way or another you are going to participate in it. The latter communicates that we are willing to give school time away in order to punish disobedience because it is not that important.

PUNISHMENT CONTRASTED TO LOGICAL AND NATURAL CONSEQUENCES

In discussing consequences for rule violations Dreikurs and Grey (1968) contend that students tend to perceive punishment as an unfair use of power and they then seek revenge. Logical and natural consequences are more useful. Whereas punishment tends to be arbitrary and represent the power of authority, logical consequences are consistent with the nature of the situation. For example, an assigned mathematics lesson must be completed. Those who goof off will have to do the mathematics assignment during recess. Natural consequences are those that occur automatically without authority intervention. For example, students pushing one another around inevitably end up with someone hurt and angry. The teacher's role here may best be served by making certain that a connection is made between the behavior and its consequences.

Dreikurs and Gray (1968) offer 103 examples of logical and natural consequences to be employed by teachers and parents. The difference between punishment and logical consequences is illustrated by the following incident.

Malingering

It was test day, and when the boys and girls entered the room there was less than the usual exuberance. The students' mouths were more tense and many didn't talk to anyone, just hurried to their seats for a final scan. When everyone settled down, Ms. Tuna began to pass out the test, then noticed that the four boys who normally sit in the back seats were absent. She asked, "Where is the back row battalion today?" The students looked about quizzically. "Dunno, Josh and Kerry were in our third period English class." "Justin was in P.E." Ms. Tuna continued to pass out the examination, commenting, "I hope they aren't too late; this test will take the full period."

With about 15 minutes remaining in the period, the four boys entered, dropped a note on Ms. Tuna's desk, and went to their seats, where they immediately picked up their tests. Ms. Tuna read the note, which explained that the boys had reported to the Dean's office between periods, complaining of stomach cramps. However, they seemed okay now, so they were going to remain in their classes. The side glances among the four boys and to others in class suggest that this illness had been quite convenient.

Ms. Tuna noted to herself, "This fish isn't going for that bait." She said to the class, "Boys and girls, I need to talk to Justin, Kerry, Josh, and Scott in the hall for a minute; please continue with the test just as you would if I were here." She motioned to the boys to go out in the hall.

Justin began, "Gosh, Ms. Tuna, sorry we missed the test but we have a good reason. We got terrible pains. It must have been that junk food we get in that dumb lunchroom." The others nodded in agreement.

Ms. Tuna decided not to challenge the illness story. There was no way to win and everyone would just end up angry. She said, "You all seem to be in good health now. Since you missed but saw the test, I'll have to make up a new one. When . . ."

Kerry interrupted: "But Ms. Tuna, we were sick and have a health excuse, so we shouldn't have to take the test."

Ms. Tuna: "Oh, you have to take the test all right, but I can't give you the short-answer test everyone else had; you'll have to take an essay test tomorrow. You had better study hard tonight, because make-up written tests are almost always harder. I'm really sorry that you boys were ill and missed the regular test. Let's go in."

This may appear to be a case of punishment, and as such it shouldn't work because some of the several necessary conditions noted by Azrin and Holz (1966) in their review of research for successful punishment are missing. On the other hand, if the reader reviews the conditions established by Redl (1980) you will find that these four boys have a basis for feeling anger, blaming themselves as a cause of the consequence, and resolving to behave otherwise.

Perhaps more relevant to the issue is Dreikurs and Grey's (1968) differentiation of punishment from logical consequences. As they would direct, Ms. Tuna communicated a positive, accepting attitude toward the boys and the class. Despite her suspicions she demonstrated a respect for their views, corrected them when they were wrong, but refrained from belittling either them or their actions. The more difficult alternative test was not administered as retaliation or as a weapon to maintain the teacher's status. The essay test is just a logical consequence of the circumstances, which were created by the boys themselves. The teacher's position is on the side of order and organization. Ms. Tuna's disposition and manner as illustrated here are quite different from that of a punitive teacher who would challenge the students, make them pay for their behavior with aversive effects, and prove to them that authority (power) is not to be trifled with.

Malingering is a very serious problem for American industry. The cost in the gross national product is enormous. Punishment does not stop it. Do you think the four boys in Ms. Tuna's class will miss the next test with stomach cramps?

Assertiveness is a process for dealing with aversive interpersonal situations. We need to also consider what actions might be taken when the adversary relations extend beyond verbal exchanges.

COPING WITH DANGEROUS BEHAVIOR

Occasionally circumstances are such that a student's behavior could endanger the teacher's physical safety. In such situations there are a few absolutes that should be heeded.

Touching someone who is angry can be dangerous and should be avoided if at all possible. Give angry people at least one arm's length of space.

Stepping between two angry youngsters is also to be avoided. If a fight is observed, walk in, don't run. Although fighting is intolerable, it is not usually a catastrophe unless weapons are involved. If the teacher is calm and resolute the chances of escalation are less likely. Furthermore, if one or the other of the combatants has gotten in a good whack, much of the steam is taken out of both participants. They are more apt to be reasonable. Whatever is done, the fewer people observing, the better. Therefore, a good first move is to disperse the observers. If that is not possible, the removal of one of the combatants may be possible.

If two students are fighting and you feel that you must intervene, rather than stepping between the assailants, approach the smaller one from behind. Briskly walk up to this individual and put your arms around him at elbow height. The idea is to pin his elbows against his body. While holding onto this student, pivot in a half circle off one of your feet so as to spin the student away from his opponent. Most often such a sudden move relaxes the situation enough to permit a discussion of the issues.

If you feel that you are physically endangered, here are some additional suggestions.

(a) Don't be afraid to leave. You are not getting combat pay.
(b) If you are under attack do not back up, move in a circle.
(c) If confronted with an angry student, move so that you are facing one side rather than straight on. Thus, you will only have to contend with one arm and one leg.
(d) Turn sideways so that the student is primarily facing only one side of you. You will be more agile and less of a target.
(e) If attacked it is easier to brush a blow aside than to stop it with your hands.
(f) Allow an escape route. Don't stand between the student and the door or stairway exit. Particularly if the student is frightened, he would rather run than attack.

An exercise recommended by Curwin and Mendler (1980) offers a fitting conclusion to our discussion of assertiveness. Curwin and Mendler assert that most of us are driven by our perceptions of school policy, our rights, expectations of others, and the role of teachers, and maintaining our reputations. These perceived mandates are translated into "I have to" beliefs. To check your perceptions write down a list of those things that you feel that you have to do. That is, complete the sentence "I have to" until you have exhausted your list. Now consider each of the "I have to" statements and change them wherever possible to "I choose to" statements. That is, "I choose to" represents what you would feel comfortable doing if you were in full control of your situation, that which is consistent with your philosophy and goals of teaching.

If the "I have to" statements translate easily and comfortably into "I choose to" statements, then why not openly and honestly state them as such? Such statements will not only help you to feel a greater sense of control, but they communicate your position to students more positively and accurately.

Analyze each of the "I have to" items that you could not easily and comfortably convert to "I choose to" statements. These represent areas of conflict for you. First, are your "I have to" statements real and necessary? Sometimes if we check out our assumptions about obligations and school regulations we find that they are not real. We can dispose of them without any negative consequences.

Decide what to do with the remainder: Is it possible to alter conditions so that you do not have to perform duties and act in ways contrary to your wishes? Is your discomfort such that you ought to act so as to alter the situation? What are the real consequences if you should default on the "I have to" commitments? Allowing ourselves to be buried in the "I have to" commitments is a prime cause of teacher burnout.

RECOMMENDED READINGS

Dreikurs, R., B.B. Grunwald, and F.C. Pepper. *Maintaining sanity in the classroom.* New York: Harper and Row, 1982.

Kounin, J. *Discipline and group management in classrooms.* New York: Holt, Rinehart, and Winston, 1970.

Rinne, C.H. *Attention: The fundamentals of classroom control.* Columbus, OH: C.E. Merrill, 1984.

12

ORGANIZATION, INTERACTION AND STUDENT BEHAVIOR

SCHOOLS AS UNIQUE INSTITUTIONS

The implications thus far have been that if we properly implement some combination of management strategies, behavioral problems would be eliminated. It is as if we have been searching for a combination of methods by which we might free classrooms of mischievous behavior. Alas, the elimination of problem behaviors will never be.

Schools have a number of built-in features that make problems inevitable. Most classrooms are seriously overcrowded. Students have little privacy and little personal space. One teacher cannot simultaneously monitor all students, meet individual needs, and provide a challenging, meaningful curriculum appropriate for every student. The participants come from diverse ethnic backgrounds with wide variations in commitments, expectations, attitudes, and habits. Many of the students and some of the teachers are distracted by emotional burdens. School attendance is compulsory, and particularly in the upper grades many of the students would prefer to be elsewhere. School furniture is uncomfortable and for many students ill-fitted. The demands of school are contrary to many natural psychological needs for social interaction and striving for independence. Physiological growth and youthful energy press for stretching and large-muscle activity. Learning naturally encompasses some frustration. Failure, occasional for many and continual for some, is endemic to the system. Much of the legitimate school activity seems irrelevant to many of the students.

The inescapable result is occasional behavior contrary to the wishes of school authority.

Some folks believe that law and order will prevail only if a rigorous set of rules is established, students are warned that violations will inevitably lead to prescribed harsh consequences, and appropriate graduated punishments are meted out. The evidence is clear: Few of the underlying conditions of behavioral problems are removed by punishment. Students are distracted from academic tasks by punishment so that more, not less, off-task behavior follows. In punitively oriented schools (as contrasted to student-oriented schools), teachers spend more time monitoring behavior and administering punishment.

Duke (1980) suggests that given the nature of the typical school described above, a more realistic strategy is to establish a program to manage problems as they occur. He offers eight procedures whereby a school might fruitfully deal with control problems:

1. Implement a comprehensive, schoolwide system.
2. Develop and publicize school rules.
3. Collect and disseminate information regarding behavior.
4. Establish procedures for resolving conflict.
5. Develop a team approach to resolve discipline problems.
6. Involve parents to develop a prosocial community.
7. Involve students in the task of governing student behavior.
8. Resort to the last resort: exclusion.

The rationale and procedures for implementing each of these procedures will be briefly discussed.

IMPLEMENTING A COMPREHENSIVE SCHOOLWIDE PROGRAM

Although various elements within the school (e.g., physical education, lunch room, hall passages, and academic classrooms) involve different behaviors, certain prescriptions ought to pervade the entire school community. Duke (1980) offers four reasons for a schoolwide approach.

(a) The majority of serious student behavioral problems occur out of class. The use of weapons, drugs, coercion, and overt aggression most frequently occurs in toilets and halls, in the cafeteria, on school buses, and at extracurricular events.

(b) Parents and students are upset by apparent inconsistent responses to student behavior. In most schools there is little collaboration or uniformity in terms of what constitutes appropriate behavior and what happens when problems arise.

(c) Legal sanctions based on the abridgement of student rights are becoming more prevalent. The challenge of court actions mandates that teachers and school administrators develop and become aware of school-wide policies that not only establish order but protect student and teacher rights.

(d) Schoolwide programs work best. Phi Delta Kappa (1980) commissioned Leonard Gregory to find out what makes some schools unusually successful. Eight exceptional schools in eight large midwestern cities were identified as exemplary of the respective school districts by the central administration. Gregory then interviewed teachers, parents, students, and the principals. He reviewed records and test results. The selected schools were found to be unique in a number of ways, but not in specific programs or in the training and years of experience of the personnel. The schools were unique in that the teachers and principal worked closely together, and decisions were made collaboratively. The roles of the principal, teachers, parents, and students were cooperative, mutually supportive, and explicit. People knew what to expect of one another. The principals of the exemplary schools were most often visible in the halls, classrooms, cafeteria, and in the neighborhood. Of all the known factors that characterize schools, the most critical are the roles and relationships among the people.

Rutter et al. (1979) came to similar conclusions from their intensive study of 12 high schools over a three-and-a-half-year period. Rutter et al. were seeking to identify causative factors for academic achievement, school attendance, overt behavior, and delinquency. The conclusions of this extensive study may be summarized as follows:

> All of the analyses were in agreement in showing that the characteristics of the school itself were by far the most important of all of the variables considered. We may conclude that school processes constituted the predominate influence on children's behavior in the classroom and the playground (1979: 166).

The means for developing, coordinating, and implementing such a systematic school program is the task described in the next seven procedures.

DEVELOP AND PUBLICIZE SCHOOL RULES

Everyone must realize that schools are a rule-governed organization. Students get into trouble because they fail to observe rules. Teachers and certain administrators spend enormous amounts of time and energy in an effort to enforce rules. Paradoxically, little attention is given to the generation and clarification of rules. Hargreaves et al. (1975) found in their school observations that administrators and teachers do little to develop and disseminate rules. Teachers seemed to be in doubt about what, if any, school rules exist.

Englander (1982) questioned all of the principals of a given school district regarding their practices of informing teachers about rules and regulations. All of the principals contended that they communicated the school regulations to their teachers each year. When pressed for details, over one-half admitted that the procedure was to make certain that beginning teachers had a copy of the faculty handbook, which contained among several other things, the school board regulations. Interestingly, although most of the administrators utilized corporal punishment on occasions and defended their actions by referring to school board regulations, none was aware that such a regulation did not exist.

Many students come to school with little experience or understanding of how rules are generated, what they mean, how they are connected with behavior, and the payoff for obedience. Many families are not rule-governed. Some children never have the opportunity to learn that proper behavior is rewarded. A person reared in a power-oriented home learns to protect himself in a variety of ways, but that does not mean that he learns the meaning or function of rules. Many students have only learned how to deal with an authoritarian parent or a hostile neighborhood. The development and publicizing of school rules involves more than posting a list of rules and the punishments that will be meted out for alleged disobedience. The nature of a democratic, rule-governed society must be taught. Several principles have been documented for implementing the establishment of school rules.

(a) Collaborative development results in better rules, more rule conformity, and higher morale. Abundant evidence from industry, family life, and education categorically demonstrates that participant collaboration increases productivity, satisfaction, pride, personal growth, and regulation abidance. Just as the whole education enterprise would function better if teachers were openly consulted on a variety of issues, so too would school behaviors and attitudes reflect the involvement of students.

Participation in governance will increase pride and feelings of belonging and ownership of the organization. Duke (1980) contends that the collaboration and discussion ought to extend to rules that govern adult behavior. As an example, a simple and just rule that most students would value is that teachers must distribute test days. Sometimes students are forced to take three or four major tests on the same day.

(b) The importance of rule-governed institutions will be better comprehended and respected if rules are discussed and illustrated in a variety of settings. The curricula of English and social studies offer natural opportunities, but equally appropriate opportunities exist in any discussion of student concern. Friendship, dating behavior, playing games, and test taking are but a few issues that naturally lend themselves to rule discussion. Reality education and values clarification are excellent examples of processes for such education. Kohlberg (1975) describes how the Just Community School integrates discussions of rules, rights, and justice into a wide variety of curricula and living segments of education.

(c) School rules must apply equally to everyone. If rules are enforced only intermittently or when violated by certain individuals, then the institution is not rule-governed. How can students respect rules when everyone knows that some persons are privileged to ignore them? A common illustration is the no smoking rule in which two areas are exempted, the teacher's hangout and the alley where students can sneak off for a quickie. At the height of the publicity regarding the health hazards of smoking, the students of one high school petitioned for absolute enforcement of the no smoking rule. As it happened, when the petition was presented to the school board, which was meeting in the school gymnasium, three members of the board had lighted cigarettes in their hands. There was some embarrassment, a lot of laughter. The recommendation supported by the student petition was tabled and never officially mentioned again. Meanwhile, health classes continued to point out the hazards of smoking, and any student apprehended with one foot in the school or its steps while holding a cigarette was automatically given five whacks with a paddle. Multiple repeaters were suspended from school. Such a system cannot expect students to learn to value rules.

(d) Enforcement is facilitated and deviancy is minimized if the rules are few in number. The *raison d'être* for rules is order. Although chaos is intolerable, the overemphasis of rules may be equally counterproductive.

Deviancy cannot exist without rules. Behavior is deviant only when it violates a rule. Behavior is most often considered to be deviant by observers, but not so by the behaving person. It follows that the more rules and the closer the monitoring, the more deviancy. If we recall Gold's (1970) study of delinquency and other references, we realize that rules can easily be overemphasized, to the decrement of good behavior.

(e) Periodic review and updating of rules facilitates observance. Hargreaves et al. (1975) found that most classroom rules are established within three days. However, many students are often transferred in or out after this three-day period. The result is that throughout the school year many students learn about certain rules only by violating them and suffering the subsequent punishment.

Rules are most likely to be obeyed if they are visible. Highway speed signs repeatedly remind us of the speed law and thereby help us to drive within its limits. Repetition is a basic tenet of advertising. If people are told a simple message over and over again they are more likely to recall and act on it.

In summary, rules should be collaboratively developed, few in number, periodically reviewed, consistently enforced, and taught in a variety of ways.

COLLECT AND DISSEMINATE INFORMATION REGARDING BEHAVIOR

Although life in the typical classroom is very complex, few of us systematically note what is happening. Of course the teacher is too busy at the time to meticulously record much of what is occurring. However, few take advantage of videotape recorders or trained nonparticipant observers. In appraising what happened we rely on the recollections of our limited perceptions. In contrast to the classroom teacher, coaches have used film and videotape recordings for years to pinpoint and analyze who did what and to give feedback to the participants. Such information is invaluable for skill development or planning and executing new processes. A simple and useful mechanism that any teacher can employ is to invite a valued colleague to sit in class and record the teacher's location every three minutes. It may surprise you to learn how little territory you can cover in an hour.

The process is simply to represent the classroom on a piece of paper. The room is divided into nine equal parts. The teacher's location at the end of each three-minute period is recorded by placing sequential numbers in the appropriate sections. The successive numbers are connected to show location and movement.

Proximity control (periodically being within an arm's reach of a student) is a powerful inhibitor of misbehavior. Teacher movement is a critical variable, however, and an experienced observer can also pick up other valuable information about classroom interaction regarding who is called on for recitation, what kinds of questions are asked which students, and the nature of feedback given to students. Good and Brophy (1984), in observing ongoing teacher–student interactions, found significant differences in teacher behavior, depending on the identity of the recipient student.

Duke (1980) recommends that schoolwide records ought to be more closely analyzed. Every school records attendance and most record such events as suspensions and truancies. However, the information is seldom summarized and shared with teachers, students, or parents. Data regarding frequency and cirumstances of various other critical misbehaviors is not generally available. Such records could be an excellent basis for establishing policies, alerting everyone to troublesome factors, pinpointing the causes of alleged problem behavior, clarifying misconceptions, and suggesting means for resolving problems. The purpose of the records is to diagnose and prescribe appropriate treatments for the underlying problems.

Duke (1980) offers several suggestions for collecting and using data for effective behavioral management. First, a specific person should be given the responsibility for receiving, analyzing, and disseminating the data. Second, standardized forms and reporting procedures would be helpful. The forms should be such as to allow analysis of such pertinent data as: frequency of particular behaviors, the identity of offending students, time and circumstances of misbehavior, the culprit's perception of the situation and the behavior, the nature of the corrective action, and recidivism. The result would be a cumulative record of the school. The point of the tally is not to accumulate evidence for individual files. The status of problem students in terms of sex, academic achievement, class level, and nonacademic participation is important for generating policies and applying preventitive/corrective processes.

Data on student behavior should be regularly reviewed. Much time and energy is devoted to resolving behavioral problems. Allegedly, many students are dissipating educational opportunities. Thus, it is a good idea for schools to plan changes based on student behavior and contextual conditions. Duke suggests that schools establish a task force to monitor the data and decide when and how it should be made known to whom. Such a task force ought to include students and teachers as well as an administrator.

ESTABLISH PROCEDURES FOR RESOLVING CONFLICTS

Conflicts in schools, as in every other phase of living, are to some extent unavoidable. Since conflicts are a natural, frequent phenomenon in human relations, educators need to not only resolve in-school conflicts but teach students reasonable, civilized, productive processes for conflict resolution. The worst of all worlds for educators would be to bury conflict by rendering learners so powerless that they must suppress their feelings and needs.

Mutually satisfying methods for resolving conflicts are possible and they can be utilized in classrooms as well as in other circumstances of human interaction. Gordon (1974) offers a no-lose model that extends the concepts of assertion to problem solving. DeCecco and Richards (1974) offer a second practical method, negotiation. Each of these will be described in some detail.

No-Lose Model

When the teacher is nonassertive the student wins and the teacher loses. The conflict is resolved when the teacher acquiesces. The price is too high. The teacher feels uncomfortable. The student becomes more demanding and less manageable. Paradoxically, student morale diminishes as students feel guilty and lose respect for the teacher, seeing him as weak and incompetent rather than a nice guy.

On the other hand, when the teacher is authoritarian, insisting that things go his way, the teacher seemingly wins while the students lose. Very often the battle is won but the war is lost. The students may be obedient, but feelings are generated and acting-out behavior follows when students feel powerless. In the end everyone loses. Behaviors that are generated out of debilitated self-esteem can only be interpreted as the antithesis of school objectives.

Gordon (1974) recommends that conflicts be resolved through a no-lose process that embodies assertiveness and listening skills. In contrast to each person vying to satisfy his needs, exercise his will, and push a solution, the no-lose method strives to resolve problems in ways acceptable to everyone.

The key is communication. The teacher sends "I" messages of "I feel" and "I want" while ascertaining similar messages from students. The process resembles the time-honored six-step problem-solving model.

1. Define the problem. Problems exist when conditions are different from those desired. Therefore, the first step involves the identification of two elements: what is and what is wanted (e.g., "There is a lot of commotion and noise in here with so many students talking and out of their seats" is

a statement of a condition that is not in itself a problem). Only when the teacher continues, "I want it to be quiet enough for everybody to be able to read and study without being distracted" do we have both elements of a problem statement. Such a statement readily lends itself to analysis and resolution.

2. Generate possible solutions. The generation of multiple solutions with input from several participants is important. It works best if student suggestions are elicited before the teacher offers his. It also helps if the proposed solutions are visible; write them on the blackboard. Furthermore, during this stage no solution should be challenged or evaluated. It doesn't cost anything to list all suggestions as possibilities. The practice spawns additional ideas and builds student respect for teachers.

3. Eliminate the impractical and unserving alternatives. The respective "I want" statements of both students and the teacher ought to be used as criteria. Gordon recommends that any solution that is rejected by anyone ought to be eliminated. However, we must also listen to advocates and encourage each to give the pros and cons of various solutions. Open discussions with decision making based on possible consequences will pay off.

4. Select the most logical means for achieving desires and protecting rights. Do not vote, because voting encourages power moves and inevitably has winners and losers. Work toward consensus. It takes more time but most often creates better solutions and higher morale. Discourage capitulation to group pressure. Ask the people to imagine what it would be like if such and such a solution were selected. Be tentative ("I would be willing to try"). Solutions ought not be cast in bronze.

5. Operationalize a selected solution. Spell out the details of what the teacher will do and what the students will do. It may be helpful to write down desires and a proposed solution.

6. Assess the consequences of the solution. After a period of time bring up the issue again and ask, "Has the solution we proposed worked out to everyone's satisfaction? If not, should we make some changes?"

Let's pick up on the problem of the noisy classroom:

Teacher's problem defined.	*Teacher:* There is a lot of commotion and noise in here with so many students talking and out of their seats. I want it to be quiet enough for everyone to be able to read and study without being distracted. *Sally:* We'll try to be quieter.

Teacher: I know that you are trying, but I think we have to do better than just try.

Sarah: Sometimes it is necessary to ask someone a little question about work that isn't clear.

Student perceptions clarified.

Sam: When we raise our hands sometimes you are busy and don't see us. We just sit there wasting time with our hands in the air.

Sue: I don't want to ask permission every time I want to sharpen a pencil. It makes me feel like a baby.

Shawn: But if everybody just gets up and does what he wants it gets so noisy you can't hear yourself think.

Teacher: If it gets too noisy we can't do our work, but you want freedom to do some things without raising hands to get permission. So, what can we do? Let's jot some ideas down on the board. We'll write down all of the ideas we can come up with and then select those that seem to have the most merit.

1. *Sally:* Let people do whatever they want as long as they are quiet.

Generate possible solutions.

2. *Sue:* Every 15 minutes take a three-minute break to do things.

3. *Shawn:* Have stricter rules. No getting out of seat and no talking.

Class: Boo.

4. *Smitty:* Punish kids who are too noisy.

5. *Sam:* You face the class all of the time so that when we raise our hands you can see us.

6. *Steve:* Raise hands to talk or to leave seat, but if the teacher doesn't say anything by the time you count slowly to six then you quietly do what you wanted to do.

Teacher: That is a pretty good list. Let's eliminate those we don't want. [Nos. 1, 3, and 4 are quickly rejected. After some discussion all agree that Sue's no. 2 sounds good, but sometimes you can't wait 15 minutes. Finally, the class and teacher agree to try nos. 5 and 6.]

Impractical solutions eliminated.

Solutions selected.	*Teacher:* Numbers 5 and 6 seem to be acceptable. Are we all agreed? Sam? Sue? Okay. I'll make a strong effort to face the class and notice when hands are raised. You will not talk or leave seats without my responding to your raised hands or you have slowly counted to six.
Solutions operationalized.	*Sue:* I think that we should have a signal system. Raise your right hand to talk to the teacher and both hands to leave our seats. That way we won't need to disturb everybody by saying out loud what we want.
	Teacher: That might work. Can you remember to do it that way?
	Class: Yeah, let us try.
Follow-up is planned.	*Teacher:* Okay, as long as it works. We will review our plan on Wednesday to see if the commotion has been kept down. Now, let's get back to the books.

The process takes time, but so do repeated reprimands. There are no guarantees that it will work, but relationships improve. There are mutual respect, positive feelings, commitments, and some creative ideas. Concerns are uncovered and attended. Students get a better idea of the meaning of cooperation and mature interaction.

Negotiation Model

DeCecco and Richards (1974) found that negotiation offers a valid alternative. Negotiation is based on four unalienable rights of all individuals within a democratic society. The four rights as identified by DeCecco and Richard are:

Dissent: To criticize, protest, or refuse to take part in an activity that one believes is immoral.

Equality: To get an equal chance in life regardless of your race, religion, sex, or economic status.

Decision making: To have a voice in the nature of rules and how they are enforced.

Due process: To have a fair chance to defend oneself.

To check the importance of these alleged rights, DeCecco et al. interviewed a large number of students, their parents, and teachers. A variety of typical incidences involving conflict were presented and the interviewees were asked to speculate about the critical factors causing the conflict. The issue of unilateral adult rule making and rule enforcement was identified by two-thirds of the students as the basis for apathy, aggression, and destructive acts. Government by the people is one of the most cherished principles of our society. Youth places a very high value on it.

When values collide a viable alternative to coercive control and vindictive retaliation is needed. Negotiation involves a realistic identification of common and opposed interests and the need to sacrifice some of the latter in order to gain more of the former. The gains will tend to offset the losses if individuals view their conflicts from all of the varying perspectives.

The DeCecco–Richards model for negotiation includes three stages: "(1) the statement of issues by each side made with direct, verbal expression of anger; (2) agreement by all sides on a common statement of issues—they agree to disagree; and (3) bargaining in which each side makes concessions" (DeCecco and Richards 1974: 189).

The initial step of negotiation is to try to get the entire issue on the table. Everyone presents his (their) perception of the issue without holding back expressions of emotions. Among other things this confrontation has a cathartic effect that lessens the probability of later outbursts and hidden resentment. Another payoff is that rumors can be quickly laid to rest. Strangely, such open expression of views and emotions can have a trust-building effect. The acceptance of another person's expressed emotions without a counterattack has a powerful salutary effect.

The second step involves sorting out the different positions without challenging the authenticity of them. Most desirable is to play down insinuations of "I'm right and you are wrong, let me explain the error of your thinking." Attempts to convince the other party to give up his views in favor of yours most frequently fail to succeed. It is better to attempt to identify areas in which you agree and then areas of disagreement. Establish relevance. Some aspects of given issues are subsidiary and not really within the focal point of the conflict. Next, try to prioritize the specific valid issues of disagreement.

The final step is to strike a bargain whereby the gains are optimized and those losses that do exist are held to a minimum for all parties. Bargaining is different from a capitulation in which one side either has insufficient power to demand his point or decides the issue is not worth the effort. Bargaining involves making reasonable concessions in order to gain optimum benefits. The primary focus should be to optimize the common gains.

Let us see how negotiation might work in a school situation.

Mr. Halt, the parent of one of the fourth-graders, came storming into Ms. Glass's room. He could hardly contain his anger. "What are you trying to do to my son, putting him in that dummy class for nonreaders? I will not stand for it. Josh may not be the best reader, but he is not dumb." Ms. Glass resisted the temptation to point out that she would have discussed the entire matter at the recent parent–teacher conference, but the Halts did not show up. Instead she said, "I'm pleased to know of your concern for Josh's reading because I'm equally concerned. I recommended that he be given some special instruction in reading because I fear that without it he is going to have academic difficulties in the future."

Mr. Halt retorted, "You are not going to label him. Once you people put a label on a kid he never lives it down. It happened to his brother. Absolutely no special classes for Josh."

Ms. Glass persisted, "Josh has some special deficiencies that hinder his reading. With 28 other students in class I cannot give him the special experiences he needs. We have the program and—"

"If you teachers did your job you wouldn't need special programs."

"Now listen, I am a good teacher and I know my job. I am becoming angry with your insinuations about my professional capabilities and goals."

After several more minutes of expressed conflicting views Mr. Halt conceded, "You have Josh's best interest in mind, but I still do not want him in special education."

"I appreciate your concern. Let's see if we can identify those things that we both want. Then we can agree on those things about which we disagree."

"We both want Josh to do well in school."

"And we both want Josh to feel good about himself. Self-concept is very important."

"But we seem to disagree on how to best help Josh. As I understand it you want him to remain in the regular class. I want him to work in the remedial reading program."

"Tell me more about the program."

"Well, it is a full-time program that diagnoses reading difficulties to—"

"I don't want him labeled as a special student."

"It is very important to you that Josh maintain his identity as a regular student."

"Yes, that is right."

"Let's see if we can strike an agreement. Something that we both feel will be best for Josh."

"Could he be in the program part-time?"

"I don't know. How about this? Suppose we have the reading specialist give him a battery of reading tests. It takes about two days. Then, you, the reading teacher, and I can go over it together to see if we can work out a plan which will keep him in a normal status, but give him the help he needs. Could we meet again next Monday?"

"Yes, that seems fair. I'll see you Monday at 3:00 p.m."

In order for negotiations to succeed a couple of requisite abilities are necessary and a back-up mediator is sometimes needed. Let's first look at the two required abilities.

The ability to decenter is very helpful. *Decentering* refers to the ability to perceive issues from another's point of view. This ability is necessary if each person is to recognize common interests and to discern the other's interest as being reasonable but distinct from his own. Thus, the person who decenters can better consider choices, better perceive that others are simply pursuing their own interest. Piagetian psychology alleges that decentering occurs when cognitive development enters the concrete operational stage at about six years of age. However, many adolescents and some adults do not always decenter, especially when threatened or emotional. Thus, the teacher must sometimes offer special help with decentering.

Second, differentiating and sequencing of events is important. Some of our youngsters have had little experience in untangling events as to time, order, and cause-effect relationships. The absence of this ability is not a sound basis for discontinuing negotiation. Contrariwise, it is even more desirable that time be taken to do so, as this is an important cognitive lesson to be mastered. If conflict did not naturally occur it would be wise to include it within our curricula so that students could practice the analyses of episodes in terms of separating, ordering, and then relating the events. Both decentering and the differentiating and sequencing of events can only be learned through experience.

Sometimes mediators (outside, objective third parties) are needed to satisfactorily resolve a conflict. If a mediator is brought into the situation, certain precautions are necessary. DeCecco and Richards (1974) recommend that

1. All parties must accept the selected mediator as a fair choice.
2. The mediator should be someone other than those already involved in the conflict.
3. The conflicting parties need to agree to the role of the mediator and how his recommendations will be used in the final resolution.

4. Sometimes the mediator can be most useful if he hears the respective views of each party in isolation from the other.
5. The role of the mediator is to gather information and clarify issues, not to make decisions.
6. If the mediator is a subordinate to either or both of the conflicting parties, care must be taken to ascertain that the relationship now or in the future will not be reflected in this conflict resolution.
7. The mediator's task is to support each party in expressing his respective views and feelings. Encourage all parties to anchor views in explicit events and help link the issues to events.
8. The mediator ought to help each party decide what he can concede. Care is taken to assure that neither party loses face if concessions are made.

Go back to the conflict between Mr. Halt and Ms. Glass. Does the remedial reading specialist qualify as a mediator?

DEVELOP A TEAM APPROACH FOR RESOLVING DISCIPLINE PROBLEMS

We teachers are peculiar people. We have one of the most complex, difficult jobs in the world and we isolate ourselves from help. We read books, we take courses at the university, we go to meetings, and we meet with colleagues regularly in the lounge for short breaks or a quick lunch. In all of these instances, however, we wall off the nagging, serious problems of our classrooms. We seldom invite anyone to enter our workplace. Moreover, we only superficially mention problem students and teaching dilemmas to other teachers.

As an illustration of the point let's consider the views of the teachers of a small high school. As part of a survey the teachers were asked to write down the names of three super students as defined by the individual teacher. The teachers were then asked to note the names of three problem students. The next task was to list the good and poor qualities of each of the six students.

Perhaps not surprisingly, the list of good qualities for the super students and the list of poor qualities for the problem students were extensive, but the lists were very short regarding the poor qualities of super students and good qualities of poor students. For example, one teacher could think of only one negative feature for her first choice of a super student: "She is as homely as sin." Another listed "a nice sister and family" as the sole redeeming quality of a problem student.

The dozen or so teachers assumed they knew everything about everybody in this small community. What a surprise it was to learn that some of the youngsters who were on the super student list of one or two teachers were listed as problems by other teachers. A number of implications are apparent from this data, but the point here is that had these teachers met and seriously discussed their successful and problem students, they might have learned a great deal from one another. Some were successful with individual students that others were struggling with.

How might teachers collaborate?

(a) Meet regularly and trouble-shoot on preidentified students. In many hospitals the staff comes together once a week to share expertise and experiences with regard to a specific patient. Teachers could be equally helpful to one another. Particularly in the secondary schools, teachers in different subject areas become isolated from one another, although within the respective track they frequently work with the same students and groups. Case conferences on individual students would serve two purposes: sharing information of successful strategies and generating new ideas. Several heads working together and sharing will come up with more good ideas than will a single teacher.

Such case conferences ought to have a format. A particular student is predesignated as the case to be studied. Specific details as to behavior, the settings, and the immediate antecedents ought to be the first item. Each teacher shares his experience regarding the student. Identify events that seem to stimulate good or deviant behaviors. Establish a plan of action with specific teachers assuming responsibility for executing the plan. Follow up in two weeks with a report of the consequences to solidify or reformulate plans.

(b) Develop an inventory of resources and agencies available to the community. Many communities have already published such a list, so the task may be simple. Surprisingly, most teachers are unaware of the variety of available services.

(c) Establish a help line. It is frequently more profitable to bring a resource into one of your meetings instead of referring the problem elsewhere. First, you need help with the student in the context of your classrooms. The service will be of maximum help to you and perhaps the student if it can be focused on the current problems in the classroom. Furthermore, such a procedure extends your knowledge and expertise for working with other such problems in the future.

How can such help be acquired? Even now, some federal and state money is available to the schools for mental health problems. Graduate students and faculty from nearby universities, experts from medical centers, and service organizations have skills and knowledge that could be useful. Such personnel are available for occasional meetings without charge or for a modest honorarium. Finally, the school psychologist, counselors, and social workers are all able to contribute useful expertise.

Perhaps more important than the explicit techniques that teachers can share is the spirit that develops when a faculty works together. Several researchers, for example, Seeman and Seeman (1976) and Rutter et al. (1979), report that student behavior and academic achievement are superior in those schools in which teachers as a group are actively involved in resolving school problems. The quality of school life is dependent on the staff working harmoniously together, with the senior colleagues taking the lead in setting and maintaining school goals and participating in critical decision making.

INVOLVE PARENTS IN DEVELOPING A PROSOCIAL COMMUNITY

Parent Education

Behavior within schools is a reflection of the behavior in the community. The more violence, sex, and drug-alcohol consumption that is shown on TV, the more we are going to witness it in the schools. The more hostile, greedy, and amoral the behavior of the adults, the more apparent it will be so in school.

Educators have no way of controlling TV programming. However, parents can control the knob to some extent and thus what their children see. Parents need and want help in achieving this control.

In the 1982 Gallup poll of public attitudes toward education over 75 percent of the parents indicated that they favored evening courses to help them help their children. Ninety percent of those surveyed expressed a willingness to serve on a parent–school advisory team.

The Higher Horizons Program dramatically improved attendance, academic achievement, student behavior, and student aspiration in a New York inner-city junior high school. One of the most applauded elements of the program was parent–teacher collaboration. Evening and weekend classes on how to live with and help your teenager were well attended.

Parents will support schools if schools support parents. The schools in Flint, Michigan have had little difficulty with taxation and bond support from the community. Why? The best explanation is that most schools are open from before breakfast until near midnight. People from the age of 3 to 83 are enrolled in every conceivable educational experience. The commitment to education in Flint began when the schools opened their doors wide to broaden education.

The one thing schools do not need is another layer of tasks and responsibilities. However, many parents are ignorant about how to help their children with school, how to discipline them, how to communicate, and otherwise deal with the children's feelings and needs. The schools are charged with the education of the community. As such, it ought to confront ignorance wherever it exists.

The foundation for good education (and in particular, social behavior) begins in the home. Elkind (1975), a noted child psychologist, indicated that social behavior begins with patterns of agreements in the home. Some agreements are relatively simple bargains: "If I come home right after school can I go over to Jimmy's house?" Some agreements are like a contract by which the youngster gets a regular allowance in exchange for keeping his room clean, washing the dishes, or some such achievement. Most important are the subtle contracts by which children develop values and commitments through interaction with parents.

Contracts for living together have three components:

(a) Responsibility earns freedom. Parents give freedom to their youngsters as they demonstrate responsibility to use it. The contract is: "As you behave appropriately you will be given more freedom and opportunity to do things." The contract is seldom stated as such, but in a variety of give-and-take situations its essence is established. The freedom expands and changes with age, as does the sense of responsibility and responsible behavior. As the child ages he wants more freedom, and the parents are able to demand more responsible, self-controlled behavior in exchange.

(b) Achievement earns rewards. The children are given rewards in terms of affection, attention, privileges, and goodies as they achieve the developmental task as assigned by the parent and society. The tasks include a wide variety of behaviors, including bowel control, coming when called, eating properly, showing interest in reading, having the right kind of friends, and doing various chores. Parent reinforcement not only increases the probability that the right behaviors will be learned, but more importantly, the child learns early in life about the pleasure of good performance.

(c) Commitment earns loyalty. In this the parent demonstrates his commitment to the welfare and the future of the child and for this the child is loyal to parental values and beliefs as well as to the parents themselves. If the parent should demonstrate little commitment to the child as a person then the child is less apt to internalize the parents' value system or comply with parental wishes.

Incidental infringement on the contracts can be ignored and often is. However, continued abuse of the contract leads to estrangement. This may not manifest itself until the onset of adolescence, when the individual feels he has the power to move against or away from the parents. Numerous children run away from home annually. Most, however, stay and fight with the resentful feelings, generalizing to the school. Much of the passive resistance and overt aggression teachers see is misdirected hostility toward parents.

Elkind contends that the contract, based primarily on a reward system, is primarily a middle and upper socioeconomic class arrangement. In lower economic homes the contract tends to be based more on punishment for nonperformance or wrongdoing rather than a reward for performance. Consequently, students from such homes tend to test limits to find out how little can be done or how much one can get away with before punishment is levied. The lower socioeconomic child is most apt to strive to avoid punishment and perceives school work, rules, and the teacher from this perspective. By contrast, the middle-class teacher perceives the social order as an arrangement whereby if a person does the right thing he will be rewarded. The disparate expectations are the basis for much misunderstanding.

Students from lower socioeconomic homes must learn how to function within the reward contract arrangement. The middle-class contract is not only more humane, but it is more productive, and finally is more consistent with the commercial world in which promotions come from achievement. It is more critical that the lower socioeconomic child adapt to the positive payoff contract than it is that the middle-class teacher revert to the punishment arrangement with which the child has lived in the past. Unfortunately, most often the teacher resorts to the punitive pattern with all its consequences. When teachers say "punishment is the only thing they understand," they may be correct. However, the function of schooling is to teach proper understanding, not to perpetuate the ones the students bring to school. The contents of this book illustrate that many alternatives to punishment exist.

Elkind's allegation that the issue is socioeconomically differentiated may be in error. Nevertheless, we know that many of our students and teachers are punishment-for-failure oriented; we would do well if we were able to convert this orientation to performance payoff. If we could help parents understand the Elkind agreement–contract system and institute it in family relations, we would help the parents, students, and ultimately ourselves. One way to help the parents and the students is to model a good example. For example, send home positive complimentary letters for achievement or good behavior in contrast to repeated indications of failure.

If the schools were to model respect and empathy when dealing with student feelings, encourage students to establish behavioral plans and thence to be responsible to them, focus adult response on desired behavior, demonstrate assertiveness in an authoritative mode rather than an authoritarian way, then parents would be more likely to follow.

Parent–teacher conferences are an important means for encouraging parents to support educational goals. The objective isn't simply to give the parent a report of the student's progress, although that is an important function. Parents are the most important people in a student's life. As such, they continually have a powerful impact on values, goals, and behavioral patterns. Parents could be a teacher's most important ally in eradicating ignorance and promoting appropriate social behavior. We not only need to obtain parental support, but need parents as part of the educational team.

Many teachers are a little afraid, suspicious, and disdainful of parents; but remember the reverse is also true. Many adults recall their own schooling experience as threatening, boring, punitive, lonely, and degrading. When a parent comes to school to see a teacher, these old memories are recalled. Second, parents often see teachers as a threat to a hoped-for bright future for their children. A bad grade or a negative comment from a teacher clouds hopes and fantasies. Still another basis for parental hostility is jealousy. If a student admires a teacher, the parent may feel inferior by comparison. After all, teachers are often better educated, better dressed, and more sophisticated than parents. Moreover, in some instances teachers are younger and nicer-looking than are the parents. A youngster's comment about any of these factors may cause a parent to feel inferior and hostile.

Meaningful communication is difficult when people are hostile, fearful, or suspicious. It is up to the teacher to be patient and skillful in building a trusting relationship. The most important element in building trust is to listen and attempt to help the other person to get what he wants. What do parents want? It is a fair guess that most parents want their children to do well in school.

The parents of those students who need the most help are often the ones who do not come in to work with the teachers. The faculty of a junior high school in Bloomington, Indiana decided to alter that situation. A counselor was assigned the task of getting the parents to school for a visitation night. She sent the usual letters home and followed this up immediately with a phone call to personally invite the parents. She didn't mention the students at all but just emphasized that she wanted to meet the parents, say hello, and show them around the school. Of course, teachers would be available for conferences. The night before the meeting, she once again called each parent to confirm their intention to come, tried to get some idea of the time she could expect them, and mostly restated that she was looking forward to seeing them. Attendance exceeded 90 percent. It was much higher than they had ever had previously. Perhaps parents just have to be convinced that school visitations are safe and that they are truly welcome.

Parents tend to consider school as someplace where they send their children. They sense that the school belongs to the teachers and the principal. The result is that they are indifferent to school problems unless money or their own children are involved. But since the community and parents are part of the problem, they should be part of the solution. To this end the people must feel that the school is owned by them as part of the community. Several examples of how this can be achieved are included here.

Community Relationships

A Los Angeles junior high school had a serious problem of vandalism, particularly damage during off-school hours. A new principal was employed and one of his most noteworthy strategies was a daily stroll through the neighborhood. He introduced himself to everyone he met. They discussed the weather, local businesses, some things that were happening in the school, and the problem of vandalism. People began making appointments with him on the street corners and serving coffee and cookies on front porches. As the principal of the school became more accepted as a member of the community, the vandalism dropped dramatically. In a couple of years the principal was promoted to a larger school and his successor did not have time to walk around the neighborhood. Soon the vandalism was back to its original level.

In a similar way, Vera Cogan, the principal of Akron's Perkins Junior High, made a point of picking up some of the troublesome students after school and driving them home. Conversations were casual and did not dwell on school or the students' problems, but rather focused on events and the neighborhood to convey friendliness. In addition to opening up an important new dimension of her relationship with the students, Ms. Cogan learned about the individual student's perception of the community. She also frequently had a chance to informally meet the parents and establish a basis for further communication.

In Billings, Montana, a junior high school with parental help and support started a work program for those youngsters who seemed prone to trouble. For example, one of the projects was a bicycle shop in the school. One of the results of the program was a drop in the cost of replacing broken windows from $1500 to $100 per year.

These examples illustrate what is found in numerous excellent American schools. An important ingredient is caring and reaching out for community support. A critical segment of the community influence is peer culture. We will now consider ways in which peer culture can be important in behavior management.

INVOLVE STUDENTS IN THE TASK OF GOVERNING STUDENT BEHAVIOR

In most public schools the prevailing assumption is that adults must control student behavior. Several ongoing programs clearly demonstrate that given the opportunity students can govern their own behavior.

Peer Social Reinforcement

McGee et al. (1977) reviewed a number of studies that looked at the issue of the effects of peer reinforcement. Two conclusions were drawn from a multitude of studies in a variety of settings. First, peer approval has a profound influence on the acquisition and maintenance of behavior that is deviant in the eyes of authority. One series of observations showed that within institutional settings 70 percent of peer approval was given to individuals specifically for delinquent behavior. That is, if an individual was to be reinforced by his peers, in the majority of situations it was for misbehavior. Second, reported evidence showed that social acceptance was highly correlated with the rate of giving or receiving reinforcement. It is fair to assume that students, like most people, want to be popular. According to these studies, the best way to be popular is to reinforce others or to be reinforced. Since delinquent behavior is that most frequently reinforced, it follows that deviancy, as defined by authority, is the vehicle for popularity. It appears that it is not the behavior that is satisfying but the frequency of reinforcement. The task is to get youth to reinforce the behavior that we as teachers value. The kids get the popularity, we get the behaviors we desire. Inasmuch as we have thoroughly discussed reinforcement, the task of focusing peer reinforcement on productive behavior is left to the reader. We will therefore focus on other forms of student help.

Four Prototypes of Student Self-Management

Several schools in Sacramento have Conflict Management Patrols. The patrols are students who have been trained to listen and encourage others to express their views. The training focuses on two items: (a) Sensitivity to impending problems. Responding to cues of potential danger and trying to intervene before behavior erupts. (b) Interceding by active listening. Encouraging offending students to state their grievance, clarify issues, and moderate their behavior while seeking satisfaction. The Conflict Management Patrols deal mostly with rumors, fights, and kids in a bad mood. I recently experienced an instance in which a Conflict Management Patrol may have been very useful. While I was visiting a high school, a girl confided in me that she and another girl were going to have a big fight behind the girls' gym right after school. I decided not to act on the information and soon forgot it. At 3:20 the principal announced over the loudspeaker that about 200 students were gathered behind the school. When we got there the fight was well under way. Although none of the teachers or administrators had heard of the impending fight, apparently most of the students knew about it. Had a Conflict Management Patrol been in operation, the members would have known about it and interceded. The intervention is nonthreatening and respectful of the students' position. The only goal is to find nonviolent resolution to conflicts.

The process is simple enough. If an incident occurs, the students are given the time and privacy to talk out their quarrels without adult interference or a student audience. The students soon recognize that if a student Conflict Management Patrol member can resolve the problem there is no recrimination from the teachers. Wayward students would much rather talk it out with another student than face a teacher or principal. The program saves teachers from getting involved in nasty situations. Most important, students learn some valuable citizenship lessons.

When Robert Tafoya introduced the idea in an elementary school, the teachers were skeptical. However, as evidence of its success became known, several other schools soon established programs of their own.

Three additional examples of responsible student action will be presented to illustrate both the constructive potential and power of students.

At the height of the black power movement in the early 1970s a group of young adult male Black Panthers entered Crispus Attucks High School in Indianapolis. They brushed by the armed guard and were moving about the halls. While the principal was considering the pros and cons of summoning the city police, the student council president asked if he could handle the situation. The principal, fearing a riot if armed police came to clear the school, agreed not to call the police, with the provision that the Black Panthers vacate the school. The student leaders told the Panthers that they were going to call an all-student meeting to discuss the issue and asked the Black Panthers to wait outside. They complied and a meeting was held. No adult was present. Most of the Crispus Attucks students were black and many favored the Black Panther movement. However, they recognized that the school would be destroyed if it were the focus of a conflict. The meeting lasted over an hour and in the end the students voted to tell the Black Panthers to stay out of the school and off of the grounds because the school belonged to the current student body. The Black Panthers, many of whom had attended Crispus Attucks, respected the student wishes and left the grounds.

In Watertown, Connecticut, school superintendent King recommended that a custodian's position be eliminated and the money be awarded to the student council to use in any manner and for whatever purposes it decided. Two stipulations were added. Expenditures by the student council were to be audited by the school administration and any damage to the school due to vandalism was to be repaired immediately and the cost was to be deducted from the account. The custodian's salary, $9048 plus adjustments for inflation, was placed in the student activity fund.

King later reported, "The strategy worked, our lavatories now look better than they have in 15 years." In addition:

1. The student council has become revitalized, growing from a few self-appointed students to 80 representatives of all factions within the student body.
2. The students have become more aware of their own actions, those of other students, and the consequences.
3. Student and teacher morale is markedly improved.
4. Students have a broader appreciation of governmental operations and political processes.

In El Paso, Texas, students of Riverton High School produced a program of filmstrips and videotapes to demonstrate the risks of alcohol and drug abuse to be shown to elementary school students. The target population was sixth-graders because high school students recalled that sixth grade was a critical time for them. The high school students not only scripted and produced the materials, they also made the presentations. In and of itself it was an excellent educational experience. Moreover, the program came across much better than anything the teachers had been able to present because the high school students had more credibility among the sixth-graders.

Positive Peer Culture Program

A program worthy of a detailed description is the positive peer culture program (PPCP). Unlike most programs that strive to rehabilitate youth, PPCP does not ask members to be receptive to adult help, just that each be willing to give help.

PPCP is based on seven underlying assumptions:

1. Each individual would prefer to succeed, or at least stay out of trouble. No one enjoys failure and the negative consequences of goofing up are perceived as a hardship by everyone.

2. Peer pressure has a powerful influence on youth behavior and orientation. Peers offer an affirmation of right and wrong and thereby help clarify values during the transition from parental control to independence.

3. Group affiliation and feelings of contributing to others' welfare are rewarding. Each person enjoys and will respond to the opportunity to make a positive contribution to a group of which he is a member. Most people sense virtue in helping others. Recall our discussion of self-concept. Esteem is partly a function of influencing others and feeling virtuous. Furthermore, each person needs to feel that he is valued and respected by others. Group cohesion is an important factor in productive behavior. People in a group, feeling responsible for others and themselves, build group cohesion.

4. Reformed people are the most committed change agents. When a person resolves his own problems and is functioning within the limits of a new order, he has the insights, patience, and will to help others with the same problems.

5. People will most likely adapt and internalize values in an atmosphere of trust and openness. Youth, particularly those who are exhibiting

behavioral problems, are more apt to trust their peers than adult professional personnel.

6. Change will occur most readily in a socio-emotional condition in which change is expected and encouraged by peers. There is ample evidence that statements like "I don't want you to skip class because I don't want you to fail" or "Come on, we'll help you make it" are powerful supports for adopting desired behavior.

7. A focus on immediate conditions is more productive than delving into the past for solving current problems. Likewise, fantasizing about the future is distracting. The groups find it more valuable to confront the situation as it is, the consequences of present behavior and the value of alternatives.

The heart of the PPCP is tough caring. The program assaults such attitudes as "Most people do not care what happens as long as it doesn't happen to me" and "It is cool to care less." Positive caring is foreign to a number of youth. Learning the what and how of caring is a major thrust of the program. Caring might be defined within a group as doing what one can to promote what is best for other individuals. Vorrath and Brendtio (1985), the originators of the PPCP, refer to love "not as the sweet sugar-coated kind, but the unselfish love that makes a marine crawl on his belly into enemy fire to save a wounded buddy." Thus, the caring of this program is more "I am concerned about what happens to you" than "tender loving care." This concern, once established, enables one person to confront an offending person with "What are you doing and what will be the consequences of it?" without the other person feeling reproached and hostile. Shared caring is the critical ingredient. Without it, the effects are negligible.

The process begins with the formation of small groups. Each group is composed of from 9 to 15 members. The respective groups discuss behavior and its consequences. It soon becomes apparent that much of the behavior isn't paying off. It just gets people into trouble. So, the question comes up, How can a person stay out of trouble? If someone is cutting class, becoming a behavioral problem in a class, or doing poorly academically, instead of administrative discipline the issue is referred to his group. The peer group then confronts the wayward individual with his behavior and the consequences. The discussions are confidential, the business of no one outside of the group. It is a family affair.

Does PPCP work? Henry Vorrath initially used it successfully with male delinquents in a reform school. The program has been equally successful in public schools. Vorrath and Brendtio (1973) report success in a midwestern high school that formerly had been overridden by riots. A cadre of armed police roamed the halls. Everyone knew that the police were using student undercover agents. The dropout rate was high and no one trusted anyone. No one was happy with the situation. A positive peer culture program was initiated and all students were assigned randomly to groups of nine. Reportedly, in this previously troubled school, students of diverse cultural and ethnic backgrounds are no longer warring but now naturally work together to solve problems. They have learned to take care of each other. Teachers once again focus their attention on teaching.

More explicitly, Peer Culture Development, Inc. of Chicago, a non-profit organization supported primarily by private funds, reports the following results:

Truancy	Reduced 40 percent
Discipline	Reduced 59 percent
Thievery	Reduced 78 percent
Assault	Reduced 74 percent
Intoxication	Reduced 35 percent

The PCD corporation has worked primarily with disaffected youths who are causing more than their share of disruption in junior and senior high school. Students in these programs are enrolled in a credit course that meets daily. Currently, the corporation is monitoring about a dozen programs in Chicago and Detroit.

In conclusion, a number of programs demonstrate unequivocally that given responsibility, students respond energetically, positively, and productively. The responsibility is not that of suffering the consequences of their behavior, but the responsibility of governing their own behavior. The programs recognize that people, particularly youth, need respect, compassion, support, and other people to resist impulses, control emotions, and to work out appropriate behaviors. The evidence consistently demonstrates that if given the opportunity and trust, that youth can accomplish the task. The most important question may be: will adults who are concerned about their own authority allow it?

RESORTING TO THE LAST RESORT: EXCLUSION

Occasionally, an individual's antisocial and unchanging behavior is such that society has no choice but to exclude him from normal affairs.

Some people are incorrigible. School personnel have neither the training nor the time to treat those who do not respond to the variety of strategies noted in this text.

The message to such an individual should be, "We are sorry, but your behavior is incompatible with the goals of this institution. Our efforts to help you find a responsible role in the school have failed. Therefore, we are denying you the right to continue as a student." Such a message ought not be delivered as a threat or punishment, but as a statement of fact. Obviously, for legal and ethical reasons such a statement should only be made after a number of alternate treatments have been unsuccessful. To dissociate an individual from normal affairs is a serious but sometimes necessary act.

Duke (1980) contends that most serious behavioral problems occur out of classrooms. Nevertheless, classroom disruptions are numerous and costly. Kounin (1970) identified several ways that teachers can and do eliminate such disturbances.

THE ORCHESTRATION OF CLASSROOM ACTIVITIES

Through an elaborate observation program of functioning classrooms Kounin (1970) and his associates arrived at an astonishing conclusion: Teacher desist messages, in any shape or form, are equally ineffective means for establishing desired student behavior. The only apparent effect seemed to be student emotional discomfort as a function of expressed teacher anger. Unfortunately, the student discomfort results in an increase in disruptive behavior.

Although desist message appear to have little positive effect, Kounin discovered that teacher behavior is a prime factor in determining the degree of on-task behavior. Classrooms differ markedly in the frequency of disruptive and off-task behavior. The critical elements are twofold: frequency of interruptions and the teachers' ability to maintain student involvement. Kounin's studies have been replicated in a variety of settings, locations, and grade levels. Although his findings have been refined and clarified, the thrust of his conclusions has been confirmed.

Interruptions

Any time anything interrupts ongoing class activity (announcements over the speaker system, an outsider appearing at the door, a sudden change of activities, roll call, passing out new materials, or the teacher making an announcement), productive work is delayed as much as eight minutes. Wayson and Pinnell (1980) found that 80 percent of the behavioral disruptions in the typical classroom are the result of some dysfunction in the way the school or the classroom is run.

Involvement

Even if classrooms were free from external interruptions and students were intrinsically motivated to participate in class activities, the complex nature of the teacher's task invites behavioral problems. Kounin identified four such factors: group focusing, overlapping, monitoring, and activity transitions.

Group focus

One of the several pitfalls confronting a teacher is that he is frequently called on to work simultaneously with groups and individuals within groups. The teacher is responsible for establishing and maintaining a group focus in which the class forges ahead on the assigned task. Kounin found that teachers differ in the way two potential traps are handled. The first is recitation. While a given student is reciting others often become bored and restless. Furthermore, recitation can be threatening to those students who fear exposure or frustrating to those eager to repeatedly demonstrate their expertise. Good teachers are alert to these dangers and carefully keep everyone involved by such means as calling on a variety of individuals to comment on another student's response, to explain why a response was correct or incorrect, to summarize periodically what has been said, and cueing various students by name (e.g., "Dale, listen carefully to Scott's answer because I am going to ask you about his ideas.").

Overlapping

The second potential problem arises out of the need to deal simultaneously with two or more events. For example, while a teacher is busy with a subgroup on one activity, a student from a different subgroup frequently comes up for help with a problem from his activity. Instead of allowing this to be an intrusion to the ongoing group activity, the successful teacher simply signals the group to continue while he quickly deals with the disruption, then returns as if nothing had happened. The danger is in having students wait while the teacher is attending to a multitude of interruptions. Some teachers tend to become so involved with one student's problems or brilliance that others are left sitting unattended for several minutes at a time. The result often is mischief.

Monitoring

Kounin found that the monitoring and responding to the minor misbehaviors that naturally occur is a critical factor in classroom management. This is a finely tuned dilemma for teachers. From our knowledge of reinforcement we know that if an activity is rewarding, such as chatting with a friend, this behavior will be continued. Likewise, a student may behave in such a way as to excite others to the point of spreading the misbehavior. Therefore, some teachers feel compelled to immediately respond to any misbehavior. However, Irving and Martin (1982) show that such teacher responses have a diverse effect. Teachers who are ever alert and respond immediately to moments of off-task behavior often stimulate more misbehavior. You will recall that this is precisely the finding of Becker et al. (1975): the more frequently teachers told students to sit down, the more frequently they stood up.

Kounin reports that only about two percent of the classroom deviancies are serious or have the potential for escalation. He warns against teacher nagging, pointing out that the more effective teachers often ignore minor deviancies.

Successful teachers communicate that they know what is going on and that they are in control, not by punitive action after the act, but by frequently scanning the class, establishing eye contact with those students who are watchful to see if the teacher knows, and by anticipating problems when students appear restless or bored. During seat work, unless occupied with a subgroup, the teacher should be moving about the room, tuning into those who need special assistance. Such help should be brief. Brophy and Evertson (1981) report that teachers can be overly intrusive and verbal while making rounds during seat work. Limit interventions to student requests or to times when a student is obviously off track. The point is to keep students involved primarily through positive interaction rather than reprimands.

Activity transitions

Perhaps the most critical factor in student involvement, other than student motivation, is the degree to which the teacher maintains momentum.

Kounin found the typical classroom to be a busy, complex organization with an average of 33.2 major changes in ongoing academic activities each morning. If a teacher is in a self-contained classroom or is utilizing one of the new National Science Foundation Curricula or any of the Social Studies Inquiry Projects or is operating an open education classroom, he must manage considerable activity movement. He is like an orchestra leader initiating, sustaining, and terminating various activities that sometimes overlap and frequently involve groups in various combinations. For some changes, students are moved from one part of the room to another and for others, the change involves storing one set of materials, which is then replaced by another. All such changes create a psychological shift for the participants because each activity is unique in its work demands and attractiveness.

We ought not be surprised to learn that within each of such transitions lay a number of teacher traps. Students are more relaxed and thus more distractable while changing from one activity to another. In addition, there is a natural confusion with storing and retrieving materials, changing seats, and shifting intellectual gears from one activity to the next. In many classrooms, the potential for mischief is compounded by teacher error. Through his observation, Kounin identified five critical teacher behaviors that could prompt problem behavior. He called the five teacher behaviors *stimulus boundness, thrusts, dangles, overdwelling,* and *fragmentation.* Each of these teacher behaviors could occur at any time but they seemed to occur more frequently during transition times. The effects of the teacher errors were not only the disruption that occurred at the time but the overall impact on continued operation of the classroom. Those classes in which errors were recorded were found to be more prone to general chaos and student misbehavior.

Stimulus boundedness.   Teachers sometimes lock into particular stimuli that seem to be unrelated to the ongoing curricula. Such events were observed to occur suddenly while the teacher was otherwise involved with students. Some minutia—a piece of paper on the floor, a noise outside of the room or a student with poor posture—would divert the teacher's attention. The point is not that the teacher noted such events but that he dwelled on them so they became a significant intrusion into the class's ongoing activity. Everything seemed to stop as the teacher focused attention on this otherwise passing event. Since it was unconnected with student work activity, the intrusion disrupted the whole class.

Thrusts. Kounin (1970) found that some teachers suddenly, without warning, changed the ongoing activity. Students might be deeply engrossed in doing mathematics and the teacher announces, "All right, everybody, put away your mathematics books, take out your geography books. Hurry up now, we don't have any time to lose." Another example might be, "I would like to hear your views on why the British acted as they did at the Boston Tea Party." Several hands are raised and the teacher calls on Sue. After Sue presents her view several other hands go up but the teacher says, "Okay, now let's talk about what was happening in Philadelphia" without either following up on Sue's comments or acknowledging the other students.

Dangles. Kounin (1970) called teacher behavior "dangles" when the teacher starts an activity, wanders off into something else, and then returns to the original activity. For example, Mr. Shok starts the spelling test. "The first word is complement, complement. The second word—Oh, before I forget it, we will be having our six-week test next Friday—Where was I? Oh, yes, the next word is implement, implement."

Whereas stimulus boundedness, thrusts, and dangles give the class activity a sense of jerkiness, the next two categories, overdwelling and fragmentation, drag things out. The effect is that the class becomes unsettled and momentum is lost. In the case of overdwelling and fragmentation a feeling of lethargy sets in as the students wait and wait and wait.

Overdwelling. Overdwelling exists when the teacher focuses attention on an event long beyond the point of student understanding. As the teacher drones on, the student reaction is "Okay, okay, we've got the message." Overdwelling comes in different forms. When it focuses on student behavior it might be called nagging. For example, two boys quietly whispering in the back of the room are repeatedly told to stop wasting time and get to work. Each time, the whole class is interrupted because the teacher's voice stops everybody's concentration. Finally, the teacher takes three minutes to explain that people cannot do their work and visit with one another at the same time. Finally, the class is allowed to return to their work. The boys once again return to whispering with one another.

In a different way the teacher gets hung up on some detail or part of the lesson. Explanations go well beyond the point of diminishing returns.

Fragmentation. In fragmentation the task is separated into smaller parts, whereas a directive or explanation could be best achieved as a whole unit.

For example, "Get your mathematics books out of your desks. Hurry up, we are all waiting. Okay, place your books on your desks now. Everyone, get a piece of paper and place it next to your book. Now, we will all need a pencil. Does everyone have a pencil? Okay, we are ready to go. Everyone, open your book to page 296. We're waiting. Find exercise 96. That is it. See question one. Read question one. Who can give us the answer to question one?"

The movement errors are self-evident. However, many of us are guilty of stop-start and delay actions. They are expensive. Not only is time lost but behavior problems are much more apt to exist in those classes due to general misbehavior. A well-organized program with minimum distraction or delay to student on-task behaviors results in maximum student achievement and minimum misbehaviors.

In conclusion, Kounin's work in school has shown that the success of a formal lesson rests on two conditions: The delivery of signals in support of appropriate behavior and the prevention of inputs that may encourage inappropriate behavior. The teacher needs to be alert to support the proper behavior with cues and reinforcement. Likewise, he must monitor the activities so as to block out the potentially distracting stimuli.

RECOMMENDED READINGS

Gotts, E.E. and R. Purnell. *Home school communication.* Bloomington, IL: Phi Delta Kappa Fastbacks, 1985.

National School Resource Network. *Resource handbook on discipline codes.* Cambridge, MA: Deleschlager, Gunn, and Hain, 1980.

Seeley, D. *Education through partnership.* New York: Harper and Row, 1981.

13

EXEMPLARS OF STRATEGIES FOR SCHOOL DISCIPLINE

In order to obtain closure and simultaneously demonstrate that the processes we have discussed work, we will now consider a number of exemplars. Each of these was conducted in the natural setting of schools by teachers and other school personnel. These are not fictitious cases and each illustrates that with confidence and skill teachers can significantly change the behavioral style of aberrant students. Each of the cases presented here speaks for itself.

Hopefully, each of you now has an understanding of the rationale and processes of the various strategies that one might employ to manage student behavior for educational development.

Table 13.1 identifies the exemplars by title for each of the strategies we have studied.

UNRULY STUDENTS CONTROLLED BY THE GOOD BEHAVIOR GAME

Outside observers described the students within two chaotic elementary school classrooms as destructive, disruptive, and unmotivated. The teachers felt helpless in their varied attempts to bring these youngsters under control long enough to instruct them. Johnson et al. (1980) suggested that the students might shape up if their behavior cost them something.

The teachers instituted the Good Behavior Game. The respective classes were divided into teams. The names of the respective team members were placed on the board and whenever a child misbehaved his team was given a black mark. At the end of the day the black marks for each team

Table 13.1. Index of exemplars: application of identified strategies

Strategies	*Titles*
Punishment	Unruly Students Controlled by the Good Behavior Game
	Logical Consequences Reduce Aggression
	Punishment: Successful but Often Temporary
Deal with feelings	Enhancing Student Communication Skills
	Working Off Excess Energy
	In-School Suspensions: "The Slammer"
Reality education	
Value-moral development	Values Clarification Reducing Adolescent Smoking
Reinforce desired behavior	
Selective Reinforcement	Encouraging Shy Students to Participate
Extinction	Roll-Call Clowning Extinguished
Token economy	Token Economy Helps Problem Adolescents
Cost effectiveness	Living by Rules Pays Off
Self-management	A Teacher Gives Behavior Modification a Try
	Carla
	Tess
Contingency-contracting	Jim Stops Stealing and Everyone Wins
	The Failure to Success Contract
Control of stimuli	
Stimulus control	Assaultive Behavior Controlled through Stimulus Control
Time out	Time Out for Crying
Stress control	A High School Student Learns to Attend School
Models	Modeling to Reduce Impulsive Hyperactive Behavior
Satiation	High School Student Gives Up Wastebasket Game
Building Congruent Self-Concepts	Using Peer Groups to Build Positive Self-Concepts
	A College Student Serves as an Aid to Building a Student's Self-Concept
	Reinforcing Positive Self-Concepts
Assertiveness	Assertiveness: Not Easy, but Good
School–community programs	Enhancing the Community's View of the School
Classroom organization	Putting a Hold On Hyperactive Students: Use Seat Belts

were tallied and the team with the fewest marks was awarded a special treat. The treats included such events as an extra ten minutes of recess, fruit, or just the opportunity to line up first for lunch the next day.

The students selected names for their respective teams and seemed to have a sense of pride in their team's record. After two weeks, because the behavior change was slower than expected, the teachers indicated that the winning team had to have ten or fewer black marks.

The disruptive behavior dropped from the original 100 percent of the time to 8 and 15 percent in the respective classes. Furthermore, the teachers relaxed and began to attend to the more appropriate behavior. At the end of 30 days the teachers felt confident enough to end the program.

Alas! A follow-up seven weeks later found that conditions were again as they had been in the first place. Teachers were nagging and students were disruptive, destructive, and unmotivated.

Unlike reinforcement, punishment does not easily lend itself to the weaning process. The authors suggested that had the game been paired with reinforcers, the teachers might have naturally weaned the students and thereby achieved enduring positive effects. On the other hand, the teachers could have focused on good behavior right from the beginning. That is, instead of issuing black marks for disruptive behavior they might have given marks for good behavior and counted the positive behaviors to determine the winners. Accentuating the positive leads naturally to good dispositions, is more effective, and allows a nondisruptive tapering off of the program. Finally, the effects of reinforcement could have been more emphatically brought to bear since the teacher could give individual selective reinforcement each time a student responded so as to build points for his team.

LOGICAL CONSEQUENCES REDUCE AGGRESSION

Webster (1976) tells how a very aggressive 13-year-old student's behavior changed following a series of episodes in which he was removed from class and isolated following assaultive acts. The boy had a long history of behavioral problems. Despite extended psychotherapy he remained wild and uncontrollable. Just prior to the program described here, he had attacked two boys on the playground and injured one so severely that he had to be hospitalized. His assaults included biting, kicking, throwing objects, and hitting with his fists or anything he could pick up. He averaged about four such assaults a day.

Treatment involved three processes. First, he was told in a matter-of-fact way that his behavior was disruptive and intolerable. The teachers explained that in the future, acts of aggression would necessitate isolation from other students. They indicated that they would interpret his behavior and the consequences and explain why he was placed in isolation. Second, for a period of one week any aggressive act on his part was stopped and consequences on the other students was explained. Third, since the aggression continued, on each outburst he was removed from class and taken to an 8 x 12 windowless room that was equipped only with a single desk. He could take his books with him. At the end of the period he was to go on to his next class. On each instance he was informed of the unacceptable behavior and escorted to the isolation room where he was left alone. He was informed that when he stopped physically attacking others without provocation the isolation trips would end, since their only purpose was to protect others from the disturbance he had been causing.

During the first two weeks he spent an average of 65 minutes a day in isolation. During the third week his aggression dropped significantly and he only averaged 18 minutes per day. His behavior steadily improved and in the seventh week the teachers found no reason to isolate him. At the end of the tenth week his teachers were satisfied that his aggressive tendencies were controlled. Meanwhile, his academic work had improved sufficiently so that he could be reinforced for this spontaneous involvement.

The punishment was quick, consistent, of short duration, and administered for specific behavior. The student could eliminate it by known behavior, that is, by controlling his assaultive acts. When the teachers administered the punishment they did so without anger or expressing blame. They simply explained the consequence of the behavior in terms of the disruption and unfairness to others in class.

PUNISHMENT: SUCCESSFUL BUT OFTEN TEMPORARY

A case when punishment seemed to work but didn't is recorded by Sulzbacher and Houser (1968). The situation occurred in an elementary special education class of six- to ten-year-old students. The problem was an obscene gesture accompanied by a variety of oral embellishments. A baseline was established after which the teacher put ten cards, numbered one through ten, on a holder in front of the room. The students were told on the morning of the first day that a special ten-minute free recess would be given at the end of each day. However, a card would be flipped over each time the teacher saw "the naughty finger" or heard any reference to what it stood for. The ten-minute recess would be reduced by the number of minutes showing on the last flipped card. The frequency of the finger sign and the oral description dropped dramatically, and at the end of 18 days it had completely disappeared. The contingency was removed and the original problem slowly increased until it was soon back at the original level.

It is possible that control could have been reinstated on a short-term basis and the desired ends reestablished with only an occasional booster shot. We do not know, however, as it was not reported.

One of the continuing problems with using punishment in school is that the effects end when the threat of punishment ends. Perennial surveillance and often repeated administration is necessary for maintenance. Surprisingly, weaning people from punishment is not easy.

ENHANCING STUDENT COMMUNICATION SKILLS

Minuchin et al. (1967) utilized a number of procedures to help students attend to teacher messages and respond more appropriately to tasks. The target of the program was children from disorganized families. Some parents tend to respond and direct children in global and erratic terms. The children never learn the nature of rules or a reward system for behaving appropriately. The children have not learned antecedent-behavior-consequence relationships or how to control events to get what they want. In solving conflicts the children seek answers in the immediate overt reactions of others. Although words may be used, the message is primarily nonverbal: push, shove, hit, and yell. Thus, attention is paid to the person rather than to the meaning of words for the context of the message.

Since teacher communication is primarily verbal, in which the meaning of words conveys the message, such children are often in conflict, confused, and unresponsive.

A curriculum of ten lessons for small groups was instituted to establish communication skills: listening, taking turns, staying on the topic, asking relevant questions, seeking and using information, and role playing. Such games as "Simon Says," in which winning was dependent on listening, were included in each lesson. Other activities included receiving a telephone message, waiting over a period of time with intervening activities, and then repeating the contents of the message. Another interesting, though simple, lesson: Each student is given a part of a familiar nursery rhyme. The task is for each to say his line in sequence. To do so, he must listen and wait his turn. Finally, the logic, sequence, and meaning of stories and give-and-take conversations were analyzed.

Students not only participated in the activities but also served as recorders and judges of their peers' communication. Pennies were often given as reinforcement.

The authors report substantial change in such communication elements as listening, taking turns, remembering, and following directions. This unusual, concentrated emphasis on communication paid off. We are reminded that many students are not ignorant, cantankerous, or mean. They just don't have the appropriate experience and orientation to function within the boundaries of school. When such is the case, we must arrange appropriate lessons.

WORKING OFF EXCESS ENERGY

When certain emotions are aroused, students become more energetic. Furthermore, many youngsters are just hyperactive. Some teachers recognize this and routinely introduce some form of calisthenics when students show signs of restlessness, particularly on rainy days. Standing up and stretching or deep knee bends are very helpful for converting tense feeings to relaxation.

Allen (1980) routinely employed jogging to help elementary students start the day in a relaxed mood. First thing each day students limbered up and then either walked or jogged around the school yard for ten minutes. Students recorded their respective distances. Although no pressure was put on the students, they were encouraged to increase their distances. Awards were given when a student passed the 5, 10, 25, and 50-mile marks. The teacher reported the class to be closer and more cooperative as a consequence of the jogging, and such misbehaviors as hitting, name calling, and interruptions were cut in half over a six-week period. As in most classrooms the behavior tended to worsen as the day progressed. Perhaps the jogging or calisthenics session would be most helpful at midday.

IN-SCHOOL SUSPENSIONS: "THE SLAMMER"

In-school suspension rooms are typically unattractive. By design, in-school suspensions are supposed to be unstimulating, authoritarian, and work oriented. Englemann (1969) goes so far as to recommend a small closet. A sentence to in-school suspension is meant to be punitive.

In contrast, Lynnfield School's suspension room, known as "the Slammer," is bright, sunny, and strewn with plants, posters, and seasonal decorations. It is a pleasant room. Study carrels, work tables, file cabinets, and bookcases give a workplace orientation. Two part-time teachers with flexible shifts offer tutoring, advice, and listening ears.

Students sometimes arrive angry, just mildly upset, belligerent, or terrified. Upon arrival students cool off and are privately informed of the highly structured program, with simple but specific rules and some privileges. Mostly the orientation attempts to positively communicate an understanding of student feelings, support, and an offer of help. In some respects the orientation resembles Glasser's reality education. An attempt is made to nonjudgmentally ascertain "What happened?" from the students' point of view. The students can blame, vent anger, or whatever else they want. The bottom line, however, is: "Okay, you're here now and we can make good use of the time to get a leg up on academic assignments and problems; we are here to help." It is a workplace.

An open folder is established for each student. The folder contains a letter to the parents explaining that the student is temporarily in the in-school suspension room. Also, a contract is made that includes statements of expectations from both the student and the teachers' points of view as well as responsibilities.

Work materials include texts, resource books, remedial-basic skill workbooks, magazines, and newspapers. Teachers are contacted for assignments and suggestions for special problem work. Games are sometimes played both as educational vehicles and therapeutic opportunities. As much as possible a one-on-one student–tutor operation is established for the time of suspension. Therefore, the number of students in the in-school suspension program is limited.

The point of this suspension is rehabilitation. Each student is explicitly informed that he is expected to live within the school rules, but a caring, helping relationship is formed whereby academic help is given and counseling is available. Although the room is perceived as punishment, it is not retaliation for past misdeeds nor is it designed to derogate personal self-image. The emphasis is on justice and helping the wayward student to get on track. To some extent it is a retreat for troubled youngsters. For more information see Martin (1980).

VALUES CLARIFICATION: REDUCING
ADOLESCENT SMOKING

Smoking and drug use are perennial problems in many secondary schools. Despite punishment, books, parental pressure, and health courses, teenagers continue to be big users. Education programs have had limited impact on curbing adolescent smoking.

Greenberg and Deputat (1978) compared three programs for discouraging smoking: a scare approach, an information approach, and a peer attitude approach. High school students who admitted smoking a minimum of five cigarettes a day were randomly assigned to one of four health classes.

In the scare class, lectures and films depicted the deadly consequences of smoking on the heart and lungs. Demonstrations illustrated how nicotine induced cancer in animals. Homework assignments included papers on how it would feel to choke to death and more personally each student was asked to identify family members who smoked and subsequently perished by cancer or a heart attack.

In the information class, facts and figures regarding the incidents of cancer and heart attacks among smokers were presented. Pamphlets published by the Lung Association, the American Heart Association, and the Department of Education were read and discussed. The point of the program was to logically convince students of the hazards of tobacco and the health and aesthetic advantages of abstaining from smoking.

The attitude group spent the first part of the semester working on communication skills. Then class activities focused on peer discussion of the values inherent in smoking. Papers were written, shields were designed, artwork was produced, and letters were written to friends about the effects of nicotine on various organs of the body. In all cases what was produced was shared with peers and discussed. That is, work was not simply submitted to the teacher for grades. Instead, the primary goal was to use the produced materials as part of class discussions. Positive reasons for smoking were considered as well as the negative consequences. For instance, in one exercise each student was asked to list three ideas that might be used to encourage a friend to smoke.

The fourth group, as a control, was assigned to a class that omitted any curricula regarding the use of tobacco.

The immediate effect showed that the scare tactic was superior. The largest initial drop in smoking occurred in that group. However, a seven-week follow-up showed that only in the values clarification group did students continue to abstain. Twenty-nine percent of the students who dealt with attitudes were no longer smoking.

ENCOURAGING SHY STUDENTS TO PARTICIPATE

Two phenomena are observable in most classrooms: (a) Even though most teachers have been taught the value of reinforcement, various observers note that reinforcement occurs only at the rate of about two per hour per class. (b) A few students carry the burden of discussions or more critically few other students seldom volunteer.

Hosford (1969) tells about a program to simultaneously counter both tendencies. Each of the social studies teachers in a junior high school was asked to select three quiet students from each of their classes. One of the three was then identified as a target for reinforcement. Anytime this student spoke out he was given both verbal and nonverbal reinforcements. Even negative verbal student comments were reinforced thus: Student: "We have too much homework in this class." Teacher: "Thanks for bringing that up. Teachers need that kind of feedback to help us decide what is a fair assignment." The nonverbal reinforcers were nods, smiles, and other approval signals.

In addition, each student was interviewed twice by the school counselor to discuss career programs during the third and fourth week of the program. Any student comment about class discussion signaled a counselor-positive response and an extra display of interest. During the second interview the experimental students were told, "Mr. So and So happened to mention to me how pleased he is with your interest in social studies these days."

As a consequence of these treatments the students became more active in class discussions and teachers were found to use reinforcement to a significantly greater degree.

ROLL-CALL CLOWNING EXTINGUISHED

Dreikurs et al. (1982) tell about this logical means for extinguishing a student's playfulness during roll call. Certain logistic details like lunch counts and attendance must be taken care of as efficiently as possible. This particular teacher called roll first thing in the morning in order to make some sort of contact as well as to take attendance.

On the first day of school the teacher was relatively confident that all of her students were in class, but no one answered when she called Rafael Thomas. She called the name a second time without receiving any response. She decided to ignore it and continue on with roll call. The next day Rafael once more did not respond when his name was called. The teacher again ignored him. On the third day Rafael's name was not included on roll call. Rafael called out, "Hey teacher, you didn't call my name." The teacher explained, "For the last couple of days you didn't answer when your name was called, so I thought you didn't care. If it matters, I'll call your name tomorrow." The next day Rafael's name was included at roll call and he responded, "Present!" at the top of his voice. The other students laughed heartily and the teacher had to wait a few minutes before resuming class. The teacher recognized that Rafael had been well reinforced for his behavior. The next day his name was omitted. He immediately stood up and yelled, "You didn't call my name again." The teacher ignored the outburst and continued on. Rafael's name was omitted for the next several days. He did not respond in any way except to closely watch the teacher during roll call. After a week the teacher decided to try once more. As part of the roll call Rafael Thomas' name was included. When his name was called Rafael immediately and pleasantly said, "Here." The teacher had no more trouble with Rafael during roll call.

TOKEN ECONOMY HELPS PROBLEM ADOLESCENTS

Stein et al. (1976) describe a special program for a group of 22 male adolescents whose behavior was such that they had been expelled from the regular public high schools. The boys exhibited a variety of excessive behavioral problems, such as drug use, school truancy, hyperactivity, and physically attacking others within the community and the schools.

The boys were enrolled in an alternative high school with the following conditions.

Enrollment in the program was voluntary, but a contract signed by parents, the boy and the school stipulated free schooling, transportation, and a hot noon meal. On the other hand, the attendance rule indicated two consecutive unexcused days of absence or four unexcused absences during the five-month period automatically resulted in termination. Five sick days required that the parental excuse be supplemented by a physician's letter.

No punishment was intentionally administered. A point system was established whereby each consecutive 15-minute period of on-task behavior earned 1 point. No points were awarded if the student was off-task at any time during the period. Similarly, points were awarded for appropriate behavior on the bus, during lunch, and during free time.

Points could be used to buy a variety of privileges. A 15-minute smoke, 15 points; 30 minutes in the swimming pool, 60 points; or a day off from school for 500 points. Other events such as arts and crafts, horseback riding, a fishing trip, bowling, and movies could also be purchased.

When they entered the program, some of these adolescents were reading at the first-grade level, although the average for the basic skills was fifth grade. The average academic gain per year was 1.4 years, and all subjects but spelling exceeded 1.5 years. The attendance rate over two years was 88 percent compared to 90 percent for the normal high school population. This is remarkable, inasmuch as 15 of these boys had been expelled from school for excessive truancy. Ninety-five percent of the group remained in school throughout the first year, and 82 percent stayed through two years. Twelve of the students returned to the regular high school within two years.

In summary, a structured token economy enabled a class of disruptive, unpredictable adolescent boys to behave appropriately and achieve substantial academic growth. The program was considerably less expensive than the cost of supporting uneducated and delinquent youth. The unmeasured effects in terms of self-control, responsibility, self-concept, and citizenship are undoubtedly the most important products of the program.

LIVING BY RULES PAYS OFF

Hegerle et al. (1979) report a simple but logical way to reduce off-task behavior. Make it a game.

The class was divided into teams. Each team started off each period with 100 points. Points are lost each time a team member violates a specific rule.

(1) Raise hands before volunteering information.
(2) Raise hands to get permission to leave seat.
(3) Do not talk to other students during seat work.

The team that loses the fewest points wins. Winning is backed up with extra recess, parties, and special privileges. At the end of five weeks talking out and out-of-seat behavior were reduced by 80 percent.

We shouldn't knock success, but probably the same results would have occurred had points been awarded for instances of rule obedience. That is, the teams could win points for each occasion in which a member acted in accordance with the above rules. The teacher would not only accentuate the positive but encourage the students to think in terms of doing what is right, which is different from not getting caught for rule transgressions. Finally, the effects of reinforcement could have been more emphatically brought to bear, since the teacher could give individual selective reinforcement each time an individual responded so as to build points for his team.

A TEACHER GIVES BEHAVIOR
MODIFICATION A TRY

Laura was a seventh-grade student. She was bright, she did her assignments conscientiously, and she always recited well in class. But Laura had a severe behavior problem in terms of relating to her fellow students.

In addition to the difficulties of relating to others, Laura was also handicapped by sight, hearing, and speech defects. Her thick glasses didn't seem to help much, and in addition to her hearing problem, she had a serious speech impediment, so it was difficult to understand her. All of these handicaps made Laura different, of course, but other children who had many of the same problems had learned to adjust to the classroom. Laura seemed to be continually squabbling with other students. I checked with our school nurse and former teachers trying to learn more about her. Laura's parents, I learned, were just as odd as their daughter.

Possibly, if Laura had been in a different class she could have achieved some degree of adjustment, but unfortunately she was in a class of known troublemakers who thrived on upsetting her. She could not cope with the heckling, teasing, and imitation. She overreacted by flying into a blind rage, screaming, hitting, and kicking at everyone and everything. No one was safe from her attacks, not even me. A small incident, such as someone touching her hair as they passed her desk, would set her off again. As a result, Laura spent part of many class periods cooling off in "Time Out."

As I mentioned, Laura was capable of better-than-average grades, and she loved to read. I decided that reading would be my key to helping her learn to cope with the other students. I explained the idea of a contract. If she could behave properly in the classroom, she would be awarded a special library pass, effective the next class period. At first she didn't understand, but I wrote three contract examples to show her how the idea worked. In order to increase the probability that the process worked, I suggested that our first contract would be for only one day. I indicated that if all went well for one day, the following day she would go directly to the library at the regular class time, check out whatever books she wanted, and remain in the library reading her books for the remainder of the period. To get Laura to take even more responsibility for her actions, I asked her to write the contract details for behaving properly in class.

The following morning, ten minutes before the first bell, Laura gleefully handed me her contract. She watched as I signed it and I watched as she signed it. All went well that first contracted day. The most testy teaser in class could not bait her; she just gave him a superior grin and continued on task. The next day, Laura happily showed me the library books and asked if she could try another contract. Of course, I agreed. We made many contracts, each time stretching the time that Laura would be "good" in class before she received her much-coveted library pass.

In time, the contracts were no longer necessary, but the warm smiles and verbal approval continued until the last day of school. Of course, she continued to receive her library passes on a regular basis. Although Laura wasn't in my class every day because of the library passes, these absences didn't adversely affect her academic progress. As her relations with classmates improved so did her grades.

Although Laura's behavior improved greatly in my class, I don't know if she is now a well-adjusted junior high student.

Below is an example of one of Laura's contracts.

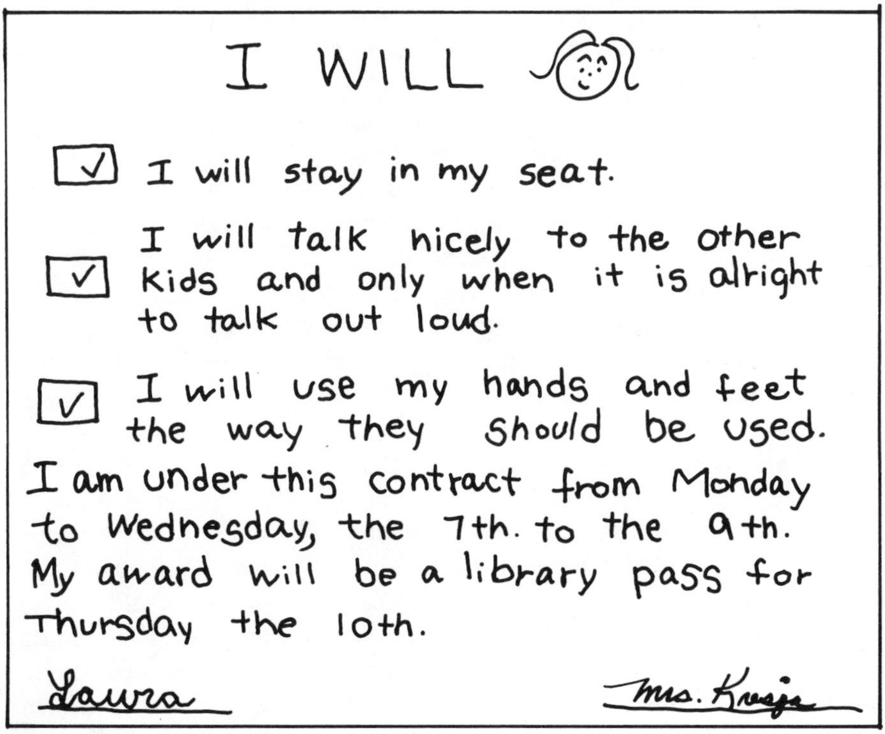

Thanks to Ann Krejsa, Lake Village, Indiana

Figure 13.1. Sample "contract" prepared by the student.

JIM STOPS STEALING AND EVERYONE WINS

Brooks and Snow (1972) report this incident: Jim, a ten-year-old boy, was accused of stealing; he often was in possession of or caught trying to pass off stolen materials. He also had a tendency to be off-task; his classroom performance was weak. The teacher believed that much of his behavior was due to social isolation and a desire to be accepted.

With Jim present, the teacher explained to the class that Jim was having trouble completing his work and some other unmentioned things. The students were asked if they would help him change. The teacher introduced this plan. Every time that Jim completed an assignment or worked effectively within a group activity through its completion he would receive a point; whenever he accumulated ten points the whole class could have 15 minutes free time to play a game, read, or do whatever they wished. On the other hand a penalty clause was added: If Jim failed to complete an assignment or left the group, one minute would be deducted from the class's next recess. In private Jim was told that he would be given ten cents for each ten points he earned.

Jim earned ten points on the first day and each of the next five days. The other students responded positively to his efforts and success. After one week the teacher congratulated Jim and the class and indicated how good it was to see everyone work together. He announced that Jim had really changed so the program was ended.

Jim had changed. Throughout the remainder of the school year he seemed to be more motivated. He participated more readily in class activities, completed more assignments. The stealing stopped.

THE FAILURE TO SUCCESS CONTRACT

Brooks (1974) reports a program whereby habitually truant students become regular in attendance. The program was used with both males and females, but we will report only the case of Mary, a 15-year-old senior. Mary missed school or specific classes about 40 percent of the time. Some weeks she was out four of the five days. All of this occurred over the strong objections of her mother. The mother whipped her with a belt, restricted her to her room full-time, and threatened to remove her from school, all to no avail. Mary continued to be truant at every opportunity.

Mary was bruised and restricted to her room when the school counselor consulted with Mary and her mother. The following contract was written:

Mary will do the following in exchange for the rewards stated below: (1) Mary will attend every class for which she is scheduled. (2) Mary will have her teacher initial an attendance card at the end of each period. (3) Mary will turn the attendance card in to the attendance office at the close of each school day. (4) Mary will record her attendance on a chart in the counseling office indicating the classes she has attended. (5) Mary will attend a group rap session once each week.

If Mary does as noted above: (1) At the end of week one, Mary will be taken off of restriction for four (4) hours on Friday night. (2) At the end of week two, Mary will be taken off of restriction for four (4) hours Friday night and six (6) hours Saturday. (3) At the end of week three all restrictions will be removed. (4) At the end of three weeks a conference will be held to determine a new reinforcement schedule.

The contract reportedly worked fine and at the end of six weeks it was terminated, since Mary was attending classes regularly. She reported a better attitude toward school and a desire to enter post–high school training. Her mother was pleased with Mary's change of attitude and their improved relationship.

ASSAULTIVE BEHAVIOR CONTROLLED THROUGH STIMULUS CONTROL

McCullough et al. (1977) explain how a high school student learned to control his temper.

Larry had a long history of losing control of his temper easily, frequently, and with very unfortunate consequences, despite repeated and harsh punishment. Just prior to the treatment described below, Larry had been suspended from school for publicly berating a teacher, and then when confronted by the principal, he stalked out of the office in the middle of the discussion.

The program involved several steps that you will recognize as segments of a number of the strategies that we have discussed.

The counselor discussed with Larry one at a time the circumstances of each of several instances in which he lost control of his temper. In the beginning Larry was defensive and justified his acts by blaming others and circumstances. The counselor never condemned Larry, but focused his remarks on the consequences: "What did that get you?" Finally, Larry saw the light. He admitted to not knowing how to control his temper and that this had been a lifelong problem.

Once Larry admitted that *he* had a problem and that *he* was going to have to change, the second phase of the rehabilitation was initiated. In order to identify some of the antecedent components to the temper outbursts, Larry was asked to describe the feelings, thoughts, and bodily sensations that he experienced in a variety of episodes. Together with the counselor, Larry identified the following sequence of events that seemed to occur prior to temper outbursts:

(a) He would curse himself when confronted with another person in any stressful situation.
(b) He became defensive and resisted complying with requests from the other person in these situations.
(c) He felt a tingling cool streak up his back.
(d) His body began to tense up, starting at his feet and gradually spreading over his whole body.
(e) His right arm muscles became tense and his muscles flickered.
(f) When his right arm tension built up he attacked others either by striking them or through verbal abuse.

Larry was then asked to reenact the conflicts he had had with the teacher and principal that had led to his suspension. A videotape record was made of the role-playing reenactment. When Larry viewed the playback he was somewhat dismayed, when he noted that his body language was more provoking than his words.

The fourth phase required Larry to again role play conflict with school authorities, but this time rather than reenact his typical behavior he was told to avoid profanity, to speak calmly, to relax and to tone down his aggressive posture. In each of several episodes the counselor played the role of authority: a teacher or school administrator. When Larry viewed these tapes he could analyze his own behavior and the positive effects on others when he controlled himself.

Next, Larry had to learn to control the chain of events that heretofore had preceded his aggression. Three particular cues were selected for change: Larry learned to say "Stop!" whenever he started to curse himself. When he felt his body tensing up he was to tense his whole torso and relax repeatedly in rapid succession and then breathe deeply and exhale. In the event of tension in his right arm he was to turn and leave the scene until he felt calm once again. Larry also learned how to be assertive; to use I-messages to convey his feelings and wants. Larry practiced each of these processes until he felt comfortable and could easily do each.

Finally, Larry and the counselor constructed a written contract that clearly spelled out his behavior in the event of confrontation with someone, and what he was to do with respect to the "signals."

The contract was shown to teachers and the principal and agreed that whenever Larry walked away to avoid a blowup, they would not pursue the conversation until he returned and calmly stated that he was ready to discuss the issue. Teachers gave him permission to leave the classroom to stand in the hall when he felt the pressure building. All school personnel agreed to verbally praise him when he handled a stressful situation without losing his temper.

The counselor checked daily with teachers and supervisors to count the frequency of breakdowns and the number of times Larry successfully managed stressful situations. During the remainder of the semester Larry lost his temper a total of three times. During the next year he lost control only twice.

This program was complex but straightforward, and did not involve anything that we have not covered. The program was time consuming, but inexpensive compared to the probable consequences had Larry simply been punished and allowed to reenter without treatment. An uncontrolled temper bodes evil for both the aggressor and the recipients.

TIME OUT FOR CRYING

When someone is hurt we tend to want to comfort them. Thus, when a child cries, nurturant people tend to respond with tender loving care, the assumption being that the child is either hurt or frightened. The case reported here by Teel (1971) emphasizes the need to interpret the causes of behavior before responding.

This six-year-old boy cried almost constantly, which suggested that he was neither hurt nor frightened, but was being reinforced by others for crying. Surprisingly, the reinforcement was scolding and corporal punishment.

The time-out procedure involved putting the child in a vacant room (called the time-out room) for five minutes whenever he cried. If he stopped crying within the five minutes he could return to his seat. If at the end of five minutes he was still crying he was brought back to his seat. If he stopped crying he stayed in his seat as long as he didn't cry. If, when brought back, he continued to cry after two minutes, he was returned to the time-out room. The teacher did not talk during the process and took care not to have any eye contact with the child while he was crying.

Within two days the heretofore nearly continuous crying was greatly reduced. In another few days it stopped completely.

The author points out that this procedure needs close monitoring because if the procedures described here are inconsistent, the effects are an even greater resistance to the elimination of the undesired behavior. The teacher complained that the procedure was very time consuming. In this case about three hours was lost during the week in which the crying was eliminated. That is expensive for one child. However, the cost in time, the psychological drain on the teacher and other pupils, and the prognosis for the crying child had he been allowed to continue crying are on the other side of the choice.

A HIGH SCHOOL STUDENT LEARNS TO ATTEND SCHOOL

Fears surrounding school attendance are more common than most of us probably realize. About five percent of school-age children develop psychosomatic reaction to school severe enough that extensive attendance becomes nearly impossible. Nausea, vomiting, cramps, headaches, and even blurred vision are reported. LeAnes and Siemsglusz (1977) tell how a paraprofessional was used to help a high school student overcome school phobia.

University students are often required or just wish to extend their practical experience. They are energetic and highly motivated and therefore are an excellent source of help.

In this case a ninth-grade girl found school intolerable. Parental threats, bribes, spankings, and giving in to her demands had no effect. She missed 50 of the first 90 days of high school. She had a record of poor grades and few friends. Any attempt to force her to attend school resulted in screaming, kicking, vomiting, and fighting.

A university psychology major volunteered to work with the girl for a project. On their first meeting the volunteer brought a matching pin and a pennant which stated "I am somebody." The parents were removed from the conflict because the volunteer picked the girl up at home every morning and delivered her to school. Nonetheless, each day began with bitter crying, begging, and threats of vomiting. In the second week the volunteer was given permission to deliver the girl late for school so that a drive around town could precede school. Short but pleasant and interesting tours were taken. The drive served to desensitize the girl and soon they were shortened and then eliminated. Meanwhile the volunteer picked up the girl after school each day and together they went to an ice cream parlor and discussed the day's events. This was supplemented by role playing.

After two months attendance was perfect and the pick-up and return had been gradually withdrawn. School achievement was reportedly improved, although the girl remained shy and without friends. Additional paraprofessional help was later employed to increase assertiveness and social skills.

MODELING TO REDUCE IMPULSIVE HYPERACTIVE BEHAVIOR

Hyperactive students are often impulsive, easily distracted, and have short attention spans. Drugs or positive reinforcement programs are used frequently to control these combined tendencies. Douglas et al. (1976) thought that a combination of modeling and self-directed messages might help such youngsters not only control their overactive behavior but improve general problem-solving skills as well. The authors also believed that to be successful the students would need to learn the controls in a variety of circumstances in order to obtain a broad sense of how they work.

The study was conducted with 18 hyperactive impulsive elementary school boys. However, the same program ought to be equally if not more successful with secondary students and young adults. The training period involved two one-hour training sessions per week over 12 weeks. Both parents and teachers worked with the students and served as models.

The process was for an adult to work with one or two students on any one of a wide variety of tasks, including academic work and games. The boys were told that they were smart enough, but they often got into trouble at home and school because they didn't use certain "tricks" that they would now be taught. They were told that the tricks would work in all kinds of situations. The tricks included various steps in defining a problem, considering alternative solutions, checking work, calmly correcting errors, sticking to tasks, and congratulating oneself for good work.

The sessions involved the adults and students working together on some task. The adult talked to himself and the student as they went about the task. For example, while solving a puzzle the teacher or parent might say: "It is important that I stop and think before I begin." "What plans could I try now?" "I wonder, how would it work if I did it this way rather than . . ." "Gee, I made a mistake there, so I'll erase it and start over." "Now, have I included all of the steps, let's check that." And finally, "Hey, I (we) did a pretty good job on that."

In addition to cues regarding searching, focusing, and attending to one's own acts and materials, special emphasis was given to noting facts. For instance, during a card game an adult might say aloud, "He is asking me for all of my threes, so I gotta remember that he has threes in his hand." The adult models set time estimates for completing tasks and paced themselves to use all of the time. As training progressed, students set time estimates and were encouraged to increase their length.

To sum up, if a teacher wants to be a model he must do more than simply be a good person. Modeling involves acting out the intended behavior and also simultaneously verbally confirming the acts by pointing out what is being done and reinforcing himself for doing it correctly. Signals must be utilized to bring the proper behavior into focus. Furthermore, the process or behavior should not be situation specific. The wider the variety of contexts in which the models are observed the greater the probability of imitation.

The program described here resulted in reduced aggression, more tolerance for frustration, better listening skills, and oral comprehension. The effects were apparent immediately following the program and were still present in a three-month follow-up.

A HIGH SCHOOL STUDENT GIVES UP
WASTEBASKET GAME

Rich sat up front by the teacher's desk and repeatedly tossed paper at the wastebasket. He made about 90 percent of his shots and didn't disrupt the class. However, as I pointed out to him, if I let him "shoot" from there, then the guy behind him will want to shoot, and then the guy behind and the guy behind him, and so on. I never really convinced him, however, and he continued the practice. I decided to try another approach.

The next day Rich took a shot at the basket with about 20 minutes left in the class period. I had just stopped lecturing and most students were about to get started on their homework. I called Rich over to the side of the room and asked him to sit in a chair that I had placed about 10 or 12 feet from the corner. I placed the wastebasket in the corner and picked up a piece of yellow paper from my desk. I wadded it up and gave it to Rich and told him he was to spend the rest of the class period shooting at the wastebasket. After each shot, hit or miss, he had to retrieve the yellow paper, go back to his desk and shoot again. This seemed like a neat idea to him and the rest of the class as they all were watching. After about five minutes most of the class was back to work and Rich spent the rest of the period shooting baskets. At the rate of three shots per minute, he shot 60 times and had to make 60 trips to the wastebasket to retrieve the paper wad. Would this repetition with little reinforcement from others lead to satiation?

For the next 12 days Rich did not throw any paper toward the wastepaper basket. On the 13th day he was doing his homework, and having realized he had made a mistake, wadded his paper up and tossed it into the wastebasket from his seat. Immediately he cringed and put his hands up to his face realizing what he had done. Despite his argument that it was unintentional, which I thought it was, I reestablished the chair, and the wastebasket over at the side of the room, where he spent the last 15 minutes shooting paper. He has not shot a paper-wad basket since, at least in my class.*

USE PEER GROUPS TO BUILD POSITIVE SELF-CONCEPTS

Self-esteem rests on self-evaluation in terms of affiliation, power, competence, and virtue. Washington (1977) based a program for building self-concepts on these elements. He reports that such programs are particularly helpful when working with inner-city minority groups who have received little positive feedback compared with many signals of inferiority.

The initial step is to develop a feeling of oneness among the students. Washington does this by asking group members to respond to such questions as "Describe a critical moment in your life," "What kinds of things make you feel good?" and "What goals are you setting for yourself?" As students share their own and listen to others' great moments, feelings, and fantasies, they feel affiliated, trusting, and trustworthy. They become close to one another.

The second set of exercises involves the sharing of successes. The teacher begins by sharing with the groups some things that make him feel proud and good about himself. Following this each participant lists on paper five successes he has experienced. Success is defined broadly and includes not only awards, but any sense of achievement from school, home, community, or church. Each individual then tells about one or more of these success experiences, during which the teacher encourages elabora-

---

*Thanks to James Brickley

tion. Finally, at the conclusion of each presentation, other members of the group are asked to identify particular strengths and virtues connected with this particular success. Thus, each individual learns that he contributed to his own success by merit of his qualities.

In summary, Washington's strategy for building self-esteem is consistent with what is known about self-psychology. The ingredients of self-esteem include feelings of power to control events, competence to achieve, and affiliation with others. The sources of information are recognizing what one has achieved and positive feedback from significant other people.

A COLLEGE STUDENT SERVES AS AN AID TO BUILDING A STUDENT'S SELF-CONCEPT

Margolis et al. (1977) report the use of reality education to increase achievement and reduce misbehavior for a high school boy.

Mark lived with his mother and two sisters, but he occasionally slept at his father's because of conflicts with the mother. However, the mother felt the father was a bad influence and she did all she could to resist the father–son relationship. Mark sometimes visited his uncle, but it was strongly suspected that the uncle supplied Mark with drugs and liquor.

The school was concerned about Mark's repeated disobedience of conduct rules, his acting out of emotions in front of and on peers, and neglect of academic responsibilities. A college student volunteered to work with Mark.

First a trusting relationship was established. They began with general neutral topics or small talk. Soon they discussed his interests and hopes for the future in the armed services, as an auto mechanic, and as a lawyer. They went to the school's weight-lifting room, where Mark explained and instructed the student on weight-lifting techniques.

Second, they discussed concerns about what seemed to be happening at school and the probability that Mark could make it if he developed reasonable goals.

Third, work periods were established during which all of the relationship was devoted to task-oriented activities. Concepts were explained, efforts were praised, and Mark's ability to succeed were stressed.

Finally, a mastery program was instituted whereby new assignments were undertaken only after Mark demonstrated achievement in the ongoing assignment.

Mark showed improvement in each of the school's areas of concern.

Three months later his behavior remained appropriate and he was making progress toward graduation.

The college student, rather than dwelling on the past record or Mark's difficulties, set standards and attended to Mark while he attained them. Most important, she showed respect for his needs and talents and made him feel valued.

REINFORCING POSITIVE SELF-CONCEPTS

Self-confident people tend to achieve more, make friends more easily, are more apt to be group leaders, and are more likely to be happy than are people who lack this self-confidence.

Hauserman et al. (1976) utilized a reinforcement strategy to help elementary schoolchildren become more aware of their positive qualities. Thirty students were selected for treatment for low self-esteem based on teacher ratings and scores on self-report self-esteem scales.

The treatment was simple and lasted 40 school days. Any time one of the targeted children completed a task, responded to a school rule, helped another child, or was obviously successful at something the teacher or his aide would say, "Tell me something good about yourself." After the child replied positively he was given a hug or pat and a statement was made, such as, "I'm really proud of you" or "It is nice to work with people like you." If a student couldn't think of anything, then an idea to be repeated was modeled: for example, "Well, how about 'I'm good because I try to get my work done on time.' " When the student repeated the statement, he was reinforced. This set of procedures was repeated for each of the children about eight times each day.

After the 40 days no further requests for self-praise were given and the class routine settled back to normal operations. Four weeks later the self-esteem test was administered once again. Every one of the 30 children showed an improvement on measured self-esteem.

ASSERTIVENESS: NOT EASY, BUT GOOD

Peterson et al. (1979) discuss in some detail the use of I-messages to increase on-task behavior and reduce disruptive behavior. Most often when people are confronted with the abrasive behavior of others they blame the others for the resultant feelings. The message is "You. . . ." Typically the verbal message is accompanied by punitive actions or at least poorly disguised, hostile, nonverbal behavior. Unfortunately, the reaction is likely to be counterproductive. When a teacher accuses or otherwise retaliates for student misbehavior with such statements as "You continually interrupt when I'm talking with other students," or "No matter how many times I tell you, you . . .," or "Your behavior is so immature that I don't know what I'm going to do with you," the student is most apt to reciprocate with aggressive behavior. If the teacher attack is powerful enough, the student may become temporarily subdued, but at best, passive aggression follows.

In contrast to the you-message an I-message focuses on the way the teacher feels. It is simply an honest statement of the teacher's reaction to given student behavior. I-messages recognize that it is not just this student's behavior that is aggravating, but that if anyone behaved this way it would be disturbing and that "I do not like the resultant feelings." Most often when a person is angry, hurt, or disappointed, he acts out these feelings by attacking the offending person. Instead of acting out the emotion, with the I-message the person *owns* the emotion. For example, "I am angry," "I become hurt," or "I feel disappointed."

Peterson et al. (1979) worked with a fifth-grade teacher and a sixth-grade teacher in the following way (a) The nature of the I-message was discussed in detail. (b) The teacher repeated the I-message in a number of controls: "(name of student), when you _____ I feel _____ because _____." (c) I-messages were demonstrated for a variety of kinds of situations, students, and feelings. (d) The teachers practiced I-messages in role-playing situations.

As a result, when this technique was employed in the classroom, the fifth-grade teacher reduced disruptiveness by 50 percent and increased on-task studying by 25 percent. Unfortunately, the teacher reverted to you-messages and students soon returned to their pretreatment behaviors.

The sixth-grade teacher maintained the I-message with eight targeted students. Six of the eight students reduced the frequency of disruptive behaviors and half of the students significantly increased study time.

ENHANCING THE COMMUNITY'S VIEW OF THE SCHOOL

Olivero (1977) tells about a number of interesting ways that schools have bridged the school–community gap. Three examples are included here.

An Idea from Japan

A school in Japan was having a hard time gaining parent support for the regular activities of the school. The parents were normally tied up in their jobs during the normal school hours, seemingly giving low priority to the school and its activities.

This school decided to change the school week twice annually. On the special weeks students attended Thursday through Monday (with time out for church services Sunday morning), rather than from Monday through Friday. Because of the changed schedule, many parents were able to participate in weekend field trips, were able to offer services (like those at the computer center), were available to offer specific courses, and were able to gain a better feel for the school and its operations.

Complimentary Cards

In a school in Tustin, California, complimentary cards have paid excellent dividends. Each student in school is given a set of complimentary cards (they look like a business card) which states, "You have just been served by (student's name), a student at (school's name) School."

When students perform a service in the community, a card is given to the individual served. The school often receives letters from senior citizens and others who tell the principal how helpful a student has been. More often than not, the students are those not known for their academic progress. Complimentary cards have been helpful to students, the school, and the community. This is a process worth considering!

ONE POSITIVE EXPERIENCE

A school in Huntsville, Alabama, took on the philosophic principle of assuring each person in school of at least one successful experience each day. Sounds easy, but try it!

To achieve their mission, ten minutes was set aside at 3:00 p.m., the end of each day, for everyone, including teachers, secretaries, students, and custodians to write on an index card one successful experience he or she had during the day. Students quickly found if they had a successful experience two or three days in a row, there was a good possibility the next day would also hold for them a positive happening. The hypothesis becomes self-fulfilling.

PUTTING A HOLD ON HYPERACTIVE STUDENTS: USE SEAT BELTS

Hyperactivity is a common problem in most special education classes and in many regular classrooms. Goodman and Hammond (1975) report a clever, nonpunitive tactic that paid off with a class of 16 primary-age, learning-disabled boys.

Out-of-seat behavior had become so common that seat learning was seriously hindered. The children were not malicious, but just couldn't seem to remember to stay in their seats. As a result of short attention spans, their distractability, and impulsivity, they were unable to remain seated long enough to complete even short assignments that they otherwise could do. Even most continuous verbal reminders were not enough to keep these students in their seats. They needed a constant reminder.

In a discussion of auto safety the use of seat belts was introduced as a means to keep from being hurt. The next day, to their surprise, the students found that each of their desks was equipped with a seat belt to help them stay in their chairs. The children liked the idea that their school desk was like a car seat. The desk seat belts were in reality pieces of string tied to the back rings of the chairs. The ends were loosly tied in a bow knot in front of each.

As each child received his assignment, he sat down and his "seat belt" was tied. Almost immediately, extraneous movement about the room was diminished. As soon as the student started to stand, without any teacher reaction whatsoever, a tug around the middle reminded the student to sit back down. At times the teacher had to redirect attention to the assigned task. However, the spontaneous movement was eliminated.

Subsequently, real seat belts, picked up at little cost from an auto wrecking company, were installed. These seat belts were better because students were able to independently buckle and unbuckle themselves. The seat belts were never used punitively and the students seemed to perceive them as a helpful cue for good behavior. Unhappiness due to the restrictiveness imposed by the belts was not evident. The authors believe that with the seat belts the otherwise hyperactive students could stay and function in regular classrooms. The authors further stated that they thought such mechanisms could be used in regular classrooms for those students who need reminders for staying in their seats.

Cautionary note: The seatbelts must be easily releasable by the student in case of emergency.

RECOMMENDED READINGS

First, J. and Mizell, M.H. (Eds.) *Everybody's business.* Capitol Station Columbia, S.C.: South Eastern Public Education Program, 1980.

Galloway, D. *Case Studies in Classroom Management.* New York: Longman, 1976.

Millman, H.L., Schaefer, C.E. and Cohen, J.J. *Therapies for school behavior problems.* San Francisco: Jossey-Bass, 1980.

IN CONCLUSION

Teaching, working simultaneously with from 20 to 40 youngsters, each unique in critical ways, has to be the toughest game in town. The task is compounded by the nature of schools and by the near isolation of individual teachers from professional aid. The primary task of teaching, academic learning, can only be achieved if the school and classroom environment are free of emotional and behavioral distractors. Thus, a share of teacher attention has to be devoted to those elements that distract learners from achieving their academic goals. This secondary task requires that we create an environment whereby learners not only behave properly but also develop the personal qualities that enable them to govern their own behavior, respect the rights of others, and feel pride in themselves.

The purpose of this book is to help teachers develop a comprehensive, systematic, consistent, and efficient program to achieve these secondary objectives.

In Part I, we carefully considered punishment and concluded that though it is natural, common, and effective under specified circumstances, it is not efficient because of its complexity and cost.

In Part II, we noted that many people are trapped in a conflict cycle that attempts to protect the self but winds up perpetuating misbehavior, hostile reactions, and negative self-images. Teachers are able to intervene in the conflict cycle by (a) dealing with learner feelings, (b) confronting learners with their moral responsibility to control their own behavior, (c) structuring the environment to reinforce proper behavior, and (d) enhancing individual self-esteem.

In Part III, we identified several factors that seem to induce misbehavior in schools. Fortunately, we were also able to identify means to counteract these factors.

Will these strategies work? Empirical studies reported in the professional literature suggest that they do. In chapter 13 we presented exemplars from schools across the country that testify that the strategies are used effectively. Thus, it appears that we do have a comprehensive, systematic, consistent, and effective program with which teachers can both control disruptive behavior and promote the development of desired personal qualities in their learners. However, the final and most critical test is your classroom and school. Be patient. Few things work the first time, and nothing works every time.

BIBLIOGRAPHY

Adler, A. *Problems of neuroses*. New York: Harper Torchbooks, 1964.

Allen, J. Jogging can modify disruptive behaviors. *Teaching Exceptional Children,* 1980, *12,* 66–70.

Alberti, R.E. and Emmons, L. *Your perfect right*. San Luis Obispo, CA: Impact, 1978.

Alschuler, A.S. *School discipline: A socially literate solution*. New York: McGraw-Hill, 1980.

Aronfreed, J.M. Aversive control of socialization. In W.J. Arnold (Ed.), *Nebraska symposium on motivation*, 271–320. Lincoln, NE: University of Nebraska, 1968.

Aspy, D.N. The relationship between selected student behaviors and teachers' use of interchangeable responses. *The Humanistic Educator,* 1975, *14,* 3–11.

Atkinson, J. and Raynor, J. *Motivation and achievement*. Washington, D.C.: Winston, 1974.

Azrin, N. and Holz, W. Punishment. In W.K. Honig (Ed.), *Operant behavior areas of research and application*. New York: Appleton-Century-Crofts, 1966.

Bandura, A. *Social learning theory*. Englewood Cliffs, NJ: Prentice-Hall, 1977.

Bandura, A., Ross, D., and Ross, S.A. Imitation of film-mediated aggressive models. *Journal of abnormal and social psychology,* 1963, *66,* 3–11.

Becker, W.C., Engelmann, S., and Thomas, D. *Teaching 1: Classroom management*. Chicago, IL: Science Research Associates, 1975.

Berne, E. *Beyond games and scripts*. New York: Grove, 1976.

Bessel, H. and Palomares, U.H. *Methods in human development*. El Cajon, CA: Human Development Training Institute, 1970.

Biehler, R. and Snowman, J. *Psychology applied to teaching*. Boston, MA: Houghton Mifflin, 1982.

Blatt, M. and Kohlberg, L. The effects of classroom moral discussion upon children's level of moral judgment. In Kohlberg, L. and Toriel, E. (Eds.), *Recent research in moral development*. New York: Holt, Rinehart and Winston, 1973.

Bonjean, C.M., Schneider, L., and Lineberry, R.L. *Social sciences in America*. Austin, TX: University of Texas Press, 1976.

Broden, M., Hall, R.V., and Mitts, B. The effects of self-recording in the classroom behavior of two eighth grade students. *Journal of Applied Behavior Analysis,* 1971, *4,* 191–199.

Brodinsky, B. *Critical issues report: Student discipline problems and solutions.* American Association of School Administrators. Sacramento, CA: Education News Service, 1980.

Brooks, B.D. Contingency contracts with truants. *Personnel and Guidance Journal,* 1974, *52,* 316–320.

Brooks, R.B., and Snow, D.L. Two case illustrations of the use of behavior modification in the school setting. *Behavior Therapy,* 1972, *3,* 100–103.

Brophy, J. Classroom management as instruction: Socializing self-guidance in students. *Theory into practice.* 1985, *24,* 233–240.

Brophy, J. and Evertson, C. *Student characteristics and teaching.* New York: Longman, 1981.

Brophy, J. and Rohrkemper, M. *Teacher's specific strategy for dealing with hostile aggressive students.* East Lansing, MI: Institute for Research on Teaching, 1980.

Canfield, J.T. and Wells, H.C. *100 ways to enhance self-concepts in the classrooms.* Englewood Cliffs, NJ: Prentice-Hall, 1974.

Canter, L. Discipline: You can do it! *Instructor.* 1979, *89,* 108–111.

Canter, L. and Canter, M. *Assertative discipline.* Seal Beach, CA: Canter and Associates, 1976.

Carkhuff, R.R. *The art of helping.* Amherst, MA: Human Resource Development, 1983.

_____. *The skills of helping: An introduction to counseling.* Amherst, MA: Human Resource Development, 1979.

Carnegie, D. *How to win friends and influence people.* New York: Simon and Schuster, 1937.

Chase, N.F. *A child is being beaten: Violence against children, an American tragedy.* New York: Holt, Rinehart and Winston, 1975.

Clarizio, H.F. *Toward positive classroom discipline.* New York: John Wiley, 1980.

Clark, D., et al. *Why do some urban schools succeed?* Bloomington, IN: Phi Delta Kappa, 1980.

Clement, P.W. Training children to be their own behavior therapists. *Journal of school health,* 1973, *43,* 615–620.

Coleman, J.S., Campbell, E., Mood, A., Weinfield, E., Hobson, C., York, R., and McPartland, J. *Equality of educational opportunity.* Washington, D.C.: U.S. Government Printing Office, 1966.

Committee to End Violence Against the Next Generation, Inc. *The last (?) resort.* Berkeley, CA, 1983.

Cooper, B.S., Dreyfuss, G.O., and Boekhuff, H.R. Incentives that work: An administrative innovation in the Dade County Schools. *Phi Delta Kappa,* 1980, *61,* 523–524.

Coopersmith, S. *The antecedents of self-esteem.* 2nd. Ed. Palo Alto, CA: Consultant Psychologists, 1981.

Coopersmith, S. and Feldman, R. Fostering a positive self concept and high self-esteem in the classroom. In Coop, R.P. and White, K. (Eds.). *Psychological concepts in the classroom.* New York: Harper and Row, 1974.

Covington, M.V. and Berry, R. *Self-worth and school learning.* New York: Holt, Rinehart and Winston, 1976.

Crutchfield, R.S. Conformity and character. *American Psychologist,* 1955, *10,* 191–198.

Curwin, R. and Mendler, A. *The discipline book.* Reston, VA: Reston, 1980.

Davis, R. The impact of self-modeling on problem behavior of school age children. *School Psychologist Digest,* 1979, *8,* 128–132.

DeCecco, P. and Richards, A.K. *Growing pains.* New York: Aberdeen, 1974.

DeCecco, P. and Richards, K. Civil war in the high schools. *Psychology Today,* 1974, *9,* 51–56, 120.

deCharms, R. *Enhancing motivation.* New York: Irvington, 1976.

Dewey, J. Ethical principles underlying education. In *The Herbart Society Third Yearbook.* Chicago, IL: University of Chicago, 1897.

Dil, N. *Sensitivity of emotionally disturbed and emotionally nondisturbed elementary school children to emotional meanings of facial expressions.* Unpublished doctoral dissertation, University of Indiana, 1971.

Dobson, J. *Dare to discipline.* Wheaton, IL: Tyndale House, 1970.

Douglas, V., Parry, P., Morton, P., and Garson, C. Assessment of a cognitive training program for hyperactive children. *Journal of Abnormal Child Psychology,* 1970, *4,* 389–410.

Doyle, E. Making managerial decisions in classrooms. In Duke, D. (Ed.), *Classroom management.* Seventy-eighth Yearbook of the National Society for the Study of Education. Chicago, IL: University of Chicago, 1979.

Doyle, W. *Classroom management.* West Lafayette, IN: Kappa Delta Phi, 1980.

Dreikurs, R., Grunwald, B.B. and Pepper, F.C. *Maintaining sanity in the class-room,* 2d ed. New York: Harper and Row, 1982.

Dreikurs, R. and Grey, L. *A new approach to discipline: Logical consequences.* New York: Hawthorne Books, 1968.

Duke, D. *Managing student behavior problems.* New York: Teachers' College, 1980.

Duke, D.L. (Ed.). *Helping teachers manage classrooms.* Alexandria, VA: Association for Supervision and Curriculum Development, 1982.

Duke, D. and Meckel, A. *Classroom management.* New York: Random House, 1983.

Elardo, R. *Behavior modification in an elementary school: Problems and issues.* Phi Delta Kappa, 1978, *59,* 334–338.

Elkind, D. Socio-economic variations in value rule learning. Colloquium, Indiana University, 1975.

Emmer, E.T., Evertson, C., Sanford, S.P., Clements, B.S., and Worsham, M.E. *Classroom management for secondary teachers.* Englewood Cliffs, NJ: Prentice-Hall, 1984.

Engelmann, S. *Preventing failure in the primary grades.* New York: Simon and Schuster, 1969.

Englander, M. Teacher management of classroom misbehavior. In Harris, J.J. and Bennett, C. (Eds.), *Student discipline.* Bloomington, IN: University of Indiana, 1982.

––––––. Evaluation of northern California secondary school guidance programs. Educational Defense Act (PL 864), 1965.

Epstein, C. *Classroom management and teaching.* Reston, VA: Reston, 1979.

Erikson, E.H. *Identity, youth and crisis.* New York: W.W. Norton, 1969.

Estes, W. An experimental study of punishment. *Psychological monographs,* 1944, *57* (whole no. 263).

Evertson, C.M., Emmer, E.T., Clements, B., Sanford, J.P., and Worsham, M.E. *Classroom management for elementary teachers.* Englewood Cliffs, NJ: Prentice-Hall, 1984.

Farson, R. Praise reappraised. *Explorations,* 1966, *5,* 13–21.

Feather, N.T. *Values in education and society.* New York: Free Press, 1975.

Feingold, B.F. *Why your child is hyperactive.* New York: Random House, 1975.

Felker, D. *Building positive self-concepts.* Minneapolis, MN: Burgess, 1974.

Feshbach, N. Studies in developing empathy. In B. Maher (Ed.), *Progress in experimental personality research*. New York: Academic, 1978.

Fiordaliso, R., Griedman, R., and Filipczak, J. Teacher assertiveness: Its effect on student grades and on-task performance. *American Educational Research Association Meeting,* Toronto, 1978.

First, J.C. and Mizell, M. (Eds.). *Everybody's business: A book about school discipline.* Columbia, SC: Southeastern Public Education Program, 1980.

Fitts, W.H., and Hammer, W.T. *The self concept and delinquency.* Nashville, TN: Marshall and Bruce, 1969.

Gallup, G. The eleventh annual Gallup poll of the public attitudes toward the public school. *Phi Delta Kappan,* 1979, *60,* 33–45.

Gazda, G.M., Asbury, F.R., Balzer, F.S., Childers, W.C., and Walters, R.P. *Human relations development,* 3rd ed. Boston, MA: Allyn Bacon, 1984.

Gilligan, C. Woman's place in man's life cycle. *Harvard Education Review,* 1979, *49,* 431–446.

Ginott, H. *Teacher and child.* New York: Macmillan, 1972.

Glasser, N. (Ed.) *What are you doing? How people are helped through reality therapy.* New York: Harper and Row, 1980.

Glasser, W. *Stations of the mind: New directions for health therapy.* New York: Harper and Row, 1981.

_____. *Schools without failure.* New York: Harper and Row, 1975.

Gold, M. *Delinquent behavior in an American city.* Belmont, CA: Brooks/Cole, 1970.

Good, T. and Brophy, J. *Looking in classrooms.* 3rd ed. New York: Harper and Row, 1984.

Goodman, G. and Hammond, B. Seatbelts control hyperactivity. *Academic Therapy,* 1975, *11,* 51–52.

Gordon, T. *TET: Teacher effectiveness training.* New York: Wyden, 1974.

Gotts, E.E. and Purnell, R. *Home school communication.* Bloomington, IN: Phi Delta Kappa, 1985.

Gray, G., Graubard, P.S., and Rosenberg, H. Little brother is changing you. *Psychology Today,* 1974, *8,* 43–46.

Greenberg, J.S. and Deputat, Z. Smoking intervention: Comparing three methods in a high school setting. *Journal of School Health,* 1978, *48,* 498–502.

Gregory, T. and Smith, G. The impact of social climates: Differences between conventional and alternative schools. *Educational Horizons,* 1982, *60,* 83–89.

Guba, E. and Lincoln, Y. *Effective evaluation*. San Francisco, CA: Jossey-Bass, 1981.

Guilford, J.P. *The nature of human intelligence*. New York: McGraw-Hill, 1967.

Hamachek, D.E. *Encounters with the self. 2nd ed*. New York: Holt, Rinehart and Winston, 1978.

Hansford, B.C. and Hattie, J.E. The relationship between self and achievement/ performance measures. *Review of Educational Research*, 1982, *52*, 123–142.

Harbach, R.L. and Asbury, F. Some effects of empathetic understanding on negative student behaviors. *Humanistic Education*, 1976, *15*, 19–24.

Hargreaves, D.H., Hester, S.K., and Mellor, F.J. *Deviance in classroom*. London: Routledge and Kegan Paul, 1975.

Hartshorne, H. and May, M. *Studies in the nature of character: I, studies in deceit*. New York: Macmillan, 1928.

Hauserman, N., Miller, J.S., and Bond, F.T. A behavioral approach to changing self-concept in elementary school children. *The Psychological Records*, 1976, *26*, 111–116.

Hawley, R.C. *Value explorations through roleplaying*. New York: Hart, 1975.

Heal, K.H. Misbehavior among school children. *Policy and Politics*, 1977, *6*, 321–332.

Hegerle, D.R., Kesecker, M.P., and Couch, J.V. A behavior game for the reduction of inappropriate classroom behaviors. *School Psychology Digest*, 1979, *8*, 339–343.

Helmreich, R. Stress, self-esteem and attitude. In King, B.T. and McGinnies, E. (Ed.), *Attitude, conflict and social change*. London: Academic Press, 1972.

Hersh, R.H., Miller, J.P., and Fielding, G.D. *Models of moral education*. New York: Longman, 1980.

Hickey, J. Effects of an experimental program on the moral development of prisoners. In Kohlberg, L. and Turiel, E. (Eds.), *Collected papers on moral development and moral education*. Cambridge, MA: Harvard Graduate School of Education, 1973.

Homme, L. *How to use contingency contracting in the classroom*. Champaign, IL: Research Press, 1970.

Hosford, R.E. Teaching teachers to reinforce student participation. In Krumboltz, J.D. and Thorsen, C.E. (Eds.), *Behavioral Counseling Cases and Techniques*. New York: Holt, Rinehart and Winston, 1969.

Hunt, D.E. and Sullivan, E.V. *Between psychology and education*. Hinsdale, IL: Dryden, 1974.

Irving, O. and Martin, J. Withitness: The confusing variable. *American Educational Research Journal*, 1982, *19*, 313–319.

Jacobson, E. *Anxiety and tension control*. Philadelphia, PA: Lippincott, 1964.

Johnson, M.R., Turner, P.F., and Konanski, E.A. The good behavior game with unruly students. In Millman et al. (Eds.), *Therapies for school behavior problems*, San Francisco, CA: Jossey-Bass, 1980.

Kaeser, S. *Orderly schools that serve all children*. Cleveland, OH: Citizens Council for Ohio Schools, 1979.

Kaplan, H.B. *Deviant behavior in defense of self*. New York: Academic Press, 1980.

Kauffman, J. and Nussen, J. Children as therapeutic change agents: Reinforcement intervention paradigms. *Review of Educational Research*, 1977, *47*, 447–451.

Kazden, A.E. *The token economy: A review and evaluation*. New York: Plenum, 1977.

Kirschenbaum, H. and Simon, S. *Readings in values clarification*. Minneapolis, MN: Winston Press, 1973.

Kohlberg, L. Moral stages and moralization. In Garrod, A., Bartell, R., Rampaul, W., and Siefert, K. (Eds.), *Perspectives on teaching, learning and development*. Dubuque, IA: Kendall/Hunt, 1984.

_____. The cognitive-developmental approach to moral education. *Phi Delta Kappan*, 1975, *56*, 670–677.

Kounin, J. *Discipline and group management in classrooms*. New York: Holt, Rinehart and Winston, 1970.

Kounin, J. and Gump, P. The comparative influence of punitive and non-punitive teachers upon children's concept of school misconduct. *Journal of Educational Psychology*, 1961, *52*, 44–49.

Krumboltz, J.D. and Krumboltz, H.B. *Changing children's behavior*. Englewood Cliffs, NJ: Prentice-Hall, 1972.

Lande, N. and Slade, A. *Stages: Understanding how you make your moral decisions*. San Francisco, CA: Harper and Row, 1979.

LeAnes, A. and Siemsglusz, S. Paraprofessional treatment of school phobia in a young adolescent girl. *Adolescence*, 1977, *12*, 115–121.

Lefkowitz, M.M., Eron, L.D., Walder, L.O., and Huesmann, L.R. *Growing up to be violent.* New York: Pergamon, 1977.

Leonetti, R. *Self-concept and the school child.* New York: Philosophic Library, 1980.

Lewin, K. *Field theory and social science.* New York: Harper and Row, 1951.

Lickona, T. (Ed.). *Moral development and behavior.* New York: Holt, Rinehart and Winston, 1976.

Lockwood, A.L. The effects of value clarification and moral development curricula on school age subjects. *Review of Educational Research,* 1978, *48,* 35–64.

Long, J.D. and Frye, V.H. *Making it til Friday.* Princeton, NJ: Princeton Book, 1981.

Macht, J. *Teacher/teachum: The toughest game in town.* New York: John Wiley and Sons, 1975.

MacMillan, D.L., Forness, S., and Trumbull, B.M. The role of punishment in the classroom. *Exceptional Children,* October 1973, *40,* 85–86.

Margolis, H., Mublfelder, C., and Brannigan, G. Reality therapy and underachievement: A case study. *Education,* 1977, *98,* 153–155.

Martin, B. The slammer: An in-school suspension program. *Educational digest,* 1980, *45,* 36–40.

Martin, G. and Pear, J. *Behavior modification: What it is and how to do it.* Englewood Cliffs, NJ: Prentice-Hall, 1978.

Masters, J.C., Gordon, F.R., and Clark, L.V. Effects of self-dispersed or externally dispersed model consequences on acquiring spontaneous and exposited imitation. *Journal of Personality and Social Psychology,* 1976, *33,* 421–430.

Maurer, A. Corporal punishment. *American Psychologist,* 1974, *29,* 614–626.

McClelland, D.C. Toward a theory of motive acquisition. *American Psychologist,* 1965, *20,* 321–333.

McCullough, J.P., Huntsinger, G.M., and Nay, N.R. Treatment of aggression in a sixteen year old male. *Journal of Consulting and Clinical Psychology,* 1977, *45,* 322–331.

McGee, C.S., Kaufman, J.M., and Nussen, J.L. Children as therapeutic change agents: Reinforcement intervention paradigms. *Review of Educational Research,* 1977, *47,* 451–577.

McLaughlin, T.F. Self control in the classroom. *Review of Educational Research,* 1976, *46,* 631–663.

McLaughlin, T.F. and Malaby, J.E. Intrinsic reinforcer in a classroom: Token economy. *Journal of Applied Behavior Analysis,* 1972, *5,* 263–270.

Meichenbaum, D. *Cognitive behavior modification: An integrative approach.* New York: Plenum Press, 1977.

Metcalf, L. (Ed.). *Values education: Rationale, strategies and procedures.* Washington, D.C.: National Council for the Social Studies, Forty-First Yearbook, 1971.

Milgram, S. Behavioral study of obedience. *Journal of Abnormal and Social Psychology,* 1963, *67,* 371–378.

Millman, H.L., Schaefer, C.E., and Cohen, J.J. *Therapies for school behavior problems.* San Francisco, CA: Jossey-Bass, 1980.

Minuchin, S., Chamberlain, P., and Gaubard, P. A project to teach learning skills to disturbed, delinquent children. *American Journal of Orthopsychiatry,* 1967, *37,* 558–567.

Moos, R. *Evaluating correctional and community settings.* New York: Wiley and Sons, 1975.

Murray, H. *Explorations in personality.* New York: Oxford Press, 1938.

Nash, R. *The teachers' perception and the students' performance.* Boston, MA: Routledge and Kegan Paul, 1973.

_____. Corporal punishment in an age of violence. *Educational Theory,* 1963, *13,* 295–308.

National School Resource Network. *Resource handbook on discipline codes.* Cambridge, MA: Oeleschlager, Ginn, and Haim, 1980.

Nucci, L. Conceptual development in the moral and conventional domains: Implications for values education. *Review of Educational Research,* 1982, *52,* 93–122.

O'Connor, R. Modification of social withdrawal through symbolic modeling. *Journal of Applied Behavioral Analysis,* 1969, *2,* 15–22.

O'Leary, D. and Becker, W. The effects of the intensity of a teacher's reprimands on children's behavior. *Journal of School Psychology,* 1968, *7,* 8–11.

Olivero, J. *Discipline . . . #1 problem in the schools? 40 positive prescriptions for those who care.* Burlingame, CA: Association of California School Administrators, 1977.

Parke, R. Punishment in children, effects, side effects, and alternate strategies. In H. Hom and P. Robinson (Eds.), *Psychological Processes in Early Education*. New York: Academic, 1977.

Peck, R. and Havighurst, R. *The psychology of character development*. New York: Wiley, 1960.

Peterson, R., Loveless, S., Knapp, T., Loveless, B., Basta, S., and Anderson S. The effects of teacher use of I messages on student disruptive and study behavior. *Psychological Record*, 1979, *29*, 187–199.

Phi Delta Kappa. *Why do some urban schools succeed?* Bloomington, IN: Phi Delta Kappan, 1980.

Phillips, E.L., Phillips, E., Wolfe, M., and Fixen, D. Achievement place: Development of an educated management system. *Journal of Applied Behavioral Analysis*, 1973, *6*, 541–561.

Power, C., Higgins, A., and Kohlberg, L. *The influence of moral atmosphere on student behavior*. Paper presented at the meeting of the American Educational Research Association, New York, March 1982.

Purkey, W. *Inviting school success: A self concept approach*. 2nd ed. Belmont, CA: Wadsworth, 1984.

Raths, L., Harmin, M., and Simon, S. *Values and teaching: working with values in the classroom*. Columbus, OH: C.E. Merrill, 1966.

Rathus, S. Assessing assertive behavior. *Behavior Therapy*, 1973, *4*, 398–406.

Redl, F. The concept of punishment. In N. Long, W. Morse, and R. Newman (Eds.), *Conflict in the Classroom*. 4th ed. Belmont, CA: Wadsworth, 1980.

Redl, F. and Wattenberg, W. *Mental hygiene in teaching*, 2d ed. New York: Harcourt, Brace, and Co., 1959.

Reardon, F.J. and Reynolds, R.N. A survey of attitudes toward corporal punishment in Pennsylvania schools. In Hyman, I.A. and Wise, J.H. (Eds.) *Corporal punishment in American education*. Philadelphia: Temple University, 1979.

Rinne, C. *Attention, the fundamentals of classroom control*. Columbus, OH: C.E. Merrill, 1984.

Rogers, C. *Carl Rogers on personal power*. New York: Dell, 1978.

Rokeach, M. *The nature of values*. New York: Free Press, 1973.

_____. Long range experimental modification of values, attitudes and behavior. *American Psychologist*, 1971, *26*, 453–459.

Rose, T.L. Current uses of corporal punishment in American public schools. *Journal of Educational Psychology*, 1984, *76*, 427–41.

Rosenberg, M. *Conceiving the self*. New York: Basic Books, 1979.

Rossman, P. *After Punishment, What?* Cleveland, OH: Willin Collins, 1980.

Rutter, M., Maughan, B., Mortimore, P., and Ousten, J. *Fifteen thousand hours*. Cambridge, MA: Harvard University Press, 1979.

Satir, V. *Peoplemaking*. Palo Alto, CA: Science & Behavior Books, 1972.

Schmuck, R. and Schmuck, P. *Group processes in the classroom*, 4th ed. Dubuque: Wm. C. Brown, 1984.

Seeley, D. *Education through partnerships*. New York: Harper and Row, 1981.

Seeman, A. and Seeman, M. Staff processes and pupil attitudes. *Human Relations*, 1976, *29*, 25–40.

Selman, R. Level of social perspective taking and the development of empathy in children: Speculations for a social-cognitive viewpoint. *Journal of Moral Education*, 1975, *5*, 35–43.

———. *The growth of interpersonal understanding*. New York: Academic Press, 1980.

Sheban, J. *The wisdom of Gibran*. New York: Bantam Books, 1973.

Shevelson, R. and Stuart, K. Self concept: Validation of construct interpretation. In M. Lynch, K. Gergen, and A. Norem-Herbeisen (Eds.), *Self concept*. Boston, MA: Balanger Press, 1980.

Silberman, M. and Wheelan, S. *How to discipline without feeling guilty*. New York: Hawthorne, 1980.

Simon, S., Howe, L., and Kirschenbaum, H. *Values clarification: A handbook of practical strategies for teachers and students*. New York: Hart, 1972.

Snygg, D. and Combs, A. *Individual behavior*. New York: Harper & Row, 1959.

Southern, S. and Smith, R. Managing stress and anger in the classroom. *Catalyst for Change*, 1980, *10*(1), 4–7.

Staines, J. The self-picture in the classroom. *British Journal of Educational Psychology*, 1958, *28*, 97–111.

Staub, E. Personality: Basic aspects and current research. Englewood Cliffs, NJ: Prentice-Hall, 1980.

Stein, K. A contingency management day program for adolescents excluded from public school. *Psychology in the Schools*, 1976, *13*, 185–191.

Sulzbacher, S. and Houser, J. A tactic to eliminate disruptive behaviors in the classroom: Group contingent consequences. *American Journal of Mental Deficiency*, 1968, *1*, 182–187.

Sulzer, B. and Mayer, G.R. *Behavior modification procedures for school personnel*. Hinsdale, IL: Dryden Press, 1972.

Tanaka, J. *Classroom management: A guide for the school consultant*. Springfield, IL: Charles C. Thomas, 1979.

Teel, S. The use of time out procedures in diminishing crying behaviors. *School Application of Learning Theory*, 1971, *3*, 27–31.

Thomas, J.W. Agency and achievement: Self management and self regard. *Review of Educational Research*, 1980, *50*, 213–240.

Thoresen, C. and Mahoney, M. *Behavioral self control*. New York: Holt, Rinehart and Winston, 1974.

Vorrath, H. and Brendtio, L. *Positive peer culture*. 2nd ed. Chicago, IL: Aldine Press, 1985.

Walters, R., Parke, R., and Cane, V. Timing of punishment and the observation of consequences to others as determinants of response inhibition. *Journal of Experimental Child Psychology*, 1965, *2*, 10–30.

Washington, K. Success counseling: A model workshop approach to self concept building. *Adolescence*, 1977, *12*, 405–409.

Wayson, W. and Pinnell, S. The discipline context inventory. In J. First and M.H. Mizell (Eds.), *Everybody's Business: A Book about School Discipline*. Columbia, SC: South Eastern Public Education Program, 1980.

Wayson, W.W. and Pinnell, G.G. *Developing discipline with quality schools*. Cleveland, OH: Citizens Council for Ohio Schools, 1978.

Weber, W. Classroom management. In J. Cooper (Ed.), *Classroom Teaching Skills: A Handbook*. Boston, MA: D.C. Heath, 1977.

Webster, R. A time out procedure in a public school setting. *Psychology in the Schools*, 1976, *13*, 72–76.

Weiner, B. The role of affect in rational (attributional) approaches to human motivation. *Educational Researcher*, 1980, *9*, 4–11.

Weinstein, G. and Fantini, M. *Toward humanistic education*. New York: Praeger, 1970.

Wells, L. and Marwell, G. *Self-esteem: Its conceptualization and measurement*. Beverly Hills, CA: Sage Publications, 1976.

Winn, M. *Children without childhood.* New York: Penguin, 1983.

Wise, J. *Proceedings of the conference on corporal punishment in the schools: A national debate,* February 18–20, 1977. National Institute of Education, U.S. Department of Health, Education and Welfare, pp. 9, 13.

Wolfgang, C. and Glickman, C. *Solving discipline problems.* Boston, MA: Allyn & Bacon, 1980.

Wolpe, J. *The practice of behavior therapy.* New York: Pergamon, 1969.

Zahavice, A. The effect of verbal instruction on preschool children. *Journal of School Psychology,* 1978, *16,* 146–153.

Zentali, S. Environmental stimulation model. *Exceptional children,* 1977, *44,* 502–510.

Zimmerman, B. and Jaffee, A. Teaching through demonstration. *Journal of Educational Psychology,* 1977, *69* (6), 773–778.

Indexes

NAME INDEX

353

SUBJECT INDEX

ABOUT THE AUTHOR

Meryl E. Englander has been a professor at Indiana University for eighteen years. Prior to that, he taught at California State University, Sacramento, and at the University of Michigan.

Professor Englander has written and lectured extensively on the recruitment, selection, and education of teachers. His teaching and research has been directed toward instructional processes, teacher-learner relationships, and the management of classroom behavior.

Professor Englander received his Ph.D. from the University of Michigan in 1957.